DOS/VSE
JCL

Second Edition

D1594911

Concepts • Job control •
VSE/POWER • Data management •
Program development • Utilities

Steve Eckols
Michele Milnes

Mike Murach & Associates, Inc.

4697 West Jacquelyn Avenue
Fresno, California 93722
(209) 275-3335

DOS/VSE
JCL

Editorial team

Anne Prince
Tim Schaldach

Production team

Steve Ehlers
Peggy Warkentine

Related books

DOS/VSE ICCF by Steve Eckols
DOS/VSE Assembler Language by Kevin McQuillen and Anne Prince

20 19 18 17 16 15 14 13 12 11 10 9 8 7 6 5 4

Library of Congress Catalog Card Number: 88-62699

ISBN: 0-911625-50-X

Contents

Preface

This book is designed to teach you how to use DOS/VSE, an operating system that's used to control thousands of IBM mainframe computer systems. If you've tried to learn about DOS/VSE from IBM's documentation, it was probably a frustrating experience. The information you need is distributed throughout several reference manuals. And because they're reference manuals, they present every detail of every feature; they don't help you learn what's useful and what isn't. In contrast, *DOS/VSE JCL* presents all the basic information you need and stresses the important elements. So if you want to learn a practical, professional subset of DOS/VSE—whether you're a student, a programmer, a computer operator, or a systems analyst—this book is for you.

Why you should have this book if you're a DOS/VSE novice

One of the most difficult parts of developing a working knowledge of DOS/VSE is learning job control language (JCL). Although knowing how to code JCL is a basic skill for a DOS/VSE user, none of the IBM manuals really teach it. This book is unique because it presents JCL so you can easily understand it and so you can use it right away to create production jobs.

But as we said, coding JCL is a basic skill. Beyond this, *DOS/VSE JCL* teaches you to use many of the more advanced features of DOS/VSE and its supplementary products. For instance, you'll learn how to use the spooling facilities of VSE/POWER, how to do terminal work with the DOS/VSE time-sharing system, ICCF, and how to use an array of service and utility programs. No other training materials combine all this information in one book.

Although the IBM manuals aren't meant for training, they do contain a wealth of advanced DOS/VSE information. But to use them effectively, you must have a broadly based background in DOS/VSE concepts. As a result, *DOS/VSE JCL* presents not only what you need to know to use the system effectively, but also the conceptual background that will let you do deeper independent study.

Why you should have this book if you're an experienced DOS/VSE user

If you're an experienced DOS/VSE user, you already know what you need to know to do your job. For example, if you're a programmer, you know how to compile and test an application program. But how much do you know about DOS/VSE facilities beyond the minimum? If you work in a typical shop, you probably don't have the time to learn the features that aren't essential, but that can make your job easier. And even if you do have some time for study, it may not be at the top of your list of things to do. If you're like us, you don't want to search randomly through the manuals in the futile hope of finding something new and useful. With this book, however, you can use the little study time you have efficiently; you'll learn just what's useful and you'll learn it quickly.

For day-to-day use, *DOS/VSE JCL* contains dozens of sample jobs you can adopt as models for similar jobs. So whether you want to define a VSAM ESDS, create a test file with VSE/DITTO, or code POWER JECL, you'll find not just the syntax of the control statements you need, but also a job stream model that's probably close to what you want. Then, you can use it with minor modifications to meet your needs.

Required
background

To learn how to use DOS/VSE from this book, you only need an elementary background in computing. Specifically, you need to know the basic functions of computer equipment and you need to understand, in general terms, the kinds of applications that are common on business data processing systems. If you've taken an introductory computer science course or a business data processing course, you have that background. Or, if you have experience as a programmer or computer operator (on IBM equipment or otherwise), you probably have the background you need.

How to use this
book

We organized this book in what we think is the most logical sequence for a new DOS/VSE user. As a result, if IBM mainframe systems—and DOS/VSE in particular—are new to you, we recommend you read the chapters in sequence. And no matter what your background is, we recommend you read chapters 1 through 5 in sequence.

Although we think it's best to read the entire book in sequence, you can read chapters 6 through 18 in any order you like. For example, if you need to know how to code JCL for tape processing, you can turn to chapter 11 without reading chapters 6 through 10 first. But because each chapter contains DOS/VSE information you should know, your background will be lacking if you don't read the entire book. As a result, we encourage you to read all of the chapters sooner or later.

Notes on the second edition

The original version of DOS was introduced more than 20 years ago and since then has evolved continuously. That means a book about DOS/VSE (or about any other data processing subject) is likely to have a limited life. In fact, soon after the first edition of *DOS/VSE JCL* was published in 1985, IBM introduced a new release of VSE called VSE/AF Version 2.1, which included some major enhancements. Although most of the content of the first edition of *DOS/VSE JCL* still applied to VSE/AF 2.1, it didn't address any of the new features of the software.

This book, the second edition of *DOS/VSE JCL*, covers all of the important features and facilities of VSE/AF 2.1. Although much of the content of this book is the same as that of the first edition, substantial portions have been rewritten and new sections have been added to cover what you need to know to work with VSE/AF 2.1. Because VSE/AF 2.1 is in widespread use today, this is the book for you if you work with a DOS system.

Many of the other components that make up a complete VSE system, such as VSAM, ICCF, and POWER, have been enhanced as well. The most current release of each of these products is covered in this book. In comparison to the changes that came with the new release of VSE/AF, however, the enhancements to these products are minor.

All of these components—VSE/AF, VSAM, ICCF, and POWER, as well as others—are included in the new release of VSE/SP, VSE/SP Version 3.1. VSE/SP (SP stands for System Package) is a collection of system components packaged as a single product. Don't confuse VSE/SP with VSE/AF, however; VSE/AF is only one component of VSE/SP. So, if the system administrator tells you that your system is running under VSE 3.1, she's referring to VSE/SP, not VSE/AF.

Related reference manuals

Although you won't have to rely much on IBM manuals when you use this book, you'll still need to refer to them occasionally. Depending on the releases of DOS/VSE and its related components your shop uses, the IBM reference manuals you may need can vary. As a result, we're not going to recommend specific publication numbers. Instead, we'll give you titles you should look for. Although the titles may vary slightly too, you should be able to find the manuals you need in your shop's reference library.

Throughout this book, you may want to refer to two manuals: *VSE/Advanced Functions System Management Guide* and *VSE/Advanced Functions System Control Statements*. For chapters 3, 9, and 14, you'll probably want to refer to *VSE/Interactive Computing and Control Facility Ter-*

minal User's Guide. And for chapters 13 and 18, you'll find *Using VSE/VSAM Commands and Macros* to be helpful. When we raise points in the text that may need more discussion, we'll refer you to these and other manuals.

Conclusion Obviously, we believe this book will help you learn DOS/VSE better than any other. But we'd also like to know what you think about it. As a result, we encourage you to use the postage-paid comment form at the end of the book to let us know how you use it, how it compares with the IBM manuals, and what topics you think need more coverage—or less. In short, we'd appreciate any ideas or thoughts you have about *DOS/VSE JCL.*

Steve Eckols   Michele Milnes
San Diego, California   Berkeley, California
November, 1988   November, 1988

Section 1

Introduction

Before you can begin to learn DOS/VSE JCL, you need some specialized background. So that's what you'll learn in the three chapters in this section. Chapter 1 introduces you to the hardware components that can make up a DOS/VSE system and shows you how they're combined in system configurations. Chapter 2 presents the concepts and terminology you need to know that relate to DOS/VSE and its associated software products. And chapter 3 teaches you how to enter text at a terminal on a DOS/VSE system so you can apply this skill as you read subsequent chapters.

If you've already had experience with a DOS system, you may be familiar with much of the material in this section. In that case, you can review the objectives and terminology list at the end of each topic to see whether you need to study the topic.

Chapter 1

An introduction to IBM mainframe systems

This chapter presents what you need to know about IBM mainframe hardware components (topic 1) and system configurations (topic 2). If IBM mainframe systems are new to you, you should certainly read this chapter. Even though some of the concepts and terms may be familiar to you from experience or previous study, you'll benefit from reading about them as they apply specifically to DOS/VSE.

On the other hand, if you're already familiar with IBM hardware and configurations, much of the material in this chapter will be review. If that's the case, you might want to skip one or both topics. To find out if you should, review the terminology and objectives at the end of each topic. If you're comfortable with them, you can probably skip the topic.

TOPIC 1   Hardware components

A *mainframe system* is a large collection of computer equipment. Just what "large" means, though, is debatable. Usually, mainframe systems support many applications and require staffs to operate and maintain them. In contrast, minicomputer and microcomputer systems usually support a smaller number of applications and often don't require staffs for operations and systems troubleshooting. The terminology is imprecise, however, because the smallest mainframe systems are smaller than the largest minicomputer systems. But in general, a mainframe system is expandable upward to create a large configuration, while a minicomputer system is more limited.

IBM manufactures dozens of hardware devices for mainframe systems. Moreover, most are available in different models with a variety of features. As a result, this topic won't try to teach you about all the devices that can be part of an IBM mainframe system. Instead, it describes three general types of components.

The first group is processors, the central components in mainframe systems. The second group includes all the peripheral devices that are used to transmit data to and receive data from the processor. The third group consists of intermediate devices, called channels, that transfer data between peripheral devices and the processor.

PROCESSORS

The center of a mainframe system is the *processor*; all the other devices that make up the system configuration attach in some way to it. For the purposes of this book, you can think of the processor as consisting of two main parts: the central processing unit and main storage. The *central processing unit* (or *CPU*) is a collection of circuits that perform machine service functions and execute program instructions for calculation and data manipulation. *Main storage* (or *main memory*) is the high-speed, general-purpose electronic storage area that contains both the data the CPU operates upon and the program instructions it executes.

DOS/VSE runs on processors that are members of the *System/360-370* family. The System/360-370 family is a group of general-purpose processors that have been developed over a 20-year span, beginning with the System/360 models of the mid-1960s and continuing with the System/370s and 3030s of the 1970s. The 9370s and 4300s are current today. And we can expect new models in the future.

Of course, as IBM has developed new System/360-370 processors, it has used contemporary technologies to create better, faster, and cheaper machines. Although the mainframe processors IBM manufactures today are direct descendants of the System/360s of the mid-1960s, those older machines are all but obsolete.

Processors that do support DOS/VSE are the System/370, 3030, 3080, 4300, and 9370 processors. Although there are significant technical differences in the way these processors operate, it doesn't matter much which one your shop uses. DOS/VSE is essentially the same no matter which processor it runs on.

Models in the 4300 series are the most common type of DOS/VSE processor. As a result, this book emphasizes 4300s. Nevertheless, the information it presents applies if your shop uses a System/370, 3030, 3080, or 9370.

INPUT/OUTPUT EQUIPMENT

The second group of mainframe devices consists of the *peripheral equipment* connected to the processor. Collectively, they're called *input/output devices*, or just *I/O devices*. Input devices provide data to the processor, and output devices receive data from it. Some machines can perform both functions. Common types of I/O units on IBM mainframes are (1) printers, (2) card devices, (3) magnetic tape devices, (4) direct access storage devices, and (5) terminal devices. Because so many different I/O devices can be part of a DOS/VSE system, I'm not going to try to cover them all. Instead, I'm going to focus on some details you need to know for magnetic tape and direct access storage devices.

Magnetic tape devices

A *tape drive*, or *magnetic tape unit*, reads and writes data on a *magnetic tape* that's a continuous strip of plastic coated on one side with a metal oxide. The amount of data a reel of tape can contain depends on how long the tape is and on the *density* used to record the data. Density is a measurement of how many bytes are recorded in one inch of tape. Tape densities on standard reel tapes can be 556, 800, 1,600 or 6,250 *bytes per inch* (*bpi*). The last two are the most common.

Of course, meaningful data on a tape isn't a random collection of bytes. A number of bytes are strung together along the tape to form a *record*, which is a collection of related data. Between individual data records on a tape are spaces where no data is recorded called *inter-record gaps*, or *IRGs*, as you can see in figure 1-1.

When a technique called *blocking* is used, more than one record is stored between IRGs. Then, the group of records stored together is called a *block*, and the IRG is called an *IBG*, or *inter-block gap*. Figure 1-2 shows a segment of a tape file that uses a *blocking factor* of five; the blocking factor is the number of records per block.

Blocking can significantly reduce the amount of wasted space on a tape. However, there is an extra cost involved when blocking is used: a buffer is required in storage to contain the entire block. As a result, the larger the block, the more main storage it requires.

Blocking also affects tape processing speed, because the usual way a tape drive operates is to stop and start again each time it encounters a gap. This is called the *start-stop mode* of operation. When records are blocked, the tape drive doesn't have to start and stop so often.

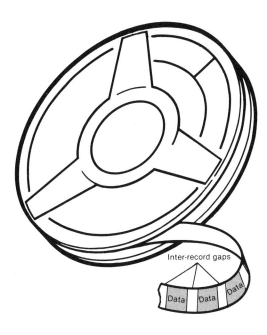

Figure 1-1   Inter-record gaps on a magnetic tape

Gap	Record 1	Record 2	Record 3	Record 4	Record 5	Gap

Figure 1-2   Blocked records on tape

Although all tape units can operate in start-stop mode, one IBM tape drive, the 8809, can also operate in *streaming mode*. This is a specialized, high-speed method of operation that can be used when the data going to the tape drive can be supplied in a continuous stream and won't require the drive to stop. As a result, streaming mode is normally used when disk data is backed up onto tape.

Of course, tape processing has one serious drawback: it must be sequential. In other words, to read the 50,000th record on a tape, it's necessary to read the preceding 49,999 records first. As a result, tape is ill-suited for applications that require direct access to stored data.

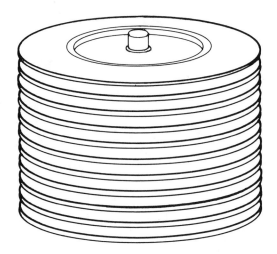

Figure 1-3   A disk pack

Direct access
devices

A *direct access storage device* (*DASD*) makes it possible to access any record quickly. Because DASDs, regardless of their type, allow direct and rapid access to large quantities of data, they've become a key component of mainframe systems. They're used not only to store user programs and data, but also to store programs and data for operating system functions.

Characteristics of DASD processing   The most common type of DASD is the *disk drive*, a unit that reads and writes data on a *disk pack*. A disk pack, illustrated in figure 1-3, is a stack of metal platters that are coated with a metal oxide material. Data is recorded on both sides of the platters.

Several of the DASD models that can be part of a DOS/VSE system use removable disk packs, but the trend with newer IBM DASDs is for the pack to be fixed in a permanent, sealed assembly inside the drive. When an application requires that DASD data be available at all times, it doesn't make much difference if it's stored on a fixed pack or on a pack that can be removed, but never is. And that, of course, is the case with many interactive applications.

On each recording surface of a disk pack, data is stored in concentric circles called *tracks*, as illustrated in figure 1-4. Although the number of tracks per recording surface varies with device type, the surface illustrated in figure 1-4 has 200 tracks, numbered from 000 to 199.

The data stored on a track is read by the DASD's *access mechanism*, an assembly with one read/write head for each recording surface. Figure 1-5 shows a side view of an access mechanism. As you can see,

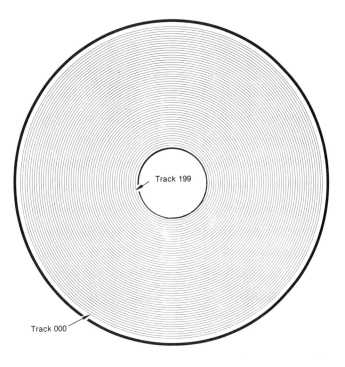

Figure 1-4   Tracks on a disk surface

the access mechanism is positioned over the same track on all record-ing surfaces at the same time. As a result, all of these tracks can be operated on, one after another, without the access mechanism having to move.

The tracks that can be accessed by a single positioning of the access mechanism make up a *cylinder*. As a result, there are as many cylinders on a disk pack as there are tracks on a single recording surface. So if there are 200 tracks on each recording surface of a disk pack, the entire pack contains 200 cylinders. When a systems designer plans the location of data on a DASD, she usually thinks in terms of how many cylinders it will require.

IBM mainframe DASD types   In concept, one DASD's operation is about the same as another's, although they vary in speed and capacity. Even though you don't need to know the technical distinctions among all types of IBM DASDs, you do need to understand two broad cate-gories into which they're grouped: count-key-data devices and fixed-block architecture devices.

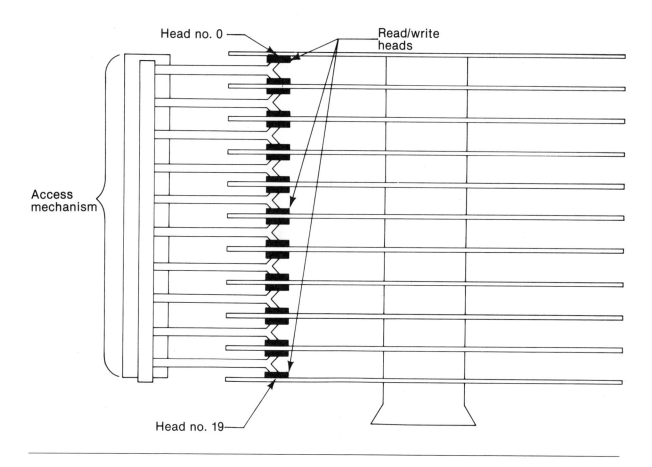

Figure 1-5   Side view of a DASD access mechanism

Count-key-data (*CKD*) devices can be found on most IBM mainframe systems, DOS/VSE or not. On a CKD device, tracks and cylinders are identified by numbers. Figure 1-6 illustrates the track and cylinder organization of a typical IBM CKD DASD, the 3350. As you can see, the 3350 has 555 tracks on each of its 30 recording surfaces. That means the 3350 pack has 555 cylinders available for user data. The cylinders are numbered from 0 to 554 as the headings across the top of the figure show. Within a cylinder, the 30 tracks it contains are numbered from 0 to 29. Any track can then be specified by naming both the cylinder number and the track number within the cylinder.

As you'll see later in this book, you need to be able to specify a track on a CKD DASD not with two numbers, but with just one. You can do that with a *relative track number*. The relative track number indicates the displacement of the track from the beginning of the disk pack when you count down each cylinder. To calculate a relative track number, multiply a track's cylinder number by the number of tracks per cylinder on that device type. Then, to the result of that multiplication,

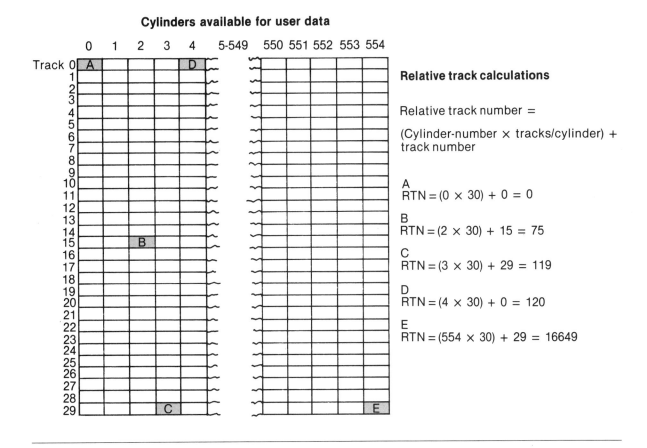

Cylinders available for user data

Relative track calculations

Relative track number =

(Cylinder-number × tracks/cylinder) + track number

A
RTN = (0 × 30) + 0 = 0

B
RTN = (2 × 30) + 15 = 75

C
RTN = (3 × 30) + 29 = 119

D
RTN = (4 × 30) + 0 = 120

E
RTN = (554 × 30) + 29 = 16649

Figure 1-6   Cylinders and tracks on the 3350 DASD

add the number of the track within its cylinder. Figure 1-6 shows the relative track number calculations for five tracks: 0, 75, 119, 120, and 16649.

To calculate a relative track number, you have to know how many tracks each cylinder contains on the DASD you're using. As a result, figure 1-7 gives the number of tracks per cylinder for several CKD DASDs that can be part of a VSE system today. You'll use this information later in this book. (If you're using a device that isn't listed in figure 1-7, find out from another resource how many tracks each of its cylinders contains.)

Fixed-block architecture (*FBA*) devices are less common than CKD devices. At present, only two FBA devices are in use: the 3310 and the 3370. When you use one of these drives, addressing is simple. You can think of the entire range of storage available on an FBA DASD as a string of blocks starting with block 0 and extending up to the capacity of the unit. Each block contains a fixed number of bytes that are available for

DASD type	Tracks per cylinder
2311	10
2314	20
2319	20
3330	19
3333	19
3340	12
3344	12
3350	30
3375	12
3380	15

Figure 1-7   The number of tracks per cylinder on common CKD DASDs

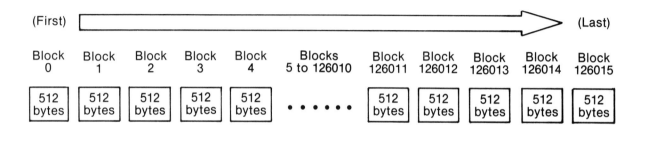

Figure 1-8   Blocks on an FBA DASD

user data: 512. To illustrate, figure 1-8 shows how you can think of the blocks on the 3310: they start at block 0 and extend up to block 126015. The organization of blocks on the 3370 is the same, only they extend up to block 557999.

As you might expect, the physical organization of data on an FBA DASD is more complex than the simple block addressing scheme in figure 1-8 might lead you to believe. In fact, FBA blocks are mapped onto the tracks of an FBA DASD, but that's transparent to you. When you use FBA devices, you don't need to understand their cylinder and track organizations, as you do with CKD devices.

CHANNELS   When I said before that a particular device can be attached to the processor, I simplified the relationship between the processor and the I/O devices. Although it may seem like a peripheral device is attached directly to the processor, it's actually attached to an intermediate device called a *channel*. A channel is a small computer that executes I/O instructions called *channel commands*. Because the channel performs the I/O operations, it frees the processor to execute other instructions. As a result, processing and I/O operations can overlap, and overall system performance is improved.

A channel on an IBM mainframe may be one of three types: (1) a selector, (2) a byte multiplexer, or (3) a block multiplexer. A *selector channel* is designed to operate with only one device at a time, and transfers data byte by byte. In contrast, *a multiplexer channel* operates with more than one I/O device at the same time by alternating between the devices. A *byte multiplexer* is usually used to attach several low-speed I/O devices (like card devices and printers) to the processor. It transfers data one byte at a time. A *block multiplexer* is used to attach higher-speed devices (like tape units and DASDs) and transfers data in blocks rather than bytes.

DISCUSSION

The information in this topic certainly isn't a comprehensive treatment of the hardware components that might be on your system. It just presents some details you need to know about hardware to use DOS/VSE. If you want more information about the devices that can make up a DOS/VSE system, you might be interested in the *IBM Input/Output Device Summary*.

Terminology

mainframe system
processor
central processing unit
CPU
main storage
main memory
System/360-370
peripheral equipment
input/output device
I/O device
tape drive
magnetic tape unit
magnetic tape
density
bytes per inch
bpi
record
inter-record gap
IRG
blocking
block
IBG
inter-block gap
blocking factor

start-stop mode
streaming mode
direct access storage device
DASD
disk drive
disk pack
track
access mechanism
cylinder
count-key-data
CKD
relative track number
fixed-block architecture
FBA
channel
channel command
selector channel
multiplexer channel
byte multiplexer
block multiplexer

Objectives

1. List the three general types of components that make up an IBM mainframe computer system.

2. Describe how blocking can improve I/O efficiency.

3. Compare the techniques used to specify the locations of data on CKD and FBA DASDs.

TOPIC 2   Hardware configurations

With such variety in the types of IBM mainframe processors and input/output devices, the number of possible *system configurations* is practically limitless. As a result, one IBM mainframe configuration is likely to be different from another, even if the two systems do similar processing. In this topic, then, I'm going to present a particular configuration to help you understand the systems you may use.

Figure 1-9 represents a small 4300 configuration. This configuration is much smaller than the average 4300 installation's. At the center of the system is a 4331 Model 1 with 1M of main memory. (M is the abbreviation for *megabyte*, about one million bytes.) Attached to the processor is a collection of devices you might find on a small DOS/VSE system.

I want to discuss this configuration in detail because it illustrates the I/O adapters on smaller 4300 models (4321, 4331, and 4361) and device addresses. And because it's a small system, you can see how all the parts work together.

I/O adapters

Although multiplexer channels are standard equipment on larger 4300 processors, they're optional on smaller 4300 models. An alternative to using multiplexers on smaller models is to install *I/O adapters*. I/O adapters are housed inside the processor cabinet and perform functions similar to multiplexers, but they're limited because only a few types of devices can be attached to them.

Six different adapters can be part of the smaller 4300 models. As you can see, the configuration in figure 1-9 includes four of them: (1) the DASD adapter, (2) the 8809 Magnetic Tape Unit adapter, (3) the Display/printer adapter, and (4) the Communication adapter. The other two, which this system doesn't include, are the Loop adapter and the 5424 adapter.

The DASD adapter allows 3310, 3370, and 3340/3344 disk devices to be attached to the 4300 processor. In figure 1-9, the devices attached are 3310s. The 3310 is a small FBA DASD that may house one or two drives. In this case, two of the units in the configuration have two drives, and one has one. The capacity of each drive is 65M, so the total capacity of this DASD bank is 325M. This amount of storage isn't likely to be adequate for most business installations.

The 8809 Magnetic Tape Unit adapter allows direct attachment of up to six 8809s, but the 8809 is the only tape unit that can be attached to this adapter. As you can see in figure 1-9, our system includes only one 8809 tape drive.

The Display/printer adapter (DPA) allows direct attachment of local terminals and printers. The configuration in figure 1-9 shows six devices

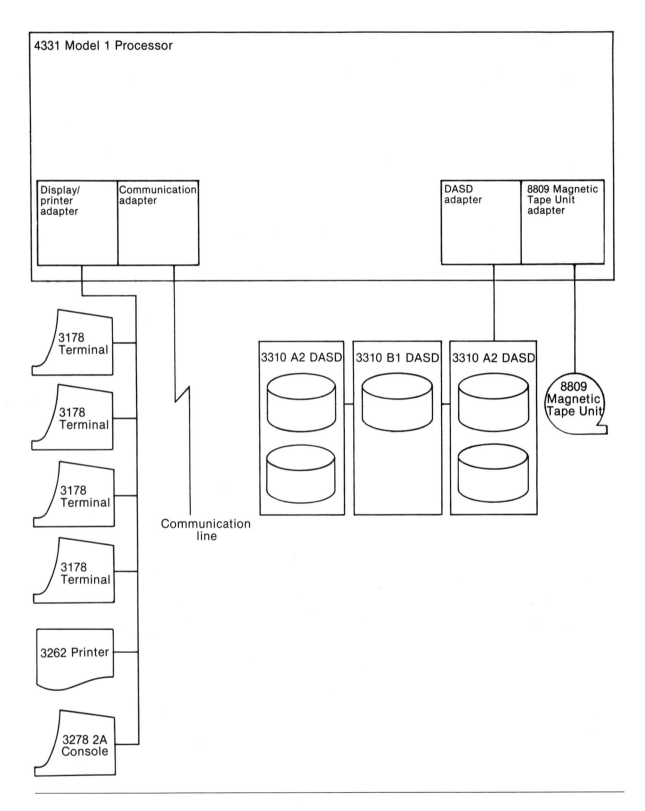

Figure 1-9   A small 4300 configuraton

attached to the DPA: the 3278-2A system console, a 3262 band printer, and four 3178 display stations.

The fourth adapter that's part of the configuration in figure 1-9 is the Communication adapter (CA). The CA can be configured to support up to eight lines, each with different communications options. Here, only one line is configured.

The other two adapters that can be part of a small 4300 system are the 5424 and Loop adapters. The 5424 adapter allows 96-column card devices to be attached to the processor. The Loop adapter allows up to 80 terminals to be attached to the system. By the way, if you use either one of these adapters, you can't use the other.

Device addresses

In the chapters that follow, you'll see that under DOS/VSE you need to know the *device addresses*, or just *addresses*, of your system's hardware components. Although device addresses depend on the hardware installed on your system, there are some general points you should know about them.

Figure 1-10 shows the same configuration as figure 1-9, but it includes the device addresses for the components that make up the system. Notice that the device addresses are all three characters long. Actually, they're three digits long, but the digits are hexadecimal (base 16) instead of decimal. Hex digits range not from 0 to 9, but from 0 to F, where A corresponds to 10, B to 11, C to 12, D to 13, E to 14, and F to 15.

The first of the three digit positions in a device address represents the channel address of the device. On the smaller 4300s, channel 0 is the byte multiplexer channel. In addition to supporting the byte multiplexer, channel 0 is used to address devices attached to the Display/printer adapter, the Communication adapter, and either the Loop adapter or the 5424 adapter. As a result, all of the devices attached to a 4300's byte multiplexer or any of these adapters have addresses beginning with 0.

As you can see in figure 1-10, each of the adapters on channel 0, plus the byte multiplexer, has its own range of two-digit device addresses. These are appended to the channel address (0) to create the unique three-digit address for each system component.

For the configuration in figure 1-10, six devices (four terminals, the system console, and the system printer) are attached to the DPA. Since the address range for the DPA is 09 to 1F, all the devices on the DPA have addresses between 009 and 01F. If you look at the actual addresses for these six devices, you'll see that the 3178s have addresses 00A, 00B, 00C, and 00D; the 3262 is at address 00E (a standard address for the system printer on a DOS/VSE system); and the system console is at address 01F (the standard address for the system console). One communication line is active on the CA, and its address is 030.

On channel 1 are devices attached to the system's block multiplexer. But on this system, the block multiplexer isn't installed.

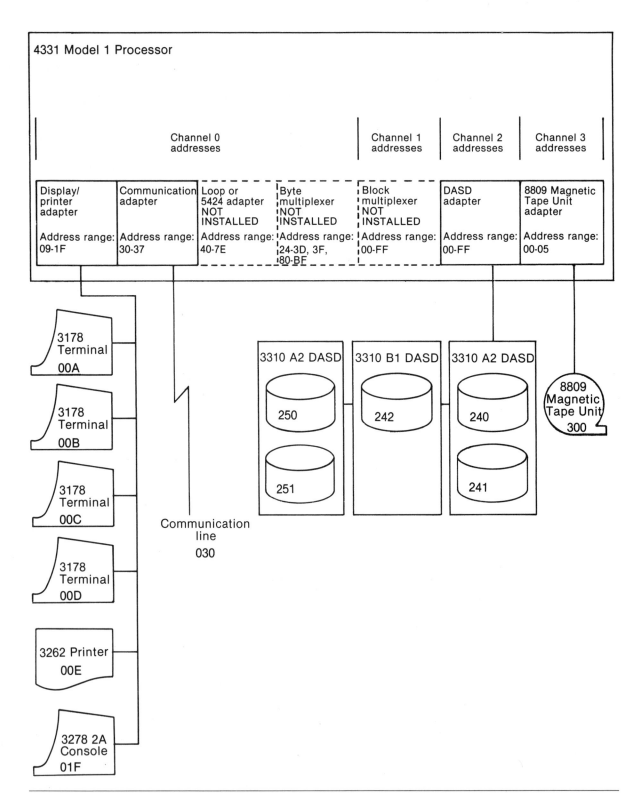

Figure 1-10   Typical device addresses on a small 4300 configuration

On channel 2 is the DASD adapter. The specific two-digit device addresses used for the DASD adapter depend on the device types attached to it and how they're arranged. On this system, the addresses for the five drives in the three 3310 units are 240, 241, 242, 250, and 251.

On channel 3 is the 8809 Magnetic Tape Unit adapter. This adapter can support up to six 8809s, addressed from 00 to 05. Since this system has only one 8809, its address is 300.

On larger 4300 systems, channels 4 through 6 can be used to attach other devices, so other addresses are common. And addresses differ on System/370 machines. Even so, this small 4300 configuration should give you a good idea of how device addresses are formed.

Discussion   Although you need to understand the information this chapter has presented, hardware types and configurations aren't what this book is intended to teach you. Instead, you're reading it to learn how to use the operating system that makes the hardware configuration work as an efficient computing system. So the next chapter introduces you to the VSE operating system.

Terminology   system configuration
megabyte
I/O adapter
device address
address

Objectives   1. Given the devices attached to a typical IBM mainframe system, explain how their device addresses are formed.

2. Find out what your system configuration is and what your device addresses are.

Chapter 2

An introduction to VSE

This chapter's three topics introduce you to DOS/VSE (or just VSE, as I'll call it from now on) and the other programs that make up a VSE system. Topic 1 describes how the VSE system control programs manage processor storage. Topic 2 presents some details on how VSE manages the user data it stores; this emphasizes DASD storage. Finally, topic 3 describes the VSE library structure and introduces you to the complete set of components that make up a production VSE system.

As you read this chapter, it might seem like it's a collection of loosely related subjects. From one point of view, that's true. However, I selected this information to give you a brief introduction to VSE. If you try to learn the same material from the VSE manuals, you'll find that they obscure the relationships between software elements. However, it's those relationships you really need to understand to use VSE effectively.

TOPIC 1   How VSE manages processor storage

This topic introduces VSE by describing one of its most important functions: processor storage management. First, this topic describes multiprogramming and virtual storage. Then it presents two ways VSE organizes virtual storage.

MULTIPROGRAMMING   A common feature of mainframe computer systems, VSE systems included, is *multiprogramming*. When a system provides multiprogramming, it allows a single processor to execute more than one program at the same time. Actually, that's not exactly true, because even though multiple programs are present in storage at the same time, only one is executing at a given instant. But from a user's point of view, it looks like multiple programs are executing at one time.

Because internal processing speeds are far greater than input and output operation speeds and because most business applications do relatively little processing between I/O operations, a processor that only executes one program at a time is idle a large percentage of the time while it waits for I/O operations to finish. To make better use of this otherwise wasted time, multiprogramming lets additional programs remain in storage so their instructions can be executed while the first program waits for its I/O operations to finish. As a result, multiprogramming improves the overall productivity of an installation.

The central component of VSE, the *supervisor program*, or just *supervisor*, determines what program should be executing at any moment. A program that's executing is said to be "in control" of the system. When the program that's in control of the system must wait for an I/O operation to complete, it gives control back to the supervisor. The supervisor then passes control to another program.

The supervisor uses a scheme of priorities to determine which program should execute next. *Priority* is a "rank" that determines a program's eligibility for receiving system services. If several programs are waiting to resume execution, the supervisor passes control to the one with the highest priority. This process of passing control among programs of different priorities is called *task selection*. Actually, priority isn't associated directly with a program, but rather with the partition where the program executes.

Partitions   VSE implements multiprogramming by dividing available processor storage (that is, storage not required by the VSE system control programs) into two to 12 *partitions*. Each partition may contain a user program. Under VSE, multiprogramming isn't an option: The storage available for user programs must be divided into partitions.

On a system with only two partitions, one is the *background partition* and the other is the *foreground partition*. In this case, lower priority programs run in the background partition, and higher priority programs run in the foreground partition.

It's more common, though, for a VSE system to use multiple partitions. When your VSE system was generated, your systems programmer decided how many partitions would be configured for it. The decision was based on the kind and number of programs that would be run on the system. Although the number of partitions can vary from two to 12, the number on your system is almost certainly fixed, and it's almost certainly 12.

Figure 2-1 illustrates the maximum number of partitions VSE can support. Regardless of the number of partitions configured for your system, one partition is always the background partition. All the other partitions are foreground partitions. The background partition is for the lowest priority jobs; the foreground partitions are for higher priority jobs. Among the foreground partitions, Foreground-1 is usually for the highest priority jobs, and Foreground-11 is usually for the lowest priority jobs.

VSE uses the abbreviations in figure 2-1 to refer to the partitions, not the longer names like Foreground-1. If you remember that A is the hexadecimal representation of decimal 10 and B is the hexadecimal representation of decimal 11, it's easy to see the relationship between a partition's name and its abbreviation.

The relative priorities for partitions that figure 2-1 shows are *defaults*. In other words, if your VSE systems programmer doesn't specify otherwise, these are the priorities that will be associated with each of the partitions. But it's possible for a VSE system operator to change a partition's priority. For instance, if output from a slowly running program is needed quickly, the operator can raise the priority of that program's partition. Then, the supervisor gives that partition preference during task selection.

Address space and virtual storage

All programs, including the supervisor, execute in the processor's *address space*. You can think of the address space as a string of bytes as long as the amount of storage on the system. For example, a 1M address space begins at byte 0 (numbering begins with 0, not 1) and extends to byte 1,048,575. Locations within the address space are identified by their displacement from its beginning.

As you can imagine, a multiprogramming system with a dozen active programs requires a large address space. To provide the storage required to support a large address space, VSE uses virtual storage. *Virtual storage* is a technique that allows a large amount of storage to be simulated in a smaller amount of *real storage* by using DASD space as an extension of internal storage. Under VSE, up to 16M or 40M of virtual storage can be simulated on a processor with as little as 1M of real storage. (Whether the maximum is 16M or 40M depends on the

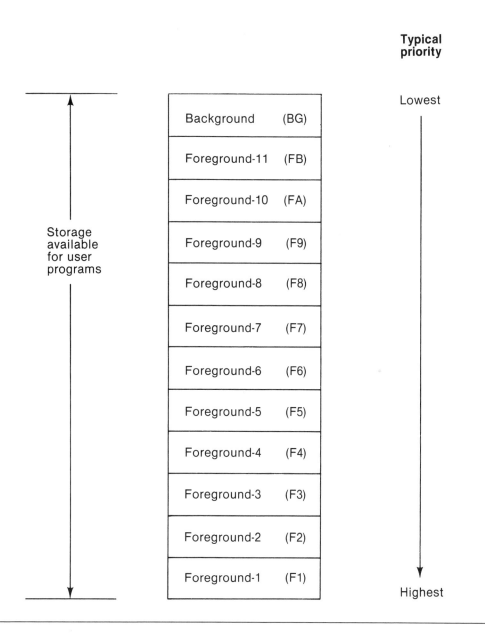

Figure 2-1   VSE partitions

machine mode in which VSE is operating; you'll learn more about machine modes later in this topic.)

The advantage of virtual storage is that it lets more programs be multiprogrammed, thus increasing the efficiency of the computer system. Although the operating system itself is less efficient because of the additional virtual storage control functions it must perform, the productivity of the system as a whole increases. Fortunately, from the application programmer's point of view, virtual storage appears to be real storage.

Virtual storage concepts   The idea behind virtual storage is that, at any instant, only the single program instruction being executed and the data areas it accesses need to be in real storage. The parts of the program that aren't currently executing can reside outside real storage on a disk drive. As additional portions of the program are required, parts that are no longer needed are written to the disk, and new ones from the disk replace them in real storage. Because it would be inefficient to transfer program instructions and the data they require back and forth from main memory one at a time, transfer takes place in blocks. These blocks are program segments called *pages*. As you'll learn in a moment, the size of a page is either 2K or 4K, depending on how VSE is operating.

The pages residing in real storage at a given instant are stored in the *page pool*. The page pool is divided into areas called *page frames*, which are the same size as the pages that are shuffled into and out of them. The pages not residing in real storage are stored on DASD in the *page data set*. (Obviously, the DASD that contains the page data set must be operational at all times on a VSE system.)

When a program requires data or instructions that aren't in real storage, a *page fault* occurs. Then, the supervisor transfers a page that isn't immediately needed in real storage to the page data set and fetches the page that contains the required data or instructions. The process of transferring pages to and from disk is called *paging, page swapping*, or just *swapping*.

Figure 2-2 illustrates virtual storage and should help you better understand this terminology. This example uses a 16M virtual storage address space as a model. As you can see, the page data set contains an image of the virtual storage address space. Logically, the page data set must be the same size as the virtual storage address space. Real storage (only 1M in this example) contains the supervisor and the page pool. The page pool contains all of the system's available page frames; each page frame contains a page from the page data set.

Although a program occupies a continuous range of virtual storage address space, it doesn't necessarily occupy a continuous group of page frames in the page pool. That's what the patchwork of page frames in the real storage section of figure 2-2 illustrates. The supervisor keeps track of what program pages are in what page frames by maintaining tables that reflect the current status of virtual storage.

Shared Virtual Area   In addition to the supervisor and the partitions, a third area uses part of the address space: the *SVA*, or *Shared Virtual Area*. In figure 2-2, the SVA appears below the representation of the F1 partition. The word "shared" in the name should help you remember that the SVA's most important function is to contain program modules shared throughout the system. Most of these are I/O modules.

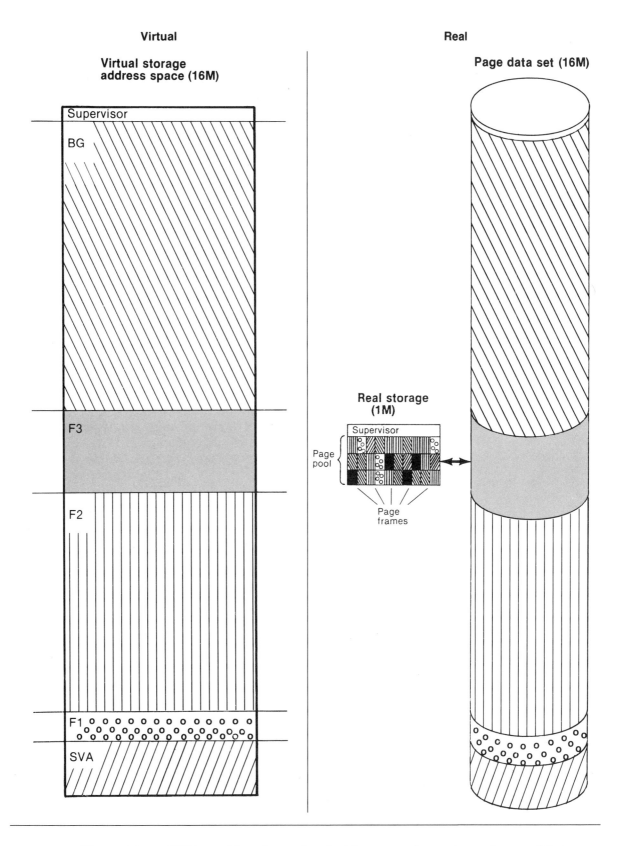

Figure 2-2   VSE provides a large virtual address space by storing an image of that space on disk (in the page data set) and transferring segments (called pages) between disk and real storage

When a module resides in the SVA, only one copy of it needs to be in storage, no matter how many partitions use it. As a result, the SVA helps optimize storage usage. The SVA also improves system performance because commonly used modules don't have to be retrieved from DASD and loaded into virtual storage each time they're needed; they're already there. Although a page fault can occur when the system needs a module from the SVA, VSE can retrieve it from the page data set much faster than it can from the module's original disk location.

Program modes   Within a partition, a program may run in one of two *program modes*: *real mode* or *virtual mode*. Program mode describes how a program uses storage. The page swapping process that's the basis of virtual storage operates for programs that run in virtual mode. As a result, they're called *pageable* programs.

In contrast, think about how the supervisor must operate. Because it has to manage the virtual storage operation, some parts of the supervisor cannot be paged. In other words, those parts must be *resident* in real storage all the time. Those parts of the supervisor must run in real mode, so they're *non-pageable*. Similarly, certain other programs, particularly those with critical time dependencies, must run in real mode.

As a result, although all of main memory is divided into page frames, not all page frames are eligible for paging. When a program that will execute in real mode is loaded, the page frames it occupies are removed from the page pool for its duration. Therefore, the size of the page pool can vary during the course of a day's processing. The page frames in the page pool at any given instant are available for application programs and for parts of the supervisor that can tolerate paging.

Machine modes   Three other modes you may hear about are *machine modes*: *370 mode, ECPS:VSE (Extended Control Program Support: VSE) mode*, and *VM mode*. Machine modes are ways that the operating system manages real and virtual storage. Any processor that supports DOS/VSE may run VSE in 370 mode. Processors in the 4300-series may also run VSE in ECPS:VSE mode. VSE runs in VM mode when it operates under the control of another IBM mainframe operating system called *Virtual Machine/System Product* or *VM/SP*. VM mode is much like ECPS:VSE mode.

Frankly, many of the differences between the 370 mode on one hand and ECPS:VSE and VM modes on the other are subtle and don't matter much unless you're involved in running special programs that require real storage. However, the mode in which VSE runs on your system does determine how its address spaces can be organized.

ADDRESS SPACE ORGANIZATION

Address space organization refers to the way available virtual storage is used. In this section, I'll first describe address space organization under ECPS:VSE and VM modes. Then, I'll describe the more complex address space organization that can be used under 370 mode.

Address space organization under ECPS:VSE and VM modes

Figure 2-3 illustrates the address space layout for a 16M four-partition system in ECPS:VSE mode or VM mode. (This is the same virtual address space layout figure 2-2 illustrated, only here I've shown more detail.) Under either of these two modes, the maximum virtual address space size is 16M. When VSE runs in ECPS:VSE mode, it uses pages (and, as a result, page frames) that are 2K. In VM mode, it uses 4K pages.

As you can see in figure 2-3, the supervisor resides in the lowest portion of the address space. In other words, the supervisor area begins at 0K and extends upward. Since a typical supervisor requires 222K, its address range here is shown as 0K to 222K.

After the supervisor comes the storage available to user programs, divided into partitions. This is the space that corresponds to figure 2-1. However, in figure 2-3, the system is configured with four, not 12, partitions. The background partition immediately follows the supervisor, and the three foreground partitions follow it. As you can see, partition sizes vary. The systems programmer decides how much address space to allocate to a partition based on the requirements of the programs that will run in it. In this case, for example, F2's programs require more storage than F1's.

Finally, the Shared Virtual Area is at the high end of the virtual address space. As I mentioned a moment ago, the SVA contains modules that can be shared among all the partitions.

GETVIS areas   Often, programs require additional storage space as they execute. To allow programs to acquire storage dynamically, VSE uses *GETVIS areas*. Figure 2-4 illustrates the locations of the two types of GETVIS areas: the system GETVIS area and the partition GETVIS areas.

As you can see, each partition has its own *partition GETVIS area*. A partition's GETVIS area occupies the highest address range within the partition. For example, in figure 2-4, the GETVIS area for F1 occupies the highest 48K bytes of storage within F1. (The minimum, and usual, size for a partition GETVIS area is 48K.) The maximum size program that may execute in a partition is the full partition size, minus the size of the partition GETVIS area. For example, in figure 2-4, the largest program that may execute in F3 is 1796K bytes (1844K − 48K).

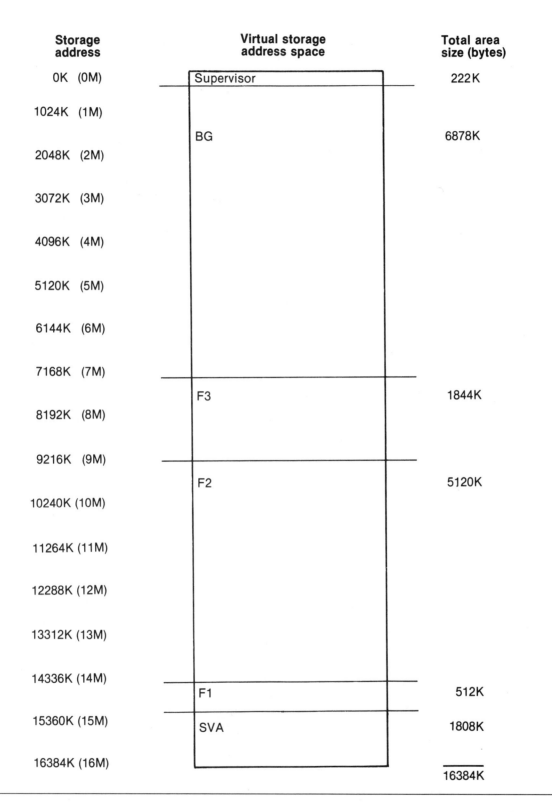

Figure 2-3 VSE address space usage on a four-partition system under ECPS: VSE mode or VM mode

Storage address	Virtual storage address space	Total area size (bytes)	GETVIS area size (bytes)
0K (0M)	Supervisor	222K	
1024K (1M)			
	BG	6878K	48K
2048K (2M)			
3072K (3M)			
4096K (4M)			
5120K (5M)			
6144K (6M)			
7168K (7M)	BG GETVIS area		
	F3	1844K	48K
8192K (8M)			
9216K (9M)	F3 GETVIS area		
	F2	5120K	48K
10240K (10M)			
11264K (11M)			
12288K (12M)			
13312K (13M)			
14336K (14M)	F2 GETVIS area		
	F1	512K	48K
	F1 GETVIS area		
15360K (15M)	SVA	1808K	464K
	System GETVIS area		
16384K (16M)			
		16384K	

Figure 2-4   Partition and system GETVIS areas on a four-partition system under ECPS:VSE mode or VM mode

The *system GETVIS area* occupies the high-address range within the SVA. It's used exclusively by VSE's system control programs. In figure 2-4, the system GETVIS area occupies 464K bytes. User programs that must acquire storage dynamically don't use the system GETVIS area. Instead, they use partition GETVIS areas.

Address space organization under 370 mode

In 370 mode, the situation is more complicated than it is under ECPS:VSE or VM mode. Under the most current versions of VSE, 370 mode can support up to 40M of virtual storage, not the 16M to which ECPS:VSE and VM modes are limited. However, this additional virtual storage is still "packaged" in 16M address spaces. What that means is that 370 mode can support not just one, but two or three virtual address spaces, all active at the same time. Like VM mode, 370 mode uses 4K pages. And like both ECPS:VSE and VM modes, 370 mode uses a system GETVIS area and partition GETVIS areas.

When a VSE system starts in 370 mode, one virtual address space exists. It contains the supervisor, the SVA, and the background partition. Then, foreground partitions are created based on the contents of start-up control statements coded by the systems programmer. Those control statements can direct VSE to create one or two more address spaces.

In 370 mode, a partition is either private or shared. A *private partition* is one that is present in only one address space. In contrast, a *shared partition* is one that is present in all of the active address spaces. Shared partitions are used for programs that need to be able to communicate with all other active partitions. Although VSE provides inter-partition communication facilities, they work only within a single address space.

(Later in this book, you'll learn about the IBM program products VSE/POWER and VTAM. Both of these products provide services for programs that can run in any of a system's partitions. To do so, they need to be able to communicate with those programs and, as a result, need to reside in a shared partition under 370 mode so they're available to any address space.)

Figure 2-5 shows how a VSE system running in 370 mode might be started so it supports three virtual address spaces, two shared partitions, and three private partitions. In part 1, the system is in its start-up condition. One address space is active, and it contains the three elements that are always present in 370 mode: the supervisor, the SVA, and the background partition. The default size for the background partition is 1M. Much of the remainder of the 16M address space is unused. Additional partitions can be created in this unused space, which is shaded in the figure.

Part 2 of figure 2-5 shows the system configuration after two foreground partitions (F1 and F2) have been started. As you can see, they reduce the amount of unused virtual storage in the address space. These

When VSE is started in 370 mode, one address space is created that contains the supervisor, the Shared Virtual Area, and the background partition

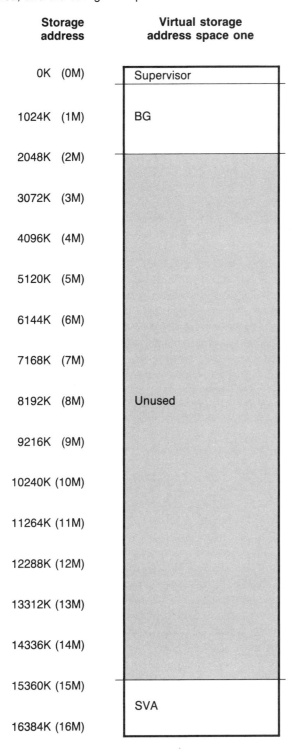

Figure 2-5   Virtual storage organization under 370 mode (part 1 of 4)

Start-up control statements allocate two shared partitions (F1 and F2)

Storage address	Virtual storage address space one
0K (0M)	Supervisor
1024K (1M)	BG
2048K (2M)	
3072K (3M)	
4096K (4M)	
5120K (5M)	
6144K (6M)	
7168K (7M)	
8192K (8M)	Unused
9216K (9M)	
10240K (10M)	
11264K (11M)	
12288K (12M)	
13312K (13M)	F2 (Shared)
14336K (14M)	
	F1 (Shared)
15360K (15M)	
	SVA
16384K (16M)	

Figure 2-5   Virtual storage organization under 370 mode (part 2 of 4)

A start-up control statement allocates the F3 partition in a second address space

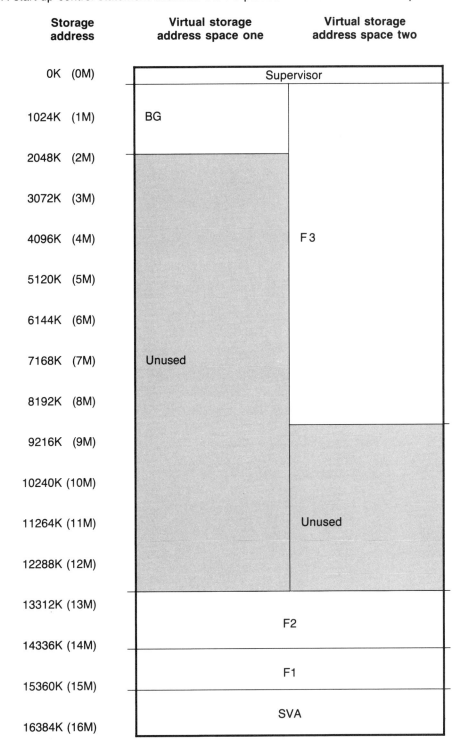

| Storage address | Virtual storage address space one | Virtual storage address space two |

0K (0M)	Supervisor
1024K (1M)	BG
2048K (2M)	
3072K (3M)	
4096K (4M)	F3
5120K (5M)	
6144K (6M)	
7168K (7M)	Unused
8192K (8M)	
9216K (9M)	
10240K (10M)	
11264K (11M)	Unused
12288K (12M)	
13312K (13M)	F2
14336K (14M)	F1
15360K (15M)	
16384K (16M)	SVA

Figure 2-5   Virtual storage organization under 370 mode (part 3 of 4)

A start-up control statement allocates the F4 partition in a third address space

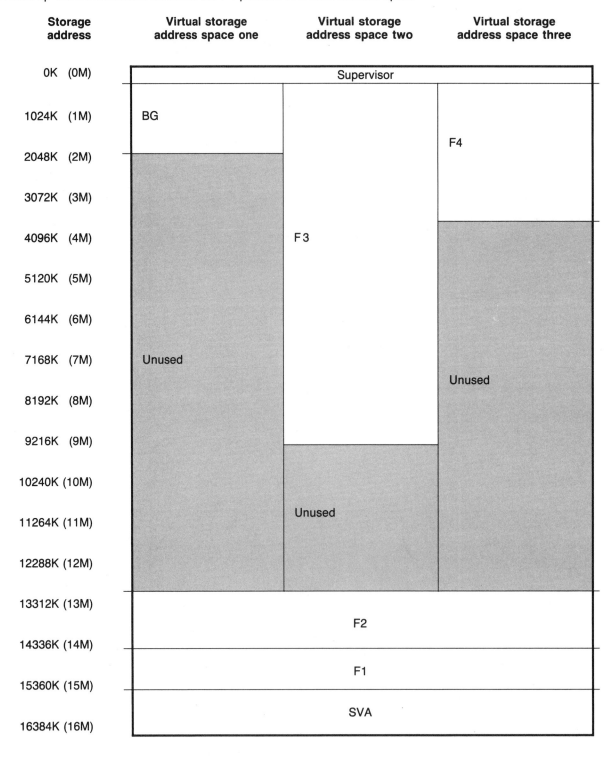

Figure 2-5   Virtual storage organization under 370 mode (part 4 of 4)

two partitions will be used for programs that must be able to communicate with all of the system's partitions, so they're defined as shared partitions. You should realize, though, that at this point only one address space is present.

Next, in part 3 of figure 2-5, a third foreground partition is allocated. In this case, however, the control statement that creates it specifies that it should be located not in the original address space, but in a second address space. As a result, VSE creates a second address space for F3. Notice here that the supervisor, the SVA, and the two shared partitions appear in both address spaces, and they use the same storage locations in the new address space as they do in the original one. Also notice, however, that the BG and F3 partitions, which are both private partitions, use storage only in their own address spaces.

Finally, in part 4 of figure 2-5, a fourth foreground partition (F4) is created. Like F3, it's a private partition. However, it's created not in the first or second address space, but in a third. At this point, all of the address spaces available under 370 mode have been activated.

Although 370 mode supports up to three address spaces, VSE still allows only 12 partitions. They can be allocated from any of the unused space in any of the three address spaces, as long as the total amount of virtual storage used for the supervisor, the SVA, the shared partitions, and the private partitions does not exceed 40M. Even though VSE is still restricted to 12 partitions, the increase in total address space size from 16M to 40M means partitions can be significantly larger under 370 mode then under ECPS:VSE or VM mode. And that's a big advantage for many shops.

DISCUSSION   To use VSE effectively, you need to understand multiprogramming and virtual storage. However, I want you to realize that VSE storage management is *not* simple. The system control programs that manage both multiprogramming and virtual storage represent many programmer-years of work. Although this topic may seem to be comprehensive, it only presents the minimum you need to know. If you want to learn the details of how VSE manages these functions, you can refer to the licensed IBM logic publications that are shipped with VSE. They should be available at your VSE installation.

Terminology   multiprogramming
supervisor program
supervisor
priority
task selection
partition
background partition
foreground partition
default

address space
virtual storage
real storage
page
page pool
page frame
page data set
page fault
paging
page swapping
swapping
SVA
Shared Virtual Area
program mode
real mode
virtual mode
pageable
resident
non-pageable
machine mode
370 mode
ECPS:VSE mode
Extended Control Program Support: VSE mode
VM mode
Virtual Machine/System Product
VM/SP
GETVIS area
partition GETVIS area
system GETVIS area
private partition
shared partition

Objectives

1. Describe how VSE implements multiprogramming.

2. Describe how VSE implements virtual storage.

3. Describe the function of the SVA.

4. Describe the difference between the real mode and virtual mode of program execution.

5. Describe the function of GETVIS.

6. Describe virtual storage organization under

    a. ECPS:VSE mode or VM mode
    b. 370 mode

TOPIC 2   How VSE manages user data

The services that manage user data are critical on a VSE system. Because data management is so important, all of the chapters in section 4 stress it. However, you need to be familiar with data management from the outset as you learn about VSE. As a result, this topic introduces you to VSE's basic data management concepts: label checking, file organizations, and access methods.

VSE LABEL CHECKING FUNCTIONS

When data is stored on disk or tape, VSE identifies it with special records called *labels*. Then, when you process the data later, you supply information in control statements that VSE compares with the label data. This insures that the correct data is processed.

You'll learn more about label processing in the chapters that follow. For now, I want to introduce the concepts of volumes and files. You need to understand both to understand the basics of label processing.

Volumes

A *volume* is a unit of a storage medium that can be mounted on an input/output device. For tape devices, a volume is a tape reel. For disk devices, a volume is a disk pack. For years, almost all volumes on IBM systems, both tape and disk, were removable. In other words, you could take a volume out of a DASD or off a tape drive and replace it with another one. Although newer DASDs use fixed packs, the terminology still applies; the packs in fixed-media DASDs are called volumes even though they can't be removed.

A typical VSE shop has many volumes, both disk and tape. As a result, they need to be labelled to insure that operators use the correct volumes at the correct times. Tape reels and removable disk packs should have *external labels* so system operators can select the proper volumes for particular applications. External labels are attached to the outside of a disk pack or tape reel. In addition, all tapes and disk packs should have *internal labels*, also called *volume labels*.

Volume labels   Unlike external labels, internal labels are stored on the recording medium, just like file records. Then, when I/O operations are to be performed on the files on a particular volume, VSE can read the internal volume label to verify that the correct volume is mounted.

Each VSE disk pack must have a standard volume label. (A *standard label* is one written in VSE format.) A tape volume probably should have a standard volume label, but it may have a non-standard label or no label at all. A volume with standard labels (either tape or disk) has a *VOL1 label*. The VOL1 label contains all the information VSE needs to perform its label checking functions on that tape or disk. A volume with standard labels may also have from one to seven supplementary volume labels called VOL2 through VOL8. However, these are strictly for information; VSE doesn't use them when it checks volume labels.

The most important data in the VOL1 label of either a tape or disk is the *volume serial number*, or *volser*. The volser is a six-character name that uniquely identifies the volume. When a new tape, disk pack, or DASD with a non-removable pack is initialized, it should be assigned a volser that's unique in your installation. The volume serial numbers of the DASD units in the configuration the last chapter described are: DOSRES (for the DASD at address 240), SYSWK1 (241), SYSWK2 (242), SYSWK3 (250), and SYSWK4 (251).

Files

The user data recorded on a volume is organized in one or more *files*. A file is a collection of related *records* that are treated as a unit. For instance, an employee file might contain one record for each of a firm's employees. Within a file, each record contains the same data elements as all the other records in the file.

The simplest file-volume relationship is a single file on a single volume. It's common for tape volumes to contain single files. For instance, one file of inventory records can be stored on one tape reel, like File-A in the top section of figure 2-6. Logically, this tape is called a *single-file volume*. It's less common for a disk volume to contain only one file, although it isn't unheard of, particularly for large files.

It's more likely that a DASD volume will hold many files. Then it's called a *multi-file volume*. The middle section of figure 2-6 illustrates a multi-file tape volume. Multi-file volumes, on both tape and disk, are common.

Some files are too large to fit on a single tape or disk volume. That doesn't mean that the file can't be stored, however, because it's possible for parts of one file to be stored on different volumes in a *multi-volume file*. This is illustrated again for tape in the bottom part of figure 2-6. Large multi-volume files can reside on DASDs, but you're also likely to find them on tape because tape is an economical storage medium for large files.

Tape file labels   Each file on a tape with standard labels must be identified at its beginning with a *file-header label (HDR1)* and at its end with an *end-of-file label (EOF1)*. It's also possible to have VSE write HDR2 through HDR8 and EOF2 through EOF8 labels. As with volume labels, however, these extra labels are for information only, so VSE ignores them when the tape is processed as input.

Figure 2-7 illustrates, in simplified form, where tape file labels are located. This example is a two-file tape. As you can see, the tape volume label (VOL1) comes first on the tape. Then, for each file, there's

Single-file volume

Tape volume

File-A	Unused

Multi-file volume

Tape volume

File-B	File-C	File-D	File-E	File-F	File-G

Multi-volume file

Tape volume

File-H (part 1 of 5)

Tape volume

File-H (part 2 of 5)

Tape volume

File-H (part 3 of 5)

Tape volume

File-H (part 4 of 5)

Tape volume

File-H (part 5 of 5)	Unused

Figure 2-6   File and volume relationships

a HDR1 label, the data, and an EOF1 label. VSE uses the HDR1 label to insure that the correct file is processed. The actual layout of a tape is a little more complicated than figure 2-7 indicates, but this figure presents all you really need to know at this point. If you'd like to learn more about the layout of tape files and labels, refer to *VSE/Advanced Functions Data Management Concepts*.

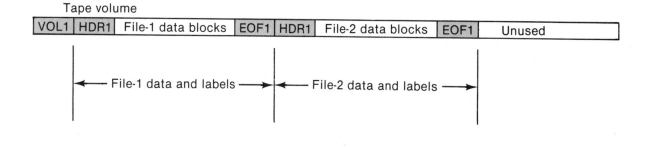

Figure 2-7   Location of tape labels

Disk file labels   Although tape files may or may not have labels (standard or otherwise), all DASD files must have standard labels. And unlike tape file labels, DASD file labels aren't stored with the file itself. Instead, they're stored in a special area on the disk volume called the *VTOC*, or *volume table of contents*. The VTOC contains one or more entries for each file on the volume. The entries identify the files and specify their locations on the volume.

Figure 2-8 illustrates this concept for a DASD volume with six files. In this example, each file is contained in one contiguous area of storage, or *extent*, although that's not a requirement for DASD files. In addition, the volume contains three free extents. Notice that the file labels aren't adjacent to the files, but are stored together in the VTOC. Each file label contains the location information VSE uses to access the file. Also, notice that the VTOC itself is a file; the records it contains are labels for the other files on the volume.

As you'd expect, figure 2-8 simplifies the organization of data on a DASD. First, a typical DASD volume contains more than six files. Second, some files in a production environment may reside in more than just one extent. And third, although figure 2-8 suggests a sequential relationship between file positions on the volume and label entries in the VTOC, that's not necessarily the case. If you want to learn more about DASD file labels, refer to *VSE/Advanced Functions Data Management Concepts*.

FILE ORGANIZATIONS AND ACCESS METHODS

In addition to label checking functions, VSE also provides you with different ways to access the data on the system. In other words, files on DASDs can be organized differently to meet different application requirements. After I introduce you to VSE file organizations, I'll describe the access methods that VSE offers to let you implement different file organizations.

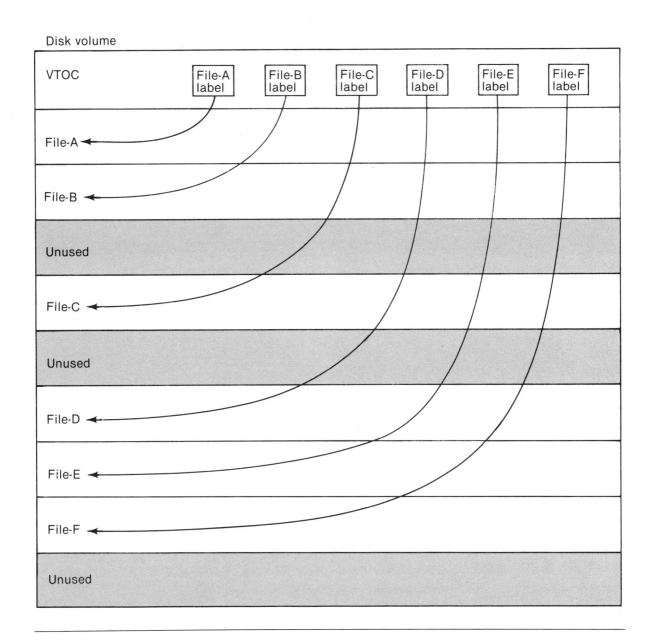

Figure 2-8   Location of DASD labels

File organizations   *File organization* refers to the way an application views a file's structure. On storage devices other than DASDs, data can only be organized sequentially. For example, in card and tape files, records follow one another in succession. To process a particular record, an application program needs to process all the preceding records in the file. For some applications, that's an efficient way to organize data.

Disk location	Social security number	First name	Middle initial	Last name	Employee number
1	213-64-9290	Thomas	T	Bluestone	00008
2	279-00-1210	William	J	Colline	00002
3	334-96-8721	Constance	M	Harris	00007
4	498-27-6117	Ronald	W	Westbrook	00010
5	499-35-5079	Stanley	L	Abbott	00001
6	558-12-6168	Marie	A	Littlejohn	00005
7	559-35-2479	E	R	Siebart	00006
8	572-68-3100	Jean	B	Glenning	00009
9	703-47-5748	Paul	M	Collins	00004
10	899-16-9235	Alice		Crawford	00003

Figure 2-9   An employee file with sequential organization

In contrast, when a file is stored on a DASD, it can be organized in more than one way. As a result, a systems designer who plans a DASD file needs to consider what the best organization for the file is. On a VSE system, there are three choices: (1) sequential organization, (2) indexed sequential organization, and (3) direct organization.

Sequential organization   Just as with data on cards and tape, data on a DASD can be stored with *sequential organization*. When that's the case, records are stored one after another in consecutive order. Often, a data element within each record contains a key value that's used to sequence the records in the file in a particular order. For instance, figure 2-9 illustrates a simple, 10-record employee file in sequence by employee social security number. In this example, the social security number field is the key field.

The key field doesn't have to be in the first position of each record. It could as well be located in the middle or at the end of the record. It might also be possible for this file to be sorted in a different sequence, such as employee last name. If so, it would still be a sequential file, only in a different order.

Sequential DASD files are most appropriate when they don't have to be accessed at random and when many of the records are changed each time the file is updated. When this is the case, sequential processing is efficient because access from one record to the next is fast. But sequential files are *not* very efficient if you want to change only a few records, because you still have to process the entire file.

Index component   **Data component**

Employee number	Disk location		Disk location	Social security number	First name	Middle initial	Last name	Employee number
00001	5		1	213-64-9290	Thomas	T	Bluestone	00008
00002	2		2	279-00-1210	William	J	Colline	00002
00003	10		3	334-96-8721	Constance	M	Harris	00007
00004	9		4	498-27-6117	Ronald	W	Westbrook	00010
00005	6		5	499-35-5079	Stanley	L	Abbott	00001
00006	7		6	558-12-6168	Marie	A	Littlejohn	00005
00007	3		7	559-35-2479	E	R	Siebart	00006
00008	1		8	572-68-3100	Jean	B	Glenning	00009
00009	8		9	703-47-5748	Paul	M	Collins	00004
00010	4		10	899-16-9235	Alice		Crawford	00003

Figure 2-10   An employee file with indexed sequential organization

Indexed sequential organization   With *indexed sequential organization*, it's possible to store records sequentially, but to access any one of them directly. To do this, an indexed sequential file contains two sections: a data section and an index section. Within the index section, each entry contains a key field value and the location of the corresponding record within the data section of the file. To use this method of file organization, each key field must have a unique value.

Figure 2-10 illustrates how the sequential file in figure 2-9 would be organized if it were an indexed sequential file. As you can see, if a record's key value is known (employee number, in this case), it's possible to access the record directly by retrieving its disk location from the index. On the other hand, it's also possible to access the records sequentially without using the index because the records were stored sequentially on the DASD in the first place. As you might expect, indexed sequential organization is more complicated than the figure indicates, but these concepts are all you need to know right now.

Direct organization   Like a record in a file with indexed sequential organization, a record in a file with *direct organization* can be accessed at random. However, unlike a file with indexed sequential organization, a file with direct organization doesn't have an index. Instead, direct organization depends on a direct relationship between data in each record and a DASD address, as figure 2-11 shows. In this case, the employee number and the disk location are the same. (Compare this to the indexed sequential file in figure 2-10 where the two fields are only indirectly related.)

In direct organization, the DASD address of a record is usually calculated using a formula that derives it from data in the record. This is called a *transformation algorithm*. When direct files are used, access to particular records is rapid. However, the programming complexities involved in using direct files often make them impractical.

Access methods

To process files with these different types of organizations, a VSE system uses access methods. An *access method* serves as an interface between application programs and the physical operations of storage devices. When you code an I/O instruction in an application program, you actually invoke an access method. Access methods relieve you of having to handle the complex technical details of using I/O devices.

The access methods available under VSE fall into two categories. In the first category are the VSE *native access methods*: SAM, ISAM, and DAM. They're a fundamental part of VSE and have been for a long time. I'll introduce you to them now, but I'll describe them in detail in later chapters. The second category includes only one access method: VSE/VSAM. Practically speaking, VSAM is now an integral part of VSE and is used for most DASD file processing. However, it's considered by IBM to be a separate software product. As a result, I'll describe it separately from the native access methods.

SAM   The *Sequential Access Method (SAM)*, as its name implies, is used to store and retrieve data sequentially. Whenever you access a card or tape unit, you invoke SAM services. Similarly, sequential files stored on DASD can be processed by SAM. SAM files on disk may reside on both FBA and CKD DASDs.

ISAM   The *Indexed Sequential Access Method (ISAM)* is used to store and retrieve data in files with indexed sequential organization. Unlike SAM files, ISAM files may reside only on DASD units. That makes sense, because direct access to individual records isn't possible on other storage units. In addition, ISAM files may reside only on CKD devices; ISAM isn't supported for FBA units.

DAM   The *Direct Access Method (DAM)* can be used to store and retrieve data on DASDs when you use direct organization. As with ISAM, DAM can only be used for files on DASDs, and then only on CKD DASDs.

VSAM   Unlike the native VSE access methods, *VSAM*, the *Virtual Storage Access Method*, can support files with any of the three organizations: sequential, indexed sequential, or direct. A VSAM file with sequential organization is called an *entry-sequenced data set*, or *ESDS*. (*Data set* means the same thing as file.) A VSAM file with indexed sequential organization is called a *key-sequenced data set*, or *KSDS*. (Although a VSAM key-sequenced data set is conceptually like an ISAM

Disk location	Social security number	First name	Middle initial	Last name	Employee number
1	499-35-5079	Stanley	L	Abbott	00001
2	279-00-1210	William	J	Colline	00002
3	899-16-9235	Alice		Crawford	00003
4	703-47-5748	Paul	M	Collins	00004
5	558-12-6168	Marie	A	Littlejohn	00005
6	559-35-2479	E	R	Siebart	00006
7	334-96-8721	Constance	M	Harris	00007
8	213-64-9290	Thomas	T	Bluestone	00008
9	572-68-3100	Jean	B	Glenning	00009
10	498-27-6117	Ronald	W	Westbrook	00010

Figure 2-11   An employee file with direct organization

file, it's implemented differently and uses a different access method.) And a VSAM file with direct organization is called a *relative-record data set*, or *RRDS*. As with ISAM and DAM, VSAM files may reside only on DASDs. However, VSAM files of any type may reside on both FBA and CKD DASDs.

VSAM offers more functions than the three native VSE access methods do. VSAM simplifies data management because it manages file creation and access through a catalog structure. In addition, VSAM manages the DASD space its files use; the native access methods don't. These advantages will be clearer to you after you've read chapter 13.

DISCUSSION   Although they may seem like the same thing, there is a difference between a file's organization and the access method that processes it. Organization is a logical concept, related to the applications that use the file. Access methods are collections of program components that let you implement file organizations. Figure 2-12 shows the relationships between the three types of file organizations available under VSE and the VSE access methods, for both sequential and random processing.

For files that require random processing, most VSE shops use VSAM key-sequenced data sets. Direct organization (implemented using either DAM or VSAM relative-record data sets) is unwieldly for most applications. And ISAM is relatively inefficient. For sequential processing, both SAM and VSAM entry-sequenced data sets are used. (For tape files, SAM is the only option.) As a result, what you really need to learn are SAM for sequential files and VSAM for key-sequenced data sets. ISAM and DAM are both antiquated. However, they are a part of VSE, and some shops still use them.

Sequential processing

Organization	SAM	ISAM	DAM	VSAM
Sequential	Supported			Supported
Indexed sequential		Supported		Supported
Direct				Supported

Random processing

Organization	SAM	ISAM	DAM	VSAM
Sequential				Supported
Indexed sequential		Supported		Supported
Direct			Supported	Supported

Figure 2-12   Access methods and supported file organizations for sequential and random processing

Terminology	label	sequential organization
	volume	indexed sequential organization
	external label	direct organization
	internal label	transformation algorithm
	volume label	access method
	standard label	native access method
	VOL1 label	Sequential Access Method
	volume serial number	SAM
	volser	Indexed Sequential Access Method
	file	ISAM
	record	Direct Access Method
	single-file volume	DAM
	multi-file volume	VSAM
	multi-volume file	Virtual Storage Access Method
	file-header label	entry-sequenced data set
	HDR1 label	ESDS
	end-of-file label	data set
	EOF1 label	key-sequenced data set
	VTOC	KSDS
	volume table of contents	relative-record data set
	extent	RRDS
	file organization	

Objectives

1. Explain the function of volume and file labels.

2. Describe the three file organizations available under VSE.

3. List the VSE access methods that can be used for each type of file organization supported by VSE.

TOPIC 3   Components of a complete VSE system

The material this chapter has presented so far has been related to basic VSE concepts. To really understand a production VSE system, though, you need to be familiar with a variety of files and software products and their interrelationships. So this topic introduces the other files and software components you're likely to find on your VSE system.

First, you'll learn about VSE libraries. These are the specialized DASD files whose main purpose is to store programs in various forms. Second, I'll introduce you to the system files VSE requires. Third, I'll give you quick descriptions of the other software products that supplement VSE on a typical production system.

VSE LIBRARIES

The software components that make up a complete VSE system number in the hundreds, and they're all stored on DASD. As you can imagine, managing all of them as separate DASD files would be inefficient and could easily get out of control. So to help systems personnel keep track of program components, VSE components are stored in special files called libraries.

Each VSE *library* is a DASD file that contains one or more *sublibraries*. Each sublibrary contains a collection of sub-files, or *members*. And each member can be one of several *member types*. You identify a specific member by its library, sublibrary, member name, and member type. Figure 2-13 shows the hierarchical structure of a VSE library.

Each library and sublibrary has a directory that lists its contents. Each *library directory* contains information on its sublibraries. And each *sublibrary directory* contains information on its members, including the members' names, types, DASD locations, and sizes.

In addition to the VSE components that must reside in your system's library space, you can also store user-written applications in libraries. In fact, you will probably be working more directly with libraries and sublibraries that contain components you've written yourself than with those that contain operating system components. To store your own members in libraries, you need to understand how sublibraries and their members can be organized.

Members

As I just said, the members of a sublibrary can be identified by name and member type. The member types are related to a standard series of steps you go through when developing a program on a VSE system. First, you code the program. Second, you compile (or assemble) it. Third, you link edit the program. And fourth, you code the control statements that will invoke it. (You'll learn more about these steps later;

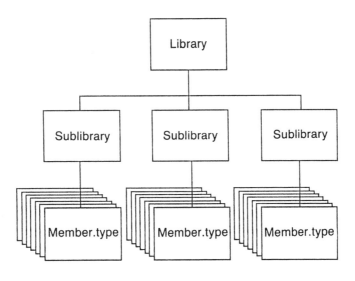

Figure 2-13   The hierarchical structure of VSE libraries

for now, I just want to mention them in the context of libraries.) As figure 2-14 shows, the member types in VSE libraries correspond to the output of each of these four steps.

Source books   The output of the coding step is a source program in whatever language you use (such as COBOL, assembler, or PL/I). When a source program is complete, it's typically stored in a sublibrary. A source program that's a member in a sublibrary is called a *source book*.

When the same segments of source code are used in several programs, it's efficient to store them in a sublibrary. Then, they can be copied into your source program at compile or assembly time. Source books that are used like this are called *copy books*.

Object modules   The output of the compilation (or assembly) step is an *object module*. If an object module will be used by a number of different programs, you will probably store it as a *subprogram* in a sublibrary. That way, you only need to write, translate, and store the module once. After the module is in object format, it is ready to be link-edited.

Phases   When an object module is processed by the linkage editor program, it is converted into code that can be executed by the machine. This module, called a *phase*, is now ready to be run.

Procedures   When a program is complete, you use job control statements to invoke it. Frequently used sequences of job control statements can be written as *procedures*. The procedures can then be stored in a sublibrary and used again and again.

Dumps   When a program *abends* (ends abnormally), the system produces a *dump*. The dump includes the contents of the parts of internal storage that the failing program was using or that were related to it. This system data can often help you analyze the program failure. Under DOS VSE/AF version 1, dumps were written to an alternate dump file defined by the user. Under DOS VSE/AF version 2.1, however, dumps are standardized library members that the system automatically writes when an abend occurs.

User-defined members   In addition to the five predefined member types, you can also assign your own member types to any members in a library. The only restriction is that a member type be between one and eight alphameric characters long. (IBM defines alphameric characters as the letters A through Z, the integers 0 to 9, and the characters @, $, and #.) *User-defined member types* can be used, for example, to store several versions of the same procedure. To do that, you would give each version a different user-defined member type, except for the current version; it would have the procedure member type.

Sublibraries

You can use sublibraries to store programs, procedures, dumps, or any other data files that may be needed on the system. Any or all of the file types may be stored in a single sublibrary. So you can store all related members together in one sublibrary. For example, if you are developing a large application program, you can define a sublibrary to contain its source books, object modules, phases, and associated procedures.

The library structure in the old version of DOS (VSE/AF version 1) had no sublibraries. Instead, there were four different types of libraries whose contents were restricted to a particular type of member. The new version of DOS (VSE/AF version 2.1), however, has made the VSE library structure more flexible by letting an installation customize its library structure.

Because of the increased flexibility of the VSE 2.1 library structure, it's important that you plan the organization of your libraries carefully. I recommend you store the different members of each application together in a single sublibrary, as in the above example. But there are other ways to organize them that will work as well. The important thing is that you make a plan and stick to it.

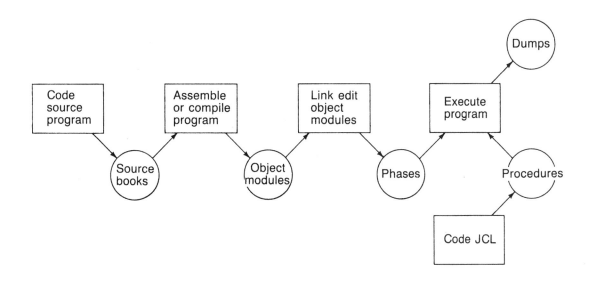

Figure 2-14   Program development and VSE library member types

The system library
and private libraries

VSE provides two different types of libraries: the system library and private libraries. Although their contents are different, both the system library and private libraries have the same logical structure; each contains sublibraries and members.

Every VSE system installation contains the *system library* with at least one system sublibrary. Located in this sublibrary are all the system programs needed for start-up and operation. The system library and the system sublibrary within it reside in a special file called the *system residence file*, or just *SYSRES*.

All other libraries are *private libraries*. Private libraries are usually located on disk volumes other than the SYSRES volume. In this case, "private" simply means that a library is outside the SYSRES file; it doesn't mean that access to a private library is necessarily restricted.

VSE FILES

To function properly, VSE requires that several system files be available. One of these that you should remember from topic 1 is the page data set. Another is SYSRES. Still others you're likely to read about in IBM manuals are the recorder file, the hard copy file, and the system history file.

The recorder file   The *recorder file* stores data IBM representatives use to resolve system problems. That data includes error codes and statistics on CPU and I/O errors. The recorder file requires about 1/3M of DASD storage on a typical system.

The hard copy file   The *hard copy file* stores all messages sent to the system console; it requires about 2M. Because all messages are stored, it's possible for the system operator to defer responding to messages that might otherwise require immediate action. Instead, the operator can retrieve them later from the hard copy file for appropriate action. This is called *asynchronous operator communication*.

The system history file   The *system history file* (also about 2M) contains a detailed record of the service that's been applied to the components of the operating system. Because VSE and its related software products are so complicated, they do have bugs. So when users encounter problems, IBM tries to correct them by issuing software updates that can be applied to an installed system. To keep an accurate record of the service that's been applied, each installation maintains its own system history file. The *Maintain System History Program* (*MSHP*), a special program supplied as part of VSE, controls the service applied to the system and the data recorded in the system history file.

VSE SOFTWARE COMPONENTS

A production VSE system uses a variety of related software products. Some of these are components of the operating system itself; others are separately licensed products. In most cases, however, the practical distinction between programs in the two groups isn't clear. A fully functioning VSE system must use some separately licensed products (like VSAM) and may not use all of the facilities of the basic operating system. As a result, in addition to being familiar with the critical components of VSE itself, you also need to know about the other IBM software products that make up a complete system.

VSE/AF   At the heart of a VSE system's software is *VSE/Advanced Functions* (or *VSE/AF*). Throughout this book, I'll describe VSE/AF facilities and functions. Thus far, you've been introduced to VSE storage management (multiprogramming and virtual storage) in topic 1, VSE data management in topic 2, and VSE libraries in this topic. Other services the programs of VSE/AF provide are system start-up, job control, operator communication, and some utility functions. In chapters 4, 5, and 6, you'll learn how to use the job control facilities of VSE.

VSE/POWER   *VSE/POWER* provides a function required for a VSE system to operate efficiently: *spooling*. Spooling manages card devices and printers for application programs by intercepting program I/O requests for those devices and routing them to or from disk files instead.

For example, if a processing program attempts to print a line on a printer, the line is spooled to a disk file. Because DASDs are faster than printers, spooling allows the processing program to resume execution more rapidly. Later, when the processing program has finished execution, the print lines temporarily stored on DASD are actually printed.

The same spooling technique is used in reverse for card input files. As cards pass through the reader, the data from them isn't immediately processed by the application program. Instead, it's stored on disk until all of the cards have been read. Then, when the processing program begins execution, records are supplied to it from the DASD file, not from the card reader.

The result of spooling is a two-fold benefit. First, programs can execute more rapidly because their I/O requests are satisfied at DASD speeds rather than printer or card device speeds. Second, and probably more important, several programs that would otherwise require exclusive control of the same card devices and printers can execute at the same time. Without spooling, a program that writes to a printer has complete control of the device until it has finished executing, so other programs that create printer output have to wait.

POWER (that's how I'll refer to VSE/POWER from now on) stands for Priority Output Writers, Execution processors, and input Readers. It runs in a high priority partition and can provide spooling services for all lower priority partitions. POWER not only provides spooling services for program input and output, but it also serves as a job scheduler. It uses a scheme of classes and priorities to determine when and in what partition a program will execute. POWER also routes output to appropriate devices and is used to control those devices.

Because POWER performs such useful system functions, you need to understand how it works and how to use it. Since much of your interaction with VSE will be through POWER, you'll learn what you need to know to use it in chapters 7, 8, and 9.

Telecommunications access methods   For a system to support any terminal devices, local or remote, it must include a *telecommunications (TC) access method*. TC access methods provide facilities for building and operating data communications applications. Although it's possible to write assembler language programs that use TC access methods directly, it's more common for them to be used through other IBM program products, such as CICS/VS, which I'll describe in a moment. On a VSE system, two TC access methods are available: *BTAM* and *VTAM*.

On smaller VSE systems, the TC access method most likely to be used is *BTAM-ES* (*Basic Telecommunications Access Method — Extended Support*). BTAM-ES provides routines that programmers can use to code telecommunications applications in assembler language.

On larger systems with heavier communications workloads, you're more likely to find VTAM in use. VTAM is part of IBM's *System Network Architecture*, or *SNA*.

VSE/ICCF   *VSE/ICCF*, or just *ICCF* (*Interactive Computing and Control Facility*), is a comprehensive time-sharing system that allows a VSE system to operate without card input and output devices. Under ICCF, users at terminals can create, maintain, and store card-image files that contain control statements, data, or source programs. ICCF stores those card-image files on DASD.

In the next chapter, I'll introduce you to ICCF. Later, sections 3 and 5 present advanced ICCF functions. For now, I just want you to recognize that ICCF runs in close conjunction with the terminal-control program that manages the terminal network, CICS/VS.

CICS/VS   *CICS/VS* (*Customer Information Control System/Virtual Storage*) not only provides ICCF terminal control services, but can also support a large network of both local and remote terminals that run a wide variety of interactive applications. *CICS* is a sophisticated *data base/data communications* (*DB/DC*) *system* that serves as an interface between interactive application programs and VSE. It controls communications between the central processor and terminals, manages concurrently executing application programs for all terminal users, and controls access to files by those programs.

DL/I   Another software product for data management that might be available on your system is a data base management system called *DL/I* (*Data Language I*). DL/I allows users to set up and maintain complex hierarchical data bases from application programs.

Language translators and the linkage editor   *Language translators* are the programs that convert source programs into object modules. One language translator, the assembler, is supplied as a part of VSE. Other language translators, the COBOL, PL/I, RPG II, and FORTRAN IV compilers, are separate products. The purpose of the language translators is to reduce the programming time required to prepare a working object program. As a result, they all print diagnostic (error) listings to help the programmer correct clerical errors. In addition, they often provide debugging statements to help the programmer test the program.

The *linkage editor* program, supplied as part of VSE, converts object modules into executable phases and combines multiple object modules into a single phase. In section 5, you'll learn how to use both the language translators and the linkage editor.

VSE Librarian   Not only does the linkage editor combine modules to create phases, but it's also used to add phases to sublibraries. In addition to the linkage editor, though, VSE includes a specialized program that performs library service and maintenance functions, the *VSE Librarian*. You'll learn how to use it in section 5.

Utility programs   Certain routine processing functions, such as copying files and sorting the records within a file, are common to most computer installations. As a result, most shops use a set of general-purpose *utility programs* (or *utilities*) to perform these functions. Then, specialized programs don't have to be created to perform common functions. Instead, you can supply parameters to a general-purpose utility program to specify the exact processing it should do. Although I won't present all of the VSE utilities in this book, I'll describe three of the most useful ones (Sort/Merge, VSE/DITTO, and AMS) in section 6.

Interactive Interface   To help you use VSE, your system may have an *Interactive Interface*. This interface is a set of menus and data entry panels that make it easier to use different VSE components like ICCF, POWER, and some utility programs. It's usually customized at each installation and sometimes even tailored to an individual user. Since this interface isn't standard on all systems, I'm not going to cover it in this book. But regardless of how it's set up at your shop, if you understand how the basic VSE components and programs work, you should have no problem working with the interface.

DISCUSSION   As you can tell by now, a VSE system is a complex collection of many components. But don't worry at this point if you're confused by the large number of terms and acronyms. They'll become second nature as you become more familiar with VSE.

Figure 2-15 should help you better understand the material this chapter has presented. It shows the address space I described in topic 1, but it also illustrates the software products typically executed in a system's partitions. Keep in mind, though, that an actual system is likely to run more partitions than the four shown in this figure.

In figure 2-15, the spooling product POWER executes in F1, the highest priority partition. As a result, it can provide spooling and job scheduling services for the other partitions. The SVA contains modules that are used throughout the system, such as SAM and VSAM components. F3 and BG are reserved for batch applications. The only reason BG is so large is that no other partitions are configured. If this system included F4 and F5, the size of BG would be reduced accordingly. Finally, F2 is used for CICS and ICCF. As you can see, CICS and ICCF require a large partition. In the next chapter, you'll learn why.

Storage address	Virtual storage address space		
0K (0M)	Supervisor		
1024K (1M)	BG	Available for low priority batch jobs	
2048K (2M)			
3072K (3M)			
4096K (4M)			
5120K (5M)			
6144K (6M)			
7168K (7M)			
8192K (8M)	F3	Available for high priority batch jobs	
9216K (9M)			
10240K (10M)	F2	ICCF and CICS	
11264K (11M)		Available for interactive program execution and time-sharing by multiple users	
12288K (12M)			
13312K (13M)			
14336K (14M)			
15360K (15M)	F1	POWER Spooling program	
	SVA	Common phases (e.g. VSAM components)	
16384K (16M)			

Figure 2-15   Partition usage in the sample system

Terminology

library
sublibrary
member
member type
sublibrary directory
library directory
source book
copy book
object module
subprogram
phase
procedure
abend
dump
user-defined member type
system library
system residence file
SYSRES
private library
recorder file
hard copy file
asynchronous operator communication
system history file
Maintain System History Program
MSHP
VSE/Advanced Functions
VSE/AF
VSE/POWER
spooling
POWER
telecommunications access method
TC access method
BTAM
VTAM
BTAM-ES
Basic Telecommunications Access Method—Extended Support
System Network Architecture
SNA
VSE/ICCF
ICCF
Interactive Computing and Control Facility
CICS/VS
Customer Information Control System/Virtual Storage
CICS
data base/data communications system
DB/DC system
DL/I
Data Language/I

language translator
linkage editor
VSE Librarian
utility program
utility
Interactive Interface

Objectives

1. List the VSE library member types and describe how they fit in the sequence of program development for a typical application.

2. Differentiate between a system library and a private library.

3. Describe the functions of:

   Maintain System History Program
   POWER
   telecommunications access methods
   ICCF
   CICS

Chapter 3

An introduction to VSE/ICCF

Much of the work you do on a VSE system requires that you key in text and data. On early systems, that entry work was done almost exclusively by keypunching. Today, keypunching is a thing of the past. Instead, you'll enter text and data interactively at a display station.

To use the VSE features in this book, you'll need to know how to use a display station. In many VSE shops, the program product VSE/ICCF is what you'll use to do this terminal work. As a result, this chapter presents the basics of ICCF—just enough so you'll be able to work with it to use the other VSE elements this book presents. In later chapters, I'll describe some advanced features of ICCF that you may want to use. For now, though, I just want you to learn the elementary terminology and concepts of ICCF (topic 1) and how to use ICCF's editing facilities to key in data (topic 2).

If your shop runs VSE under VM, you may use CMS (the Conversational Monitor System) and its text editor XEDIT to do terminal entry. However, since VM, CMS, and XEDIT are subjects unto themselves, I'm not going to cover them in this book. If CMS is what's available on your system, I suggest you skip this chapter and read my book *VM/CMS Commands and Concepts* instead.

TOPIC 1   Basic ICCF concepts and commands

In this topic, you'll learn the essential concepts you need to work with ICCF. In addition, you'll learn how to use basic ICCF commands. Although you can learn about ICCF by studying IBM manuals, that can be confusing and frustrating for two reasons.

First, some ICCF components have names that sound like VSE counterparts. As a result, unless you're thoroughly familiar with both VSE and ICCF, they can confuse you. In this topic, I'm going to stress the terminology that can be particularly troublesome.

Second, ICCF is complicated. It's a powerful program product with a large set of commands and features. However, you'll only need a small subset of them most of the time. Unfortunately, the IBM manuals present the ICCF commands as though they're all important. They're not. In this topic and the next, I'll describe only the commands you really need to know. If you want to learn more about ICCF, I recommend you read my *DOS/VSE ICCF* book.

How ICCF uses processor storage

To understand ICCF, you need to be familiar with the way it uses processor storage and how it services the commands you issue. Of course, ICCF executes in a VSE partition. But the way ICCF uses the virtual storage in its partition is more complex than the way a routine application program uses storage. This is illustrated in figure 3-1. You can think of the ICCF partition as being divided into four parts: (1) the terminal control program, (2) the ICCF main control program, (3) ICCF command processors, and (4) interactive partitions.

As you interact with ICCF at your display station, terminal I/O is handled by the terminal control program. Recall from chapter 2 that CICS serves as the terminal control program and executes in the same partition as ICCF.

ICCF functions other than terminal control are managed by the ICCF main control program. The ICCF command processors interpret and handle the commands you issue. When you enter commands or text, the main control program, the terminal control program, and the command processors work together to fulfill your requests.

In ICCF terms, the interactive work you do is *foreground processing*. This processing takes place within the ICCF partition under control of the ICCF main control program, the terminal control program, and the ICCF command processors. However, don't confuse ICCF foreground processing with the work done in a VSE foreground partition. Remember that the ICCF partition is itself a VSE foreground partition.

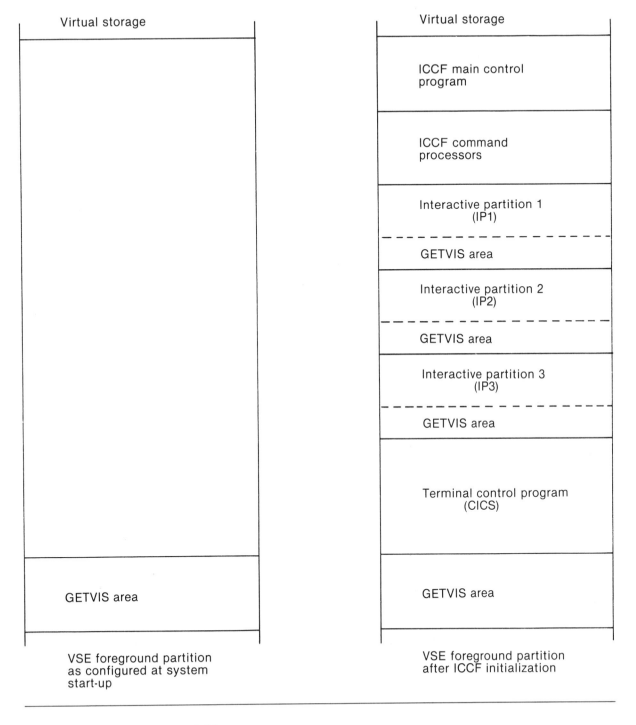

Figure 3-1   ICCF storage usage

You might assume that if you can do foreground processing within ICCF that you can also do *background processing,* and you can. While ICCF foreground processing is characterized by continuous interaction with you at your terminal, basic background processing is essentially independent of your terminal. In fact, it's even possible to detach your terminal from a background execution and do foreground work while it runs. As you can imagine, then, ICCF background processing has a lower priority than foreground processing.

Background processing takes place in *interactive partitions,* which are actually contained within the larger ICCF partition. Don't let the "interactive" in "interactive partition" confuse you, however. An ICCF interactive partition is used to do batch work entirely within the ICCF environment; it's not typically used to run programs that interact with the user. Although ICCF can support up to 35 interactive partitions, only three are configured in the example in figure 3-1.

Interactive partitions do have some characteristics in common with VSE partitions. For example, you can run programs in them and they have their own GETVIS areas. As you'll see later in this book, you can use interactive partitions to translate programs at your terminal and to execute other programs.

The ICCF library

ICCF records all users' data in a large DASD file called the *ICCF library file.* The ICCF library file, also called *DTSFILE* (DTS is the VSE prefix for ICCF), is central to the functions of ICCF. As a result, it's important that you understand what it is and how it's used.

One of the most confusing parts of ICCF terminology is the use of the term "library." So I want to be sure you understand how it's used before I describe the other elements of ICCF. The ICCF library file is *not* one of the VSE libraries. VSE libraries are processed by the VSE Librarian, but the ICCF library file is processed only by the components of ICCF. And although there can be any number of VSE libraries on a system, there can be only one ICCF library file in use at one time.

The confusion is compounded because on a typical VSE system, similar data can be stored in both the ICCF library file and in a sublibrary of a VSE library. For example, some source programs may be stored in a VSE sublibrary, while others are stored in the ICCF library file. In general, it's easier to store text (like source programs) in the ICCF library file than in a VSE sublibrary. This is because when text is stored in the ICCF library file, it's a simple matter to retrieve or modify it; that's not so easy when it's stored in a VSE sublibrary. However, in a shop with heavy ICCF use, limiting the size of the ICCF library file may be an important concern—one that's serious enough to dictate that completed source programs be stored elsewhere. Since standards for the use of the ICCF library file vary from installation to installation, find out what they are in your shop.

The distinction between the ICCF library file and VSE libraries is confusing enough. But the confusion is compounded because within the ICCF library file are subdivisions that themselves are called *ICCF libraries*, or just *libraries*. In fact, when you read the term "library" within the context of ICCF, it almost always refers to one of these subdivisions. Remember, though, that these libraries, identified by numbers, don't exist as independent files; they're all contained within the ICCF library file.

As an ICCF user, you will have one of the ICCF libraries designated as your *primary library*. You may have exclusive use of it, or you may have to share it with other users. In addition, you may be able to access other libraries, but that varies from shop to shop.

Some ICCF libraries have specialized purposes. For example, library 1 is usually used for system administration, and library 2 is usually a *common library*. The common library contains data available to all users at all times.

Within each library, ICCF stores data in *library members*, or just *members*. You can store any kind of data you wish in a library member: program source code, job streams, test data, or object code. The only restriction is that the data stored in a library member has to be in 80-character card-image format.

A simple ICCF terminal session

To begin an ICCF terminal session, you key in

    ICCF

and tap the enter key. Then, you have to log on to use the system.

Logging on   To log on, you supply your ICCF *user-id* and *password*. Both are specified in your *user profile*, a record that contains information that identifies you to ICCF. Your user profile also contains information about how you can interact with ICCF and what ICCF facilities and resources you can use. For instance, the user profile always specifies your primary library. The user profile is created by the *ICCF administrator*, who is a systems programmer responsible for controlling access to ICCF and for insuring that it works at optimum levels for your environment.

You issue ICCF commands by keying them in on the top line of the screen and tapping the enter key. To log on, I enter

    /LOGON STEV

Here, /LOGON is an ICCF command and STEV is my user-id. As you might guess, ICCF accepts only user-ids that have already been defined in a user profile. If you try to log on with a user-id that isn't defined in a user profile, ICCF doesn't let you continue. Since STEV is defined in my user profile, ICCF proceeds and prompts me for my password.

The password is up to six characters long, and it's also assigned to you by the ICCF administrator. Depending on your user profile, though, you may be able to change your password yourself. After ICCF

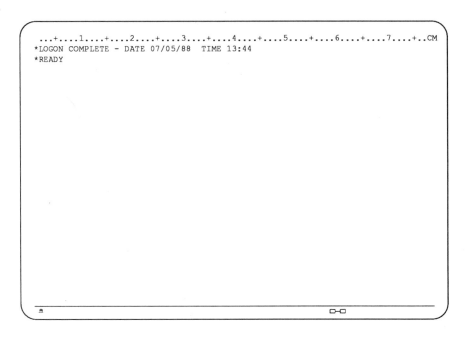

```
...+....1....+....2....+....3....+....4....+....5....+....6....+....7....+..CM
*LOGON COMPLETE - DATE 07/05/88  TIME 13:44
*READY
```

Figure 3-2   The ICCF completed log on screen

validates the password you enter against your user profile, you'll see the screen shown in figure 3-2. This lets you know the log on process is complete and you can start work.

Command mode   During and just after your log on, ICCF is in *command mode.* (That's what the CM in the upper right corner of the screen in figure 3-2 means.) In command mode, you can issue *system commands* or enter other modes. You'll learn about two other modes later in this chapter.

An ICCF system command consists of a slash followed by a brief *operation code* that indicates the command's function. Usually, you can also enter *operands* on a system command that provide more specific information about what the command should do. For example, in the command I entered to log on, /LOGON is the operation code and STEV, the user-id, is the operand. Figure 3-3 presents the most useful of the more than 60 ICCF system commands. Once you've seen how a few work, they're all easy to understand.

A system command you'll use often is /LIB. In its simplest form, it displays a directory list of the members in your primary library. Figure 3-4 shows what the output of the /LIB command might look like. The first line identifies the primary library (15), gives the current date and time, and shows how many directory entries are available in the library (0006).

Command	Function
/LIB	List the directory of the primary library.
/LIB COMM	List the directory of the common library.
/LIST name	List text in the specified member without line numbers.
/LIST	List text in the input area without line numbers.
/LOGON user-id	Begin an ICCF terminal session.
/LOGOFF	End an ICCF terminal session.
/PURGE name	Delete the specified member.
/RENAME name new-name	Change the name of the specified library member to the new name.

Figure 3-3   Basic ICCF system commands

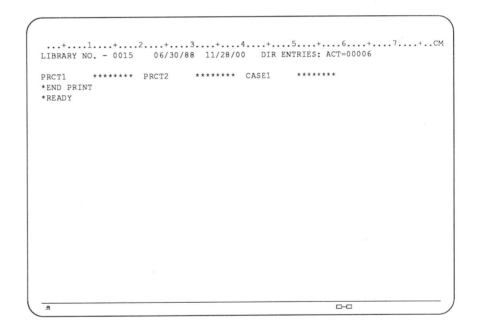

```
   ...+....1....+....2....+....3....+....4....+....5....+....6....+....7....+..CM
   LIBRARY NO. - 0015    06/30/88  11/28/00   DIR ENTRIES: ACT=00006

   PRCT1    ******** PRCT2    ******** CASE1    ********
   *END PRINT
   *READY
```

Figure 3-4   Output of the ICCF /LIB command

As you can see, you don't have to use all the available directory entries. In this case, there are three members: PRCT1, PRCT2, and CASE1 in a six-entry library. The three rows of asterisks in the figure represent unused directory entries. As new members are added to this

```
...+....1....+....2....+....3....+....4....+....5....+....6....+....7....+..LS
       IDENTIFICATION DIVISION.
       *
       PROGRAM-ID. TRANLST.
       *
       ENVIRONMENT DIVISION.
       *
       CONFIGURATION SECTION.
       *
       INPUT-OUTPUT SECTION.
       *
       FILE-CONTROL.
           SELECT ARTRANS  ASSIGN TO SYS005-UR-2540R-S.
           SELECT TRANLIST ASSIGN TO SYS006-UR-1403-S.
       *
       DATA DIVISION.
       *
       FILE SECTION.
       *
       FD  ARTRANS
           LABEL RECORDS ARE OMITTED
```

Figure 3-5   Output of the ICCF /LIST command

library, the available directory entries are used. Then, new directory entries are created as they're needed.

Notice the member names in figure 3-4. When you create a member in an ICCF library, you have to name it. The name can be from one to eight characters long and must begin with a letter.

List mode   To view the contents of a library member, you can use the /LIST command. For example, if I key in

```
/LIST PRCT1
```

and tap the enter key, ICCF displays the screen in figure 3-5. As you can see, the library member PRCT1 contains a COBOL source program. If the member is too long to be displayed on one screen, as in figure 3-5, your terminal goes into *list mode*. (That's what the LS in the upper right corner of the screen in figure 3-5 means.) Then, you tap the enter key to refresh the screen with the next section of text.

To page through the member, you tap the enter key repeatedly until you find the section you're interested in. You can continue to tap the enter key until you reach the end of the member. Then, the terminal returns to command mode. Alternatively, you can press the PA2 key on the display station's keyboard at any time to end list mode and return immediately to command mode.

Logging off   To end your terminal session, all you do is key in the system command

    /LOGOFF

and press the enter key. Be sure to log off when you're finished with a terminal session to prevent other users from working under your user-id.

Discussion

To use ICCF effectively, you need to understand libraries and foreground and background processing, and you need to be able to issue the system commands in figure 3-3. However, as an ICCF user, you'll spend most of your terminal time entering text using the full-screen editor. So that's what the next topic teaches you.

Terminology

foreground processing	member
background processing	user-id
interactive partition	password
ICCF library file	user profile
DTSFILE	ICCF administrator
ICCF library	command mode
library	system command
primary library	operation code
common library	operand
library member	list mode

Objectives

1. Differentiate between the following terms:

> ICCF foreground processing
> ICCF background processing
> VSE foreground partition
> VSE background partition
> ICCF partition
> ICCF interactive partition

2. Differentiate between the following terms:

> VSE library
> ICCF library file
> ICCF library
> ICCF library member

3. Given your ICCF user-id and password, log on, use the system commands in figure 3-3, and log off.

TOPIC 2   How to use the ICCF full-screen editor

The ICCF *full-screen editor* lets you enter data and store it in a library member. In addition, it lets you retrieve data from a library member and make changes to it. Although ICCF provides other ways of entering and storing data (such as the line-oriented *context editor*), the full-screen editor is the simplest to use and the most powerful. As a result, I'm going to show you how to use the full-screen editor, not the other techniques.

How to invoke the full-screen editor

You invoke the full-screen editor with the ICCF supplied macro called ED. (A *macro* is a series of ICCF commands stored in a library member. When you run a macro, the commands it contains are processed by ICCF one by one, just as if you entered them at the terminal interactively. However, you only need to enter the macro name to invoke them.) You do this by keying in

    ED

The ED macro, by the way, is stored in the common library, so it's available to all ICCF users.

When you use the full-screen editor, you can process text in two ways. First, you can work directly on a library member. When you do, any changes you key in are recorded in the library member as you work. To invoke the full-screen editor to edit an existing library member, you enter a command like this:

    ED MNT5200

This command causes the full-screen editor to begin and to use the member MNT5200 in your primary library.

A second way to use the full-screen editor is to edit a temporary work area called the *input area*. Each user has a separate input area that ICCF maintains in the library file. If you invoke the full-screen editor without specifying a member name, you'll be editing your input area.

ICCF uses the input area for a variety of functions, so depending on what you've done during your terminal session, your input area may or may not already contain text. Figure 3-6 presents the screen ICCF displays when you invoke the full-screen editor to edit the input area and the input area is empty. Here, the indicators for the top and the end of the file are together. If the input area had contained text, the text would appear between those indicators.

I want you to notice the parts of figure 3-6 I've labelled. The second line of the screen contains a *scale line* you can use to identify column

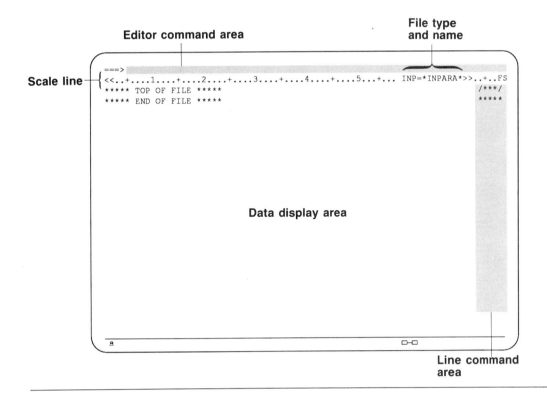

Figure 3-6   Areas on the ICCF full-screen editor screen

positions within the text you edit. Embedded in the scale line is a field that displays what you're editing. In this figure, the value

```
INP=*INPARA*
```

indicates that I'm editing the input area. If I were editing a library member, it would look something like

```
MEM=MNT5200
```

where MNT5200 is the member name. The FS on the right side of the scale line indicates that ICCF is in the full-screen editor.

The other two labelled areas in figure 3-6 are command entry areas. You can use the top line of the screen to enter editor commands just as you enter system commands. This is the *editor command area*. You can use the area on the right side of the screen to enter special full-screen editor commands. This is the *line command area*. As their names imply, you enter different types of commands in these two areas.

How to use commands for the full-screen editor

Editor commands   *Editor commands* are entered at the top of the full-screen editor screen. As with system commands, there are more editor commands for the full-screen editor than I'm going to cover; in all, there are more than 80. However, those in figure 3-7 are the essential ones. As you can see, I've divided the commands in figure 3-7 into four groups: commands to (1) manage library members, (2) scroll the text, (3) search for text, and (4) end the full-screen editor.

Commands in the first group let you retrieve text from an existing member and store text you've created. Of these four commands, the two you'll use most often are GETFILE and FILE.

When you use the full-screen editor to edit an existing member, any changes you make are recorded in the member as you work. For that reason, you'd be wise not to work directly on an important member, but rather on a copy of it stored in the input area. To work on a member in the input area, you invoke the full-screen editor (by entering ED without a member name); then, you use the GETFILE command to copy in the member you want to edit. Once you do this, you can edit freely without worrying about making unrecoverable changes. For example, to copy the member TRANLST into the input area, you enter

```
GETFILE TRANLST
```

in the editor command area. (Incidentally, you can abbreviate GET-FILE as GET.)

After you've finished an editing session, you can store the edited text from the input area in a new library member with either the SAVE or FILE command. For example, to store the text from the input area in a new member called TRANLST2, you enter

```
SAVE TRANLST2
```

The difference between SAVE and FILE is that FILE not only stores the text you're editing, but it also ends the full-screen editor. In contrast, when you issue the SAVE command, your editor session continues.

If you want to store the text you've been editing in a library member that already exists, you use the REPLACE command. For example, the command

```
REPLACE TRANLST
```

causes the text from the input area to be stored in the member TRANLST, replacing whatever was originally in that member.

When you're editing text that's more than a full screen long, you need to be able to move up and down in the text so the lines you want to edit are displayed on the screen. This is called *scrolling*, and is controlled by the editor commands in the second group in figure 3-7.

Commands to manage library members

Command	Function
FILE name	Store the text being edited in the specified member and end the full-screen editor (equivalent to SAVE followed by QUIT).
GETFILE name	Insert the text from the specified member at the current position.
REPLACE name	Store the text being edited in the specified member after deleting the original text in that member.
SAVE name	Store the text being edited in the specified member.

Commands to scroll the text

Command	Function
BACKWARD n	Scroll backward n screens.
BOTTOM	Scroll to the last line in the text.
DOWN n (NEXT n)	Scroll forward n lines.
FORWARD n	Scroll forward n screens.
TOP	Scroll to the first line in the text.
UP n	Scroll backward n lines.

Commands to search for text

Command	Function
LOCATE text	From the current position, locate the next line that contains the specified text.
SEARCH text	From the beginning of the text, locate the first line that contains the specified text.

Commands to end the full-screen editor

Command	Function
CANCEL	End the full-screen editor.
END	End the full-screen editor.
QUIT	End the full-screen editor.

Figure 3-7   Basic editor commands for the ICCF full-screen editor

Command	Function
An	Insert n lines (up to 999) after the indicated line.
Cn	Clear the copy work area and copy n lines (from 1 to 99), beginning with the indicated line, into the copy work area. Does not delete those lines from the member.
Dn	Delete n lines (up to 999), beginning with the indicated line.
I	Insert the text in the copy work area after the indicated line.
Kn	Copy n lines (from 1 to 99), beginning with the indicated line, into the copy work area, appending them to the text currently there. Does not delete those lines from the member.
Mn	Clear the copy work area and copy n lines (from 1 to 99), beginning with the indicated line, into the copy work area. Deletes those lines from the member.
''n	Duplicate the indicated line n times (from 1 to 999) after the current line.
/	Make the indicated line the current line.

Figure 3-8   Basic line commands for the ICCF full-screen editor

If you have a long library member and you want to locate a specific text string within it, you can use one of the two commands in the third section of figure 3-7. To locate the first occurrence of a text string anywhere in your text, use the SEARCH command. To locate a text string at a position after your current position, use the LOCATE command.

When you're finished with your full-screen editor session, you can enter CANCEL, END, or QUIT. All three end the session. Although CANCEL, END, and QUIT have different effects when you use advanced features of the full-screen editor, they're the same for the basic editing techniques this chapter presents. As I already mentioned, you can also end an editing session by entering a FILE command. This has the same effect as a SAVE command followed by QUIT.

Line commands   In addition to commands you key in at the top of the screen, you can also use *line commands* to manipulate lines within the text. Figure 3-8 illustrates the basic line commands. Although there are other line commands, they're not as useful as the ones I've listed.

```
===>
<<..+....1....+....2....+....3....+....4....+....5....+..  INP=*INPARA*>>..+..FS
***** TOP OF FILE *****                                                 A100/
***** END OF FILE *****                                                 *****
```

Figure 3-9   Entering an ICCF full-screen editor command to add 100 lines to an empty input area

You enter a line command in the line command area on the right side of the screen on the line you want it to affect. If you want to process a group of continuous lines, you enter the command on the first line you want it to affect. For instance, figure 3-9 shows how you can use a line command to insert 100 blank lines in an empty input area. To do this, type A (for add) in the line command area and follow it with the number of lines you want to add. (If you omit the number of lines, ICCF assumes you mean one.) Figure 3-10 shows the full-screen editor display after this add command has been processed. The other line commands work in a similar way.

Once you have a work area, you can key in text. Basically, all you have to do when you use the full-screen editor is key in the characters you want in the positions you want. If you want to change text displayed on the screen, you just type the new value right over the old value. You can also move the cursor around the screen using the cursor control keys. Figure 3-11 shows the full-screen editor display after I keyed in the first part of a COBOL program.

```
===>
<<..+....1....+....2....+....3....+....4....+....5....+.. INP=*INPARA*>>..+..FS
***** TOP OF FILE *****                                               /***/
                                                                      *===*
                                                                      *===*
                                                                      *===*
                                                                      *===*
                                                                      *===*
                                                                      *===*
                                                                      *===*
                                                                      *===*
                                                                      *===*
                                                                      *===*
                                                                      *===*
                                                                      *===*
                                                                      *===*
                                                                      *===*
                                                                      *===*
                                                                      *===*
                                                                      *===*
                                                                      *===*
```

Figure 3-10   The ICCF full-screen editor screen after adding 100 lines to an empty input area

```
===>
<<..+....1....+....2....+....3....+....4....+....5....+.. INP=*INPARA*>>..+..FS
***** TOP OF FILE *****                                               /***/
        IDENTIFICATION DIVISION.                                      *===*
      *                                                               *===*
      PROGRAM-ID. TRANLST.                                            *===*
      *                                                               *===*
      ENVIRONMENT DIVISION.                                           *===*
      *                                                               *===*
      CONFIGURATION SECTION.                                          *===*
      *                                                               *===*
      INPUT-OUTPUT SECTION.                                           *===*
      *                                                               *===*
      FILE-CONTROL.                                                   *===*
          SELECT ARTRANS  ASSIGN TO SYS005-UR-2540R-S.                *===*
          SELECT TRANLIST ASSIGN TO SYS006-UR-1403-S.                 *===*
      *                                                               *===*
      DATA DIVISION.                                                  /===*
      *                                                               *===*
      FILE SECTION.                                                   *===*
      *                                                               *===*
      FD  ARTRANS                                                     *===*
          LABEL RECORDS ARE OMITTED                                   *===*
          RECORD CONTAINS 80 CHARACTERS.                              *===*
```

Figure 3-11   The ICCF full-screen editor screen after entering 21 lines of text and a line command to reset the current line pointer

```
===>
<<..+....1....+....2....+....3....+....4....+....5....+.. INP=*INPARA*>>..+..FS
        DATA DIVISION.                                                   /===/*
     *                                                                   *===*
        FILE SECTION.                                                    *===*
     *                                                                   *===*
        FD  ARTRANS                                                      *===*
            LABEL RECORDS ARE OMITTED                                    *===*
            RECORD CONTAINS 80 CHARACTERS.                               *===*
                                                                         *===*
                                                                         *===*
                                                                         *===*
                                                                         *===*
                                                                         *===*
                                                                         *===*
                                                                         *===*
                                                                         *===*
                                                                         *===*
                                                                         *===*
                                                                         *===*
                                                                         *===*
                                                                         *===*

   a                                                        ▭–▭
```

Figure 3-12   The ICCF full-screen editor screen after resetting the current line pointer

After you've filled a screen, you need to scroll down to be able to enter more of the program. To do this, you can enter either a DOWN or FORWARD command in the editor command area. Or you can use the line command **/** to reset the *current line pointer*, which identifies your position within a member. In figure 3-11, the current line is indicated by the slash in the line command area on the first line (TOP OF FILE). To reset this pointer, you enter a slash on another line. Then, when you tap the enter key, that line becomes the current line, as you can see in figure 3-12. Now, you can continue to enter the program source code.

To end the editing session, I entered

```
FILE TRANLST2
```

in the editor command area. ICCF then stored the text I entered in the member TRANLST2 and returned my terminal to command mode.

Discussion   The best way to learn the ICCF commands for the full-screen editor is to use them. Once you've used a few, they'll come easily to you. To enter and edit text, you can get by with the commands you've learned in this topic. However, you might find it useful to get a copy of my *DOS/VSE ICCF* book to see what other commands are available. I'm sure you'll find some of them useful.

Terminology   full-screen editor
context editor
macro
input area
scale line
editor command area
line command area
editor command
scrolling
line command
current line pointer

Objective   Use the commands for the full-screen editor presented in this topic to enter and store text in a new member and to modify text in an existing member.

Section 2

Job control language

In this section, you'll learn what you need to code a variety of production jobs. The first two chapters in this section cover similar material, but at different levels. Chapter 4 introduces you to JCL by presenting basic job control statements at an elementary level. Then, chapter 5 gives you more information about some of the statements chapter 4 introduced and presents some additional statements. Finally, chapter 6 shows you how to use some of the more advanced features of VSE JCL: cataloged procedures, conditional JCL, and symbolic parameters.

Chapter 4

Basic VSE JCL

This chapter will teach you how to code jobs using a basic subset of VSE's job control language. Topic 1 describes the format of job control statements and the structure of a job. Then, it introduces several job control statements. Topic 2 illustrates the information in topic 1 with two complete production jobs.

In this and the following chapters, you'll learn how to code JCL to perform a variety of VSE functions. However, to learn the material in later chapters, you have to master the material in this chapter. So be sure you feel comfortable with it before you read on.

TOPIC 1   Basic VSE JCL statements

A *job* is one or more programs presented to VSE for execution as a single unit of work. Each program within a job comprises a *job step*. To define what a job is to do and to describe its system environment, you code statements from VSE's *job control language*, or *JCL*. A series of job control statements, possibly combined with some data to be processed, is a *job stream*.

Job streams may be submitted to VSE for execution in several ways. The old-fashioned way was to submit a deck of job control cards from a system card reader. Then, the job stream was called a *job deck*. Today, a job stream probably wouldn't be stored on cards. Instead, it would be stored on DASD, either in a VSE sublibrary or, more likely, in the ICCF library file.

To create a job and store it in the ICCF library file, you usually use the full-screen editor. Then, you can use ICCF's *submit-to-batch facility* to submit a job from the ICCF library file to VSE for execution. In chapter 9, you'll learn how to use the submit-to-batch facility.

With few exceptions, VSE installations use POWER as a job scheduler. When you submit a job, either from a card reader or an ICCF terminal, POWER stores it on DASD. After that, POWER schedules the job to execute in a VSE partition. Although you won't learn about POWER in detail until section 3, you should realize now that VSE jobs almost always execute under POWER's control.

No matter how job streams are stored and submitted on your system, you code job control statements in 80-character card-image format. As a result, even when JCL is stored on DASD, you can call individual JCL statements "cards" and job streams "job decks."

HOW TO CODE JCL STATEMENTS

To make it easier for you to understand how to code JCL, you can divide the 80-character statement into the seven fields figure 4-1 illustrates: (1) the name field, (2) the operation field, (3) the operands field, (4) the comment field, (5) the continuation field, (6) the sequence number field, and (7) the modifier field. Although IBM literature doesn't document all these as separate fields, it's easier to learn how to code VSE JCL if you remember them.

In practice, most statements require only the name, operation, and operands fields, as in the statement in figure 4-1. You'll seldom need to use the comment, continuation, sequence number, and modifier fields. As a result, you shouldn't feel overwhelmed by the number of fields that can make up a job control statement.

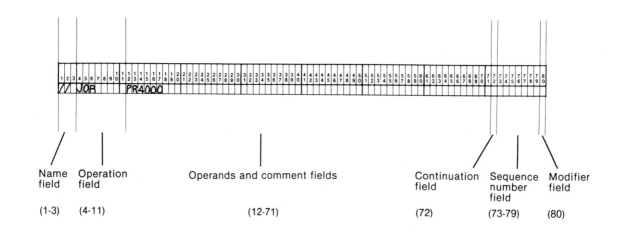

Figure 4-1   Format of a VSE job control statement

The name field   The *name field* (columns 1-3) identifies a card (or card image) as a job control statement. The name field contains two slashes followed by a space (//) in all JCL statements except five (*, /*, /&, /+, and /.). Frankly, calling the first three positions of a job control statement the "name field" is confusing, but that's how the IBM literature refers to them.

If you omit the //, VSE treats the line as a *job control command*; then, it may have a different effect than a job control statement. As a result, you should always code // unless you specifically want the line to be treated as a job control command. In this book, I'm not going to cover job control commands, because you'll seldom, if ever, need to use them.

The operation field   The *operation field* (columns 4-11) follows the name field. In it, you code a VSE JCL operation code that specifies the statement's function. Figure 4-2 lists the VSE JCL operation codes. Notice that they're all seven or fewer characters long. This topic introduces the JOB, EXEC, ASSGN, LIBDEF, DLBL, EXTENT, ID, and PAUSE operation codes. Later on, you'll learn more about these statements, as well as most of the others in figure 4-2. (By the way, you don't have to start the operation code in column 4, but I think your JCL will be more readable if you do.)

The operands field   The *operands field* begins at least one space after the operation code and can extend up through column 71. I recommend you always code the operands field beginning in column 12. The operands field is where you provide the information required for the statement to be processed properly. For some statements, the operands field can be complicated, containing a series of several *operands* (also called *parameters*) separated by commas. Since VSE assumes that the

ASSGN	LIBDEF	PWR
CLOSE	LIBDROP	RESET
DATE	LIBLIST	RSTRT
DLBL	LISTIO	SETPARM
EXEC	MTC	SETPRT
EXTENT	ON	STDOPT
GOTO	OPTION	TLBL
ID	OVEND	UPSI
IF	PAUSE	ZONE
JOB	PROC	

Figure 4-2   VSE JCL operation codes

operands are complete when it encounters a blank, make sure you don't include a blank in your operands field by accident. If you need to include a blank as part of an operand, enclose the operand value between apostrophes.

Operands may be of two types: positional or keyword. A *positional operand* must occur in a specific position in a string of parameters in a statement. That means VSE determines what an operand is by its position in the string. When you code a statement with positional operands and you omit some, you may need to account for the missing operands by coding extra commas. This will be clearer to you when you see examples later in this topic. As you'll see, some statements use positional operands only, while other statements use both positional and keyword operands.

With *keyword operands*, you don't have to account for omitted operands. Instead, you identify the operand in another way: by coding a keyword identifier in front of it. In a moment, I'll point out some examples of keyword operands.

The comment field   If you don't fill the operands field with parameters, you can code a brief comment in the remainder of the field. This area is the *comment field*. As you can see, then, the comment field doesn't have a fixed starting position; it begins wherever the operands field ends. That's why figure 4-1 shows the same range of columns for these two fields. After VSE encounters a space (not enclosed within apostrophes) in the operands field, it ignores the rest of the statement, up through column 71. So it ignores the comment field.

As a general rule, I advise you not to include comments in JCL statements. As it is, VSE JCL is difficult enough to read, and comments often make it worse. So use comments sparingly, if you use them at all.

The continuation field   Although you must code most JCL statements on a single line, ten JCL statements may be continued on one or more lines. These statements are: DLBL, EXEC, IF, LIBDEF, LIBDROP, LIBLIST, PROC, SETPARM, SETPRT, and TLBL.

To continue a line, code a *continuation character* (IBM recommends a C) in column 72, the *continuation field*. In addition, the columns between the last comma in the operands field and the continuation character must be blank. In other words, you can't include a comment in a continued statement. Subsequent lines of the continued statement must begin in column 16.

The sequence number field   If you want, you can include sequence numbers in columns 73 through 79 of your JCL statements. This is the *sequence number field*. Although sequence numbers aren't useful in most instances, you may want to code them if your shop still uses cards. Then, if you drop a job deck, you can put it back in order.

The modifier field   The *modifier field* is no longer used with the new version of DOS (VSE/AF version 2.1). Under the old version of VSE, you could use the modifier field to override a statement in a VSE cataloged procedure, but its function has been replaced by conditional JCL and symbolic parameters. (You'll learn about both of these features in chapter 6.) As a result, you should just leave column 80 blank.

Guidelines for coding JCL statements   As I've already mentioned, VSE JCL can be difficult to read. Although you can't do much to eliminate the problem, you can follow a few suggestions to make your job streams uniform. As I see it, the most useful thing you can do to make your JCL more readable is to align like elements of code. So I suggest you always code the operation code beginning in column 4 and the operands beginning in column 12.

If all you do is align your code, you'll be taking a big step toward making your job streams more readable. But you can improve them even more by following two other recommendations. First, avoid using comments since they usually make your JCL more difficult to read. Second, avoid continuation lines and sequence numbers where you can, for the same reason. If you follow these guidelines, your JCL will be easier to code, read, and maintain.

HOW TO IDENTIFY JOBS AND JOB STEPS

A job, consisting of one or more job steps (programs), is submitted as a single unit of work to VSE. To control the transitions between jobs and job steps, VSE uses its *job control program*. This program interprets your JCL and controls the execution of all application programs. Although the job control program isn't present in a partition when an application program is running, the job control program is loaded into a partition whenever it's needed.

Three job control statements delimit jobs and job steps to the job control program. The job control program identifies a new job when it encounters a JOB statement. Within a job, it identifies a job step when it encounters an EXEC statement. And it identifies the end of a job

The JOB statement

```
// JOB   job-name [accounting-information]
```

Explanation

job-name	A one- to eight-character name that identifies the job to VSE.
accounting-information	Data used by the VSE job accounting interface. If the interface is active on your system, the value you code must be 16 characters long and must be separated from job-name by one space.

Figure 4-3   The JOB statement

when it encounters the end-of-job statement (/&) or, if /& is missing, another JOB statement. After I introduce each of these statements, I'll show you how your use of jobs and job steps can affect the sequence in which programs are executed.

The JOB statement   Figure 4-3 presents the JOB statement with its positional operands. Because up to 12 jobs can be running at the same time in VSE's partitions, it's important to be able to refer to a job by name. So on the JOB statement, you should always code a one- to eight-character *job name*. Then, when VSE issues messages to the system operator, it uses that name. Also, listings produced by the job are labelled with the job name.

Because a typical VSE installation has hundreds of jobs, their names need to be descriptive and standardized. As a result, your shop probably has rules for creating job names. If so, you should find out what they are.

The second operand of the JOB statement, accounting information, is optional. You use it only if the VSE job accounting interface was specified when your system was generated. Otherwise, accounting information coded on the JOB statement is treated as a comment. If you do code accounting information, it must begin one space after the job name. Just what you'll code for accounting information depends on your shop's standards.

The end-of-job (/&) statement   At the end of each job, you should code the end-of-job statement (/&). Obviously, this is one of the five JCL statements that doesn't begin with //. If the job control program encounters a JOB statement without a preceding /&, it assumes the /& was present. Even so, it's a good practice to end each job with /&.

```
// JOB       COMPLNK                    ⎞
   .                                    ⎟
   .                                    ⎟
// EXEC      FCOBOL ⎞                   ⎟
   .               ⎬ Job step 1         ⎬ Job
   .               ⎠                    ⎟
// EXEC      LNKEDT ⎞                   ⎟
   .               ⎬ Job step 2         ⎟
   .               ⎠                    ⎟
/&                                      ⎠
```

Figure 4-4   A skeleton of a two-step job

The EXEC statement   The EXEC statement specifies the name of a program to be executed and, as a result, delimits a job step. Its basic format is

```
// EXEC     program-name
```

The EXEC statement can be more complex than this, as you'll see in the next chapter when I present its complete format. Right now, though, I just want you to understand the differences between a job (identified by a JOB statement) and a job step (identified by an EXEC statement).

To illustrate, consider figure 4-4. It's a skeleton of a two-step job that compiles a COBOL program and link edits the resulting object module. As you can see, the entire job is marked at the beginning by a JOB statement and at the end by a /& statement. Two EXEC statements specify the programs to be executed, so they mark job steps. To be complete, this job stream would require additional statements to define the program's system environment and data cards containing the COBOL source code. Nevertheless, figure 4-4 shows you the basic structure of the job.

The sequence of program execution if a job step fails   If any step in a job fails or terminates abnormally, the job control program bypasses the remaining steps in the job, and the job ends. In figure 4-4, for example, if the compile step (EXEC FCOBOL) fails, the link edit step (EXEC LNKEDT) won't be executed. That's desirable because the link edit step depends on the successful completion of the compile step.

In other situations, however, one job step may not depend so clearly on a preceding one. Then, you may not want all job steps to be cancelled when an earlier step fails. To avoid this problem you can either avoid coding unrelated job steps in a single job, or you can use conditional JCL.

If you code unrelated job steps as separate jobs within a single job stream and one program fails, the others will still execute. To illustrate,

Job stream		Next program executed if current program ends normally	Next program executed if current program ends abnormally
// JOB	A		
// EXEC	A1	B1	B1
/&			
// JOB	B		
// EXEC	B1	B2	C1
// EXEC	B2	C1	C1
/&			
// JOB	C		
// EXEC	C1	C2	D1
// EXEC	C2	C3	D1
// EXEC	C3	D1	D1
/&			
// JOB	D		
// EXEC	D1		
/&			

Figure 4-5   The sequence of program execution for a job stream with multiple jobs

consider the job stream skeleton in figure 4-5. This job stream contains four separate jobs. Two of the jobs (A and D) have only one step; one (B) has two steps; and one (C) has three steps. The column on the right side of the figure shows what program executes next if any of the job steps terminates abnormally. If you study this figure, you should develop a good understanding of how jobs and job steps are handled within a job stream.

If you use conditional JCL, you can code jobs that evaluate return codes from job steps to determine what processing has been done. Then, based on the return codes, your jobs can conditionally perform other job steps. You'll learn about conditional JCL in the second topic of chapter 6.

A job step can terminate abnormally for reasons other than a program failure. If, for example, VSE can't locate the program you specify on an EXEC statement, the job step—and the job—fails. Although VSE always searches the system sublibrary of the system library for a phase, VSE may not be able to locate a phase stored in a private sublibrary unless you provide information about that sublibrary's location in your JCL.

HOW TO ESTABLISH SUBLIBRARY SEARCH CHAINS

To cause VSE to search one or more private sublibraries for a phase, you need to establish a sublibrary *search chain* (or sublibrary *concatenation chain*). Sublibraries related in a search chain are called *concatenated sublibraries* or *chained sublibraries*. Although a search chain gives the sequence VSE uses to search sublibraries, this doesn't imply any physical relationships among the sublibraries in the chain. You can search through all the sublibraries belonging to the one library, or you can search several sublibraries located in separate libraries.

To establish a search chain, you code the LIBDEF statement in your job stream before the EXEC statements that load and execute phases stored in the chained sublibraries. Although this section introduces LIBDEF for setting up sublibrary search chains for phases, you can use the statement to set up search chains for other types of VSE library members as well. You'll learn how to do that in the next chapter.

The LIBDEF statement   The format of the LIBDEF statement to establish a phase search chain is

```
// LIBDEF  PHASE,SEARCH=(lib1.slib1,...,lib15.slib15)
```

Here, the first operand (PHASE) is positional, and the second operand (SEARCH=) is a keyword operand. The list of names you code in the keyword operand specifies the sequence of sublibraries VSE searches for a phase. Although you can code up to 15 sublibrary names in one search chain, you'll usually use fewer. The library names must be between one and seven alphameric characters long, and the sublibrary names must be between one and eight alphameric characters long. The library names must have already been defined to the system with DLBL and EXTENT statements. (I'll describe those statements in a moment.)

A typical LIBDEF statement is

```
// LIBDEF  PHASE,SEARCH=(USR1.AP2,USR3.AP3,USR2.AP4)
```

This statement establishes a search chain that begins with USR1.AP2 (USeR 1.APplication 2), continues with USR3.AP3, and ends with USR2.AP4. If you follow this LIBDEF statement with

```
// EXEC   MNT2100
```

VSE first searches the directory of USR1.AP2 for the phase MNT2100.

If VSE finds the phase, it loads and executes it. But if it doesn't find MNT2100 in USR1.AP2, VSE searches USR3.AP3. And if it doesn't find it there, it searches USR2.AP4. Finally, if VSE doesn't find the phase in the last library in the concatenation chain, it searches the system sublibrary. (Its name is IJSYSRS.SYSLIB.) If that fails, VSE displays an error message for the system operator and ends the job abnormally.

If programs in different sublibraries have the same name, it's possible to execute the wrong program if you make an error in a LIBDEF statement. You're most likely to have this problem when you maintain duplicate copies of programs in production and test sublibraries. And since it's surprisingly easy to code a LIBDEF statement that points to the wrong sublibrary, take care.

HOW TO SPECIFY A JOB'S DEVICE REQUIREMENTS

To execute a program properly, you need to do more than code an EXEC statement for it. You also need to specify its system environment. That means you have to specify the relationships between the program's I/O requests and the physical devices it will use.

When a program issues an I/O request, it doesn't specify the address of the device it will use. If it did, it would be restricted to that device. Then, if the device were out of service, the program wouldn't work. And if the same function were to be performed on different devices, a separate program with the proper device address for each would be required.

To avoid these problems, VSE uses *symbolic I/O assignment*. In other words, programs don't refer directly to the devices they use. Instead, they issue I/O requests using symbolic names called *logical units*. Then, the job stream that invokes a program must establish its processing environment by relating the logical units the program uses to the device addresses of physical units. The JCL statement you code to do this is the ASSGN statement.

The ASSGN statement and logical units   The basic format of the ASSGN statement is:

```
// ASSGN    SYSxxx,cuu
```

where SYSxxx is the logical unit name the program specifies and cuu is the address of the device you want to associate with that logical unit. All logical unit names are six characters long and begin with SYS.

The logical unit names you're likely to code in application programs, called *programmer logical units*, have numbers between 000 and 255 in the xxx position of the name. These numbers depend on how your system was generated and on your shop's standards. As a general rule, lower numbers are more common than higher ones, so you're more likely to use SYS020 than SYS200. In addition, it's common practice (although not required) to use SYS005 for a card reader, SYS006 for a printer, and SYS007 for a card punch.

The device address (cuu) is the standard VSE three-hex-digit address, where the first digit (c) is the device's channel address and the second and third (uu) are its unit address. For example,

```
// ASSGN    SYS010,300
```

relates the logical unit SYS010 (specified in the program) to the physical device at address 300.

As you'll see in the next topic, you can code other operands on the ASSGN statement and use device specifications other than the standard VSE cuu addresses. For example, you can code an ASSGN statement in the form

```
// ASSGN    SYSxxx,SYSyyy
```

to assign one logical unit (SYSxxx) to another that's already been assigned (SYSyyy). In the next chapter, I'll describe still other variations of ASSGN.

System logical units   In addition to programmer logical unit names, VSE also uses a set of *system logical unit* names. Since you'll need to use some of these in your JCL, you should be familiar with them. As a result, figure 4-6 lists all the system logical units, the device types usually associated with them, and their functions. As you can see, system logical unit names begin with SYS, just like programmer logical unit names. However, the last three characters of system logical unit names are letters that describe the function of the unit. For instance, SYSRDR refers to the system card reader, and SYSLST refers to the system printer.

You need to be familiar with system logical units because many VSE components refer to them instead of programmer logical units. For example, the job control program accepts its input from the device assigned to SYSRDR, not a programmer logical unit. As a result, when the system is started, each active partition must have SYSRDR assigned to an appropriate device. Otherwise, the job control program can't process JCL for that partition, and programs can't be run in it. On a typical VSE system, POWER provides SYSRDR input for all partitions under its control.

Don't let the term "system" logical unit lead you to believe there's only one SYSRDR or SYSLST in a system. Instead, each partition has its own set of system logical units. What must be unique is the relationship between a system logical unit and the physical device associated with it by an ASSGN statement. For example, a printer at address 00E can only be assigned to SYSLST for one partition. So if the printer is assigned to SYSLST for partition F1, no other partition may assign SYSLST (or any other logical unit) to 00E.

VSE/POWER reduces the inconveniences this sort of contention for devices can cause. When you use POWER, you assign printers and

System logical unit	Native device type	Function
SYSCAT	DASD	VSAM master catalog
SYSRES	DASD	System residence file
SYSREC	DASD	Recorder, hard copy, and system history files
SYSLNK	DASD	Input to the linkage editor
SYSRDR	Card reader	Job control input
SYSIPT	Card reader	Data input
SYSIN	Card reader	Combines SYSRDR and SYSIPT
SYSPCH	Card punch	Punch output
SYSLST	Printer	Print output
SYSOUT	Tape unit	Combines SYSLST and SYSPCH
SYSLOG	Terminal	Operator communication

Figure 4-6   VSE system logical units

card devices to the POWER partition. Then, when a program in another partition needs to read a card record or write a print or punch record, it doesn't do so directly. Instead, POWER intercepts its I/O request and provides the necessary service. In chapter 7, you'll learn how POWER works in detail.

HOW TO SPECIFY A JOB'S DISK FILE REQUIREMENTS

Most of the jobs you code will do some sort of disk file processing. For files on DASD (and also on tape, in some instances), VSE performs data security functions to insure that files are properly accessed. As you learned in chapter 2, data security functions center on label processing. For disk files, you code DLBL and EXTENT statements to supply the information VSE uses to perform its label-processing functions.

When you create a new DASD file, VSE uses the label information you supply to (1) generate the label for the new file and (2) insure that the area for the new file isn't already in use by another current file. When you access an existing file, VSE compares the label information from the JCL with the information in the file label to insure, for example, that the correct tape reel or disk pack is mounted on the assigned device and that the file you need is actually present.

The label information you code in DLBL and EXTENT statements is stored temporarily in VSE's *label information area* in the system residence file. Since it's possible to make permanent entries in the label information area, you may not have to code the same DLBL and EXTENT statements over and over for frequently used files. For instance, you'd almost certainly want to store label information permanently for sublibraries used in LIBDEF statements throughout an installation. So in chapter 10, I'll show you how to make permanent entries in the label information area.

Whether or not you store label information permanently, you'll need to code DLBL and EXTENT statements at some times to access DASD files. So right now, I'll give you the information you need to code simple DLBL and EXTENT statements for SAM files. Then, in section 4, I'll present what you need to know to code more complex label statements for SAM files as well as for other types of files.

The DLBL statement

The DLBL statement names a file and describes its characteristics. Its basic format with two positional operands is

```
// DLBL     file-name,'file-id'
```

Although the DLBL statement has other operands you may need to use under certain circumstances, you don't need to learn them all now. Instead, I'll present them in chapters 12 and 13.

The file-name operand   This is the only required operand of the DLBL statement. It's one to seven alphameric characters long and begins with a letter. Note, though, that the value you code doesn't refer to the file's label; instead, it refers to the symbolic name the processing program uses for the file. In assembler language, the symbolic name is the DTF (Define The File) name; in COBOL, it's the name in the SELECT clause; and in PL/I, it's the name in the DECLARE statement with the FILE attribute. When you get specifications for a job that uses disk files, you must find out the names the job's programs use for them.

The file-id operand   The name in the file's physical label is what you code for file-id. You can omit the file-id, but if you do, VSE substitutes the value you coded for file-name. So almost always, you'll need to code file-id. It can be up to 44 alphameric characters long, and it must be enclosed within apostrophes.

The EXTENT statement

In addition to naming a DASD file with a DLBL statement, you also need to specify its location. To do this, you use the EXTENT statement. When you include an EXTENT statement in a job stream, you code it immediately after the DLBL for the file so VSE knows the DLBL and EXTENT statements refer to the same DASD file.

Although you code only one DLBL statement to identify a DASD file, you may need to code more than one EXTENT statement. That's because a DASD file can reside on more than one disk area, or extent. If it does, you code one EXTENT statement for each extent. The basic format of the EXTENT statement is

```
// EXTENT   logical-unit,,,,location,size
```

As with DLBL, this basic format doesn't include all of EXTENT's operands; you'll learn the others in chapter 12.

As you can see, the operands of EXTENT are positional. In other words, if you omit one and include a succeeding one, you should account for the omitted one with a comma. The four commas in the basic format I've just shown indicate that there are three omitted positional operands between logical-unit and location.

The logical-unit operand   This is a six-character operand that specifies the logical unit for the file. This unit should already have been associated with a device address by an ASSGN statement. If you omit the logical-unit operand, the one from the preceding EXTENT statement is used. And if you omit the logical-unit operand on the first EXTENT statement in a job, the symbolic name specified in the application program is used as the default. To avoid possible confusion, I recommend that you always code the logical-unit operand.

The location and size operands   The location operand specifies where a file extent begins. On an FBA DASD, you give the number of the first block the file uses; on a CKD DASD, you give the relative track number of the first track the file uses.

To specify how large a file is, you use the size operand of the EXTENT statement. For an FBA device, you code the total number of blocks the file uses. For a CKD device, you code the number of tracks the file uses.

For a file on an FBA DASD,

```
// EXTENT   SYS014,,,,75000,1500
```

locates the file on the device already assigned to SYS014. The file begins at block 75000 and uses 1500 blocks. This type of statement will work for both types of FBA DASDs (3310 or 3370).

For a file on a CKD DASD,

```
// EXTENT   SYS014,,,,6000,480
```

locates the file on the device already assigned to SYS014. Assuming that this device is a 3350, the file begins at track 0 on cylinder 200 and occupies 16 cylinders. In this case, the relative track number is the cylinder number (200) multiplied by the number of tracks per cylinder (30), plus the track number on the cylinder (0), or 6000. The size of the file in tracks is the number of cylinders (16) multiplied by the number of tracks per cylinder (30), or 480.

Although the DLBL and EXTENT statements may seem complicated at this point, there really isn't much to them. Just remember that both are required to define DASD files that use native VSE access methods. In contrast, as you'll see later, VSAM files don't require

EXTENT statements because the location and size information for them is stored by VSAM.

Also, keep in mind that DLBL and EXTENT statements insulate your application programs from VSE's requirements. For instance, an application program can refer to an inventory master file as INVMAST and expect to find it on a DASD associated with programmer logical unit SYS019. But to VSE, that information by itself is meaningless. VSE only knows that there is a file with the name INVENTORY.MASTER.FILE stored on the FBA DASD with address 251 that's located at block 45000 and uses 5000 blocks. In your JCL, then, you correlate your program with VSE by coding

```
// ASSGN    SYS019,251
// DLBL     INVMAST,'INVENTORY.MASTER.FILE'
// EXTENT   SYS019,,,,45000,5000
```

With this information, VSE can identify INVENTORY.MASTER.FILE as the file your program calls INVMAST.

HOW TO INCLUDE DATA IN A JOB STREAM

Many job streams contain *in-line data*. In figure 4-7, for example, you can again see a job that shows the steps necessary to compile and link edit a COBOL program. To compile a program with a job like this, you include COBOL statements in the job stream right after the EXEC statement that invokes the compiler. Then the COBOL statements are treated as in-line data and are processed as input by the COBOL compiler.

When data is included in a job stream, it is considered to be a series of card-image records in 80-character format. So as long as data is in card-image format, you can include it in a job stream. Just be sure to mark the end of the in-line data with the end-of-data statement (/*). The /* statement is another one of the five job control statements that doesn't begin with two slashes.

HOW TO SUPPLY USER IDENTIFICATION

If your shop uses VSE's Access Control Facility, you need to supply both your user-identification and your password to execute a job. To do that, you code the ID statement in a job stream before you code any ASSGN statements.

The ID statement   Figure 4-8 gives the format of the ID statement with its keyword operands. The values you code for both operands are assigned to you by the systems programmer responsible for system security. Both are alphameric. User-id must be four characters long; password must be between three and six characters long.

For example, if my user-id were STEV and my password were ECKOLS, I'd code

```
// ID       USER=STEV,PWD=ECKOLS
```

```
// JOB      COMPLNK
   .
   .
// EXEC    FCOBOL
      IDENTIFICATION DIVISION.
   *
      PROGRAM-ID.  PR4100.
   *
      ENVIRONMENT DIVISION.
   *
      CONFIGURATION SECTION.
   *
   .
   .
/*
   .
   .
// EXEC    LNKEDT
   .
   .
/&
```

Figure 4-7   A two-step job with in-line data

The ID statement

```
// ID      USER=user-id,PWD=password
```

Explanation

user-id   The four-character user identification assigned to the user.

password   The three- to six-character password assigned to the user.

Figure 4-8   The ID statement

Because this user-id and and password are obvious, it's unlikely that they'd be used in a shop that's serious about access control. It's more likely that at least your password will be some cryptic combination of characters.

HOW TO COMMUNICATE WITH THE SYSTEM OPERATOR

In general, a job should be able to execute without operator intervention. But occasionally, you may want to tell an operator what a job's doing. Or, you may want to stop a job so an operator can ready an I/O device or verify that processing should proceed. To provide these facilities in your jobs, you can use the comment and PAUSE statements.

The comment (*) statement   The comment statement causes VSE to display messages on the system console. To include a comment in a job, you code an asterisk in column 1 and a space in column 2. Then, the rest of the statement is available for the message. As you can see, the comment statement is another one of the five job control statements that doesn't begin with //.

Because comments can distract an operator, you should only use comment statements when you really need them. So don't use them for job documentation. If a job contains many comments, the operator might miss more important messages. And because comments are displayed on the system console, they're also stored in the hard copy file. As a result, comments can cause the hard copy file to fill up faster than it should. So although it may be tempting to include comments in your job streams, don't do so without a good reason.

The PAUSE statement   If a message is important enough to warrant a comment statement, you may want to stop the job when it's displayed. For instance, you may want to let the operator mount a tape or verify that processing should proceed. When you want a job to pause, you code the PAUSE statement. Its format is

```
// PAUSE
```

A typical use for the PAUSE statement is this:

```
// PAUSE    MOUNT ICCF BACKUP TAPE ON UNIT AT 300
```

Note, here, that you can use the rest of the PAUSE statement for an operator message. As a result, this is the only statement that I advise you to code comments on. If you can fit a complete and understandable message on the PAUSE statement, you should. Otherwise, you can code as many comment statements as you need before the PAUSE statement, as in figure 4-9.

DISCUSSION   At this point, you've been introduced to the most important VSE job control statements. And you know enough to understand and code fairly complicated jobs. To help you get a better idea of how the statements you've learned work together, topic 2 presents two complete

```
     .
     .
*            THIS JOB WILL RESTORE THE DASD AT ADDRESS 250
*            FROM THE BACKUP TAPE MOUNTED ON THE UNIT AT ADDRESS 300.
*
*            TAP ENTER IF YOU ARE SURE YOU WANT TO PROCEED.
*
*            OTHERWISE, CANCEL THIS JOB.
// PAUSE
     .
     .
```

Figure 4-9   Using PAUSE and comment statements together to prompt the system operator

production jobs. As you read topic 2, many of the questions you may have about how these statements work will be answered.

Even though this chapter has covered a lot of new material, you've only begun your JCL training. In the next chapter, you'll continue by learning some new statements and some new operands for the statements to which you've already been introduced.

Terminology

job
job step
job control language
JCL
job stream
job deck
submit-to-batch facility
name field
job control command
operation field
operands field
operand
parameter
positional operand
keyword operand
comment field
continuation character
continuation field
sequence number field
modifier field
job control program
job name
search chain

concatenation chain
concatenated sublibraries
chained sublibraries
symbolic I/O assignment
logical unit
programmer logical unit
system logical unit
label information area
in-line data

Objectives

1. Describe three ways you can submit a job for execution on a VSE system.

2. Describe the format of a JCL statement.

3. Distinguish between a job step, a job, and a job stream.

4. Explain why programs that execute under VSE specify logical units rather than physical device addresses for I/O operations.

5. Describe the functions of the JOB, /&, EXEC, LIBDEF, ASSGN, DLBL, EXTENT, /*, *, and PAUSE statements.

6. Explain how you can include in-line data in a job stream.

7. Explain how you supply user and password identification for a job to be executed on a system with VSE's Access Control Facility.

8. Explain how you can communicate with a VSE system operator through JCL.

TOPIC 2   Examples of typical job streams

This topic presents two complete VSE job streams that use the JCL you learned in topic 1. To make sure you understand them, I'll explain each job stream line by line. As you'll see, these aren't typical textbook examples—they're realistic production jobs. The first is a payroll edit-update application. The second is an accounts receivable report-preparation application.

An edit-update application

Figure 4-10 is the system flowchart for a payroll application that reads card input transactions, edits them, and uses the edited transactions to update a master file. As you can see, the flowchart gives the functions and names of the application's programs and files.

Figure 4-11 is a system structure chart that illustrates the hierarchical relationship between the entire job (PR4000) and its programs (PR4100, PR4200, PR4300, and PR4400). Although you don't have to know how to create system structure charts, they're important documentation in many shops, so you should be familiar with them.

In this example, program PR4100 copies the payroll input data from cards to disk. However, PR4100 does more than just copy the card deck to DASD. It also reformats the card records. That's necessary in this application because the payroll transaction record is too large to fit on a single card; instead, it requires three cards for each record. As a result, PR4100 combines the data from each set of three cards into a single DASD record. In addition, it converts numeric data from display to packed decimal usage to improve the processing efficiency of the other programs in the application.

After PR4100 produces the DASD file called PRTRANS, PR4200 edits each record in it, looking for detectable errors. If it doesn't find any, it combines each transaction with data from the payroll rate table file (PRTABLE) and writes the new records to another transaction file, PREDTTR. If it does find an error, it writes a line on its error listing. Then, the error listing is returned to the data entry department so the invalid transactions can be corrected.

After editing, the transactions in PREDTTR are used to update the payroll master file. In this application, the update is sequential, so records from the master file and the transaction file are processed from beginning to end and matched along the way. After a master record is read from the original file, it is modified based on its matched transaction and it is written to a new copy of the master file.

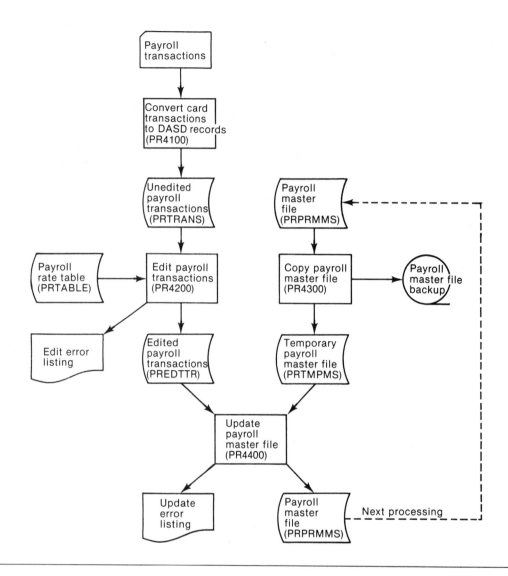

Figure 4-10   System flowchart for the edit-update application

Because this application requires two copies of the master file during the update step, the system uses an intermediate file preparation step. When the job is complete, the new copy of the master file needs to be located where the old copy was. But the old master file needs to be available as input for the sequential update program. As a result, this application first copies the old master file (PR4300). Then, it uses the output file of this step (PRTMPMS) as input to the update program (PR4400). As PR4400 executes, the new master file can be written over the original version, and it will be in the right location when the job is complete.

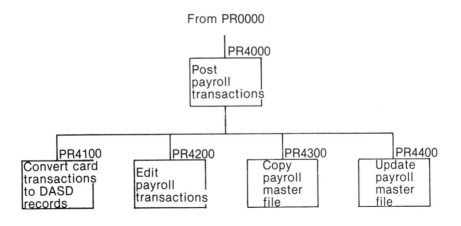

Figure 4-11   System structure chart for the edit-update application

---

To copy a file, you can use a VSE utility program. For this application, though, the system designer decided to make a backup copy of the master file on tape as well as to copy it to another DASD file. Although you can also use a utility to copy a DASD file to tape, both the disk and the tape copy functions require that the entire master file be read from beginning to end. As a result, it is more efficient to use a program that performs both functions at the same time. So that's why PR4300 reads the old master file (PRPRMMS—PayRoll PeRManent MaSter) and creates both the DASD file that will be used in the update step (PRTMPMS—PayRoll TeMPorary MaSter) and the backup tape.

After PR4300 prepares the master file for update, the update program itself (PR4400) is executed. This program uses the edited transactions (PREDTTR) and the temporary master file (PRTMPMS) as input and creates a new copy of the master file (PRPRMMS) as output in its original DASD location. It also creates an error listing that reports transactions that were found to be in error during the update run.

To write the JCL for this application, you need some additional documentation. First, you need to know what logical unit names the job's programs use. Of course, if you developed the programs yourself, you would know the names you used. But if you didn't, you need to get a complete listing of all logical units referenced by all programs in the job stream. Also, you need to know the addresses of the devices that will be assigned to those logical units. For this application, figure 4-12 gives that information. Note, here, that the backup tape is unlabelled so you don't have to supply label information for this file when you create the JCL for this job.

For each DASD file, you need to know still more: the file name the programs use to refer to it, the file id from its physical label, and its location and length. So figure 4-12 also gives the file ids for the DASD files this application requires. Then, figure 4-13 shows where those files

Program	Logical unit	Device	Program file name	File id	Flowchart file name
PR4100	SYS005	Card reader	None		
	SYS010	DASD at 251	PRTRANS	PAYROLL.UNEDITED.TRANSACTIONS	PRTRANS
PR4200	SYS006	Printer	None		
	SYS010	DASD at 251	PRTRANS	PAYROLL.UNEDITED.TRANSACTIONS	PRTRANS
	SYS010	DASD at 251	PRTABLE	PAYROLL.TABLE	PRTABLE
	SYS010	DASD at 251	PREDTTR	PAYROLL.EDITED.TRANSACTIONS	PREDTTR
PR4300	SYS011	DASD at 250	PRPRMMS	PAYROLL.MASTER.FILE	PRPRMMS
	SYS011	DASD at 250	PRTMPMS	PAYROLL.TEMPORARY.MASTER.FILE	PRTMPMS
	SYS012	Tape at 300	None	Unlabelled	
PR4400	SYS006	Printer	None		
	SYS010	DASD at 251	PREDTTR	PAYROLL.EDITED.TRANSACTIONS	PREDTTR
	SYS011	DASD at 250	PRTMPMS	PAYROLL.TEMPORARY.MASTER.FILE	PRTMPMS
	SYS011	DASD at 250	PRPRMMS	PAYROLL.MASTER.FILE	PRPRMMS

Notes

1. All programs are stored in the sublibrary USRSLE.PAYROLL.

2. All DASDs are FBA units.

Figure 4-12   Logical units, device assignments, and file ids used by the programs of the edit-update application

reside on the DASDs. It also gives the size of each file. For instance, the file PRTRANS resides on an FBA DASD at address 251. It begins at block 15764 and uses 1000 blocks. Although you usually won't get a diagram like this when you create the JCL for a job, I included it to help you visualize where the files the job uses are located and how large they are relative to the total capacity of the DASD.

The JCL for the job   Figure 4-14 shows the JCL for the payroll application. As you can see, it's fairly brief. Before I explain each statement, though, I want you to notice that this job can be divided into two parts. The first part defines the system environment for the job (it ends with the last EXTENT statement). The second part, beginning with the first EXEC statement in line 12, causes the application programs to be executed.

In my opinion, it's good to divide your jobs like this if you can. If several programs in a job use the same libraries, devices, and files, it makes sense to define them once at the start of the job rather than with each job step. Of course, some jobs will contain steps with different system environment requirements, as you'll see in the second example in this topic. When that's the case, you code the varying statements with each job step.

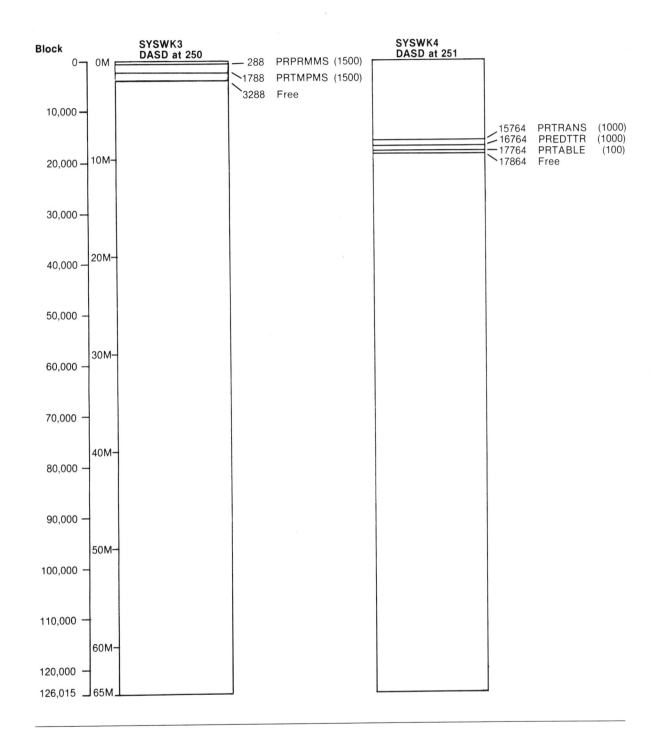

Figure 4-13   DASD layouts for the edit-update application

```
 1 // JOB      PR4000
 2 // LIBDEF   PHASE,SEARCH=(USRSLE.PAYROLL)
 3 // ASSGN    SYS005,SYSRDR
 4 // ASSGN    SYS006,SYSLST
 5 // ASSGN    SYS010,251
   // ASSGN    SYS011,250
 6 // ASSGN    SYS012,300
 7 // DLBL     PRTRANS,'PAYROLL.UNEDITED.TRANSACTIONS'
   // EXTENT   SYS010,,,,15764,1000
 8 // DLBL     PREDTTR,'PAYROLL.EDITED.TRANSACTIONS'
   // EXTENT   SYS010,,,,16764,1000
 9 // DLBL     PRTABLE,'PAYROLL.TABLE'
   // EXTENT   SYS010,,,,17764,100
10 // DLBL     PRPRMMS,'PAYROLL.MASTER.FILE'
   // EXTENT   SYS011,,,,288,1500
11 // DLBL     PRTMPMS,'PAYROLL.TEMPORARY.MASTER.FILE'
   // EXTENT   SYS011,,,,1788,1500
12 // EXEC     PR4100

13    PAYROLL TRANSACTION CARDS ARE INCLUDED HERE IN THE JOB STREAM

14 /*
15 // EXEC     PR4200
16 // PAUSE    MOUNT BACKUP TAPE FOR PAYROLL MASTER FILE.
17 // EXEC     PR4300
18 // EXEC     PR4400
19 /&
```

Figure 4-14   JCL for the edit-update application

Now, let me explain how this job works, statement by statement.

1. The job name is from the system structure chart (PR4000). This job stream contains only one job. If it contained several, each would be identified with a separate JOB statement.

2. The LIBDEF statement establishes the phase sublibrary search chain that's in effect for this job. In this case, only one sublibrary is in the chain: USRSLE.PAYROLL. The library USRSLE was defined to VSE during system start-up with DLBL and EXTENT statements; if it hadn't been, this job would have included those statements before the LIBDEF statement.

3. This is the first of five ASSGN statements that relate physical devices to the programmer logical unit names used in the programs in the job. This statement relates SYS005 (specified in PR4100) to a card reader. Rather than specify the actual address of a card reader, though, this statement indicates that the assignment in effect for the system logical unit SYSRDR should be used. In this example, you can assume that SYSRDR was

permanently assigned to a POWER-simulated card device during system start-up.

4. This ASSGN statement relates SYS006 (specified in both PR4200 and PR4400) to a printer. As with the preceding ASSGN, this statement doesn't specify a particular device address. Instead, it indicates that the assignment in effect for this partition's system logical unit SYSLST should be used. In this case, you can assume that SYSLST was assigned to a POWER-controlled printer during system start-up.

5. The next two ASSGN statements relate the logical units SYS010 and SYS011 to two DASDs, the ones at addresses 251 and 250. The DASD at 251 contains the payroll transaction files and the payroll table file (PR4100, PR4200, and PR4400 all use SYS010). The DASD at 250 contains the payroll master files (used by PR4300 and PR4400).

6. The last ASSGN statement relates the logical unit SYS012 (used in PR4300) to the tape drive at address 300.

7. Next are five pairs of DLBL and EXTENT statements that identify the DASD files the job requires. The first pair identifies the unedited payroll transaction file (PRTRANS) created by PR4100. Because the EXTENT statement specifies SYS010, the operating system uses the DASD at 251 (specified earlier in the job in an ASSGN statement) for this file. The file begins at block 15764 and is 1000 blocks long.

8. The second pair of DLBL and EXTENT statements identifies the edited payroll transaction file (PREDTTR) created by PR4200. Because the EXTENT statement specifies SYS010, this file will also reside on the DASD at address 251. This file begins immediately after PRTRANS (at block 16764) and is the same size (1000 blocks).

9. The third pair of DLBL and EXTENT statements identifies the payroll rate table file (PRTABLE) used by PR4200. Because the EXTENT statement specifies SYS010, this file too resides on the DASD at address 251, beginning immediately after the edited payroll transaction file at block 17764. It only requires 100 blocks, however.

10. The fourth pair of DLBL and EXTENT statements identifies the payroll master file (PRPRMMS) used by PR4300 and PR4400. Because the EXTENT statement specifies SYS011, this file will reside on the DASD at address 250. The file begins at block 288 and requires 1500 blocks of storage.

11. The last pair of DLBL and EXTENT statements identifies the temporary payroll master file (PRTMPMS) created by PR4300 and used as input by PR4400. Because the EXTENT statement specifies SYS011, this file will also reside on the DASD at address 250. Like the permanent file, it requires 1500 units of DASD storage. It begins right after the permanent file, at block 1788.

12. This EXEC statement marks the first job step in the job and causes the program PR4100 to be loaded and executed. PR4100 is fetched from the sublibrary USRSLE.PAYROLL.

13. Immediately following the EXEC for PR4100 in the job stream are the payroll transaction data cards.

14. The end-of-data statement (/*) marks the end of the payroll transaction cards in the input stream.

15. This EXEC statement marks the second job step and causes the program PR4200 to be loaded from USRSLE.PAYROLL and executed.

16. The PAUSE statement causes the job to stop and wait for an operator to reply before continuing. Here, the PAUSE statement prompts the operator to mount the tape reel required for the payroll master file backup. After the operator mounts the tape, readies the drive, and responds to the PAUSE statement, the job resumes.

17. This EXEC statement marks the third job step and causes the program PR4300 to be loaded from USRSLE.PAYROLL and executed.

18. This EXEC statement marks the fourth job step and causes the program PR4400 to be loaded from USRSLE.PAYROLL and executed.

19. /& marks the end of the job PR4000.

A report-preparation application

Figures 4-15 through 4-18 present the specifications for a report-preparation application that uses the basic JCL elements this chapter has presented. Figure 4-15 shows a system flow chart for this application. Here, the first application program (AR7100) creates a file with data from two master files (a customer file and an accounts receivable file). Before this program can be run, the receivables file, stored in invoice number sequence, is sorted into invoice number within customer number sequence. Then, AR7100 can match records from the sorted receivables file with records from the customer file, which is already stored in customer number sequence.

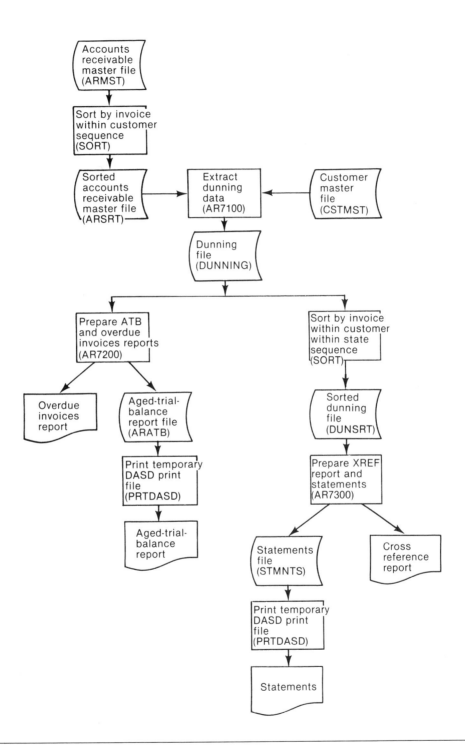

Figure 4-15   System flowchart for the report-preparation application

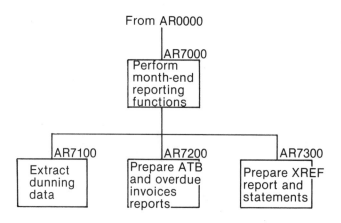

Figure 4-16 System structure chart for the report-preparation application

The output of the AR7100 program is the dunning file. It is used to produce customer statements and three reports. Two of the reports (an overdue-invoices report and an aged-trial-balance report) are prepared in the dunning file's original sequence: invoice within customer. Because both of these reports are prepared from the same file, a single program (AR7200) prepares them so the file only needs to be read once.

But preparing two reports simultaneously presents a problem. If both reports were assigned to the system printer (SYSLST), lines from them would be mixed. Most of the lines would be aged-trial-balance report lines, but a few overdue-invoices report lines would print too. To avoid this problem, only one of the reports is assigned to the printer (the overdue-invoices report). The other (the aged-trial-balance report) is written by the program to a DASD file (ARATB). That DASD file, in turn, is processed by a user-written utility program (PRTDASD) that copies the DASD print file to the printer. In section 3 of this book, you'll learn a more sophisticated way of printing two or more reports from a single program using POWER. But for now, my intent is to show you the basic VSE JCL for a job like this.

The other two reports the application produces require that the dunning file be sorted into a different sequence: invoice within customer number within state. So after a sort program is run, AR7300 uses the sorted dunning file to prepare a cross reference listing, which is printed directly from the program, and statements, which are stored temporarily on DASD. Then, this DASD print file is printed by the PRTDASD program. Here again, both reports could be prepared in a more sophisticated way using POWER.

The system structure chart in figure 4-16 gives the hierarchical structure for this application. Here, the top-level box represents the job stream for this application, while the lower-level boxes represent application programs, or job steps. In contrast to the system flowchart, this is

Program	Logical unit	Device	Program file name	File id	Flowchart file name
SORT	SYS015	DASD at 250	SORTIN1	ACCOUNTS.RECEIVABLE.MASTER.FILE	ARMST
	SYS015	DASD at 250	SORTWK1		SORTWK1
	SYS015	DASD at 250	SORTOUT	SORTED.ACCOUNTS.RECEIVABLE. MASTER.FILE	ARSRT
AR7100	SYS015	DASD at 250	ARSRT	SORTED.ACCOUNTS.RECEIVABLE. MASTER.FILE	ARSRT
	SYS015	DASD at 250	CSTMST	CUSTOMER.MASTER.FILE	CSTMST
	SYS015	DASD at 250	DUNNING	DUNNING.FILE	DUNNING
AR7200	SYS015	DASD at 250	DUNNING	DUNNING.FILE	DUNNING
	SYS015	DASD at 250	ARATB	AGED.TRIAL.BALANCE.REPORT.FILE	ARATB
	SYS006	Printer	None		
PRTDASD	SYS015	DASD at 250	PRTFILE	AGED.TRIAL.BALANCE.REPORT.FILE	ARATB
	SYS006	Printer	None		
SORT	SYS015	DASD at 250	SORTIN1	DUNNING.FILE	DUNNING
	SYS015	DASD at 250	SORTWK1		SORTWK1
	SYS015	DASD at 250	SORTOUT	SORTED.DUNNING.FILE	DUNSRT
AR7300	SYS015	DASD at 250	DUNSRT	SORTED.DUNNING.FILE	DUNSRT
	SYS015	DASD at 250	STMNTS	STATEMENTS	STMNTS
	SYS006	Printer	None		
PRTDASD	SYS015	DASD at 250	PRTFILE	STATEMENTS	STMNTS
	SYS006	Printer	None		

Notes

1. SORT is stored in SOFTLIB.SYSUTIL1.

2. PRTDASD is stored in USRSLE.USRUTIL1.

3. All other programs are stored in USRSLE.ACCTRCV.

4. All DASDs are FBA units.

Figure 4-17   Logical units, device assignments, and file ids used by the programs of the report-preparation application

another way of looking at the relationship between the programs and jobs of the system.

Figures 4-17 and 4-18 give you the information you need about the files that will be accessed in this procedure. The files' system logical units, devices, and programmer logical unit assignments, along with the file-ids and flowchart names, are summarized in figure 4-17. Then, figure 4-18 shows the layout of the DASD where these files are stored.

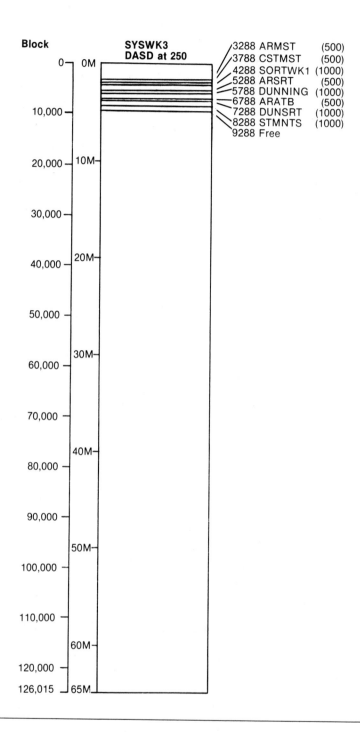

Figure 4-18   DASD layout for the report-preparation application

The JCL for the job   Figure 4-19 gives the JCL for this report-preparation application. Compared with the JCL for the edit-update application, this job stream is more complex. That's largely because file naming isn't consistent among the programs in this application. As a result, it isn't possible to code all the DLBL and EXTENT statements at the beginning of the job. Instead, they have to be coded for each step.

Although this is a more complicated job stream, you shouldn't have any trouble understanding it. So let's take the JCL statements one at a time.

1. The job name, AR7000, comes from the system structure chart. This job stream contains only one job.

2. The LIBDEF statement indicates the sublibraries that should be searched for the required phases, beginning with USR-SLE.ACCTRCV, and continuing with USRSLE.USRUTIL1 and SOFTLIB.SYSUTIL1. In this application, the AR programs reside in USRSLE.ACCTRCV; the user-written print utility, PRTDASD, resides in USRSLE.USRUTIL1; and the IBM Sort/Merge program resides in SOFTLIB.SYSUTIL1. This assumes that the DLBL and EXTENT statements that defined the libraries those sublibraries are located in were processed when the system was initialized. Otherwise, the job stream would have included them before this LIBDEF statement.

3. This application requires only two devices: the system printer (SYS006) and the DASD at address 250 (SYS015). As figure 4-17 shows, all of the programs that produce printed output specify SYS006 as the logical unit for the printer, and all that do DASD processing specify SYS015 as the logical unit for the disk unit.

4. Three files are used by the sort program in the first step of this job: SORTIN1 for input (the accounts receivable master file), SORTOUT for output (the sorted accounts receivable master file), and SORTWK1 (a work file). So three pairs of DLBL and EXTENT statements define them. Notice that I didn't code a file-id for SORTWK1. That's because I can let the default value be used for it (the file-name SORTWK1 from the DLBL statement).

5. This EXEC statement marks the first step in the job and causes the Sort/Merge program to be loaded from SOFT-LIB.SYSUTIL1 and executed. Both USRSLE.ACCTRCV and USRSLE.USRUTIL1 were searched for SORT before it was retrieved from SOFTLIB.SYSUTIL1.

```
 1 // JOB      AR7000
 2 // LIBDEF   PHASE,SEARCH=(USRSLE.ACCTRCV,USRSLE.USRUTIL1,SOFTLIB.SYSUTIL1)
 3 // ASSGN    SYS006,SYSLST
   // ASSGN    SYS015,250
 4 // DLBL     SORTIN1,'ACCOUNTS.RECEIVABLE.MASTER.FILE'
   // EXTENT   SYS015,,,,3288,500
   // DLBL     SORTWK1
   // EXTENT   SYS015,,,,4288,1000
   // DLBL     SORTOUT,'SORTED.ACCOUNTS.RECEIVABLE.MASTER.FILE'
   // EXTENT   SYS015,,,,5288,500
 5 // EXEC     SORT
 6          SORT   FIELDS=(16,5,CH,A,1,5,CH,A),WORK=1
            RECORD TYPE=F,LENGTH=80
 7 /*
 8 // DLBL     ARSRT,'SORTED.ACCOUNTS.RECEIVABLE.MASTER.FILE'
   // EXTENT   SYS015,,,,5288,500
   // DLBL     CSTMST,'CUSTOMER.MASTER.FILE'
   // EXTENT   SYS015,,,,3788,500
   // DLBL     DUNNING,'DUNNING.FILE'
   // EXTENT   SYS015,,,,5788,1000
 9 // EXEC     AR7100
10 // DLBL     DUNNING,'DUNNING.FILE'
   // EXTENT   SYS015,,,,5788,1000
   // DLBL     ARATB,'AGED.TRIAL.BALANCE.REPORT.FILE'
   // EXTENT   SYS015,,,,6788,500
11 // EXEC     AR7200
12 // DLBL     PRTFILE,'AGED.TRIAL.BALANCE.REPORT.FILE'
   // EXTENT   SYS015,,,,6788,500
13 // EXEC     PRTDASD
14 // DLBL     SORTIN1,'DUNNING.FILE'
   // EXTENT   SYS015,,,,5788,1000
   // DLBL     SORTWK1
   // EXTENT   SYS015,,,,4288,1000
   // DLBL     SORTOUT,'SORTED.DUNNING.FILE'
   // EXTENT   SYS015,,,,7288,1000
15 // EXEC     SORT
16          SORT   FIELDS=(43,2,CH,A,1,5,CH,A,50,5,CH,A),WORK=1
            RECORD TYPE=F,LENGTH=80
17 /*
18 // DLBL     STMNTS,'STATEMENTS'
   // EXTENT   SYS015,,,,8288,1000
   // DLBL     DUNSRT,'SORTED.DUNNING.FILE'
   // EXTENT   SYS015,,,,7288,1000
19 // EXEC     AR7300
20 // DLBL     PRTFILE,'STATEMENTS'
   // EXTENT   SYS015,,,,8288,1000
21 // EXEC     PRTDASD
22 /&
```

Figure 4-19   JCL for the report-preparation application

6. The two data lines are sort control statements. They're read by the sort program and define the processing it's to do. Since I'll explain the sort program in chapter 16, you don't have to worry about what these control statements do now.

7. The end-of-data statement (/*) marks the end of the in-line data (the sort control statements).

8. The next three pairs of DLBL and EXTENT statements define the files that AR7100 uses: the sorted receivables file (ARSRT), the customer master file (CSTMST), and the output dunning file (DUNNING). If you look at the three EXTENT statements, you can see that all three files reside on the DASD assigned to the logical unit SYS015, but at different locations.

9. This EXEC statement marks the second step in the job and causes AR7100 to be loaded from USRSLE.ACCTRCV and executed.

10. The next two pairs of DLBL and EXTENT statements define the files required by the first reporting program (AR7200): the dunning file (DUNNING) and the temporary file that will contain the aged-trial-balance report (ARATB). Notice that the DUNNING file has to be specified for AR7200, even though it was specified with the same name in the previous job step. That's because if any files are defined in a job step, all previous temporary definitions are lost. On the other hand, if no files are defined in a job step, those in effect for the previous step remain in force. (That was the case with the payroll edit-update application.) You'll learn more about how this works when you read about the label information area in chapter 10.

11. This EXEC statement marks the third step in the job and causes the first report-preparation program (AR7200) to be loaded from USRSLE.ACCTRCV and executed.

12. This pair of DLBL and EXTENT statements defines the input file for the PRTDASD program. Since the program expects its input file to be defined with the name PRTFILE, new label statements for the aged-trial-balance report file are required. If the program expected its input file to be named ARATB, these two statements would be unnecessary, because the definition from the previous job step could be used.

13. This EXEC statement marks the fourth step in the job and causes the print program (PRTDASD) to be loaded from USRSLE.USRUTIL1 (after USRSLE.ACCTRCV was searched unsuccessfully) and executed.

14. The next three pairs of DLBL and EXTENT statements define the files required by the second sort in the job.

15. This EXEC statement marks the fifth step in the job and causes the Sort/Merge program (SORT) to be loaded from SOFTLIB.SYSUTIL1 and executed.

16. The two data lines are sort control statements.

17. The end-of-data statement (/*) marks the end of the in-line data (the sort control statements).

18. The next two pairs of DLBL and EXTENT statements define the files required by the second report-preparation program (AR7300): the sorted dunning file (DUNSRT) and the temporary statements print file (STMNTS).

19. This EXEC statement marks the sixth step in the job and causes the second report-preparation program (AR7300) to be loaded from USRSLE.ACCTRCV and executed.

20. This pair of DLBL and EXTENT statements defines the input file for the second execution of the PRTDASD program. Here, the file name PRTFILE is related to the temporary DASD print file that contains statements. As with the first execution of the PRTDASD program, if it were expecting the input file to be defined with the name STMNTS, the DLBL and EXTENT statements for that file from the previous job step could be used, and these two would be unnecessary.

21. This EXEC statement marks the seventh and last step in the job and causes the print program (PRTDASD) to be loaded from USRSLE.USRUTIL1 and executed.

22. /& marks the end of the job.

Discussion   The examples in this topic are typical of jobs you might find in a VSE shop. Because you'll have to learn how to code jobs like these, I didn't try to present unrealistic, simple examples in this topic.

These two jobs should make it clear how important file handling is in VSE JCL. For instance, in the report-preparation job, 30 of the 48 lines are either DLBL or EXTENT statements. As you can imagine, then, you'll have to learn more details about file handling before you master VSE JCL. So that's what section 4 of this book presents.

You should also have noticed that I referred to both permanent and temporary labels in my descriptions of the job streams. In both jobs, in fact, labels for the libraries listed in the LIBDEF statements had already been stored permanently. In contrast, the labels used during the job were temporary, and they were lost between job steps when new labels were defined. More than just labels can be defined either temporarily or permanently, though. You also saw that logical unit assignments can be either temporary or permanent.

In the next chapter, then, I'll describe how to use temporary and permanent options. I'll also present some advanced features of the EXEC statement that you'll need to know to develop production VSE job streams. Finally, I'll present several new statements that you'll find useful in your basic job streams.

Objective   Given complete specifications for a job, code its JCL using the statements this chapter presented.

Chapter 5

Advanced VSE JCL

In chapter 4, you learned elementary forms of the most important VSE job control statements and saw how to use them to create production job streams. This chapter extends that knowledge. Topics 1, 2, and 3 present advanced features of the EXEC, LIBDEF, and ASSGN statements and introduce related statements. Then, topic 4 presents other statements that affect how your jobs may execute; they all use an area of storage called the partition communication region.

TOPIC 1   Advanced VSE JCL to manage program execution

You learned in the last chapter that the primary function of the EXEC statement is to invoke a program during a job step. Although you can also use EXEC to invoke a job stream stored in a VSE procedure library, I'll explain that in the next chapter. This topic presents the additional operands of EXEC you can code to specify how a program should execute.

Advanced operands of the EXEC statement

Figure 5-1 illustrates the full format of EXEC to invoke a program. Since the operands of EXEC are keyword operands, you don't have to account for them with commas if you omit some. However, the operands you do code must be in the order in figure 5-1. Although you can code one or two continuation lines for EXEC, you'll seldom need to under normal circumstances.

The REAL operand   Some programs, particularly those with critical time dependencies (like parts of the supervisor), must execute in real rather than virtual storage. When you want to run such a program, you need to code the REAL operand on the EXEC statement for the program. However, because application programs almost always execute in virtual storage, you'll seldom need to code REAL.

The SIZE operand   You should recall from chapter 2 that each VSE partition has its own GETVIS area to which VSE allocates 48K by default; the rest of the partition is the program area. Although that's adequate for some programs, many other programs, including all those that use VSAM files, require larger GETVIS areas. In these cases, when you need a larger GETVIS area than the default provides, you code the SIZE operand on the EXEC statement.

Frankly, the different ways you can code SIZE can be confusing. But if you study figure 5-2, the alternatives should be manageable. In each example in figure 5-2, a 96K program named UPDTA is loaded into a 480K partition. As you can see, storage usage in the partition varies depending on what the SIZE operand specifies.

In the first example, the EXEC statement doesn't include the SIZE operand, so the program space within the partition is 432K (the full partition size, 480K, minus the VSE default for the GETVIS area, 48K). Because the program requires only 96K, 336K of unused address space is available in the program area. (That's the shaded portion of example 1.)

The EXEC statement to execute a program

```
// EXEC     [[PGM=]program-name][,REAL][,SIZE=size][,GO][,PARM='value']
```

Explanation

program-name   The one- to eight-character name of the phase to be executed. You may omit PGM = .
                    This operand is required unless the phase you are executing was just created by
                    the linkage editor; in that case, you omit it.

REAL   Specifies that the phase is to execute in real storage. If you don't code REAL, the
                    phase executes in virtual storage.

SIZE = size   Specifies the size of the program area of the partition. You may code this operand
                    in one of five ways:

                        SIZE = {nK | mM}
                        SIZE = phase-name
                        SIZE = (phase-name,{nK | mM})
                        SIZE = AUTO
                        SIZE = (AUTO,{nK | mM})

                    See the text for a description of these options.

GO   The GO operand is used in program development job streams. If you use the GO
                    operand on the EXEC statement for the language translator, you don't code sepa-
                    rate steps for the link edit and the test execution.

PARM = 'value'   Allows you to pass data to the application program. For value, you may code up to
                    100 characters of data. The value must be enclosed within apostrophes. If the value
                    includes an apostrophe, code it as two apostrophes.

Figure 5-1   The EXEC statement to execute a program

In example 2, the EXEC statement includes a SIZE operand that uses the first variation in figure 5-1:

```
SIZE=96K
```

In this case, the size of the program area is set to the value specified on the SIZE operand (96K), and the remainder of the partition is available as GETVIS space (384K). Because the SIZE operand specifies exactly the proper amount of storage for the program, the entire program area of the partition is used. In contrast, the SIZE operand of example 3 specifies more storage than the program requires, so a 48K portion of the program area isn't used.

In example 4, I use the SIZE=phase-name option. When you use this variation of the SIZE operand, the program area uses exactly the amount of space the program requires according to its sublibrary directory entry. As a result, the same amount of space is allocated to the

**Sublibrary
directory entries**

Phase   Size

.   .
.   .
.   .
UPDTA   96K
UPDTB   96K
UPDTC   192K
UPDTD   144K
UPDTE   48K
.   .
.   .

In each example, a 96K
application program executes
in a 480K virtual partition.

Shading indicates unused
virtual storage.

Example 1

EXEC UPDTA

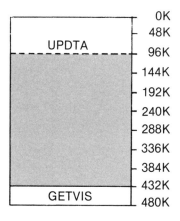

Example 2

EXEC UPDTA,SIZE = 96K

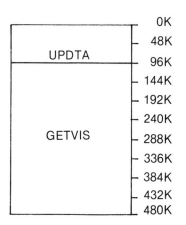

Example 3

EXEC UPDTA,SIZE = 144K

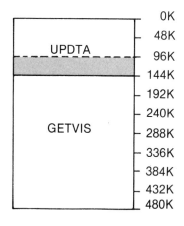

Figure 5-2   The effect of the SIZE operand of EXEC on storage usage (part 1 of 2)

Example 4

EXEC UPDTA,SIZE = UPDTA

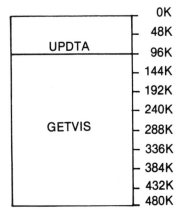

Example 5

EXEC UPDTA,SIZE = (UPDTA,48K)

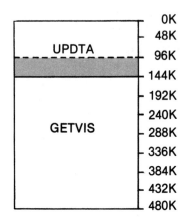

Example 6

EXEC UPDTA,SIZE = AUTO

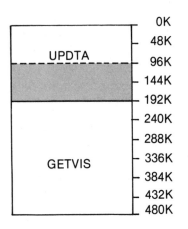

Example 7

EXEC UPDTA,SIZE = (AUTO,48K)

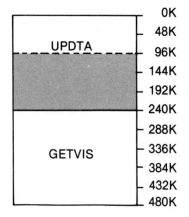

Figure 5-2   The effect of the SIZE operand of EXEC on storage usage (part 2 of 2)

program area in example 4 as in example 2. The difference is that in example 4, I didn't have to know the size of the program because VSE determined the space required when it loaded the program.

Example 5 illustrates the SIZE=(phase-name,nK) option. This works like SIZE=phase-name, only nK bytes are added to the program area. In this case, the SIZE option specifies that 48K should be added to the size of the phase to be executed, so the program area is 144K.

In example 6, I coded AUTO for the SIZE operand. Although AUTO works much like the phase-name option, it differs because the program area size isn't determined by the size of the specific phase to be executed. Instead, the program area size is the size of the largest phase in the sublibrary with the same first four characters in its name as in the name of the phase that's actually going to be loaded and executed.

To understand, look at the sublibrary directory in part 1 of figure 5-2. You can see that it contains entries for five phases that begin with the letters UPDT. Because example 6 specifies AUTO on the SIZE operand, the sublibrary directory is searched to determine the size of the largest phase that begins with the letters UPDT. Here, that's UPDTC: a 192K program. As a result, 192K is the size of the program area in example 6, although the program to be executed, UPDTA, requires only 96K.

Finally, in example 7, I coded AUTO as the SIZE operand, but I also specified that the program area should be increased by 48K. As a result, the program area in this example is 240K.

It might seem strange to you that storage is allocated based on phase names, but it makes more sense if you're familiar with the idea of *multi-phase programs*. If a program is too large to fit in a single partition, it can be written in segments that are stored as separate phases. Together, all the segments make up a complete program. To run a multi-phase program, the program area of the partition must be large enough to contain its largest phase. Because it's a VSE naming convention that the phases of a multi-phase program have names that begin with the same four characters, SIZE=AUTO insures that enough storage is available for all parts of a multi-phase program. I want you to realize, however, that new multi-phase user programs are rare. Today, virtual storage provides partitions that are large enough for practically any application program.

Although you won't have much chance to use SIZE=AUTO to run multi-phase application programs, it's standard practice to code SIZE=AUTO on EXEC statements that invoke programs that use VSAM files. And for some programs, you'll need to allocate additional program space. For instance, if you want to run a COBOL program that does an internal sort and accesses VSAM files, you need to allow for automatic size calculation for VSAM. In addition, you need to add at least 32K to the program area to accommodate the Sort/Merge utility program along with the application program. So you could code SIZE=(AUTO,32K). In other instances, you'll need to specify a particular program area size to meet program requirements.

In any case, if any of the phases or programs executed by your job require more storage than is available in the partition, your job will fail. So make sure you always use a partition that has enough space for the largest phase or program in your job.

Notice in figure 5-1 that you can specify the size as mM as well as nK. For instance, you can code SIZE=1M or SIZE=1000K to specify the same program area size. In either case, just be sure that the size you indicate isn't greater than the size of the partition. In addition, both m and n must be integers, and n must be a multiple of 4. If it's not, VSE will round it up to the next highest integer that is.

The GO operand   If you're an application programmer, you know how often you run jobs to translate and test new programs. Under VSE, that kind of job has three steps: (1) translation, (2) link editing, and (3) test execution.

When you code GO on the EXEC statement for the language translator, you don't need to code these three functions as separate job steps; they're done automatically. Then, if the translation step ends abnormally, the link edit and execution steps are bypassed, just as if they'd been coded as separate job steps. Similarly, if the link edit step fails, the execution step will be bypassed. In chapter 14, I'll show you an example of a job that uses the GO operand of EXEC when I describe program development.

The PARM operand   The last operand of EXEC is PARM. If you need to pass data from your job stream to an application program, you can code up to 100 characters as the value for PARM. To do this, you must enclose the value within apostrophes. And if the value itself contains an apostrophe, you must code it as two apostrophes. If programs developed in your shop require that data be passed to them from JCL, you are likely to use the PARM operand frequently.

Discussion   As you can see, most of the complexity of the EXEC statement is in how you code the SIZE operand. But that's not as complicated as it may seem. For programs that use VSAM files, you know that you code SIZE=AUTO. And if a program requires special storage allocations, the job specifications should indicate it.

Terminology   multi-phase program

Objective   Given the requirements for a program, code an EXEC statement for it using any or all of the REAL, SIZE, GO, and PARM operands.

TOPIC 2   Advanced VSE JCL to manage sublibrary search chains

In the last chapter, you learned how to code the LIBDEF statement to establish sublibrary search chains for phases. This topic will show you how to set up search chains for other member types. In addition, it will introduce two new statements for library management: LIBLIST and LIBDROP.

Advanced operands of the LIBDEF statement

Figure 5-3 shows all the operands you can code on the LIBDEF statement. The member-type and SEARCH operands should look familiar from the LIBDEF examples presented in chapter 4. The CATALOG operand is only required when you produce a system dump or use the linkage editor. As a result, I'll show you how to code it in topic 4 of this chapter and in chapter 14. I've only included CATALOG in figure 5-3 for completeness. The TEMP and PERM operands are new, and I'll cover them in this topic.

The member-type operand   Because the format of the LIBDEF statement presented in the last chapter was for setting up phase search chains, it specified PHASE for the member-type operand. But you can code other values for the member-type operand to set up search chains for source books, object modules, and procedures. You won't set up search chains for dump and user-defined member types, though. Dump member types are only used with the CATALOG operand. And user-defined member types can't be specified on a LIBDEF statement at all.

When you develop programs, it's often efficient to include sections of commonly used source code in copy books. Then, you can include that code in application programs at compile or assembly time. To specify the sublibraries that your language translator should search, you have two options for the member-type operand. You can code one of the single characters A..Z, 0..9, -, $, or @, or you can code SOURCE. The single characters are used when your source book members are collected into related groups. For instance, you can give the member type $ to all the source books used for payroll applications. As you can see in Figure 5-4, the letters A through I, P, R, and Z are reserved by IBM for system components; you should avoid using these letters for user-written source books. Your installation probably has guidelines for choosing source member types, so check with your supervisor to see which characters you can use. If you code SOURCE for the member-type operand, all source member types are searched.

The LIBDEF statement

```
// LIBDEF  member-type
           [,SEARCH=(lib1.slib1,lib2.slib2,...,lib15.slib15)]
           [,CATALOG=lib.slib]
           [,TEMP|PERM]
```

Explanation

member-type	Specifies the type of member:

PHASE	phases for execution
OBJ	object modules for the linkage editor
SOURCE	source books
PROC	cataloged procedures
*	all types except dumps and user-defined
DUMP	system dumps

SEARCH	Lets you establish a search chain of up to 15 sublibraries. If there is more than one sublibrary to be searched, the list of sublibrary names must be within parentheses, and commas must separate the sublibrary names. The value you code for a library name (the lib*n* component of the complete sublibrary name) is the one- to seven-character file name on a DLBL statement, unless you are specifying the system sublibrary. Then, you code IJSYSRS.SYSLIB. In addition, you may specify the system directory list in a phase search chain by coding SDL.
CATALOG	Specifies the sublibrary to receive output from the linkage editor or dump.
TEMP	Specifies that the LIBDEF statement is to be in effect only for the duration of the job.
PERM	Specifies that the LIBDEF statement is to be in effect for the partition permanently.

Figure 5-3   The LIBDEF statement

When you link-edit a program, you may need to identify the sublibraries in which the object modules to be linked are stored. To do that, you code a LIBDEF statement just as you would to define a phase search chain, except you code OBJ for the member-type operand. You'll need to define search chains for object modules most often when you write programs that call subprograms.

If you want to execute a procedure that's stored in a VSE sublibrary, you need to identify the sublibraries to be searched for the procedure. To do that, you code a LIBDEF statement with PROC for the member-type operand. I'll have more to say about procedures in the next chapter.

If you store all of the members for a specific application in the same sublibrary, as I recommend, you'll also want to know about the wild card option available for the member-type operand. If you code *, all of the member types that can be used in search chains—PHASE, OBJ,

Sublibrary	Contents
A	Assembler source books
B	ACT/VTAM network definitions
C	COBOL source books
D	Assembler source books (alternate)
E	Assembler edited macros
F	Assembler edited macros (alternate)
G	Reserved for future use by IBM
H	Reserved for future use by IBM
I	Reserved for future use by IBM
P	PL/I source books
R	RPG II source books
Z	IBM-supplied sample programs

Figure 5-4   Source book member types used by IBM

SOURCE, and PROC—are searched. So, for example, if all of the source programs, object modules, phases, and procedures for an application are stored in the sublibrary named USR1.AP1, you can access all of the members by coding

```
// LIBDEF *,SEARCH=(USR1.AP1)
```

The SEARCH operand   In the last chapter, you saw this example of how to code a LIBDEF statement to establish a phase sublibrary search chain:

```
// LIBDEF  PHASE,SEARCH=(USR1.AP2,USR3.AP3,USR2.AP4)
```

This sets up a search chain that begins with USR1.AP2 and continues with USR3.AP3 and USR2.AP4. Although this example uses only three sublibrary names, you can code up to 15. If there is more than one sublibrary to be searched, you code the list of sublibrary names within parentheses, and you separate the sublibrary names with commas.

Special considerations for phase search chains   For all member types, VSE automatically searches the system sublibrary (IJSYSRS.SYSLIB) for the specified member if it doesn't find it in any of the private sublibraries you named in the LIBDEF statement. When you code PHASE as the member type, however, the situation is more complex.

As figure 5-5 shows, the statement

```
// LIBDEF  PHASE,SEARCH=(USR1.AP2,USR3.AP3,USR2.AP4)
```

causes more than just those three sublibraries to be searched for a phase.

LIBDEF statement

```
//LIBDEF PHASE,SEARCH=(USR1.AP2,USR3.AP3,USR2.AP4)
```

Resulting search sequence

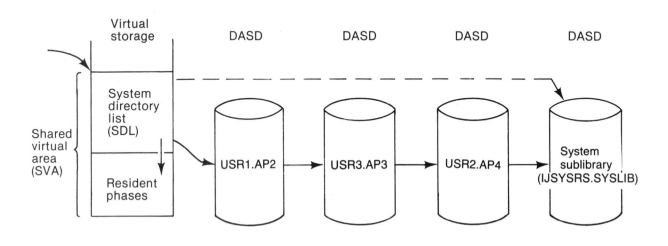

Figure 5-5   A LIBDEF statement and the resulting phase sublibrary search sequence

Before any of the sublibraries are searched, VSE searches the *System Directory List (SDL)* for the phase. Then, if neither the SDL nor the specified sublibraries contain the required phase, VSE searches the system sublibrary directory.

The System Directory List is part of the Shared Virtual Area (SVA). That means, as you should remember from chapter 2, that it resides in virtual storage. The SDL contains two types of entries. Entries of the first type point to phases that themselves reside in the SVA. Those are program components that are constantly used throughout the system and that need to be immediately available.

SDL entries of the second type also point to commonly used phases, but ones that do not reside in the SVA. Instead, entries of the second type are images of directory entries from the system sublibrary. After retrieving the phase's location from its SDL entry, VSE can retrieve the phase directly from its location in the system sublibrary without searching the sublibrary's directory first. Because the system sublibrary directory contains many entries, this can significantly improve system efficiency.

For the most part, SDL entries point to phases that are used repeatedly throughout the system, such as modules of VSAM and the job control program. User-written applications rarely have SDL entries. As a result, from a practical point of view, the entries in the SDL don't matter to you.

If you want the SDL search to be other than at the beginning of the chain, you can explicitly code SDL as one of the names in the SEARCH operand, as in

```
// LIBDEF   PHASE,SEARCH=(USR1.AP2,USR3.AP3,USR2.AP4,SDL)
```

But because SDL entries usually point to heavily used operating system components, not to user-written applications, and because the SDL scan is rapid, you shouldn't need to alter the standard sequence.

You're more likely to raise the priority of the search of the system sublibrary. If most of the programs a job executes reside in the system sublibrary, there's no reason to search several private libraries for them first. You can move the search of the system sublibrary up by coding IJSYSRS.SYSLIB at the proper location in the search chain. For example,

```
// LIBDEF   PHASE,SEARCH=(IJSYSRS.SYSLIB,USR1.AP2,USR3.AP3,USR2.AP4)
```

causes the system sublibrary to be searched for required phases before the three private sublibraries. However, the SDL search will still precede the system sublibrary search. One caution: Never code IJSYSRS.SYSLIB before SDL in a LIBDEF search chain. If you do, linkage to phases in the SVA won't work properly.

The phase search sequence is also altered when the phase is a *logical transient routine*. These are phases that the system needs to access and load quickly. They are recognizable by the $ at the beginning of their names. When the phase name begins with a dollar sign, the system sublibrary IJSYSRS.SYSLIB is searched immediately after the SDL, instead of at the end of the chain. Although you probably won't be working directly with logical transient routines, you should be aware of them and avoid giving your phases names that begin with $.

The PERM and TEMP operands   When you code a simple LIBDEF statement, its effect is temporary (for the duration of the current job only). However, it's often practical to establish permanent search chains for your system's partitions. Each partition has two sets of search chains: a temporary set and a permanent set. If you execute a job that contains a LIBDEF statement for a temporary search chain in a partition that already has a permanent search chain in effect, VSE can search along both, but it uses the temporary chain first. If the search is satisfied by one of the sublibraries in the temporary chain, the permanent chain isn't searched.

```
        .
        .
        .
// LIBDEF   PHASE,SEARCH=(MMA.PROD,PRD1.BASE,PRD1.CONFIG,SOFTLIB.SYSUTIL1),PERM
// LIBDEF   OBJ,SEARCH=(MMA.PROD,PRD1.BASE,PRD1.CONFIG,SOFTLIB.SYSUTIL1),PERM
// LIBDEF   SOURCE,SEARCH=(MMA.PROD,PRD1.BASE,PRD1.CONFIG,SOFTLIB.SYSUTIL1),PERM
        .
        .
        .
```

Figure 5-6   LIBDEF statements that establish permanent search chains

To establish a permanent search chain, you code the LIBDEF statement with the PERM operand. If you code TEMP, or let it default, a
LIBDEF statement establishes a temporary chain.

Figure 5-6 illustrates three LIBDEF statements that set up permanent search chains. These statements happen to be for the system's background partition, but similar statements are executed in each partition
of a typical system. After these statements are processed, no temporary
search chains are necessary to retrieve a phase, object module, or source
book from the sublibraries specified in these permanent chains.

Recall that in the report-preparation job stream in the last chapter,
I coded the sublibrary where the Sort/Merge utility was located explicitly
in the phase sublibrary search chain. Note, though, that if the the permanent search chains shown in figure 5-6 had been in effect for that
job, that wouldn't have been necessary. I could've just coded

```
// LIBDEF   PHASE,SEARCH=(USRSLE.ACCTRCV,USRSLE.USRUTIL1)
```

as the temporary search chain. Then, when the job control program
couldn't find the phase SORT in either of those two sublibraries, it
would've searched the sublibraries in the permanent search chain and
retrieved it from SOFTLIB.SYSUTIL1.

As a general rule, you should code PERM only on LIBDEF statements in system start-up jobs, not in routine job streams. If you execute a job that contains a LIBDEF statement with the PERM operand
in a partition that already has a permanent search chain in effect, the
new chain replaces the old one. Because many jobs may depend on
the original permanent search chain, that can disrupt system operations.

The LIBLIST   If you want to find out what search chains are currently in effect on
statement   your system, you can code a job that includes the LIBLIST statement.
The LIBLIST statement lists all the library information defined on the
system by preceding LIBDEF statements. Figure 5-7 presents the format of LIBLIST. For the member-type operand, you code the type of

The LIBLIST statement

```
// LIBLIST member-type[,partition]
```

Explanation

member-type   Specifies the type of member:

PHASE	phases for execution
OBJ	object modules for the linkage editor
SOURCE	source books
PROC	cataloged procedures
*	all types except dumps and user-defined
DUMP	system dumps

partition   Specifies the partition for which sublibrary definitions should be listed:

BG	for the background partition
Fn	for the named foreground partition (n is a hex digit between 1 and B)
*	all partitions

Omission of this operand causes a listing of the sublibrary definitions for the partition that processes the statement.

Figure 5-7   The LIBLIST statement

---

library member you want to list: PHASE, SOURCE, OBJ, PROC, or *. The wild card character * will list the current search chains for all of these member types.

After the member-type operand, you code a value to indicate the partition whose library information you want to list. Code BG for the background or Fn for one of the foreground partitions (F1 for foreground 1, F2 for foreground 2, and so on). If you code * for the partition operand, you'll get a listing of all the partitions. If you omit the partition operand, the library information for the partition where your job executes will be printed.

To see how LIBLIST works and to reinforce your understanding of temporary and permanent search chains, look at figure 5-8. It's a simple library management job that illustrates how the LIBDEF and LIBLIST statements work. Before you study figure 5-8, look back to figure 5-6 at the LIBDEF statement that sets up the permanent phase sublibrary search chain for the sample system's background partition. That chain is MMA.PROD, PRD1.BASE, PRD1.CONFIG, and SOFTLIB.SYSUTIL1.

In figure 5-8, the job contains two LIBLIST statements. One immediately follows the JOB statement. Because all temporary sublibrary search chains are lost at the end of a job, no temporary chains are in effect

JCL for the job

```
// JOB      LIBLIST
// LIBLIST PHASE,BG
// LIBDEF  PHASE,SEARCH=(USRSLE.ACCTRCV,USRSLE.USRUTIL1)
// LIBLIST PHASE,BG
/&
```

Output from the job

```
// JOB      LIBLIST
// LIBLIST PHASE,BG
```

| BG-TEMP ** NO LIBRARY INFORMATION AVAILABLE ** |

BG-PERM	LIBNAME	SUBLIB	STATUS	-PARTITIONS-
SEARCH	MMA	PROD		012
	PRD1	BASE		012
	PRD1	CONFIG		012
	SOFTLIB	SYSUTIL1		012

```
// LIBDEF  PHASE,SEARCH=(USRSLE.ACCTRCV,USRSLE.USRUTIL1)
// LIBLIST PHASE,BG
```

BG-TEMP	LIBNAME	SUBLIB	STATUS	-PARTITIONS-
SEARCH	USRSLE	ACCTRCV		0
	USRSLE	USRUTIL1		0

BG-PERM	LIBNAME	SUBLIB	STATUS	-PARTITIONS-
SEARCH	MMA	PROD		012
	PRD1	BASE		012
	PRD1	CONFIG		012
	SOFTLIB	SYSUTIL1		012

Figure 5-8   The effect of the LIBLIST statement

when a new job begins. The output from the first LIBLIST statement indicates that. It also shows the permanent chain that's in effect—it's just what you'd expect based on figure 5-6.

The next statement in the job is a LIBDEF that establishes the temporary chain USRSLE.ACCTRCV and USRSLE.USRUTIL1. Then, immediately after the LIBDEF is another LIBLIST. If you look at its output, you'll see that not only is the permanent chain in effect, but the temporary one is too.

The LIBDROP statement

If you want to delete the library information you defined in a previous LIBDEF statement, you can code the LIBDROP statement, illustrated in figure 5-9. The values you code on the LIBDROP statement correspond to the type of library member (PHASE, SOURCE, OBJ, PROC, and *) and the type of library definition (SEARCH or CATALOG) you want to delete. Figure 5-10 illustrates the effect of the LIBDROP state-

The LIBDROP statement

```
// LIBDROP member-type[,definition-type...][,TEMP|PERM]
```

Explanation

member-type   Specifies the type of member:

                  PHASE   phases for execution
                  OBJ   object modules for the linkage editor
                  SOURCE   source books
                  PROC   cataloged procedures
                  *   all types except dumps and user-defined
                  DUMP   system dumps

definition-type   Specifies the type of library definition to be dropped for the partition. You may code one or both of the following values (if you code both, separate the values with commas):

                  SEARCH
                  CATALOG

TEMP   Indicates that the specified temporary library definition is to be dropped.

PERM   Indicates that the specified permanent library definition is to be dropped.

Figure 5-9   The LIBDROP statement

ment. Here, I coded one LIBDROP statement to delete the temporary search chain the job establishes, plus a LIBLIST to show that the LIBDROP statement did indeed delete the temporary chain.

Although LIBDROP is easy to use, you probably won't need to use it much. I've already explained why you shouldn't change permanent search chains. And, because you may change a temporary search chain in the middle of a job by coding another LIBDEF statement, you won't need to drop temporary chains often. It's only in cases where you want to revert from a temporary chain to a permanent chain in mid-job that you're likely to use LIBDROP.

Discussion   If you understand the LIBDEF statement, LIBLIST and LIBDROP should follow naturally. At this point, then, you know all you need to know about coding search chains. As you'll see in topic 4 of this chapter and topic 1 of chapter 14, the remaining function of LIBDEF, specified using the CATALOG operand, doesn't establish a search chain; it identifies a single sublibrary that's used to store a system dump or a load module. As a result, it will be easier to understand within the context of those topics.

JCL for the job

```
// JOB      LIBDROP
// LIBDEF   PHASE,SEARCH=(USRSLE.ACCTRCV,USRSLE.USRUTIL1)
// LIBLIST PHASE,BG
// LIBDROP PHASE,SEARCH
// LIBLIST PHASE,BG
/&
```

Output from the job

```
// JOB      LIBDROP
// LIBDEF   PHASE,SEARCH=(USRSLE.ACCTRCV,USRSLE.USRUTIL1)
// LIBLIST PHASE,BG
```

```
BG-TEMP LIBNAME SUBLIB    STATUS  -PARTITIONS-
SEARCH  USRSLE  ACCTRCV           0
        USRSLE  USRUTIL1          0


BG-PERM LIBNAME SUBLIB    STATUS  -PARTITIONS-
SEARCH  MMA     PROD              012
        PRD1    BASE              012
        PRD1    CONFIG            012
        SOFTLIB SYSUTIL1          012
```

```
// LIBDROP PHASE,SEARCH
// LIBLIST PHASE,BG
```

```
BG-TEMP ** NO LIBRARY INFORMATION AVAILABLE **
```

```
BG-PERM LIBNAME SUBLIB    STATUS  -PARTITIONS-
SEARCH  MMA     PROD              012
        PRD1    BASE              012
        PRD1    CONFIG            012
        SOFTLIB SYSUTIL1          012
```

Figure 5-10   The effect of the LIBDROP statement

Terminology   System Directory List
SDL
logical transient routine

Objective   Given a JCL problem requiring sublibrary search chains, code the
required LIBDEF, LIBLIST, and LIBDROP statements.

TOPIC 3 Advanced VSE JCL
to manage device assignments

In the last chapter, you learned how to code the ASSGN statement
to relate the logical units specified in programs to physical devices. In
this topic, you'll learn some other features of ASSGN. In addition, you'll
learn two related statements that let you manage device assignments:
LISTIO and RESET.

Advanced operands
of the ASSGN
statement

The basic format of the ASSGN statement is

```
// ASSGN    SYSxxx,cuu
```

where SYSxxx is the logical unit name and cuu is the address (channel and unit) of the assigned device. The address in this case is the
device operand of the ASSGN statement.

As you can see in figure 5-11, you can specify the device operand
in other ways, and you can code additional operands. Figure 5-11 has
three parts. Part 1 presents ASSGN as you can code it for an assignment to any device. Parts 2 and 3 present other ASSGN operands you
can use only for assignments to tape and disk units.

The device operand   The first option for the device operand of
ASSGN in part 1 of figure 5-11 is address (channel and unit). The other
options for the device operand all eventually reduce to this, but they
provide you with more flexibility. For example, the second format lets
you assign one logical unit to another logical unit:

```
// ASSGN    SYSxxx,SYSyyy
```

In the last chapter, you saw the following examples of this kind of device
assignment:

```
// ASSGN    SYS005,SYSRDR
// ASSGN    SYS006,SYSLST
```

Here, the programmer logical units SYS005 and SYS006 are associated
with the devices already assigned to the system logical units SYSRDR
and SYSLST. You can also assign a programmer logical unit to another
programmer logical unit as in

```
// ASSGN    SYS021,SYS014
```

although you'll probably do this less often. No matter what type of

The ASSGN statement for any device

```
// ASSGN   SYSxxx,device[,TEMP|PERM]
```

Explanation

SYSxxx	Specifies the logical unit being assigned. It may be a system logical unit or a programmer logical unit.
device	Specifies the device to which the logical unit is to be assigned. You may code device in one of these formats:
	cuu SYSyyy (address-1,address-2,...address-7) device-type device-class
TEMP	Indicates that the assignment is for the duration of the current job only. It is the default value.
PERM	Indicates that the assignment is permanent.

Figure 5-11   The ASSGN statement (part 1 of 3)

unit you code in the device operand, it must have already been assigned to an appropriate physical device.

If you use the address-list option for the device operand, you can code up to seven physical device addresses. Then, when the ASSGN statement is executed, the first device in the list that isn't already in use will be associated with the logical unit. For example, if you code

```
// ASSGN   SYS015,(300,301,302,303)
```

and the devices at addresses 300 and 301 are in use, VSE assigns SYS015 to the device at address 302. On the other hand, if the device at address 300 is available, VSE assigns SYS015 to it.

A fourth way to make a device assignment is to specify device-type in the device operand. In this case, the value you code is a unit model number. When you use the device-type option, you insure that the device is of a particular type, but you don't require that a specific unit of that type be used. For instance, if you code

```
// ASSGN   SYS018,8809
```

VSE selects the first available 8809 tape drive for association with SYS018. If all of the system's 8809s are in use, VSE waits until an 8809 is free to make the assignment, even if 3420 tape units are available.

The ASSGN statement for tape units

```
// ASSGN    SYSxxx,device[,mode|ALT][,TEMP|PERM][,VOL=volser]
```

Explanation

mode	Specifies the mode in which the tape unit should operate. For details, see chapter 11.
ALT	Specifies that the assigned device is an alternate tape unit. For details, see chapter 11.
VOL = volser	Specifies that the assignment may be made only to a device with the named volume mounted.

Figure 5-11   The ASSGN statement (part 2 of 3)

The last way to assign a logical unit is to code device-class for the device operand. A device class is a grouping of units with possible values such as TAPE, DISK, CKD, FBA, PRINTER, READER, and PUNCH. It differs from device-type in that it doesn't specify a particular model number. If, for example, you code

```
// ASSGN    SYS019,TAPE
```

VSE selects the first available tape drive, regardless of the type. In this case, VSE could assign either a 3420 or an 8809 tape unit to SYS019. Generic device names, like TAPE or PRINTER, can be useful because they don't tie your job to a specific device; they let your job use whatever happens to be available at execution time.

When you code ASSGN statements that use either the device-type or device-class options of the device operand, you need to be careful. For instance, not all printers can be identified with the generic name PRINTER and not all DASD units can be properly assigned using these options. So if you're going to use these options, refer to *VSE/Advanced Functions System Control Statements*. It lists all the valid entries you can make for both device-class and device-type.

Temporary and permanent assignments   A typical assignment made through a job control statement is in effect only for the duration of the job. As a result, it's a *temporary assignment*. In addition, though, your system may be set up with *permanent assignments*. To make a permanent assignment, you code PERM on the ASSGN statement. Typically, when a system is started, ASSGN statements are used to make permanent assignments. Because many jobs depend on these permanent assignments, you shouldn't replace them in routine application jobs.

The ASSGN statement for DASDs

```
// ASSGN    SYSxxx,device[,TEMP|PERM][,VOL=volser][,SHR]
```

Explanation

VOL = volser   Specifies that the assignment may be made only to a device with the named volume
                        mounted.

SHR   Specifies that the assigned unit can be shared. Valid only for DASDs and only when
                        you use the address-list, device-type, or device-class option for the device operand.

Figure 5-11   The ASSGN statement (part 3 of 3)

ASSGN operands for disk and tape units   Parts 2 and 3 of figure
5-11 show the ASSGN operands you can code for tape unit and DASD
assignments. As you can see in part 2 of this figure, you can specify
the operational mode of a tape unit (mode) or an alternate tape unit
(ALT). You'll learn these operands when you read about advanced tape
processing in chapter 11.

For assignments to both tape and disk units, you may code the
VOL operand. This operand has two uses. First, you can use it to insure
that a specific volume is mounted on a specific device. Alternatively,
you can use it to give the operations staff greater flexibility in device
usage.

To insure that a specific volume is mounted on a specific unit, you
code an ASSGN statement with this format:

```
// ASSGN    SYSxxx,cuu,VOL=volser
```

as in

```
// ASSGN    SYS012,300,VOL=067217
```

Then, VSE lets the job continue only if the tape with volume serial
number 067217 is mounted on the tape unit at address 300. But this
technique is often too restrictive because it requires a specific volume
to be mounted on a specific device at a specific time. Although it's useful
in some circumstances, I think you're more likely to use the second
application of the VOL operand.

You use the second application by coding any of these versions
of the ASSGN statement:

```
// ASSGN    SYSxxx,(address-list),VOL=volser
// ASSGN    SYSxxx,device-type,VOL=volser
// ASSGN    SYSxxx,device-class,VOL=volser
```

For instance, this statement uses the device-type option:

```
// ASSGN    SYS012,8809,VOL=067217
```

When VSE processes this statement, it searches for the 8809 unit that has volume 067217 mounted on it. When it finds it, processing proceeds. If the volume isn't mounted on any 8809, VSE selects the first free 8809 and prompts the operator to mount the tape on it. This makes operations more flexible and efficient because the system isn't restricted to using one device for the application; it can use whatever device is available.

For disk devices only, you may code the SHR operand to specify that the device may be shared with other jobs. SHR is meaningful only when you code the address-list, device-type, or device-class option for the device operand. When you use one of these operands on an assignment to a DASD, you probably should code SHR. If you don't, your job will have exclusive use of the device, and the chances are that's not what you want.

The LISTIO statement

If you need to find out what the current device assignments are on your system, you can use the LISTIO statement. Because temporary device assignments can change rapidly as jobs execute, the output from the LISTIO statement can be inaccurate even before you get it. However, it is useful for determining permanent assignments.

Figure 5-12 gives the format of the LISTIO statement. It only has one operand: type. For type, you can code any of the options the figure indicates. These options should be self-explanatory.

Figure 5-13 shows the output of a job that executes the LISTIO statement with a foreground partition (F1) for the type operand. The output of the job shows all of the logical units associated with F1 in the column labelled I/O UNIT. The column labelled ASSGMNT indicates whether the assignment is temporary or permanent. Finally, the CHNL and UNIT columns show the assigned device address.

To get a physical device address, for example, you read the CHNL and UNIT columns together. In figure 5-13, SYSRDR is assigned temporarily to the unit at address 240. If you look back to the system configuration in chapter 1, you can see that the device at 240 is a DASD. SYSRDR, then, is temporarily assigned to a disk extent. If you briefly study figure 5-13, it should reinforce some of the facts you've learned about device assignments, hardware configurations, and system software components.

First, notice that several logical units are assigned to the DASD at address 240. Actually, though, the units are assigned to different extents on that volume. You can tell the DASD at address 240 is the system residence volume, because SYSRES is assigned to it. Also on this unit are SYSREC and SYSCAT.

The LISTIO statement

```
// LISTIO   type
```

Explanation

type   Specifies the type of assignments to be listed. May be one of the following:

ALL	List all assignments by logical unit.
ASSGN	List all assignments in the partition that processes the statement.
BG	List all assignments in the background partition.
cuu	List the logical units assigned to the device at the specified address.
DOWN	List all devices that aren't operational.
Fn	List all assignments in the specified foreground partition (n is a hex digit between 1 and B).
NPGR	List the number of programmer logical units allocated to each partition.
PROG	List all programmer logical unit assignments in the partition that processes the statement.
SYS	List all system logical unit assignments in the partition that processes the statement.
SYSxxx	List the devices assigned to the specified logical unit in the partition that processes the statement.
UA	List all devices not currently assigned.
UNITS	List all assignments by device.

Figure 5-12   The LISTIO statement

Now, look at the programmer logical units at the bottom of the output. The first three (SYS000, SYS001, and SYS002) are assigned to disk extents. Two are assigned to extents on the system residence volume (address 240) and one is assigned to the DASD at address 241. SYS003 is assigned to the system printer (address 00E) and SYS004 is assigned to a telecommunications line (address 030). Although DASD units can be assigned to more than one logical unit because they can contain many extents, other devices, like printers and telecommunications lines,

JCL for the job

```
// JOB     LISTIO
// LISTIO  F1
/&
```

Output from the job

```
// JOB     LISTIO
// LISTIO  F1

        *** FOREGROUND 1 ***

I/O UNIT ASSGMNT CHNL UNIT MODE

    SYSRDR   TEM       2    40
    SYSRDR   PER       * UA *
    SYSIPT   TEM       2    40
    SYSIPT   PER       * UA *
    SYSPCH             * UA *
    SYSLST             * UA *
    SYSLOG   PER       0    1F
    SYSLNK             * UA *
    SYSRES   PER       2    40
    SYSUSE             * UA *
    SYSREC   PER       2    40
    SYSDMP             * UA *
    SYSCAT   PER       2    40
    SYSTEM FILES
    SYS000   PER       2    40
    SYS001   PER       2    40
    SYS002   PER       2    41
    SYS003   PER       0    0E
    SYS004   PER       0    30
    SYS005             * UA *
    UP TO
    SYS099             * UA *
```

Figure 5-13   The effect of the LISTIO statement

can only be assigned in one partition at a time. As a result, this LISTIO output indicates that F1 has exclusive control of the printer and TC line.

The notation * UA * means that the logical unit is unassigned. As you can see, many of the logical units associated with this partition are unassigned. In fact, the bottom of the LISTIO output indicates that programmer logical units SYS005 through SYS099 are unassigned.

Although this system was generated so each partition may have 100 programmer logical units (numbered from SYS000 to SYS099), the VSE limit for programmer logical units in a partition is 256 (numbered from SYS000 to SYS255). It's rare that a partition needs even 100 programmer logical units, though, and it's more efficient to configure the system with a smaller number than the maximum.

The RESET statement

`// RESET    unit`

Explanation

unit   Specifies the type of assignments to be reset. May be one of the following:

    ALL   Reset all temporary logical unit assignments and library search chain definitions to their permanent assignments.

    PROG   Reset all temporary programmer logical unit assignments to their permanent assignments.

    SYS   Reset all temporary system logical unit assignments and library search chain definitions to their permanent assignments.

    SYSxxx   Reset the temporary assignment for the specified logical unit to its permanent assignment.

Figure 5-14   The RESET statement

The RESET statement

If you use the ASSGN statement to make a temporary assignment of a unit that also has a permanent assignment, you can restore that unit to its permanent assignment by coding the RESET statement. Figure 5-14 gives the format of this statement. It has one operand (unit) that may have one of the four values in the figure. Depending on the value you code for the unit operand, you can reset assignments for all logical units (ALL), all system logical units (SYS), all programmer logical units (PROG), or any specific unit (SYSxxx). The RESET statement only affects assignments in the partition in which it's processed.

Note, that if you code ALL or SYS as the unit operand on the RESET statement, all the temporary library search chain definitions in the partition will also be reset to their permanent definitions. In those two cases, the RESET statement is similar to the LIBDROP statement you learned in the last topic.

Remember, though, that an ASSGN for a temporary assignment is in effect only for the duration of a job. As a result, you don't need to code RESET unless you have to restore permanent assignments in the middle of a job. There's no need to code it at the end of a job because permanent assignments are restored automatically.

Discussion   As you can see, VSE gives you a variety of options for making device assignments. In practice, though, you only use a couple of them most of the time: ASSGN to a physical address and ASSGN to another logical unit. Nevertheless, you should know the other options for device assignment because there are occasions when they're appropriate.

Terminology   temporary assignment
permanent assignment

Objective   Given a JCL problem requiring complex device assignments, code the ASSGN, LISTIO, and RESET statements for the job.

TOPIC 4 How to code statements that use the communication region

In this topic, I'll describe several job control statements that let you manage program execution and control your jobs' system environments. These statements all have one feature in common: VSE uses an area of storage called the partition communication region to store data related to them. In this topic, I'll briefly describe the communication region. Then, I'll introduce the UPSI, DATE, STDOPT, and OPTION statements.

The partition communication region

Within the supervisor area of storage, each partition has its own *partition communication region*, or *COMREG*, that contains control information VSE uses for a variety of functions. For example, VSE stores the name of the job currently executing in a partition in its COMREG, along with other job and system information. Although you don't need to know all the details about the data VSE stores in a partition's communication region, you should have a general knowledge of the COMREG. If you do, you'll have a better understanding of the VSE JCL statements this topic presents.

Each partition's communication region uses 200 bytes in the supervisor area and is divided into more than 60 fields. Obviously, then, most of the fields are small. In fact, 45 of them are either one or two bytes long. VSE makes intensive use of the space in each partition's communication region. In several instances, one-byte fields are manipulated and evaluated at the bit level.

The UPSI statement

One of the fields in a partition's communication region is the *UPSI byte*. (UPSI stands for User Program Switch Indicators.) Application programs can evaluate the UPSI byte to determine the processing they should do. You, in turn, can code the UPSI statement to set bits in the UPSI byte to control the execution of those programs.

Figure 5-15 illustrates the format of the UPSI statement. Here, each n represents one of the eight bit positions in the UPSI byte, and each bit position is considered to be a switch. For each, you may code 0 to set the switch off, 1 to set the switch on, or X to retain the current switch setting.

The UPSI statement is valid only for the duration of a job. Whenever a JOB statement is encountered, all bits of the UPSI byte are set to off (0). As a result, when you execute a program that requires particular UPSI bit settings, you must code the UPSI statement between the JOB statement and the EXEC statement that invokes the program.

The UPSI statement

`// UPSI     nnnnnnnn`

Explanation

nnnnnnnn   Each n represents one bit position in the UPSI byte. For each position, you may code

0 to set the bit to 0 (off)
1 to set the bit to 1 (on)
X to leave the bit setting unchanged

If you don't code a value for each of the eight bit positions, VSE assumes you coded X for the rightmost positions.

Figure 5-15   The UPSI statement

If your shop's application programs use the UPSI byte, you'll need to code the UPSI statement in the job streams that invoke them. It's more likely, however, that you'll use the UPSI statement in jobs that invoke IBM system products.

For instance, the IBM utility program VSE/DITTO can be executed either from the system console (called console operation) or from a job stream (called batch operation). To determine its operational mode, DITTO evaluates the UPSI byte. If the first bit of the UPSI byte is off, DITTO begins console operation, but if it's on, DITTO begins batch operation. As a result, if you want to run a job that executes DITTO in batch mode and you don't code the UPSI statement, the job will fail.

To insure that the first bit of the UPSI byte is turned on (set to 1) and the other seven bits remain unchanged, you code

`// UPSI     1XXXXXXX`

If you don't code values for all eight bit positions in the UPSI statement, VSE assumes you coded X for rightmost positions, so their values in the UPSI byte remain unchanged. As a result, you could also code

`// UPSI     1`

to cause DITTO to execute in batch mode.

DITTO isn't the only IBM program that uses the UPSI byte. If, for example, you want to run an application program that uses DL/I, you need to code an appropriate value for the UPSI byte. Other IBM software products also use the UPSI byte, some for application-related processing, others for systems programming options.

The DATE statement

`// DATE    xx/xx/yy`

Explanation

xx/xx/yy	Date to override the system date for the job. Depending on the format of the system date on your system, you code either

       mm/dd/yy (month precedes day)

or

       dd/mm/yy (day precedes month)

Figure 5-16   The DATE statement

The DATE statement

A partition's communication region also contains a field for the system date. VSE uses the date in the communication region for accounting information and for job output identification. Under some circumstances, though, you may need to run a job with a date different from the system date. If so, you can temporarily change the date in the partition's communication region by coding the DATE statement, as illustrated in figure 5-16.

The value you code in the DATE statement replaces the date value stored in your partition's communication region; it doesn't reset the system date. The new date value you supply remains in effect only until the end of the job. Then, the system date is restored to the partition communication region's date field.

The default coding sequence is for the month to precede the day in the format mm/dd/yy. However, your system options may be set so you'll have to code the day before the month in the format dd/mm/yy. As you'll see in a moment, the format of the date is only one of several system standard options you need to be familiar with to execute some types of jobs properly.

System standard options

By providing *system standard options*, VSE is flexible in how it handles some conditions, performs some functions, and represents common data. As a result, your systems programmer can set the system standard options to meet your shop's processing requirements. These option settings are recorded in the partition's communication region.

For each option, VSE uses its *system default*, unless the systems programmer specifies otherwise. To make permanent changes to the system defaults, the systems programmer can submit STDOPT statements. If you want to make temporary changes to the system standard options, you can code the OPTION statement.

Option	Default	Description
DATE	MDY	The default format for the system date is month/day/year. Alternatively, the date can be in the format day/month/year (DMY).
HCTRAN	YES	If HCTRAN is in effect, all hard copy output to the devices assigned to both SYSLST and SYSLOG is converted to all upper case letters. If HCTRAN is not in effect, mixed case output is possible.
LINES	56	LINES specifies the number of lines written per page on the device assigned to SYSLST. The value must be between 30 and 99.

Figure 5-17   System standard options for system management

You won't often code the STDOPT statement in routine job streams because it changes system standard options permanently, which affects all the partitions on your system. In some cases, though, you'll need to temporarily override a system standard option setting for the partition where your job (most likely, a program development job) is executing. Then, you'll code an OPTION statement in your job stream. In this topic, you'll learn how both the STDOPT and OPTION statements work.

Figures 5-17, 5-18, and 5-19 list and describe the VSE system standard options. I divided them into functional groups to make it easier for you to learn them. As you can see, they fall into three groups: standard options for (1) system management, (2) job management and abnormal job termination, and (3) the language translators.

Standard options for system management   The three standard options for system management, illustrated in figure 5-17, are DATE, HCTRAN, and LINES. DATE determines the format of the system date. As you can see, the date may be stored in one of two formats: mm/dd/yy (the default) or dd/mm/yy. Most American shops use month before day (mm/dd/yy).

HCTRAN determines how data sent to the system console and to the devices assigned to SYSLST is handled. If HCTRAN is in effect, all lowercase letters are converted to uppercase before the data is written to the device. If the option isn't in effect, VSE doesn't do the conversion. Although the practical implications of this option are limited, you should keep in mind that if HCTRAN is in effect, literal values with lowercase letters in your program source listings will print as uppercase. (By the way, HC in HCTRAN stands for hard copy.)

LINES determines how many lines should be written on each page on the devices assigned to SYSLST. The default, 56, is appropriate for the continuous form paper most installations use.

Option	Default	Description
ACANCEL	NO	If ACANCEL is in effect, a job is automatically cancelled if a device assignment (ASSGN statement) or a sublibrary specification (LIBDEF statement) fails. If ACANCEL is not in effect, the system waits for operator intervention to cancel such a job.
DUMP	YES	If DUMP is in effect, jobs that end abnormally cause a dump of the registers and virtual storage to be written on the device assigned to SYSLST (usually a printer).
JCANCEL	NO	If JCANCEL is in effect, a job is automatically cancelled when a job control error occurs. If JCANCEL is not in effect, operator intervention is required to cancel such a job.
LOG	YES	If LOG is in effect, all job control statements processed are written on the device assigned to SYSLST. If LOG is not in effect, only invalid statements are written to SYSLST.
LOGSRC	NO	If LOGSRC is in effect and LOG is also in effect, the job control statements that contain symbolic parameters are written on the device assigned to SYSLST twice, once as coded and once with the substituted parameter values as processed by the job control program. If LOGSRC is not in effect, the job control statements are written as specified by the LOG option with the symbolic parameters represented by their substituted values.
SYSDUMP	NO	If SYSDUMP is in effect, dumps are written to the dump sublibrary that is active for the partition. If no dump sublibrary has been defined for the partition with a LIBDEF statement, the option SYSDUMP is ignored. If SYSDUMP is not in effect, dumps are written to the device assigned to SYSLST. The old form of this operand, SYSDMP, is also accepted.

Figure 5-18   System standard options for job management and abnormal job termination

Standard options for job management and abnormal job termination   VSE also lets you make changes to the way it manages jobs and abnormal job terminations. Six options, listed in figure 5-18, fall into that category: ACANCEL, DUMP, JCANCEL, LOG, LOGSRC, and SYSDUMP. ACANCEL determines whether a job with an invalid device assignment or invalid sublibrary specification is to be cancelled automatically or only after operator intervention (the default). Similarly, JCANCEL indicates whether or not a job with any job control errors should be cancelled automatically.

LOG causes all job control statements to be written on the device assigned to SYSLST. Even if LOG isn't in effect, though, invalid job control statements are written to SYSLST. When you specify LOGSRC in addition to LOG, the job control statements that contain symbolic parameters are written to SYSLST twice, once as coded in the source program and once with the substituted values processed by the job control program. (You'll learn about symbolic parameters in the next chapter.)

DUMP specifies whether or not information in parts of storage should be listed when a program ends abnormally. The default is for a full dump to be created and for it to be written to the device assigned to SYSLST. However, it's possible to set this option to PART so a partial dump is created.

If SYSDUMP is in effect, dumps are written not to SYSLST, but rather to the dump sublibrary which is active for the partition. But, before you can code the SYSDUMP option, you need to specify the dump sublibrary by coding a LIBDEF statement with the CATALOG operand. For example,

```
// LIBDEF   DUMP,CATALOG=SYSDUMP.BG
```

specifies SYSDUMP.BG as the sublibrary where dumps will be stored. The dump sublibrary should be defined permanently on your system; if it's not, the SYSDUMP option will be ignored.

Notice in the LIBDEF statement above that the sublibrary name identifies the partition, in this case, BG. That's because the Information/Analysis program that analyzes dumps assumes that there is only one dump sublibrary for each partition, and that it's in the library SYSDUMP with a partition identifier as its sublibrary name.

In older versions of DOS (prior to VSE/AF version 2.1) a similar option, SYSDMP, was available. That option stored the dump as a file rather than as a library member. Although you can still code SYSDMP, the dump will be stored in the dump sublibrary specified by the LIBDEF statement, just as if you coded SYSDUMP.

Standard options for the language translators   If you look at figure 5-19, you can see that system standard options for language translators outnumber options for system and job management combined. You can also see that most of the options in this group specify language translator output. In chapter 14, you'll learn more about these options; I only present them here so you can see all of the system standard options in one place.

The STDOPT statement   If most jobs in your shop require option settings other than the system defaults, your systems programmer should code STDOPT statements to change the defaults permanently. Figure 5-20 shows the format of this statement. As you can see, it can contain an entry for each option. Once STDOPT sets the options, they become permanent values and apply to all partitions. (Although the options STDOPT sets apply to all partitions, the statement can execute only in the background.)

In a typical shop, STDOPT statements are submitted in the job that starts the background partition. Because system standard options are permanent and affect all partitions, many jobs in your shop probably depend on them. So if you code a STDOPT statement in a routine job, you may alter the option values on which other jobs depend.

Option	Default	Description
ALIGN	YES	If ALIGN is in effect, the assembler will align data on halfword or fullword boundaries according to the instruction used.
CHARSET	48C	CHARSET specifies the character set the PL/I compiler will use. You may code 48C or 60C.
DECK	YES	If DECK is in effect, the language translators write their object modules on the device assigned to SYSPCH.
EDECK	NO	If EDECK is in effect, the assembler writes edited macros on the device assigned to SYSPCH.
ERRS	YES	If ERRS is in effect, the language translators write source program diagnostics on the device assigned to SYSLST.
LIST	YES	If LIST is in effect, the language translators write source program listings on the device assigned to SYSLST.
LISTX	NO	If LISTX is in effect, the language translators write hexadecimal object code listings on the device assigned to SYSLST.
RLD	NO	If RLD is in effect, the language translators print relocation dictionary information. (This is information in the object module that the linkage editor uses to combine modules in an executable phase.)
SXREF	NO	If SXREF is in effect, the assembler writes a short cross-reference listing on the device assigned to SYSLST.
SYM	NO	If SYM is in effect, the PL/I compiler will produce symbol and offset table listings, and the COBOL compiler will produce data division map listings. Output will be written on the device assigned to SYSLST.
TERM	NO	If TERM is in effect, language translator messages are displayed on the system console.
XREF	YES	If XREF is in effect, the assembler and the COBOL compiler write cross reference listings on the device assigned to SYSLST.

Figure 5-19   System standard options for the language translators

Figure 5-21 shows the STDOPT statements from the job that starts the background partition on the system I presented in Chapter 2. Since the STDOPT statement is not one of the ten JCL statements that allow continuation lines, there are three separate STDOPT statements coded. As you can see, these three lines specify most of the options, although some are set to default values. As a result, these two lines would produce the same result:

```
// STDOPT   CHARSET=60C,DECK=NO,DUMP=PART,RLD=YES
// STDOPT   SXREF=YES,SYM=YES,SYSDUMP=YES,XREF=NO
```

The STDOPT statement

```
// STDOPT   option-value[,option-value...]
```

Explanation

option-value   May be one of the following:

                                ACANCEL = NO | YES
                                ALIGN = YES | NO
                                CHARSET = 48C | 60C
                                DATE = MDY | DMY
                                DECK = YES | NO
                                DUMP = YES | NO | PART
                                EDECK = NO | YES
                                ERRS = YES | NO
                                HCTRAN = YES | NO
                                JCANCEL = NO | YES
                                LINES = 56 | nn
                                LIST = YES | NO
                                LISTX = NO | YES
                                LOG = YES | NO
                                LOGSRCE = NO | YES
                                RLD = NO | YES
                                SXREF = NO | YES
                                SYM = NO | YES
                                SYSDUMP = NO | YES
                                TERM = NO | YES
                                XREF = YES | NO

Figure 5-20   The STDOPT statement

```
       .
       .
       .
// STDOPT   ACANCEL=NO,ALIGN=YES,CHARSET=60C,DATE=MDY,DECK=NO,DUMP=PART
// STDOPT   EDECK=NO,ERRS=YES,JCANCEL=NO,LINES=56,LIST=YES,LISTX=NO,LOG=YES
// STDOPT   RLD=YES,SXREF=YES,SYM=YES,SYSDUMP=YES,TERM=NO,XREF=NO
       .
       .
       .
```

Figure 5-21   Sample STDOPT statements

These two statements specify only the options that are set to values other than the system defaults.

The OPTION statement   When you need to override a system standard option, you code the OPTION statement in your job. In contrast to STDOPT, OPTION sets an option for only the partition that processes it, and its effect is temporary. It causes values in the partition COM-REG to be changed to indicate the temporary options. When the job ends, all options are reset to their standard values.

Figure 5-22 shows the format of the OPTION statement. As with STDOPT, you need to code only the options you want to change. However, the way you code an option differs between the two statements. For example, to disable ACANCEL temporarily, you code

```
// OPTION   NOACANCEL
```

In contrast, to disable ACANCEL permanently for all partitions, you code

```
// STDOPT   ACANCEL=NO
```

If you study figure 5-22, you can see that most of the values you can code on the OPTION statement for system standard options are paired. Also, they're in the format option-name/NOoption-name. When you use OPTION, you can override all of the standard option settings except the ones for system management: DATE, HCTRAN, and LINES.

In addition to overriding system standard options, you can use the OPTION statement for some other functions. They fall into the three groups shown in figure 5-22: options to control (1) standard labels, (2) the linkage editor, and (3) the assembler's use of copy books stored in sublibraries. In chapter 10, you'll learn how to use the options for standard labels. And in chapter 14, you'll learn how to use options to control the linkage editor and the assembler.

Discussion   The four statements in this topic all affect the contents of a partition's communication region. Although you don't need to know the details of how the partition communication regions are organized, you should know that STDOPT and OPTION cause switches (bit positions) in bytes in a partition's COMREG to be turned on and off.

Terminology   partition communication region
COMREG
UPSI byte
system standard option
system default

The OPTION statement

```
// OPTION   overriding-value[,overriding-value...]
```

Explanation

overriding-value   May be one of the following:

ACANCEL	NOACANCEL	
ALIGN	NOALIGN	
48C	60C	(for CHARSET)
DECK	NODECK	
DUMP	NODUMP	PARTDUMP
EDECK	NOEDECK	
ERRS	NOERRS	
JCANCEL	NOJCANCEL	
LIST	NOLIST	
LISTX	NOLISTX	
LOG	NOLOG	
LOGSRC	NOLOGSRC	
RLD	NORLD	
SXREF	NOSXREF	
SYM	NOSYM	
SYSDUMP	NOSYSDUMP	
TERM	NOTERM	
XREF	NOXREF	

To control standard labels, you may code:

PARSTD
PARSTD = ADD
PARSTD = DELETE
PARSTD = Fn
STDLABEL
STDLABEL = ADD
STDLABEL = DELETE
USRLABEL

To control linkage editor functions, you may code:

CATAL
LINK
NOLINK

To control assembler copy library usage, you may code:

SUBLIB = AE
SUBLIB = DF

Figure 5-22   The OPTION statement

Objectives

1. Given the UPSI byte requirements for a program, code an UPSI statement that will cause the program to execute properly.

2. Given specifications for a job that requires a date different from the system date, code an appropriate DATE statement.

3. Given a job containing STDOPT or OPTION statements, identify the system standard options they set.

4. Given a job that requires a change in one or more system standard options, code appropriate OPTION statements for the job.

Chapter 6

Other features of VSE JCL

In the first two chapters of this section, you learned the basic and advanced forms of most of the VSE JCL statements you'll need to create production job streams. This chapter introduces some other advanced features of VSE JCL that will make coding job streams easier. In topic 1, I'll show you how to code and store segments of job streams as cataloged procedures and how to retrieve those procedures to use them again and again. In topic 2, I'll teach you how to use conditional JCL to alter the sequence of your job streams. And in topic 3, I'll explain how to use symbolic parameters to alter the values of the operands in your job streams and cataloged procedures.

TOPIC 1   Cataloged procedures

A *cataloged procedure* is a frequently used segment of a job stream that's stored in a VSE sublibrary. Once it's stored, VSE can retrieve it and execute it as often as needed. In this topic, I'll describe what you need to know to code, store, and execute cataloged procedures.

How to execute a cataloged procedure

Executing a cataloged procedure is much like executing a program. If the procedure doesn't reside in the system sublibrary, IJSYSRS.SYSLIB, you establish a sublibrary search chain with a LIBDEF statement. Then, you execute the procedure by coding an EXEC statement. But instead of using the program-name operand on the EXEC statement, you use the PROC=procedure-name operand.

How to establish a sublibrary search chain for procedures   Establishing a sublibrary search chain for procedures is similar to establishing a search chain for phases. The only difference is that you code PROC for the library-type operand of LIBDEF instead of PHASE. For example,

```
// LIBDEF   PROC,SEARCH=(USR1.AP2,USR3.AP3,USR2.AP4)
```

establishes a sublibrary search chain that begins with USR1.AP2 and includes USR3.AP3 and USR2.AP4. (This assumes, of course, that all three library files have already been defined with DLBL and EXTENT statements.) Once the search chain has been established, you can code EXEC statements to execute the cataloged procedures.

The PROC operand of the EXEC statement   To execute a procedure, you code the EXEC statement as shown in figure 6-1. Unlike the EXEC statement for a program, you must code the PROC= operand to execute a procedure; it's not optional. If you code

```
// EXEC     PROC=INV5200
```

for example, VSE searches the sublibraries in the active procedure search chain until it finds the member named INV5200. Then, it processes the statements in the procedure as if they were supplied in a standard job. (What actually happens is that VSE temporarily assigns SYSRDR to the sublibrary where the procedure is located and uses the procedure as input to the job control program.)

The EXEC statement to execute a procedure

```
// EXEC   PROC=procedure-name
```

Explanation

procedure-name | The one- to eight-character member name of the procedure to be executed. This operand is required, and you must precede it with PROC=.

Figure 6-1   The EXEC statement to execute a procedure

How to code a procedure

For the most part, coding a procedure is no different from coding a standard job. But you do need to remember that you code the JOB statement in the job stream that invokes the procedure, not in the procedure itself, and you end the procedure with the end-of-procedure statement (/+).

To illustrate how to code and execute a cataloged procedure, I'm going to use the simple inventory application that figures 6-2 through 6-5 present. Figure 6-2 is the system flowchart for an inventory management job that (1) copies an inventory master file from DASD to tape, (2) sorts the original file into the sequence required for a report-preparation program, and (3) prepares an inventory report. Figure 6-3 is the system structure chart for the application, and figures 6-4 and 6-5 present the detailed specifications for the logical units and files required by the programs of the application.

Figure 6-6 is a standard job stream for this application. Except for the Sort/Merge control statements it contains, you shouldn't have any trouble understanding it. To convert it to a cataloged procedure and create a job stream to execute it, you code the job streams in figure 6-7. The left side of the figure shows the job that executes the procedure. As you can see, it's simple, consisting only of a JOB statement, a LIBDEF statement to establish the correct sublibrary search chain, an EXEC statement with the PROC= operand to invoke the cataloged procedure, and an end-of-job statement. All the other statements are stored in the cataloged procedure.

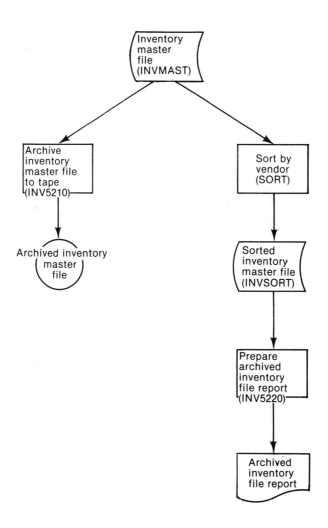

Figure 6-2   System flowchart for an inventory application

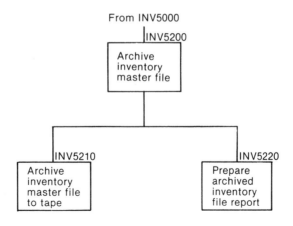

Figure 6-3   System structure chart for the inventory application

Program	Logical unit	Device	Program file name	File id	Flowchart file name
INV5210	SYS013	Tape at 300		Unlabelled	
	SYS015	DASD at 250	INVMAST	INVENTORY.MASTER.FILE	INVMAST
SORT	SYS015	DASD at 250	SORTIN1	INVENTORY.MASTER.FILE	INVMAST
	SYS015	DASD at 250	SORTWK1		
	SYS015	DASD at 250	SORTOUT	SORTED.INVENTORY.MASTER.FILE	INVSORT
INV5220	SYS006	Printer			
	SYS015	DASD at 250	INVMAST	SORTED.INVENTORY.MASTER.FILE	INVSORT

Figure 6-4   Logical units, device assignments, and file ids used by the programs of the inventory application

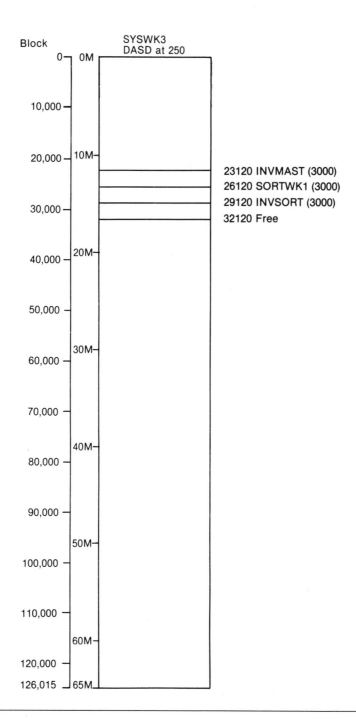

Figure 6-5 DASD layout for the inventory application

```
// JOB        INV5200
// LIBDEF     PHASE,SEARCH=(USRSLE.INVNTORY)
// ASSGN      SYS006,SYSLST
// ASSGN      SYS013,300
// ASSGN      SYS015,250
// DLBL       INVMAST,'INVENTORY.MASTER.FILE'
// EXTENT     SYS015,,,,23120,3000
// PAUSE      MOUNT TAPE FOR INVENTORY FILE ARCHIVE
// EXEC       INV5210
// DLBL       SORTIN1,'INVENTORY.MASTER.FILE'
// EXTENT     SYS015,,,,23120,3000
// DLBL       SORTWK1
// EXTENT     SYS015,,,,26120,3000
// DLBL       SORTOUT,'SORTED.INVENTORY.MASTER.FILE'
// EXTENT     SYS015,,,,29120,3000
// EXEC       SORT
   SORT       FIELDS=(21,8,CH,A),WORK=1
   RECORD     TYPE=F,LENGTH=256
/*
// DLBL       INVMAST,'SORTED.INVENTORY.MASTER.FILE'
// EXTENT     SYS015,,,,29120,3000
// EXEC       INV5220
/&
```

Figure 6-6   The inventory application job implemented as a standard VSE job

Invoking job stream

Cataloged procedure INV5200

```
                                            // LIBDEF     PHASE,SEARCH=(USRSLE.INVNTORY)
                                            // ASSGN      SYS006,SYSLST
                                            // ASSGN      SYS013,300
                                            // ASSGN      SYS015,250
                                            // DLBL       INVMAST,'INVENTORY.MASTER.FILE'
                                            // EXTENT     SYS015,,,,23120,3000
                                            // PAUSE      MOUNT TAPE FOR INVENTORY FILE ARCHIVE
                                            // EXEC       INV5210
// JOB     INV5200                          // DLBL       SORTIN1,'INVENTORY.MASTER.FILE'
// LIBDEF  PROC,SEARCH=(USRSLE.INVNTORY)    // EXTENT     SYS015,,,,23120,3000
// EXEC    PROC=INV5200                      // DLBL       SORTWK1
/&                                          // EXTENT     SYS015,,,,26120,3000
                                            // DLBL       SORTOUT,'SORTED.INVENTORY.MASTER.FILE'
                                            // EXTENT     SYS015,,,,29120,3000
                                            // EXEC       SORT
                                               SORT       FIELDS=(21,8,CH,A),WORK=1
                                               RECORD     TYPE=F,LENGTH=256
                                            /*
                                            // DLBL       INVMAST,'SORTED.INVENTORY.MASTER.FILE'
                                            // EXTENT     SYS015,,,,29120,3000
                                            // EXEC       INV5220
                                            /*
```

Figure 6-7   The inventory application job implemented as a cataloged procedure

```
// JOB      CATPROC
// DLBL     library-name,...
// EXTENT   ...
// EXEC     LIBR
   ACCESS SUBLIB=library.sublibrary
   CATALOG membername.PROC [DATA=YES]
   .
   .
   .
   procedure statements
   .
   .
   .
/+
/*
/&
```

Figure 6-8   Model job to catalog a procedure

The right side of figure 6-7 shows the cataloged procedure itself. Although it's much the same as the original job, you should notice that it doesn't contain a JOB statement and that it ends with /+, not /&. (When the job control program encounters /+, SYSRDR is reassigned from the sublibrary where the procedure is located to its permanent unit.) Otherwise, the cataloged procedure in figure 6-7 is identical to the standard VSE job in figure 6-6.

How to catalog a procedure

Once you've coded a procedure like the one on the right side of figure 6-7, you need to catalog it in a sublibrary. Although I'm not going to cover the VSE Librarian until chapter 15, I want to show you how to perform this library function now.

Figure 6-8 is a model job you can use to catalog a procedure in a sublibrary. It begins with a JOB statement, followed by DLBL and EXTENT statements that define the library in which the sublibrary is located. (If the library was defined with a permanent label during system start-up, you can omit these statements.)

The EXEC statement invoking the Librarian (LIBR), is followed by two Librarian commands: ACCESS and CATALOG. The ACCESS command identifies the sublibrary that will contain the procedure. And the CATALOG command specifies the name of the member you're cataloging in the sublibrary. If the job stream you're cataloging contains any in-line data, you must code DATA=YES on the CATALOG command; if the job stream doesn't contain in-line data, you can omit the DATA operand.

```
// JOB      CATPROC
// EXEC     LIBR
   ACCESS   SUBLIB=USRSLE.INVNTORY
   CATALOG  INV5200.PROC DATA=YES
// LIBDEF   PHASE,SEARCH=(USRSLE.INVNTORY)
// ASSGN    SYS006,SYSLST
// ASSGN    SYS013,300
// ASSGN    SYS015,250
// DLBL     INVMAST,'INVENTORY.MASTER.FILE'
// EXTENT   SYS015,,,,23120,3000
// PAUSE    MOUNT TAPE FOR INVENTORY FILE ARCHIVE
// EXEC     INV5210
// DLBL     SORTIN1,'INVENTORY.MASTER.FILE'
// EXTENT   SYS015,,,,23120,3000
// DLBL     SORTWK1
// EXTENT   SYS015,,,,26120,3000
// DLBL     SORTOUT,'SORTED.INVENTORY.MASTER.FILE'
// EXTENT   SYS015,,,,29120,3000
// EXEC     SORT
   SORT     FIELDS=(21,8,CH,A),WORK=1
   RECORD   TYPE=F,LENGTH=256
/*
// DLBL     INVMAST,'SORTED.INVENTORY.MASTER.FILE'
// EXTENT   SYS015,,,,29120,3000
// EXEC     INV5220
/+
/*
/&
```

Figure 6-9   Job to catalog the inventory application procedure

Following the Librarian commands are the statements to be cataloged. All of these statements are processed as input to the Librarian; they are not treated as job control statements during this process. Be sure the input ends with /+. Then, code /* to indicate the end of the in-line data and /& to indicate the end of the job.

Figure 6-9 presents the job I used to catalog the procedure in figure 6-7. As you can see, the ACCESS command specifies that the procedure is to be stored in the sublibrary USRSLE.INVNTORY. Since the library USRSLE was defined during system start-up, I didn't need to code DLBL and EXTENT statements for it. The CATALOG command specifies that the member name is to be INV5200. And since it's a procedure, its member type is PROC. Because the procedure contains in-line data (SORT control statements), I coded DATA=YES on the CATA-LOG command. The job stream ends with /+, /*, and /& indicating the end of the procedure, the end of the input data, and the end of the job, respectively. Again, let me stress that because the statements that make up the inventory procedure are themselves in-line data read by the Librarian program, they aren't processed by the job control program when the job in figure 6-9 is executed.

Nested procedures	You can code a cataloged procedure that executes other cataloged procedures. When procedures are coded this way they're called *nested procedures*. For example, suppose procedure A contains the statement

```
// EXEC      PROC=B
```

Then, procedure B is said to be nested in procedure A.

Procedures can be nested up to 16 levels deep. The first level, which contains the JOB statement, is called the highest level. The level that is nested deepest is called the lowest level. (IBM literature refers to the highest level as level 0 and the lowest level as level 15. However, I won't use that notation here.) To illustrate, figure 6-10 shows how procedures might be nested. At the highest level, the job NSTPROC executes procedure A. Then, procedure A executes procedure B, and procedure B executes procedure C. So in this example, procedure C is the lowest level.

Any cataloged procedure can be nested. The only restriction is that a procedure may not execute itself or any of the procedures in which it's contained. In other words, you can't execute a procedure that's at the same or higher level than the procedure that's currently executing. So, using the example above, procedure B can execute procedure C, but not procedures A or B.

Rules for using cataloged procedures

When you use cataloged procedures, you have to follow one rule: only code the statements for a single job in a cataloged procedure. If you recall that you never code the JOB statement in a cataloged procedure, but rather in the job stream that invokes the procedure, this rule should be easy to remember.

Although there are other rules for coding cataloged procedures, they have to do with complex job streams that make changes to procedure search chains. Since you'll probably never code a cataloged procedure to do that, I won't present those rules here. If you need to know what they are, you can refer to *VSE/Advanced Functions System Control Statements* for details.

Overriding procedure statements

In general, you don't catalog a procedure unless you intend to use it again and again. Sometimes, however, you need to make a temporary change to a cataloged procedure. Since it's inefficient to create a modified version and catalog it for just one run, VSE provides facilities that let you modify existing procedures at execution time.

Under the old version of DOS (VSE/AF version 1) this modification is done using *overriding statements*. These overriding statements let you delete, replace, and insert new lines into cataloged procedures.

Highest level

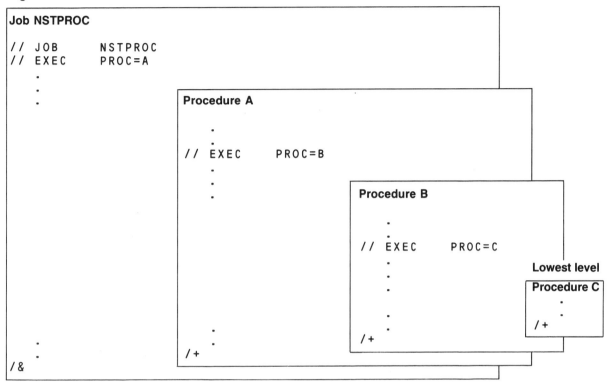

Figure 6-10   Structure of nested procedures

Although the new version of DOS (VSE/AF version 2.1) still processes these overriding statements, I recommend you use the new features of VSE, conditional JCL and symbolic parameters, to make temporary modifications to your cataloged procedures. I'll explain these features in the next two topics.

Discussion   Although cataloged procedures are a useful feature of VSE, you may not use them extensively in your shop. As you'll see, there are other ways to store procedures that are simpler and more flexible. For example, job streams can be stored in an ICCF library and submitted for execution from there. Also, commonly used jobs can be stored by POWER. In chapter 7, you'll see how.

Terminology   cataloged procedure
               nested procedures
               overriding statement

Objectives   1. Given specifications for a job that will execute a cataloged proce-
                  dure, code the JCL to invoke it.

               2. Given specifications for a job that will be stored as a cataloged proce-
                  dure, code it and add it to the specified sublibrary.

TOPIC 2   Conditional JCL

Normally, the job control program processes the statements in a job stream in sequence, from first to last. With *conditional JCL*, however, you can alter the order of execution of job control statements.

To use conditional JCL, you need to learn five JCL statements: GOTO, label (/.), ON, IF, and SETPARM. In this topic, I'll cover the first four. Then, in the next topic, I'll discuss the SETPARM statement when I explain symbolic parameters.

Conditional JCL is most effective when all the statements are used together. In fact, there isn't any reason to use a GOTO or a label command by itself; they're used in combination with ON and IF. Even so, I'll begin by presenting GOTO and label, since they're the easiest to learn. Then, after I present ON and IF, I'll present a sample job stream that uses all four statements so you can see how they work together.

The GOTO statement

The GOTO statement causes an unconditional branch in your job stream. As you can see in figure 6-11, its only operand is either the name of a label statement or the keyword $EOJ. (I'll present the label statement in a moment.) If you code $EOJ, the job control program goes immediately to the end of the job. If you code the name of a label statement, the job control program skips forward until it reaches the specified statement. For example, if you code the GOTO statement

```
// GOTO     ABLABEL
```

your job searchs for a label statement with the name ABLABEL and continues processing at that statement.

There are two things you should keep in mind when you code a label operand on a GOTO statement. First, the label statement referred to must follow the GOTO statement. In other words, you can't use a GOTO statement to branch backwards. Second, you can't use the GOTO statement to branch outside of a job or procedure. If VSE encounters an end-of-job statement (/&) before it reaches the referenced label statement, it terminates the job. And if VSE encounters an end-of-procedure statement (/+), it skips the rest of the procedure.

The label statement (/.)

The label statement (/.) is the last of the five JCL statements that don't begin with //. It's used to identify a particular location in your job stream. Its format is given in figure 6-12.

On the label statement, you code a label name. This name can be from one to eight alphameric characters long, and the first character must be alphabetic. You can reference the label name from a GOTO

The GOTO statement

```
// GOTO    {label}
          {$EOJ }
```

Explanation

label   Specifies the one- to eight-character operand of the label statement (/.) where exe-
                                   cution of the current job is to continue.

$EOJ   Specifies that the job should end immediately.

Figure 6-11   The GOTO statement

The label statement (/.)

```
/. label
```

Explanation

label   Specifies a one- to eight-character alphameric name. The first character must be
                                   alphabetic.

Figure 6-12   The label statement

statement (as described above) or from the GOTO operand of an ON
statement. (I'll present the ON statement in a moment.) For example,
the GOTO statement I just presented would search for this label
statement:

```
/. ABLABEL
```

The ON statement

When you code an ON statement, you specify a condition and an action
to be taken if the condition is true. The condition you specify is checked
by the job control program after each job statement. Because the condition remains in effect for the duration of the job, it's known as a *global
condition*. The format of the ON statement is given in figure 6-13.

There are three conditions you can test with the ON statement.
First, you can test the *return code* of a job step. The return code indicates the success or failure of a job step. It's a numerical value, ranging
from 0 to 4095 that's updated after a program executes.

The ON statement

```
         ($RC operator n)  [(OR )   ($RC operator n)]  (GOTO {label}    )
// ON    {$CANCEL       }  [(|  )   {$CANCEL       }]  {     {$EOJ }    }
         ($ABEND        )  [(AND)   ($ABEND        )]  (CONTINUE        )
                           [(&  )                  ]
```

Explanation

$RC	Represents the return code of the step.
operator	Specifies a comparison to be done:

> EQ or =
> NE or ¬ =
> GT or >
> LT or <
> GE or > =
> LE or < =

n	Specifies a decimal integer from 0 to 4095 to be compared with the return code.
$CANCEL	Specifies that the action is to be taken if the CANCEL command is given for the job.
$ABEND	Specifies that the action is to be taken if the step terminates abnormally.
GOTO label	Specifies that processing should continue at the indicated label statement if the condition is true.
CONTINUE	Specifies that processing should continue if the indicated condition is true. CONTINUE is not valid for the conditions $CANCEL and $ABEND. CONTINUE can be abbreviated as CONT.

Figure 6-13   The ON statement

The condition a return code represents depends on the program that issues it. Most system programs that you'll use, like the linkage editor, use the standard IBM codes shown in figure 6-14. You can also set your own return codes in programs you write in assembler and some high-level languages. Check your programming language reference manual to find out how to set return code values.

In the ON statement, $RC represents the return code of the last step executed. To test a return code, you compare $RC with an integer value. Figure 6-13 shows the types of comparisons you can make.

For example, suppose you code the following ON statement:

```
// ON        $RC>=4 GOTO $EOJ
```

Then, if the return code from the preceding step is 8, the condition

Return Code	Meaning
0	The requested function has been executed successfully.
4	A problem has been encountered, but it was possible to continue and complete the function.
8	The requested function has been completed, but major parts were bypassed.
12	The requested function could not be performed.
16	A severe error occurred, and the step was terminated.

Figure 6-14   Standard return codes for conditional JCL

is true and the action GOTO $EOJ is taken. If the return code is 0, the condition is false, and the next job control statement is processed.

Notice that I used spaces to separate the $RC>=4, GOTO, and $EOJ operands. The ON and IF statements are the only JCL statements that allow spaces between operands instead of commas. That's because these two statements read more like sentences than other JCL statements; they have a logical flow, unlike the others, which contain disjointed lists of operands.

The other two types of conditions you can test for are specified by the keywords $CANCEL and $ABEND. If you code $CANCEL as a condition, VSE takes the specified action when a systems operator issues a CANCEL command for the job. (I don't discuss the CANCEL command in this book, but if you want to know more about it, consult IBM's *VSE/Advanced Functions System Control Statements.*) If you code $ABEND, VSE takes the specified action when a step terminates abnormally.

Notice in figure 6-13 that you can code two conditions on an ON statement. To code a compound condition, just separate the conditions by one of the logical operators, OR, AND, or their symbolic representations, | or &. When you code OR or |, VSE will take the action you specify whenever either of the conditions are true. But when you specify AND or &, both conditions must be true for VSE to take the specified action. (If you code a compound condition, make sure you leave a space before and after the logical operator.)

For example, it's likely that you'll want to end a job if either of the $ABEND or $CANCEL conditions occur. Rather than coding these conditions in separate statements, you could code a single ON statement like this:

```
// ON      $ABEND OR $CANCEL GOTO $EOJ
```

As you'll see in a minute, however, it's not usually necessary to code this particular statement, since it specifies the default action.

You can specify the action to be taken on an ON statement in two ways. First, you can indicate a branch using GOTO, as in the above examples. You code it just like a GOTO statement. Second, you can indicate that processing should continue using the CONTINUE operand. You'll rarely code CONTINUE, since it specifies processing that will take place anyway. At times, though, you may need to use it to override an existing ON statement.

When a job starts, there are already several default ON statements in effect. They are:

```
// ON        $RC<16 CONTINUE
// ON        $RC>=16 GOTO $EOJ
// ON        $ABEND GOTO $EOJ
// ON        $CANCEL GOTO $EOJ
```

If these conditions and actions aren't what you want, you'll need to code overriding ON statements. For example, to override the first two defaults, you can code

```
// ON        $RC<8 CONTINUE
// ON        $RC>=8 GOTO $EOJ
```

When two ON statements specify the same condition but different actions, the last one issued overrides the first. Overriding a default, as shown above, is the most common situation in which you'll code the CONTINUE operand.

If you code the ON statement in a nested procedure, you should know that the ON condition is in effect not only for the level at which the statement is issued, but for all lower levels as well. For example, if you code an ON statement in the first level of your job stream, it remains in effect, unless you override it, throughout all the procedures your job executes. However, if your job executes procedure A and procedure A contains an ON statement, that ON condition is only in effect for the duration of procedure A. It does *not* remain in effect when the job control program returns to the original job stream.

The IF statement

Like the ON statement, the IF statement is conditional. But unlike ON, it's a *local condition*; it only affects the immediate execution of the job. When VSE encounters an IF statement, it executes the statement that follows it if the IF condition is true. Otherwise, VSE skips the next statement.

The condition you code on an IF statement can be either a return code comparison or a parameter comparison, as shown in figure 6-15. For a return code comparison, you can specify either $RC or $MRC. You code the $RC comparison just like you do on the ON statement.

The IF statement

```
         ($RC              operator n     )
// IF    {$MRC             operator n     }
         (parameter-name operator value)


    [(OR )  ($RC                operator n     )]
    [( |  ) ($MRC               operator n     )]  THEN
    [(AND)  (parameter-name operator value)]
    [( &  )
```

Explanation

$RC	Represents the return code of the preceding job step.
$MRC	Represents the maximum return code of all preceding steps within the current job.
parameter-name	Specifies the name of a parameter to be compared.
operator	Specifies the comparison to be done:

> EQ or =
> NE or ¬ =
> GT or >
> LT or <
> GE or > =
> LE or < =

n	Specifies a decimal integer from 0 to 4095 to be compared with the return code.
value	Specifies a character string of 0 to 50 characters to be compared with the parameter name.

Figure 6-15   The IF statement

The $MRC comparison is essentially the same, except it tests the maximum return code of all preceding steps within the current job, not just the last return code.

For example, suppose that in a job containing three steps, you don't want to execute the third step if the return code from either of the first two steps is greater than or equal to eight. Then, before the third job step, you could code the statement

```
// IF      $MRC>=8 THEN
// GOTO    $EOJ
```

and the third step would execute only if the return codes from both the first and second steps were less than eight. In contrast, if you wanted the execution of the third job step to depend only on the outcome of the second job step, you could code this statement:

```
// IF      $RC>=8 THEN
// GOTO    $EOJ
```

Coding a parameter comparison is more complicated. Here, you compare a symbolic parameter to a value you've selected. You'll learn how to code symbolic parameters in the next topic. For now, all you need to know is that both the value of the symbolic parameter and the value you compare it with are character strings that contain 0 to 50 characters. This allows you to make a *logical comparison*.

VSE performs a logical comparison by looking at the bit patterns of the character strings. But you don't need to know the bit patterns to do comparisons. All you need to know is the *collating sequence* on your system. A collating sequence ranks numbers, letters, and characters from lowest to highest and lets you compare them in the same way you compare numbers. Although the collating sequence can be tailored, most shops use this standard sequence:

```
the blank
.
(
&
$
)
-
/
,
#
'
"
the letters A-Z
the numbers 0-9
```

With this collating sequence, B/W is less than BTW, A&M is less than A-M, and RT7 is less than R66.

It's also possible to compare strings of different lengths with a logical comparison. When you do that, the shorter string is padded on the right with blanks. So MONTH is less than WEEK, even though WEEK has fewer characters than MONTH.

You may also code one of the strings in a logical comparison as a *null string*, which VSE interprets for comparison as all blanks. The literal representation of a null string is two apostrophes ('   '). When you code a null string, you can only use the comparators =, ¬=, EQ, and NE. That's because the null string will always be less than any other character string, so any greater-than or less-than comparisons are meaningless.

```
 1  // JOB      CONDJCL
 2  // ON       $ABEND GOTO ABLABEL
 3  // LIBDEF   PHASE,SEARCH=(USRSLE.INVNTORY,USRSLE.USRUTIL1)
 4  // EXEC     INV4800
 5  // IF       $RC<4 THEN
 6  // EXEC     INV4900
 7  // GOTO     $EOJ
 8  /. ABLABEL
 9  // EXEC     ABTERM
10  /&
```

Figure 6-16   Job that uses conditional JCL

As with the ON statement, you can specify compound conditions on an IF statement. Just separate them with OR, |, AND, or &. For example, in the three-step job I presented earlier, if you wanted to skip the third step if the return code from the first step was greater than or equal to eight or if the return code from the second step was greater than or equal to four, you could code this IF statement before the third step:

```
// IF       $RC>=4 OR $MRC>=8 THEN
// GOTO     $EOJ
```

As you can see in figure 6-15 and in the examples I've presented, the last thing you code on an IF statement is the word THEN. It's required, so be sure you don't leave it off.

The only other thing you need to know about the IF statement is that its effect is limited to the job or procedure that contains it. Therefore, you can't use it to skip over a JOB, end-of-job (/&), or end-of-procedure (/+) statement. If you try to do that, VSE will execute the statement anyway, even if the condition isn't true.

A sample job that uses conditional JCL

To illustrate conditional JCL, I've coded a job in figure 6-16 that uses the GOTO, /., ON, and IF statements. I'll explain how this job works, statement by statement.

1. The first statement specifies the job name as CONDJCL.

2. Following the JOB statement, the ON statement indicates that if a step terminates abnormally, processing should continue with the ABLABEL statement. This statement overrides the default condition ON $ABEND GOTO $EOJ.

3. The LIBDEF statement indicates that VSE should search the sublibraries USRSLE.INVNTORY and USRSLE.USRUTIL1 for the required phases.

4. Next, the phase INV4800 is executed.

5. The IF statement tests the return code from INV4800. If the return code is less than 4, the next statement is processed. If the return code is greater than or equal to 4, the next statement is skipped and processing resumes at the GOTO statement.

6. INV4900 will be executed only if the condition in the preceding IF statement is true. In other words, if the return code from the execution of INV4800 is less than 4, program INV4900 will be executed. Otherwise, this step is skipped.

7. The GOTO statement directs the job control program to the end of the job. Note that this statement will be processed whether or not INV4900 was executed. The only exception is if a preceding step terminated abnormally.

8. If any of the preceding steps terminate abnormally, the job control program skips down to this label statement and resumes processing. This branch is directed by the ON condition coded in line 2. Notice that I began coding the label name ABLABEL in column 4. Although this isn't required, it makes the code easier to read because it's lined up with the operation names of the other JCL statements.

9. If the job control program branches to the /. statement, processing resumes with the statement that follows it. In this case the phase ABTERM is executed. Notice that this statement is processed only if a job step terminates abnormally. If all the steps execute properly, the preceding GOTO $EOJ statement directs the processing past this EXEC statement.

10. /& marks the end of the job.

Discussion   By now, you should understand how to use basic conditional JCL to control the sequence of job steps in your job streams. Conditional JCL is a new feature, first made available with DOS/VSE version 2.1. It's a welcome convenience because it increases the flexibility of your job control coding. And when you combine conditional JCL with symbolic parameters (which the next topic introduces), you have a command language that's significantly more powerful than what basic VSE JCL offers.

Terminology   conditional JCL
global condition
return code
local condition
logical comparison
collating sequence
null string

Objective   Given specifications for a job, use the GOTO, label, ON, and IF statements as required to control its execution.

TOPIC 3   Symbolic parameters

This topic introduces you to *symbolic parameters* and shows you how they're used. With symbolic parameters, you can code operands in your cataloged procedures as variables. Then you can specify values for those variables at execution time. This lets you code generalized procedures for functions you perform frequently. You can also use symbolic parameters with conditional JCL to control your job's sequence of execution.

In this topic, I'll first show you how to code symbolic parameters. Then, I'll show you how to assign a value to a parameter with three different JCL statements. Next, I'll explain how to code concatenated parameters. Finally, I'll present a job that demonstrates how to use symbolic parameters.

How to code symbolic parameters

You code a symbolic parameter in the operands field of a JCL statement when you want an operand to have a variable rather than a constant value. You can substitute a symbolic parameter for an operand in any JCL statement except for the label statement (/.) and the PROC statement. The only other restriction is that the statement must be coded in a cataloged procedure unless it is an IF, SETPARM, or EXEC statement.

The name of a symbolic parameter can be from one to seven alphameric characters, with the first character alphabetic. To indicate that you've coded a symbolic parameter in place of another operand, you precede the parameter name with an ampersand (&). (As you'll see later, you won't always need to code an ampersand, because sometimes the job control program expects to see a parameter name for the operand of a statement.)

To illustrate, here's an example of an ASSGN statement that uses a symbolic parameter:

```
// ASSGN    SYS001,&UNIT
```

When the job control program encounters this statement, it knows that UNIT is a symbolic parameter because its name is preceded by an ampersand.

How to define symbolic parameters and assign values to them

Symbolic parameters must be assigned values before the job control program can process them. You can assign a value to a symbolic parameter in the procedure or job stream that contains the parameter or in the job that executes the procedure that uses the symbolic parameter.

The PROC statement

```
// PROC   [parameter-name=[value]][,parameter-name=[value]...]
```

Explanation

parameter-name	Specifies the one- to seven-character alphameric name of the symbolic parameter. The first character must be alphabetic. Do not code a delimiting ampersand as the first character of a symbolic-name on the PROC statement.
value	Specifies a character string of from 0 to 50 characters. This represents the value of the symbolic parameter. The string must be enclosed in apostrophes if it contains any nonalphameric characters.

Figure 6-17   The PROC statement

If you try to process a symbolic parameter that hasn't been assigned a value, the job control program will generate an error message that will probably require operator intervention.

There are three ways you can assign values to symbolic parameters. First, you can assign default values to symbolic parameters in a cataloged procedure using the PROC statement. Second, you can assign values during processing with the SETPARM statement. Third, you can assign parameter values in the EXEC statement that executes a procedure. Since you'll use all three statements for different situations, I'll explain each one in detail.

How to assign default values: The PROC statement   The PROC statement defines the default values for symbolic parameters in a cataloged procedure. On the PROC statement, you code a list of the symbolic parameter names along with the values you want to assign to them. The format of the PROC statement is given in figure 6-17.

The value you assign to a parameter must be a character string, with from 0 to 50 characters. If the string contains any spaces or special characters (ones that aren't alphameric), the string must be enclosed in apostrophes. As a result, apostrophes can't be characters in the string itself. If you want to nullify a parameter's value, you can code a null string by coding two apostrophes (' '), or by coding nothing. (You'll see how a null string can be used to affect processing in the sample job stream at the end of this topic.)

The following example illustrates how to use the PROC statement to assign default values:

```
// PROC     UNIT=250,TIME=DAY,A=,B=''
```

Here, the value 250 is assigned to the symbolic parameter UNIT, and the value DAY is assigned to TIME. Then, the parameters A and B are nullified. Notice that you don't code an ampersand in front of the parameters' names in the PROC statement. That's because you're coding the parameter name to assign a value to it, not to represent another operand.

The PROC statement should be the first statement in a cataloged procedure. You can specify up to 36 parameters and code up to six continuation lines. This gives you plenty of space to list the parameters for any procedure you're likely to code.

It's possible to omit the PROC statement or to code a PROC statement without any operands. But if you do, none of the symbolic parameters in the procedure will have default values. Then, all of the parameters must have values assigned to them elsewhere, or the job control program will issue an error message requiring operator intervention.

To prevent this, I recommend you always code a PROC statement to assign default values to all the symbolic parameters used in your cataloged procedures. Although any values you assign with the SETPARM or EXEC statements will override these values, you'll always be sure that values have been assigned to the parameters.

How to assign values during processing: The SETPARM statement
You can use the SETPARM statement to assign values to symbolic parameters at any point during processing. You can code it in the procedure or job that contains the symbolic parameter or in the job stream that executes the procedure that contains them. It doesn't matter if the symbolic parameter already has a value assigned to it; the SETPARM statement overrides any previously assigned value.

Figure 6-18 shows the format of the SETPARM statement. Like the PROC statement, you list the parameters' names and the values you want to assign to them in the operands field. Again, the maximum number of assignments you can code on a single statement is 36, and the maximum number of continuation lines you can code is 6.

The value you code for a parameter on the SETPARM statement can be a character string, coded just as you would code it on a PROC statement, or the keyword $RC or $MRC. If you code $RC, the value assigned to the symbolic parameter is the return code of the last job step executed. If you code $MRC, the parameter value is the maximum return code of all the preceding steps in the current job.

To understand how this works, consider the following statement:

```
// SETPARM LENGTH=80,B=,C=$RC
```

First, the value 80 is assigned to the symbolic parameter LENGTH. Second, the value of parameter B is nullified. Third, the return code of the last job step executed is assigned to the parameter C.

The SETPARM statement

$$
// \ \text{SETPARM parameter-name=} \left[\left\{ \begin{matrix} \text{value} \\ \text{\$RC} \\ \text{\$MRC} \end{matrix} \right\} \right] \ \text{[,parameter-name=} \left[\left\{ \begin{matrix} \text{value} \\ \text{\$RC} \\ \text{\$MRC} \end{matrix} \right\} \right] \ \text{...]}
$$

Explanation

parameter-name   Specifies the one- to seven-character alphameric name of the symbolic parameter. The first character must be alphabetic.

value   Specifies a character string of from 0 to 50 characters. This represents the value of the symbolic parameter. The string must be enclosed in apostrophes if it contains any nonalphameric characters.

$RC   Represents the return code of the preceding job step.

$MRC   Represents the maximum return code of all preceding steps in the current job.

Figure 6-18   The SETPARM statement

In the last topic, I mentioned that SETPARM is one of the five statements used for conditional processing. That's because in addition to using it to assign values to symbolic parameters that are used as procedure operands, you can also use the SETPARM statement to set parameter values that are tested by IF statements. By doing this, you can modify the sequence of your job stream processing.

For example, consider the statements coded in figure 6-19. Here, the SETPARM statement assigns the value WEEK to the symbolic parameter TIME. Then, two IF statements test the value of TIME. Since the first condition (TIME=DAY) isn't true, processing continues with the second IF statement. In this instance , the condition (TIME=WEEK) is true, and the program PROGWEEK is executed. (Notice that the parameter names in the IF statements in figure 6-19 are coded without ampersands. That's because the parameter name is a specified operand of the IF statement and not a substitute for another operand.)

How to assign values with the EXEC statement   The last way you can assign values to symbolic parameters is on the EXEC statement that executes a cataloged procedure. Like the SETPARM statement, parameter values assigned with EXEC override any default values. Although I presented this statement in the first topic of this chapter, I didn't show you how to use it to assign values to symbolic parameters. Figure 6-20 shows the complete format of the EXEC statement for executing procedures.

```
          .
          .
          .
//  SETPARM TIME=WEEK
          .
          .
          .
//  IF       TIME=DAY  THEN
//  EXEC     PROGDAY
//  IF       TIME=WEEK  THEN
//  EXEC     PROGWEEK
          .
          .
          .
```

Figure 6-19   Combining conditional JCL and symbolic parameters

The EXEC statement to execute a procedure and assign symbolic parameter values

```
//  EXEC   PROC=procedure-name[,parameter-name[=[value]]...]
```

Explanation

procedure-name	The one- to eight-character member name of the procedure to be executed. This operand is required, and you must precede it with PROC=.
parameter-name	Specifies the one- to seven-character alphameric name of the symbolic parameter. The first character must be alphabetic.
value	Specifies a character string of from 0 to 50 characters. This represents the value of the symbolic parameter. The string must be enclosed in apostrophes if it contains any nonalphameric characters.

Figure 6-20   The EXEC statement to execute a procedure and assign symbolic parameter values

Like the PROC and SETPARM statements, you code a list of the parameters and their assigned values on the EXEC statement. And you can list up to 36 parameters, coded on up to 6 lines. Notice in figure 6-20, though, that you can't code $RC or $MRC in the EXEC statement; only character string values are allowed.

To illustrate how to assign values with EXEC, suppose you code the following statement in the job JOB001:

```
// EXEC     PROC=PROC001,TIME=WEEK,X=,DATE=&DATE
```

This statement executes the procedure PROC001. The first parameter assignment assigns the value WEEK to the parameter TIME. Then parameter X is nullified. Finally, DATE=&DATE assigns the value of the parameter DATE in JOB001 to the same parameter in PROC001. Notice that the ampersand is included in front of the second DATE parameter. That's because you want the value represented by the DATE parameter in JOB001 to be assigned to the DATE parameter in PROC001; you don't want to assign the character string DATE to it.

In the example above, the values assigned to all three parameters are only in effect for the executed procedure. The assignments do not affect the values of the parameters (if they exist) in the original job stream. Sometimes, however, you'll want the value of a symbolic parameter to be passed from a job stream to a procedure and then back to the job stream after the procedure ends. To do that, you list the parameter name without an equal sign or value. For example, if I executed PROC001 using the statement

```
// EXEC     PROC=PROC001,TIME=WEEK,X=,DATE
```

the current value of DATE would be passed to PROC001. Then, when the procedure ended, the resulting parameter value would be passed back to the original job stream. When you pass a parameter value this way, I recommend you always assign a value to it first with either a SETPARM, PROC, or EXEC statement. That way, you'll be sure it contains meaningful data.

How to concatenate symbolic parameters

So far, all the examples in this topic have shown you how to code simple symbolic parameters. But you can also code complex parameters by concatenating parameters with other parameters or constants.

To concatenate two symbolic parameters, you simply code them one after the other. For instance, suppose you have two parameters M and N with values 19 and 89, respectively. If you code &M&N, the parameters are concatenated, and their value becomes 1989.

Concatenating parameters and constants is a bit more complicated. Figure 6-21 illustrates different ways to do this. For each example in the figure, I've included three things: (1) a parameter name concatenated with a constant; (2) the value assigned to the parameter; and (3) the resulting value.

There are a few things I want you to notice in these examples. First, you code a period as a delimiter when there isn't any delimiter to separate the parameter from the constant, as in &SIZE.(80), &LIBNAME.LIB, and WX&Y.Z.

Concatenated parameter name and constant	Parameter value	Resulting operand
&SIZE.(80)	SIZE=BLOCK	BLOCK(80)
&LIBNAME.LIB	LIBNAME=SLE	SLELIB
SYS&NUM	NUM=013	SYS013
&MNAME..OBJ	MNAME=PROC01	PROC01.OBJ
WX&Y.Z	Y=	WXZ

Figure 6-21   Symbolic parameters concatenated with constants

Second, if you want a period to be part of the actual value of the resulting operand, you need to code two periods, as in &MNAME..OBJ. Then, the job control program recognizes the first period as a delimiter and the second period as part of the operand. This same rule applies to coding ampersands. When you want an ampersand as part of a resulting value, code a double ampersand (&&).

Finally, notice what happens when the symbolic parameter is assigned a null value. In the last example, the constant Z is concatenated with the symbolic parameter Y, which is concatenated with the constant WX. But because Y is assigned a null value, it's as if Y was never coded.

A sample job that uses symbolic parameters

To understand how to use symbolic parameters, take a look at figure 6-22. It includes a job and the procedure it executes. Both contain conditional JCL in addition to symbolic parameters. I've numbered the steps in the order they're processed, so you can see what happens step by step.

1. The JOB statement assigns the job name SYMBPRM.

2. The ON statement specifies that if a job step terminates abnormally or a CANCEL command is issued for SYMBPRM, processing should continue with the ABLABEL statement.

3. The LIBDEF statements specify the sublibraries that are searched for phases and procedures, respectively.

4. The phase CHECKVOL is executed.

5. The SETPARM statement assigns the value of the return code from the previous step (identified by the keyword $RC) to the

Job SYMBPRM

```
 1 // JOB      SYMBPRM
 2 // ON       $ABEND OR $CANCEL GOTO ABLABEL
 3 // LIBDEF   PHASE,SEARCH=(USRSLE.INVNTORY,USRSLE.USRUTIL1)
   // LIBDEF   PROC,SEARCH=(USRSLE.USRUTIL1)
 4 // EXEC     CHECKVOL
 5 // SETPARM  RCODE=$RC
 6 // EXEC     PROC=ASSGN001,RCODE
12 // EXEC     INV8500
13 // GOTO     $EOJ
14 /. ABLABEL
15 // EXEC     ABTERM
16 /&
```

Procedure ASSGN001

```
 7 // PROC     UNIT=302,VOLUME=,RCODE=0
 8 // IF       RCODE>6 THEN
 9 // SETPARM  UNIT=300,VOLUME=',VOL=007778'
10 // ASSGN    SYS001,&UNIT&VOLUME
11 /+
```

Figure 6-22   Job that uses symbolic parameters

symbolic parameter RCODE. In other words, the return code of the program CHECKVOL is stored as the value of the parameter RCODE.

6. This EXEC statement executes the procedure ASSGN001. In addition, it specifies that the value of RCODE should be passed from the job SYMBPRM to ASSGN001.

7. This PROC statement assigns the default values for the symbolic parameters in ASSGN001. Unless other statements assign different values, the parameter UNIT will have the value 302, VOLUME will be nullified, and RCODE will have the value 0. But because RCODE was passed to the procedure by the EXEC PROC statement, it will have the value assigned to it in SYMBPRM. In other words, it is assigned the return code of the program CHECKVOL.

8. The IF statement tests the value of RCODE. If this parameter's value is greater than 6, the next statement is processed. Otherwise, the next statement is skipped.

9. The SETPARM statement assigns the value 300 to the symbolic parameter UNIT and the value ',VOL=007778' to the parameter VOLUME. These values override the values defined in the previous PROC statement. Notice that these assignments are made only if RCODE has a value greater than 6. Otherwise, this statement is skipped.

10. The ASSGN statement assigns the value of the concatenated parameter &UNIT&VOLUME to the logical unit SYS001. Depending on the value of RCODE, this parameter has the default value assigned in the PROC statement at the beginning of ASSGN001 or the value assigned by the preceding SETPARM statement. If VOLUME is a null string, the ASSGN statement will be processed as if there wasn't a VOL= operand. If VOLUME has the value ',VOL=007778', it specifies the volser to be used. Notice that a comma is the first character of the value. That's so there's a comma separating the UNIT and VOL= operands.

11. /+ marks the end of the procedure. Processing control passes back to the job SYMBPRM.

12. The phase INV8500 is executed.

13. The GOTO statement directs the job control program to the end of the job.

14. If any of the preceding job steps terminate abnormally or a systems operator issues a CANCEL command, the job control program skips down to this label statement and resumes processing. This branch is directed by the ON condition coded in line 2.

15. If control branches to the /. statement, processing begins with this statement, and the phase ABTERM is executed.

16. /& marks the end of the job.

Discussion   As I mentioned earlier in this chapter, symbolic parameters have eliminated the need for coding overriding statements to modify cataloged procedures. By coding a procedure with conditional JCL and symbolic parameters, you can easily alter the procedure at execution time. So, you won't need overriding statements, except to modify old procedures that don't contain symbolic parameters. In fact, VSE won't even process overriding statements for procedures that contain symbolic parameters.

Since overriding statements are still processed by VSE, you should avoid naming a symbolic parameter OV. This is the operand used on the EXEC statement for overriding cataloged procedures. If you were to code this as the name of a parameter, the job control program would interpret it as the override command, and your job wouldn't execute the way you intended.

Terminology

symbolic parameter

Objectives

1. Given specifications for a procedure, code it using symbolic parameters.

2. Given specifications for a job that uses cataloged procedures, code it using symbolic parameters and conditional JCL.

Section 3

VSE/POWER

You should recall from chapter 2 that VSE/POWER is an IBM software product that provides spooling services for VSE systems. Strictly speaking, POWER isn't a part of VSE; it's a separately licensed product. From a practical point of view, though, POWER is so widely used and so important in most shops that it's an integral part of a complete VSE system. As a result, to understand VSE, you need to understand POWER.

This section has three chapters. Chapter 7 introduces you to the way POWER works. Chapter 8 describes the format of the control statements you can code to use POWER's facilities, covers the most important of those statements in detail, and presents two sample job streams that show you how to combine those statements with VSE JCL. Chapter 9 shows you how to submit jobs to POWER from ICCF, monitor their progress, and retrieve output from them.

Chapter 7

POWER Concepts

VSE/POWER has two main functions: spooling and job scheduling. As you'll see in a moment, spooling and job scheduling are related functions. You should remember that spooling is a feature that improves the overall efficiency of systems that execute programs requiring card and printer I/O. Because card and printer devices are usually far slower than the internal processing of an application program, much processing time is wasted when a program accesses them directly. With spooling, unit record input and output data are stored temporarily on DASDs.

HOW POWER PERFORMS SPOOLING AND JOB SCHEDULING FUNCTIONS

Job execution under POWER involves several steps: input spooling, job scheduling, execution management, and output spooling. Although these steps happen in this sequence, they don't necessarily happen in immediate succession. There may be a delay between any of the steps, depending on system usage and how POWER's options are set.

Input spooling
Figure 7-1 shows how POWER handles a job submitted to it. Although the input stream must be in card-image format, the job doesn't have to come from a card reader. In fact, it's likely that it doesn't. For now, though, assume the simplest case: The input job stream is a physical deck read in by a card reader.

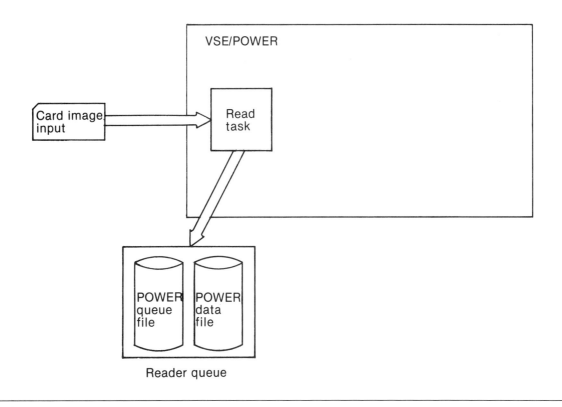

Figure 7-1   How POWER manages input spooling

As you can see in figure 7-1, a *read task* within the POWER partition reads the input stream and stores the card images on disk. Actually, POWER uses two files to store spooled data. The card images are
stored in the *POWER data file*, and another file, the *POWER queue file*,
contains pointers to the entries in the data file.

Although POWER uses two files to record spooled data, it's more
important from your point of view to know that those files are logically divided into three sections called *queues*. A queue is a list formed
by items waiting in line for some sort of system service. As figure 7-1
shows, spooled card input resides in the *reader queue*. You'll see shortly
that spooled output resides in either the *punch queue* or the *list queue*,
depending on whether it's card or printer output. You should realize,
though, that the three queues are not distinct physical entities; they
all share space in the POWER queue and data files.

Job scheduling

Once an entire job (JCL and in-line data) has been stored in the reader queue, POWER has to schedule it for execution before it can run. To make this possible, each item in the reader queue has three characteristics POWER evaluates to determine what job to schedule next: disposition, class, and priority. (Keep in mind as you read about disposition, class, and priority that entries in the punch and list queues have the same three characteristics.)

Disposition   The *disposition* of a reader queue item indicates two things: (1) whether it's available for immediate execution and (2) whether it should be deleted from or retained in the reader queue after it has executed. An item's disposition is one of the four values in figure 7-2. As the figure indicates, if a reader queue item's disposition is D or K, it's available for immediate scheduling by POWER. But if its value is H or L, the system operator must explicitly release the job before POWER will schedule it.

In the next chapter, you'll learn how to specify a job's disposition. If you don't specify a particular disposition for a job, POWER assigns it the disposition D. In other words, if you submit a job to POWER without an explicit disposition, it's available for automatic scheduling and will be deleted when it has finished executing.

Class   Before POWER schedules a job, an "appropriate" partition must be available. The *class* of a reader queue item determines what an appropriate partition is. When a VSE system is started, partitions are set up with different options and device assignments to meet the requirements of particular jobs. For some jobs to run properly, they must execute in a specific partition; if they don't, they fail. Under POWER, both jobs and partitions are characterized with single-character class codes that may be letters of the alphabet or digits. An appropriate partition for a job is one that has a class that matches the job's class.

Classes that are digits are called *partition-specific classes*. For example, class 2 is unique to F2, 3 to F3, and so on. In other words, you can't specify class 3 for F2. Although up to four classes may be associated with one partition, only one may be the partition-specific class.

The other classes that may be associated with a partition are letters. The partition classes on your system depend on the specifications your systems programmer coded in the procedure that starts the POWER partition. For instance, the background may execute jobs with class I, 0 (zero), or J; F2 may execute jobs with class L or 2; and F3 may execute jobs with class M, N, or 3. The order in which the systems programmer coded the class values for each partition determines the preference POWER gives jobs of different classes. If, for example, other factors I'll describe in a moment are equal, a job in the reader queue with class M will be executed before one with class N if the partition is set up with classes M, N, and 3.

For POWER to schedule a job, the job's class must match one of the classes specified for a free partition. If you submit a job without

	Delete from queue after processing	Retain in queue after processing
Schedule the job automatically	D(elete)	K(eep)
Schedule the job only after the system operator releases it	H(old)	L(eave)

Figure 7-2   Disposition values for items in the reader queue

specifying a class, POWER assigns it class A. Then, if your system doesn't have a partition with class A, the job can't be scheduled, regardless of its disposition. In this case, before POWER can schedule the job, the system operator has to change the job's class to one specified for one of the system's partitions. Just when the job is scheduled depends on how many other jobs with the same class have been submitted ahead of it and, more importantly, on its priority.

Priority   The third characteristic that POWER evaluates as it schedules jobs is the *priority* of a reader queue entry. Although the term is the same, don't confuse this with partition priority, which is a VSE feature. The POWER queue entry priorities can range from 0 (the lowest) to 9 (the highest); the default is 3.

When a partition becomes available, POWER checks the reader queue for jobs that are eligible to execute in it. If, for example, the background is configured for classes I, 0 (zero), and J, an eligible job has disposition D or K and class I, 0 (zero) or J. If POWER finds more than one job in the queue that meets these requirements, it schedules the one with the preferred class (in this case, I before zero before J). If it finds two with the same class, it schedules the one with the higher priority. And if two have the same priority and the same class, POWER schedules the one that was in the reader queue first. So POWER's scheduling sequence (for jobs with dispositions D or K) is class first, priority second, and time in the reader queue third.

Execution management   Once the scheduled job starts to run, it's under the control of VSE, but POWER services its unit record I/O requests. The three POWER tasks in figure 7-3 perform these functions. The *execution read task*

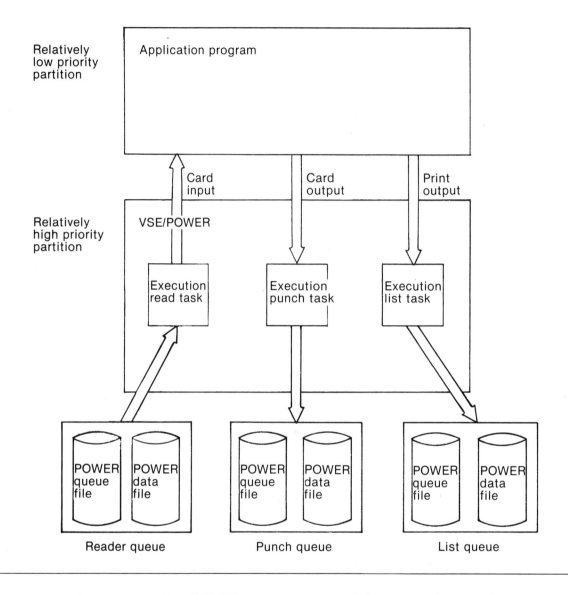

Figure 7-3   How POWER services unit-record I/O requests from application programs

retrieves records from the reader queue and passes them to the application program running in the POWER-controlled partition when it executes a read instruction for a card reader. Similarly, when the application program executes a write instruction for a card punch, an *execution punch task* intercepts the request and writes the data to the POWER punch queue. And when the application program executes a write instruction for a printer, an *execution list task* intercepts that request and writes the data to the POWER list queue.

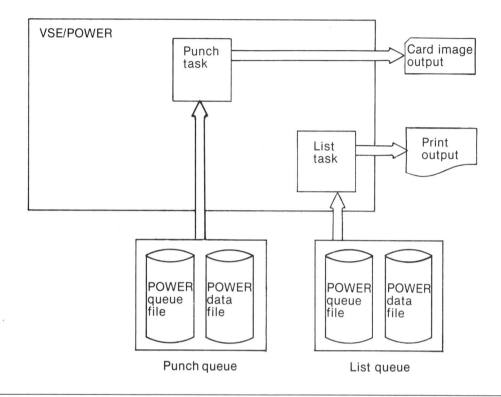

Figure 7-4   How POWER processes spooled output

When a job finishes, POWER deletes it from the reader queue if its disposition is D or H; if its disposition is K or L, POWER retains it in the reader queue. Retaining jobs in the reader queue is an efficient way to manage jobs that are executed regularly. For example, a job that's run each week to back up the system's DASDs might be stored in the reader queue so the system operator can easily release it when it's needed. This is a practical alternative to using cataloged procedures.

Output spooling   Figure 7-4 illustrates how POWER processes data stored in the punch and list queues. A *punch task* and a *list task* write data from the punch and list queues to the output devices. Just as jobs in the reader queue are scheduled and handled based on their class, disposition, and priority, so are items in the punch and list queues.

Disposition   As a general rule, output is automatically punched or printed, then deleted from its queue. In some cases, though, you may want to hold output from automatic punching or printing operations; you may also want to retain it in its queue after processing. Any

	Delete from queue after processing	Retain in queue after processing
Punch or print item automatically when an appropriate device is available	D(elete)	K(eep)
Punch or print item only after the system operator releases it	H(old)	L(eave)

Figure 7-5   Disposition values for items in the punch and list queues

combination of these functions is possible, as long as you set the item's disposition to the proper value, indicated in figure 7-5. These disposition values parallel those for the reader queue entries in figure 7-2. In the next chapter, I'll show you how to specify the disposition for an item in an output queue.

Class   To punch or print spooled output, POWER has to know what physical device to use. Recall that POWER uses classes to associate jobs in the reader queue with partitions where they can execute. It also uses classes to associate spooled output items in the punch and list queues with the devices on which they can be punched or printed.

Priority   It's possible to specify a priority for output from 0 to 9, where 9 is the highest. As for reader queue entries, the default priority for items in the punch and list queues is 3. Output is processed on a first-in, first-out basis, unless another queue item has a higher priority.

Other output management features   POWER provides you with still other ways to manage output. The ones I think you'll use most often let you specify a special form for output or that a multiple number of copies be produced. In addition, you can code control statements to (1) create output with password protection, (2) specify the number of job separator pages or cards that come between two jobs' output, (3) print user information on job separator pages, (4) notify the system operator when the output punched or printed exceeds a specified number of cards or lines, and (5) route output to specified remote users. In the next chapter, I'll show you how to code control statements to take advantage of the most useful of these features.

HOW POWER COORDINATES SPOOLING AND PROGRAM I/O REQUESTS

Figures 7-1 and 7-4 show how POWER relates to physical I/O devices. In figure 7-3, though, unit-record I/O is going on, but no unit-record devices are involved. For this to work, the application program's I/O requests must be coordinated with POWER's spooling functions. In other words, POWER must know what units for each partition are to be treated as *spooling devices*.

Figure 7-6 shows how spooling devices are defined. This figure presents segments of the jobs that start POWER and the partitions under its control on the simple system I'm using as a model in this book. Don't worry about learning the syntax of the statements in the figure. I'm only showing them to give you a better understanding of how POWER works.

The segment of the job in the top of figure 7-6 includes statements that are used for *POWER autostart*. If the control statements in the procedure weren't present, the system operator would have to key them in to start POWER properly. First, an EXEC statement invokes POWER (the phase name is DTRPOWER). FORMAT=NO means the POWER queue and data files should not be reformatted. Then, the job stream contains control statements that place the system's other partitions under the control of POWER (PSTART BG, PSTART F3, and PSTART F2).

While you're looking at the PSTART statements, notice that each specifies not only a partition identifier, but also the classes of jobs that can execute in that partition. For example, jobs with classes I, zero, and J can execute in the background. The last term coded on each PSTART is the default output class for output produced in that partition. It's A for each of the three partitions the procedure in figure 7-6 places under the control of POWER.

For each of these partitions, there's one READER statement, one PUNCHES statement, and one PRINTERS statement. These statements identify the devices for which POWER will provide spooling services for the partition. For all three partitions, the spooling devices are the same. POWER provides input spooling services for requests associated with address 02C, punch spooling services for requests for 02D, and list spooling services for requests for 02E.

Because no physical devices on the system have these addresses, they're called *dummy devices*. It doesn't matter that these spooling devices don't exist because they're only used to coordinate spooling functions between the POWER partition and the partitions under its control. If a partition causes punch output to be routed to address 02D, POWER intercepts the request and writes the punch data to the punch queue, so there's no need for a real device at address 02D. And the same is true for the dummy reader 02C and the dummy printer 02E.

You should realize, though, that the spooling devices specified in the POWER partition start-up job don't have to be dummy devices.

Statements processed in the POWER partition (F1)
during POWER autostart

```
•
•
•
// EXEC      DTRPOWER
FORMAT=NO
PSTART BG,IOJ,A
READER=02C
PRINTERS=02E
PUNCHES=02D
PSTART F3,MN3,A
READER=02C
PRINTERS=02E
PUNCHES=02D
PSTART F2,L2,A
READER=02C
PRINTERS=02E
PUNCHES=02D
PSTART LST,00E,8A,D
•
•
•
```

Statements processed in the partitions under the control
of POWER (BG, F3, and F2) after POWER autostart

```
•
•
•
// ASSGN     SYSLST,02E,PERM
// ASSGN     SYSPCH,02D,PERM
// ASSGN     SYSIN,02C,PERM
•
•
•
```

Figure 7-6   Procedure segments showing POWER start-up statements

For example, if a real reader were part of this system and had address 02C, POWER would still intercept I/O requests for partitions under its control for 02C and satisfy them from the reader queue because 02C is specified as a spooling device in the POWER autostart job stream. In other words, POWER completely isolates the application program from the unit record devices.

After the POWER start-up job in the top part of figure 7-6 has finished, the spooling devices it specified have to be properly assigned in each partition under the control of POWER. On the model system I'm using for the examples in this book, the start-up jobs for BG, F2, and F3 all contain ASSGN statements like those in the bottom part of figure 7-6. These statements associate each partition's unit-record system logical units (SYSLST, SYSPCH, and SYSIN) with POWER spooling devices. SYSIN is the combination of SYSRDR (JCL) and SYSIPT (data) input to the system. After the system start-up process is complete, any punch output produced in BG, F2, or F3 is spooled. That's because SYSPCH is permanently assigned to the spooling device 02D in each of those partitions. Similarly, printer output and card input are also spooled because SYSLST and SYSIN are permanently assigned to 02E and 02C in each POWER-controlled partition.

At this point, you should understand how POWER satisfies application program card input requests by reading card images from its reader queue. Similarly, you should understand how it satisfies application program card output requests by writing card images to the punch queue. However, you might well wonder how a job can get into the reader queue to begin with if there's no card reader on the system. And you might also ask what happens to an item in the punch queue if the system doesn't have a card punch. These are relevant questions because almost no new VSE systems are installed with card units. Moreover, many shops that do have card units are gradually phasing them out.

HOW POWER SPOOLS INPUT AND OUTPUT ON A CARDLESS SYSTEM

To let users migrate away from card-based processing, VSE, POWER, and other system components let *card image files* be processed just like physical card decks. For example, POWER can write spooled punch output not only to a card punch, but also to a tape drive. The punch data is recorded on the tape in card image format. Similarly, POWER can read a tape containing card image job streams, called a *SYSIN tape*. The jobs retrieved from the tape appear as if they had been submitted from a card reader.

Another technique is to use *inter-partition communication* to transfer spooled items between the POWER partition and another partition. For instance, figure 7-7 illustrates what happens when an ICCF user submits a job to POWER. Here, ICCF retrieves the job stream from its library file. Then, inter-partition communication between the CICS/ICCF partition (F2) and the POWER partition (F1) lets the card images that make up the job stream be transferred to POWER. POWER stores the card images in the reader queue just as if they had come from a card reader. At this point, POWER can schedule the job for execution in an available, eligible partition (probably BG). When the job begins to execute, POWER manages its unit record I/O requests as in figure 7-3.

What happens to the output of a job submitted from ICCF depends on the output's class. For instance, a listing may be printed on a system printer if it's created with the proper class. On the other hand, the item may be held in the list queue for retrieval by the ICCF user. Figure 7-8 shows how this works. When the user enters the proper

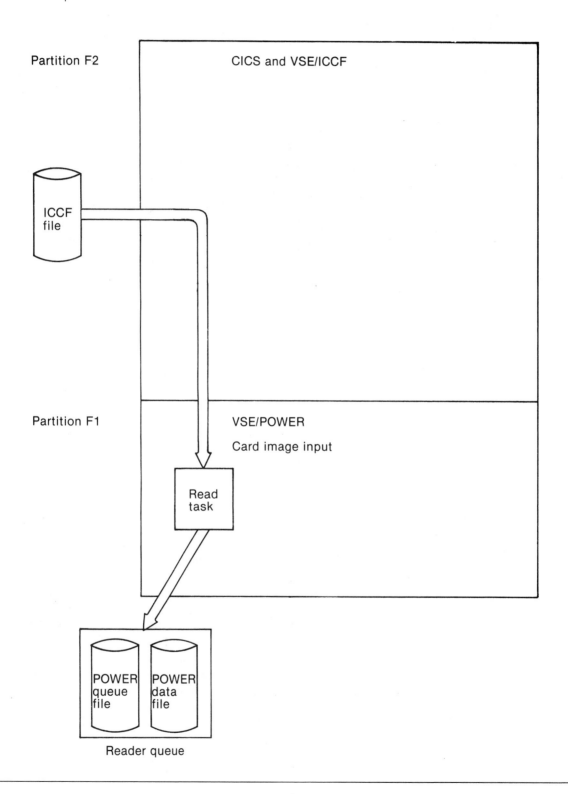

Figure 7-7   How POWER manages input spooling from another partition

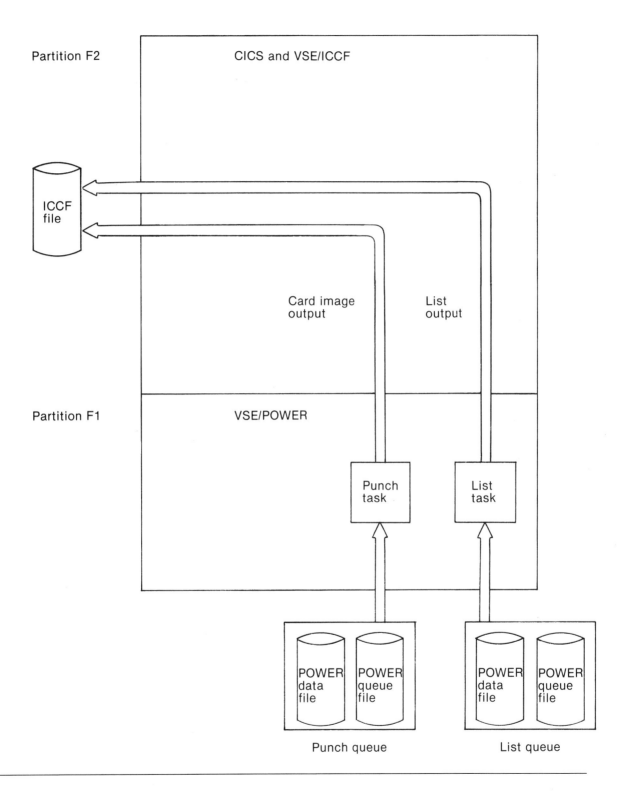

Figure 7-8 How POWER manages output spooling to another partition

command, a list or punch output item is transferred by POWER from its queue to ICCF in F2, where ICCF stores it in its library file. In chapter 9, you'll learn how to use ICCF to perform these functions.

DISCUSSION

The facilities POWER offers are vital in a data processing installation. In fact, a typical VSE shop simply can't do without them. Although POWER is considered to be separate from VSE itself, that's largely for historical reasons. Briefly, the first versions of DOS didn't include spooling facilities. Though POWER was soon added to DOS, it was clearly a distinct product. Today, POWER is an integral part of a DOS/VSE system.

When I discussed the disposition values for queue entries in this chapter, I didn't mention two new values available with POWER version 2.3 or later. Although you probably won't see them used very often, you should be aware of their existence. These two dispositions, X and Y, can be assigned by VSE during processing when a system or POWER error occurs or when requested by the user. When that happens, the entry is returned to the queue and is no longer available for normal processing. The entry remains in the queue until its disposition is changed to D or K by the systems operator. Because these dispositions are only assigned temporarily, they are called *temporary dispositions*.

At points in this chapter, I mentioned that you can override some POWER defaults by coding appropriate control statements. Those control statements are part of POWER's job entry control language (or JECL). In the next chapter, I'll describe how JECL and VSE JCL work together and how you code JECL statements for common functions.

Terminology

read task	execution punch task
POWER data file	execution list task
POWER queue file	punch task
queue	list task
reader queue	spooling device
punch queue	POWER autostart
list queue	dummy device
disposition	card image file
class	SYSIN tape
partition-specific class	inter-partition communication
priority	temporary disposition
execution read task	

Objectives   1. Describe how POWER performs its spooling functions.

2. Describe how POWER performs its job scheduling functions. Specifically, describe how a partition is selected for a job and how POWER determines when the job should be scheduled.

3. Describe how POWER works on a system with no card devices.

Chapter 8

POWER job entry control language

Just as you code statements from VSE's job control language to control VSE functions, you code statements from POWER's *job entry control language* (*JECL*) to control POWER functions. Topic 1 of this chapter introduces JECL and shows you how to use the most important JECL statements. Then, topic 2 shows you how to combine JCL and JECL statements in production job streams.

196

TOPIC 1   How to use
POWER's job entry control language

This topic explains how VSE JCL and VSE/POWER JECL complement one another and shows you how to code JECL. Then, it presents the most important JECL statements: JOB, EOJ, LST, and PUN.

HOW JECL AND VSE JCL WORK TOGETHER

Before you learn anything else about JECL, I want you to know that it doesn't replace VSE JCL in any way. Instead, it supplements VSE JCL to let you control POWER operations. The VSE features you've learned so far that require job control statements (like assigning devices, establishing sublibrary search chains, and describing files) still require JCL.

Moreover, POWER performs its spooling and job scheduling functions whether you code JECL or not. So the only time you need to code JECL is when you want to override POWER's defaults. As a result, many jobs don't contain any JECL.

When you use JECL, you combine it with JCL in the same job stream. The JCL directs VSE once POWER has scheduled the job for execution in a VSE partition. The JECL directs POWER's job scheduling and output spooling functions.

A POWER job contains one or more VSE jobs. The first two JECL statements you need to learn are those that define a *POWER job*: JOB and EOJ. They parallel VSE JCL's JOB and end-of-job statements. In this topic, when I refer to a JOB statement, I'll be talking about the JECL JOB statement, not the VSE JOB statement.

To illustrate, consider figure 8-1. Here, three VSE jobs are contained in one POWER job. The entire job stream is identified to POWER as AP5000 by a POWER JOB statement (* $$ JOB). As a result, POWER schedules the entire POWER job for execution in a VSE partition under its control that has an appropriate class. Within that partition, the three VSE jobs execute one after another, as if they'd been submitted to that partition directly from a card reader as a single job stream.

HOW TO CODE JECL STATEMENTS

From figure 8-1, it might seem to you that VSE JCL and POWER JECL statements are radically different. Actually, though, they're much the same, as you can see in figure 8-2. The top part of the figure shows the format of a JCL statement. The bottom part shows the format of a JECL statement. Notice that all of the fields you learned for a JCL statement have equivalents on a JECL statement, except for the modifier field.

```
* $$ JOB    JNM=AP5000
// JOB      AP5100
.
.
.
/&
// JOB      AP5200
.
.
.
/&
// JOB      AP5300
.
.
.
/&
* $$ EOJ
```

Figure 8-1   A skeleton POWER job that contains three VSE jobs

Name field   The name field of a JECL statement begins with an asterisk, followed by a space, followed by two dollar signs, followed by another space:

    * $$

Because the first character of a JECL statement is an asterisk, if a job with JECL is submitted directly to a partition that isn't under the control of POWER, the JECL statements are treated as comments.

Operation field   The operation field contains the POWER operation code. One or more blanks separate the operation code from * $$. I recommend you code the operation field after including one blank after the name field entry, as figure 8-2 shows.

In this book, I'm going to cover four JECL statements. You've already seen simple examples of the JOB and EOJ statements in figure 8-1. Although there's really nothing to know about EOJ other than that it marks the end of a POWER job, I'll have more to say about JOB after I describe the general format of a JECL statement. I'll also show you how to use the LST and PUN statements to specify how POWER should manage spooled output. But I won't cover any of the other JECL statements. For the most part, they're for specialized functions you probably won't need, like using source book library members with POWER jobs, and submitting jobs from diskette units.

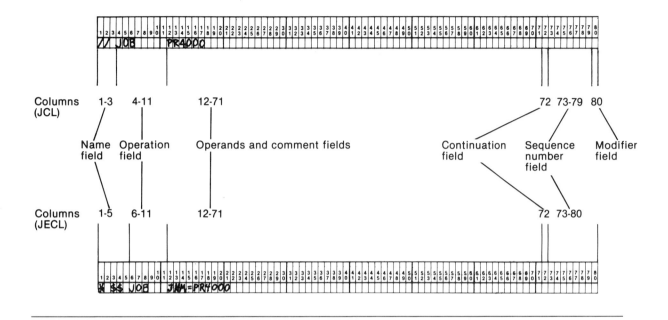

Figure 8-2   The formats of JCL and JECL statements

Operands field   After the operation code, you usually need to supply more information about how POWER should perform the requested function. In a JECL statement, you do that in the operands field. Most of the complexity of a JECL statement is in its operands field.

In early versions of POWER, you could code JECL operands in either positional or keyword format. But positional format is being phased out and isn't included in VSE/POWER version 2.3 (available with VSE/SP 3.1). So, I'm only going to cover the keyword formats in this book.

When you use the keyword format, you identify each operand with a keyword that names the operand. An equal sign and the operand's value follow the keyword as in

```
CLASS=A
```

This, of course, is true for JCL as well as for JECL.

Comment field   As with a JCL statement, you can code a comment after you code the operands field. Just be sure at least one blank separates the end of the operands field and the beginning of your comment. The comment must end before column 72.

Continuation field Column 72 is the continuation field. To continue a statement, you code any non-blank character in column 72. Then, on the next line, you begin the continued statement with * $$. To indicate that operands are continued on a subsequent line, you code the last operand followed by a comma and at least one space. (Sometimes you'll need to continue a line, but most of the time you won't.)

Sequence number field If you want to include a sequence number in a JECL statement, you code it in columns 73 through 80. These numbers must begin in column 73. But unless your JECL jobs are punched in card decks, you probably won't need to use sequence numbers.

HOW TO CONTROL JOB SCHEDULING: THE JOB STATEMENT

In figure 8-1, you saw a skeleton VSE/POWER job that began with a JOB statement and ended with an EOJ statement. The JOB statement in figure 8-1 is about the simplest you can code since its only operand is job-name. Figure 8-3 shows additional operands you can code on the JOB statement. Three of them (disposition, priority, and class) let you direct how POWER schedules a job. Because the last chapter introduced you to the characteristics POWER evaluates when it schedules jobs, you should already understand the effects of these three operands.

The job-name operand of JOB The value you code for job-name is the name POWER uses to identify your job in the reader queue, to identify it as it executes, and to identify its output in the list and punch queues. In figure 8-1, the output of the VSE jobs AP5100, AP5200, and AP5300 will all be stored under the POWER queue name AP5000. (If you submit a job without a POWER JOB statement, POWER uses the names you coded in the VSE JOB statements.)

The job-name you code must be between two and eight alphameric characters long. Don't use one-character names or the names ALL, HOLD, FREE, RJE, LOCAL, or STATUS, because they conflict with POWER operator commands. If you code a JOB statement but omit the job-name operand, POWER calls your job AUTONAME.

The disposition operand of JOB In the last chapter, you learned that the disposition of a job determines two things: (1) whether POWER schedules the job for execution automatically (D or K) or waits until the job is explicitly released by the system operator (H or L); and (2) whether POWER retains the job in the reader queue after it has executed (K or L) or deletes it (D or H).

The JOB statement

```
* $$ JOB  [JNM=job-name]
          [,DISP=disposition]
          [,PRI=priority]
          [,CLASS=class]
          [,NTFY=YES]
          [,USER=user-information]
          [,PWD=password]
```

Explanation

JNM = job-name
Specifies a two- to eight-character name that POWER uses to identify the job. If you omit job-name, POWER calls the job AUTONAME. Don't use one character names or the names ALL, HOLD, FREE, RJE, LOCAL, or STATUS, because they conflict with POWER operator commands.

DISP = disposition
Specifies a one-character value that determines if POWER will schedule the job automatically and if POWER will retain the job in the reader queue after it has executed. Values you may code are:

H	Hold for execution, delete after execution
L	Hold for execution, retain after execution
D	Execute automatically, delete after execution
K	Execute automatically, retain after execution

D is the default.

PRI = priority
Specifies a one-digit value that indicates the job's scheduling priority. You may code a value ranging from 0 (lowest) to 9 (highest). The standard default is 3, but it may differ in your shop.

CLASS = class
Specifies a one-character value that associates a job with the partition(s) in which it may execute. The default is A.

NTFY = YES
Specifies that the job originator will receive messages indicating job processing and execution status.

USER = user-information
Specifies a value of up to 16 characters used to identify a job. If the value includes any blanks, it must be enclosed within apostrophes.

PWD = password
Specifies a one- to eight-character value used to password protect a job.

Figure 8-3   The JECL JOB statement

If you don't code a value for disposition on the JOB statement, POWER automatically uses D. As a result, you don't need to code a value for a job's disposition if you want POWER to schedule it automatically and delete it when it finishes.

The priority operand of JOB   You should also remember from the last chapter that POWER evaluates a job's priority as it selects jobs for execution. The value you code for priority on the JOB statement, ranging from 0 (the lowest) to 9 (the highest), affects not only job scheduling, but also output spooling. In other words, output from a job is created with a priority that's the same as the job's priority (unless you specify otherwise on the LST or PUN statement).

If you don't code a value for priority, POWER uses its default. Although this may vary from shop to shop, 3 is the standard default value, and it's used in many installations.

The class operand of JOB   In addition to evaluating priority as it schedules jobs, POWER also considers a job's class. Remember that class lets POWER associate jobs with the partitions in which they can execute. You specify a job's class by coding the class operand on the JOB statement. If you don't code a value for class on the JOB statement and no other overrides are in effect, POWER assigns class A to a new job. If no partitions have been started that can accept class A jobs, the job doesn't execute until the system operator changes its class to one associated with an active partition.

The notify operand of JOB   Most often, you'll submit jobs to POWER through ICCF. (You'll learn how to do that in the next chapter.) When you submit a job from ICCF, you can code NTFY=YES to indicate that you want processing information sent back to your ICCF terminal. Then, you'll receive messages to notify you when POWER receives output for processing and when your job finishes executing.

The user-information operand of JOB   The value you code for user-information can be up to 16 characters long. When it's used, the value displays on the system console, is recorded in the POWER account file, and is printed on output separator pages. If you want to include any blanks in the value, you must enclose the value in apostrophes.

Your shop may require that you code a particular value for the user-information operand, perhaps so charges for system use (based on data recorded in the POWER account file) can be assigned properly. If that's the case, be sure to follow your installation's standards.

The password operand of JOB   When you code the password operand, POWER protects your job and its output from access by any user (except the system operator) who doesn't supply the password value you specified. The password value you code must be between one and eight characters long.

Other operands of JOB   There are other operands you can code on the JOB statement besides the ones in figure 8-3. I didn't present them here because you'll rarely, if ever, use them. In general, they have to do with printing ownership and destination information on separator pages, controlling the destination of a job and its print and punch output, and using diskette units for SYSIN data. For more information on these operands, refer to *VSE/POWER Installation and Operations Guide*.

HOW TO CONTROL OUTPUT: THE LST AND PUN STATEMENTS

The formats of the statements you code to manage list and punch output (LST and PUN) are so similar that I'm going to cover them together. With only a few exceptions, you can code the same operands on each with similar results. In a typical shop, you'll use the LST statement more than the PUN statement.

Figures 8-4 and 8-5 show the formats of the LST and PUN statements. Notice that you can code the disposition, class, and priority operands on both. You're already familiar with these operands from the last chapter. All the others are new to you.

The disposition operand of LST and PUN   The disposition values D, H, K, and L have the meanings you learned in the last chapter for list and punch queue items. If you omit the disposition operand, POWER assumes a value of D for spooled output. In addition, you can code two other disposition values on both LST and PUN: N and T. And you can code still another on the PUN statement: I.

If you code disposition N on the LST or PUN statement, output is produced without spooling. As a general rule, you won't use disposition N because it's seldom appropriate to produce print or punch output directly.

If you code T for disposition on either the LST or PUN statement, output is spooled not to the POWER queues, but to tape. When you code T for disposition, you must also code the tape-unit operand to specify the address of the tape drive that will receive the spooled output. I'll describe the tape-unit operand in a moment.

If you code I for disposition on the PUN statement, punch output isn't routed to the punch queue, but rather to the reader queue. This is another feature you should seldom need to use. Because you wouldn't

The LST statement

```
* $$ LST [,DISP=disposition]
        [,PRI=priority]
        [,CLASS=class]
        [,FNO=form-number]
        [,JSEP=job-separators]
        [,COPY=copies]
        [,USER=user-information]
        [,PWD=password]
        [,TADDR=tape-unit]
        [,LST=list-unit]
        [,FCB=FCB-phase-name]
```

Explanation

DISP = disposition

Specifies a one-character value that determines if POWER will print the output automatically and if POWER will retain the output in the list queue after it has printed. Values you may code are:

H	Hold for printing, delete after printing
L	Hold for printing, retain after printing
D	Print automatically, delete after printing
K	Print automatically, retain after printing
N	Print directly without spooling
T	Spool to tape (requires that you also code the tape-unit operand)

D is the default.

PRI = priority

Specifies a one-digit value that indicates the output's print priority. You may code a value ranging from 0 (lowest) to 9 (highest). If you don't code priority, the default is the priority of the job that produces the output.

CLASS = class

Specifies a one-letter value that associates list output with a device on which it can be printed. The default is A.

FNO = form-number

Specifies a one- to four-character value indicating the form on which the list output is to be printed.

JSEP = job-separators

Specifies a one-digit value indicating how many separator pages are to be printed between output from different jobs.

COPY = copies

Specifies a one- or two-digit value indicating how many copies of the list output are to be produced. The default is 1.

USER = user-information

Specifies a value of up to 16 characters used to identify print output. If the value includes any blanks, it must be enclosed within apostrophes. The user-information you code on the LST statement overrides user-information from the JOB statement.

PWD = password

Specifies a one- to eight-character value used to password protect print output. The password you code on the LST statement overrides the password from the JOB statement.

Figure 8-4   The JECL LST statement (part 1 of 2)

TADDR = tape-unit | Specifies the address of the tape unit to which spooled output is to be routed. This operand is valid only if you coded T for disposition.

LST = list-unit | Specifies the spooling device address for print output. This operand is typically used when a job produces two different print items at the same time.

FCB = FCB-phase-name | Specifies the name of a forms control buffer phase to be loaded for print output.

Figure 8-4   The JECL LST statement (part 2 of 2)

want to route list output to the reader queue, you can't code disposition I on the LST statement.

Figure 8-6 illustrates the effect of each of the values you can code for disposition. This figure shows what happens when you code different dispositions for punch output; the results are similar for list output (except for disposition I). If you code a value of D, H, K, or L for disposition, output is spooled normally into the proper output queue (in this instance, the punch queue). If you code N for disposition, output is routed directly to a unit record device. If you code T for disposition, output is routed directly to a tape drive. Finally, if you code I for disposition, punch output is spooled to the reader queue, not the punch queue.

The priority operand of LST and PUN   You can code the priority operand if you need to modify the priority of an output item. If you omit it, the item's priority is the same as that of the job that created it. Priority values range from 0 (lowest) to 9 (highest).

The class operand of LST and PUN   For both statements, you can specify the class of the spooled output by coding the class operand. Output classes are letters of the alphabet (A to Z). If you omit class, a default class is assigned (usually it's A, but it may differ on your system).

For punch output produced with disposition I, you may also code a class with a numeric value between 0 and 9. This class value becomes the class of the new entry in the reader queue.

The form-number operand of LST and PUN   You code the form-number operand to identify the paper or card type to be used for the output. The value you code may be between one and four alphameric characters. When POWER is ready to print or punch spooled output, it checks the form-number specification for the output about to be processed with the form-number last used on the appropriate device. If they don't match, POWER issues a message to the system operator to mount the required form or card type in the unit.

The PUN statement

```
* $$ PUN [,DISP=disposition]
         [,PRI=priority]
         [,CLASS=class]
         [,FNO=form-number]
         [,JSEP=job-separators]
         [,COPY=copies]
         [,USER=user-information]
         [,PWD=password]
         [,TADDR=tape-unit]
         [,PUN=punch-unit]
```

Explanation

DISP = disposition

Specifies a one-character value that determines if POWER will punch the output automatically and if POWER will retain the output in the punch queue after it has been punched. Values you may code are:

H   Hold for punching, delete after punching
L   Hold for punching, retain after punching
D   Punch automatically, delete after punching
K   Punch automatically, retain after punching
N   Punch directly without spooling
T   Spool to tape (requires that you also code the tape-unit operand)
I   Spool punch output to the reader queue

D is the default.

PRI = priority

Specifies a one-digit value that indicates the output's punch priority. You may code a value ranging from 0 (lowest) to 9 (highest). If you don't code priority, the default is the priority of the job that produces the output.

CLASS = class

Specifies a one-character value (a letter A to Z or, for output produced with the disposition I, a digit 0 to 9) that associates punch output with a device on which it can be punched. The default is A.

FNO = form-number

Specifies a one- to four-character value indicating the form on which the punch output is to be punched.

JSEP = job-separators

Specifies a one-digit value indicating how many separator cards are to be punched between output from different jobs.

COPY = copies

Specifies a one- or two-digit value indicating how many copies of the punch output are to be produced. The default is 1.

USER = user-information

Specifies a value of up to 16 characters used to identify punch output. If the value includes any blanks, it must be enclosed within apostrophes. The user-information you code on the PUN statement overrides user-information from the JOB statement.

Figure 8-5   The JECL PUN statement (part 1 of 2)

PWD = password

Specifies a one- to eight-character value used to password protect punch output. The password you code on the PUN statement overrides the password from the JOB statement.

TADDR = tape-unit

Specifies the address of the tape unit to which spooled output is to be routed. This operand is valid only if you coded T for disposition.

PUN = punch-unit

Specifies the spooling device address for punch output. This operand is typically used when a job produces two different punch items at the same time.

Figure 8-5   The JECL PUN statement (part 2 of 2)

If you omit the form-number operand, POWER assumes you coded four blanks. Four blanks is considered to be the installation's standard form for a printer or blank cards for a punch.

If you use forms of various heights, you need to be sure your printer is properly set up for them. You can do that with the FCB operand of LST. I'll describe it later in this topic.

The job-separators operand of LST and PUN   Depending on how VSE/POWER was generated on your system, it may or may not insert separator pages or cards between output from different jobs. If your system does insert job separators, you can control how many it inserts by using the job-separator operand. You can code a value between 0 and 9.

The copies operand of LST and PUN   You can use the copies operand to specify how many copies of the output item POWER should produce. To do that, you code one or two digits for the copies operand. As a result, you can specify that up to 99 copies of a report or card deck be produced. If you code 0 or 00 or omit the copies operand altogether, POWER produces one copy.

The user-information operand of LST and PUN   If you code the user-information operand, you can override the value coded for the same operand on the JOB statement. The value you code is printed on separator pages or punched in separator cards and is recorded in POWER account records.

The password operand of LST and PUN   If a job is submitted with a value coded for the password operand, users other than the system operator must provide that value to access the job's output. If you code the password operand on a LST or PUN statement, it overrides the job level password, if one's in effect.

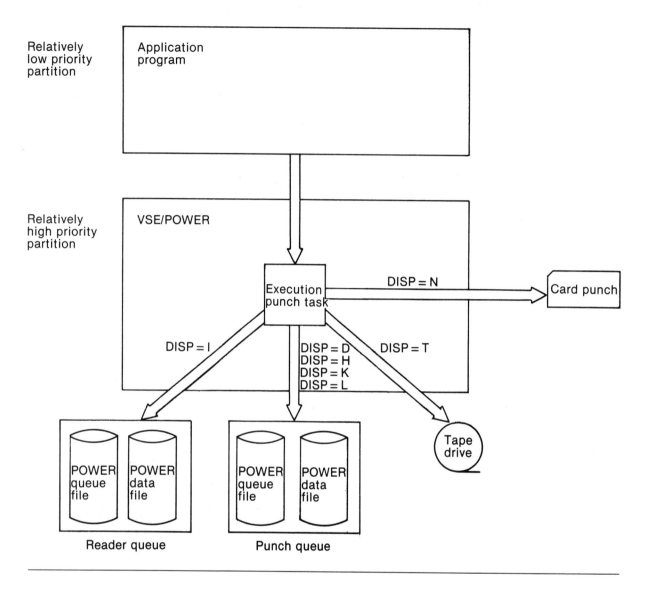

Figure 8-6   The effect of the disposition operand on punch operations

The tape-unit operand of LST and PUN   With the tape-unit operand, you code the address of a tape unit that will receive a spooled output item. You can do this only if the disposition of the item is T. The simplest way to code the tape-unit operand is as the three-hex-digit address of a tape unit. You can also specify the recording density of the output tape with this operand, but if you need to do that you should refer to the *VSE/POWER Installation and Operations Guide* for more details.

The list-unit operand of LST   In some cases, a job may produce two or more reports at the same time. If they're assigned to the same unit, regardless of whether or not POWER's spooling services are used, the lines of the reports will be mixed. To avoid mixing output from two reports, you can assign them to different spooling devices. That means two or more printers must have been specified as spooling devices for the partition when it was started under the control of POWER.

If a program produces two reports and you want one to be handled differently than the other, you need to code the LST statement with the LST operand. For the LST operand, you code the address of the spooling device that's assigned to the logical unit for the report that requires special treatment. You'll see an example of this in the next topic.

The punch-unit operand of PUN   Just as you can direct list output to two or more printers, you can direct punch output to two or more punches. If you want one item of punch output handled differently than another, you need to code the PUN statement with the PUN operand. It works just like the LST operand of the LST statement.

The FCB operand of LST   Most printers on VSE systems use a *forms control buffer* (*FCB*) to determine vertical formatting. Vertical formatting indicates both how long the form is (top to bottom) and where on it the printer may skip when printing (those locations are called *channels*).

The FCB is a phase stored in a VSE sublibrary. Different FCB phases are required for different size forms and for different printer types. When the system is started, the appropriate FCB phase for standard forms is loaded into each printer on the system.

As a standard form, most installations use the familiar continuous paper that's often printed with green and white stripes. A single page of a standard form is usually 11 inches or 8-1/2 inches high. Not all printers on one system have to use the same standard form, but the FCB loaded into a particular printer should match whatever the standard form is for that printer.

Sometimes, you need to use a form that's not the same size as a printer's standard form. When you do, make sure that the proper FCB for the non-standard form is loaded into the printer before printing starts. When you use VSE/POWER, you can do that with the FCB operand of the LST statement.

The value you code on the FCB operand is the name of the phase to be loaded into the printer. What that name is depends on the type of printer you're using and on your shop's naming conventions. When the processing requested by the LST statement has finished, the original FCB is restored, so you don't have to worry about specifying the default FCB at the end of your job or at the beginning of the next one.

Because FCB and form are so closely related, you shouldn't code FCB without FNO. However, you may code FNO without FCB. You do that when you want to use a form that's the same height as the standard form, but with a different width or with preprinted information on it. You'll see an example of how to use the FCB operand in the next topic.

Other operands of LST and PUN   Both statements have other operands you might need to code for particular circumstances. They relate to segmenting very large output items, to using alternate character bands in printers, and to remote job entry, shared spooling, and the 3800 Printing Subsystem. In addition, you can create user-defined operands for the JECL LST and PUN statements. If you want to learn more about any of these features, refer to *VSE/POWER Installation and Operations Guide*.

DISCUSSION   When you use JECL statements, they won't be a large part of the jobs you code. Your job streams are still going to be mostly VSE JCL. However, adding one or more JECL statements to some job streams can give you better control over job scheduling and output processing. In the next topic, then, I'll show you two job streams that illustrate how coding JECL can give you that added control.

Terminology   job entry control language
JECL
POWER job
forms control buffer
FCB
channel

Objective   Given job specifications, code appropriate JOB, LST, and PUN statements to control job scheduling and output spooling.

TOPIC 2   Examples of typical POWER job streams

Now that you've seen how to code the most important JECL statements, I want to show you how to use them in production job streams. The examples in this chapter are enhancements of the edit-update and report-preparation applications you saw in topic 2 of chapter 4. Although you can look back to that topic to review these jobs, you don't really need to because I'll point out the changes you should focus on here.

The enhanced
edit-update
application

The enhanced edit-update application centers on the addition of one program to the job stream: a program to prepare payroll checks and to create new payroll transactions in card format that will be spooled to tape. The new program's name is PR4500, and it resides in USRSLE.PAYROLL, just like the other application programs in the job.

The checks PR4500 produces are SYSLST output and are associated with the logical unit SYS005. As a result, you don't need to code an additional ASSGN statement for that output. Also, PR4500 doesn't use any files that aren't already identified with DLBL and EXTENT statements in the original job and aren't already associated with the correct logical units. PR4500 does, however, produce card image output that you need to provide for; it's standard SYSPCH output associated with SYS007.

Although the card output of PR4500 can be assigned to SYSPCH, the specifications for the enhanced job require that the data be stored in card image format on tape. The tape that contains that data will be sent to a central installation for additional processing. So the enhanced job should route the SYSPCH output to the tape unit at address 300 to produce this output.

Because the enhanced version of the job produces negotiable checks, it needs a higher level of security than a standard job. As a result, the specifications for the enhanced job indicate that it should execute in the background partition with the highest possible priority and class. And the job should be held in the reader queue until the system operator explicitly releases it.

To exercise more control over the check output produced by the job, it should be created with class X and disposition H so it will remain in the list queue until the system operator is ready to print it. To prevent terminal users from accessing the checks in the list queue, the list queue entry is password protected with the password PR704AQ3. On the other hand, there's no need for the other print output of the job to be password protected.

```
÷ $$ JOB    JNM=PR4000,DISP=H,PRI=9,CLASS=I
// JOB      PR4000
// LIBDEF   PHASE,SEARCH=(USRSLE.PAYROLL)
// ASSGN    SYS005,SYSRDR
// ASSGN    SYS006,SYSLST
// ASSGN    SYS007,SYSPCH
// ASSGN    SYS010,251
// ASSGN    SYS011,250
// ASSGN    SYS012,300
// DLBL     PRTRANS,'PAYROLL.UNEDITED.TRANSACTIONS'
// EXTENT   SYS010,,,,15764,1000
// DLBL     PREDTTR,'PAYROLL.EDITED.TRANSACTIONS'
// EXTENT   SYS010,,,,16764,1000
// DLBL     PRTABLE,'PAYROLL.TABLE'
// EXTENT   SYS010,,,,17764,100
// DLBL     PRPRMMS,'PAYROLL.MASTER.FILE'
// EXTENT   SYS011,,,,288,1500
// DLBL     PRTMPMS,'PAYROLL.TEMPORARY.MASTER.FILE'
// EXTENT   SYS011,,,,1788,1500
// EXEC     PR4100

   PAYROLL TRANSACTION CARDS ARE INCLUDED HERE IN THE JOB STREAM

/÷
// EXEC     PR4200
// PAUSE    MOUNT BACKUP TAPE FOR PAYROLL MASTER FILE.
// EXEC     PR4300
// EXEC     PR4400
// PAUSE    MOUNT TAPE FOR HOME OFFICE CHECK FILE.
// RESET    SYS012
÷ $$ PUN    DISP=T,TADDR=300
÷ $$ LST    CLASS=X,DISP=H,FNO=PCHK,FCB=FCB2CHKS,PWD=PR704AQ3
// EXEC     PR4500
/&
÷ $$ EOJ
```

Figure 8-7   JCL and JECL for the enhanced edit-update application

When the checks finally are released for printing, they require a special form called PCHK. Because PCHK is a non-standard size form, it's necessary to load the proper forms control buffer into the printer before the checks are printed. The FCB phase name is FCB2CHKS.

The JCL and the JECL for the job   With the enhancements in mind, take a look at the JCL and JECL for the enhanced edit-update job in figure 8-7. Here, I've shaded the statements I particularly want you to notice. First, a POWER JOB statement identifies the POWER job. In this case, it consists of one VSE job. Both the POWER and the VSE jobs are called PR4000. The POWER JOB statement is coded with a disposition of H (Hold), a priority of 9 (the highest possible), and a class of I.

Next, notice the three ASSGN statements I've shaded. These associate the three programmer logical units SYS005, SYS006, and SYS007 with the system logical units SYSRDR, SYSLST, and SYSPCH. During system start-up, these system logical units were permanently assigned to the spooling dummy devices 02C, 02E, and 02D. As a result, any I/O requests for SYS005, SYS006, and SYS007 will be intercepted by POWER and spooled.

The next two shaded statements, near the end of the job, are VSE JCL statements that prepare the system to perform punch spooling to tape. The PAUSE statement advises the operator to mount a tape for the spooling function. The RESET statement cancels the ASSGN statement that relates SYS012 to the tape unit at address 300 so that unit is available for output spooling.

Next, a POWER JECL PUN statement specifies that punch output should be routed not to the punch queue, but rather to tape (disposition T). The tape unit to be used for spooling is the one at address 300. When POWER processes this statement, it issues another message that requires the system operator to verify that the proper tape is mounted for the spooling function.

The next statement, LST, gives the operands required to manage the check print output properly. As you can see, the operands it includes match the requirements for the enhanced job that I described earlier.

After POWER's spooling requirements have been defined, the new program in the job, PR4500, can be executed. When it finishes, both the VSE job and the POWER job end as indicated by the /& and EOJ statements.

The enhanced report-preparation application

The second example of a POWER job that I want to present is an enhancement of the accounts-receivable report-preparation application in chapter 4. You should recall from the original job that two of its programs produce two list items. Each of those programs was designed so one of the list items was written temporarily to disk while the other was written to a printer to prevent the two output items from being mixed. Then, a user-written utility program called PRTDASD copied the temporary disk file to a printer in the next job step.

Although this works, it's a clumsy way to handle a common function. When you use POWER, you can take advantage of its spooling functions and produce two or more report items simultaneously without worrying about them being mixed, provided your system is properly set up. The enhanced version of this job does just that.

In the enhanced version, the programs that produce two print items are replaced by versions that create both as printer-directed files, in contrast to one printer-directed file and one DASD file. The new versions of those programs are AR7201 and AR7301, replacing AR7200 and AR7300.

```
        •
        •
        •
// EXEC DTRPOWER
FORMAT=NO
PSTART BG,IOJ,A
READER=02C
PRINTERS=02E,02F
PUNCHES=02D
PSTART F3,MN3,A
READER=02C
PRINTERS=02E
PUNCHES=02D
PSTART F2,L2,A
READER=02C
PRINTERS=02E
PUNCHES=02D
PSTART LST,OOE,BA,D
        •
        •
        •
```

Figure 8-8 Statements to start POWER showing two dummy printers for the background partition

To produce two reports simultaneously, a program must execute in a partition that has two spooling printers associated with it. Figure 8-8 shows part of the job that starts the POWER partition and provides two spooling printers for the background partition. As you can see, the background partition has not only 02E as a spooling printer, but 02F as well. Because 02E and 02F aren't addresses of physical units, both are dummy devices.

Both AR7201 and AR7301 write one report to the logical unit SYS006 and one to SYS008. One of those units is assigned to 02E and the other is assigned to 02F. As a result, POWER will initiate two execution list tasks, and the two report items will be separate.

The only change in specifications for the job is that each report is to be printed twice, except for statements; they need to be printed only once. The statements, however, require a special form called STMT. Since the statements are the same height as the printer's standard form, a different FCB phase isn't necessary. All output is to be produced as class Q and is to be deleted from the list queue after it has been printed.

The entire job is to execute in the background partition with the lowest possible priority and class. It's to be deleted from the POWER reader queue after it has finished.

The JCL and the JECL for the job   Figure 8-9 presents the JCL and the JECL for the enhanced report-preparation application. Again, I've shaded the lines I especially want you to notice.

```
÷ $$ JOB     JNM=AR7000,CLASS=J,DISP=D,PRI=0,USER='STEVE ECKOLS'
÷ $$ LST     LST=02E,CLASS=Q,DISP=D,COPY=2
// JOB       AR7000
// LIBDEF    PHASE,SEARCH=(USRSLE.ACCTRCV,USRSLE.USRUTILI,SOFTLIB.SYSUTILI)
// ASSGN     SYS006,SYSLST
// ASSGN     SYS008,02F
// ASSGN     SYS015,250
// DLBL      SORTINI,'ACCOUNTS.RECEIVABLE.MASTER.FILE'
// EXTENT    SYS015,,,,3288,500
// DLBL      SORTWK1
// EXTENT    SYS015,,,,4288,1000
// DLBL      SORTOUT,'SORTED.ACCOUNTS.RECEIVABLE.MASTER.FILE'
// EXTENT    SYS015,,,,5288,500
// EXEC      SORT
   SORT      FIELDS=(16,5,CH,A,1,5,CH,A),WORK=1
   RECORD    TYPE=F,LENGTH=80
/÷
// DLBL      ARSRT,'SORTED.ACCOUNTS.RECEIVABLE.MASTER.FILE'
// EXTENT    SYS015,,,,5288,500
// DLBL      CSTMST,'CUSTOMER.MASTER.FILE'
// EXTENT    SYS015,,,,3788,500
// DLBL      DUNNING,'DUNNING.FILE'
// EXTENT    SYS015,,,,5788,1000
// EXEC      AR7100
÷ $$ LST     LST=02F,CLASS=Q,DISP=D,COPY=2
// EXEC      AR7201
// DLBL      SORTIN1,'DUNNING.FILE'
// EXTENT    SYS015,,,,5788,1000
// DLBL      SORTWK1
// EXTENT    SYS015,,,,4288,1000
// DLBL      SORTOUT,'SORTED.DUNNING.FILE'
// EXTENT    SYS015,,,,7288,1000
// EXEC      SORT
   SORT      FIELDS=(43,2,CH,A,1,5,CH,A,50,5,CH,A),WORK=1
   RECORD    TYPE=F,LENGTH=80
/÷
// DLBL      DUNSRT,'SORTED.DUNNING.FILE'
// EXTENT    SYS015,,,,7288,1000
÷ $$ LST     LST=02F,CLASS=Q,DISP=D,FNO=STMT
// EXEC      AR7301
/&
÷ $$ EOJ
```

Figure 8-9   JCL and JECL for the enhanced report-preparation application

The first line is a POWER JOB statement. The JOB statement specifies the job's name as AR7000, which is also the name of the only VSE
job it contains. In addition, the JOB statement indicates that the class,
disposition, and priority of the job are J, D, and 0. As you can see in
the PSTART for BG in figure 8-8, J is the least preferred class for the
background partition. That, combined with priority 0, makes this a very
low priority job. Disposition D indicates that the job will be deleted
from the reader queue after it has executed.

The first LST statement indicates that all list output directed to the spooling device 02E is to be created with class Q and is to be deleted from the list queue (DISP=D) after it has printed twice (COPY=2). I coded this statement at the beginning of the job because it applies to more than one job step. However, I could just as well have coded it anywhere in the job stream before the EXEC statement for AR7201.

The two shaded ASSGN statements relate SYS006 and SYS008, both used by AR7201 and AR7301, to spooling devices. SYS008 is assigned directly to 02F. SYS006 is assigned indirectly to 02E through SYSLST. (SYSLST was permanently assigned to 02E during system start-up.)

The next shaded statement is another LST statement. This one is for output directed to the spooling device 02F. It specifies the same characteristics as the LST statement for output directed to 02E. The next JECL statement in the job stream, another LST statement, specifies the spooling requirements for the statements produced by AR7301 that are directed to the spooling device 02F. This LST statement is like the others in the job stream, except it doesn't specify COPY and it does specify FNO. As a result, one copy of the statements will be printed on form STMT.

If you compare this job stream with the one for the original job in chapter 4, you'll see some differences. First, notice that I didn't include DLBL and EXTENT statements for the AR7201 job step. That's because AR7201 doesn't use a temporary DASD file for one of the print items, as AR7200 did. And because DLBL and EXTENT statements don't have to be submitted for it, I used the label information submitted in the previous step for the file DUNNING. It's still in effect because no new label information was submitted for the current step.

Second, the enhanced job is simpler because the two job steps that invoke the PRTDASD programs aren't required. Not only did I delete those two EXEC statements, but I also eliminated the DLBL and EXTENT statements for the temporary disk print files.

Discussion

As you can see from the two examples in this topic, JECL is relatively easy to code and makes up only a small part of a typical job stream. However, to use it effectively, you need to understand POWER's job scheduling and spooling functions. At this point, you should have that understanding, and you should be able to integrate JCL and JECL in job streams to use the facilities of both VSE and POWER.

Objective

Given specifications for a job that requires non-standard job scheduling and output handling, code the job stream using the appropriate JCL and JECL statements.

Chapter 9

How to use POWER through ICCF

In a VSE shop, you probably won't keypunch job streams. Instead, you'll enter them interactively using ICCF's editing facilities. Then, you'll submit them to POWER for execution through ICCF's *submit-to-batch facility*. The submit-to-batch facility uses inter-partition communication to transfer a job stream from your library to POWER. In this chapter, I'll show you how to submit a job to POWER, how to monitor its status, and how to view and retrieve its output.

To use the submit-to-batch facility, the job stream you're going to submit must be stored as a member in an ICCF library. To create a job stream and store it, you can use the ICCF full-screen editor, as you learned in chapter 3. The job stream can include job control statements, job entry control statements, and in-line data. Figure 9-1 shows a simple job stream I've entered using the full-screen editor.

How to use the SUBMIT procedure

Once your job stream has been stored as a library member, you can submit it. At first, the submit-to-batch facility might confuse you because it involves two jobs: (1) the job you submit to POWER for execution in a VSE batch partition; and (2) an ICCF job that runs in an ICCF interactive partition to transfer your VSE job to POWER.

To submit a job to VSE, you use the ICCF SUBMIT procedure. It's a series of ICCF control statements stored in a library member that perform the steps necessary to transfer your job to POWER. Figure 9-2 shows the format of the command line you key in to run the SUBMIT procedure. You enter the procedure name SUBMIT followed by the name of the library member that contains the job you want to run.

```
===> FILE LISTLIBS
<<..+....1....+....2....+....3....+....4....+....5....+.. INP=*INPARA*>>..+..FS
***** TOP OF FILE *****                                                 /***/
// JOB      LISTLIBS                                                     *===*
// LIBLIST PHASE,BG                                                      *===*
// LIBLIST OBJ,BG                                                        *===*
// LIBLIST SOURCE,BG                                                     *===*
// LIBLIST PROC,BG                                                       *===*
/&                                                                       *===*
***** END OF FILE *****                                                  *===*
```

Figure 9-1   Creating and storing a job stream with ICCF's full-screen editor

$$\text{SUBMIT job-name} \begin{Bmatrix} \text{DIRECT} \\ \text{RETURN} \end{Bmatrix} [\text{PRINT}]$$

Figure 9-2   Format of the command line to invoke the SUBMIT procedure

Before the SUBMIT procedure transfers your job to POWER, it brackets it with POWER JECL. The first of those JECL statements is a JOB statement that specifies a class that determines the VSE partition in which POWER will schedule the job. The JECL also includes PUN and LST statements that specify how the job's output will be handled. Although the specific JECL created by the SUBMIT procedure varies from installation to installation (depending on how ICCF has been tailored), most shops use the IBM default operands in figure 9-2 to control job handling: DIRECT and RETURN.

If you want your job's output to be spooled to a printer or punch automatically, you use DIRECT. If you want the output held in the POWER queues, you use RETURN. (If you omit this parameter, the SUBMIT procedure uses DIRECT as its default.) I suspect that you'll code RETURN most of the time.

```
SUBMIT LISTLIBS RETURN PRINT
  ...+....1....+....2....+....3....+....4....+....5....+....6....+....7....+..CM
*FULL-SCREEN EDITOR TERMINATED
*READY




                                                  ▫–▫
   ▫
```

Figure 9-3   Submitting a job to POWER using ICCF's submit-to-batch facility (part 1 of 3)

As I said, how these values affect your job's processing varies from shop to shop. So if you use the submit-to-batch facility and the results aren't what you expect, don't panic. Check with your ICCF administrator or another ICCF user to find out if your shop has changed the defaults.

Another operand you can specify for the SUBMIT procedure is PRINT. If you enter PRINT, the JCL and the JECL for your job that SUBMIT transfers to POWER will be displayed on your screen. If you omit PRINT, the JCL and JECL won't be displayed.

The three parts of figure 9-3 illustrate what you see when you use the submit-to-batch facility. Part 1 of figure 9-3 shows the command line I entered to run the SUBMIT procedure to transfer the job in the member LISTLIBS from the ICCF library file to the POWER reader queue. Because I specified RETURN, the job output is held by POWER after it executes so I can view it at my terminal. And because I specified PRINT, the JCL and JECL transferred to POWER are displayed at my terminal.

When I tap the enter key, ICCF schedules the SUBMIT procedure to execute in one of its interactive partitions. Part 2 of figure 9-3 shows that my terminal is in *execution mode*. (That's what the EX in the upper

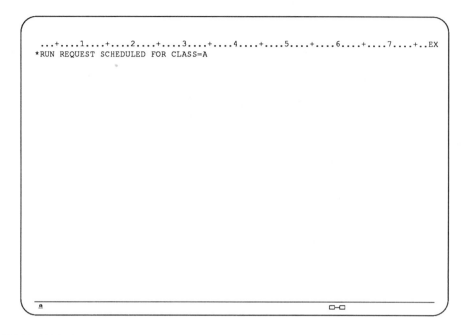

```
...+....1....+....2....+....3....+....4....+....5....+....6....+....7....+..EX
*RUN REQUEST SCHEDULED FOR CLASS=A
```

Figure 9-3   Submitting a job to POWER using ICCF's submit-to-batch facility (part 2 of 3)

right corner of the screen indicates.) The terminal remains in execution mode until the ICCF job is finished. For the SUBMIT procedure, that's probably only a moment, although the longer a job stream is, the longer it will take to submit it. While the terminal is in execution mode, you can't do other ICCF work.

When the SUBMIT procedure finishes, the screen in part 3 of figure 9-3 is displayed. Because I entered PRINT on the command line that invoked the SUBMIT procedure, the JCL and JECL transferred to POWER are displayed. Here, you can see that SUBMIT added three JECL statements at the beginning of the job stream to specify the classes that correspond to the processing I requested by entering RETURN. Then, you can see the VSE JCL that I keyed in and stored in the library member LISTLIBS. Finally, you can see that SUBMIT inserted a POWER EOJ statement at the end of the job stream.

At the bottom of the screen is a message that advises me that the job was successfully submitted. The message shows the number of statements transferred to the POWER reader queue (10) and the POWER job number assigned to the job (6828). The job name POWER uses is the name of the ICCF library member that contains the job stream, regardless of the name you code on the VSE JOB statement in your job stream. In this example, though, the library member's name and the job name in the JOB statement are the same.

```
   ...+....1....+....2....+....3....+....4....+....5....+....6....+....7....+..SP
* * * * * START OF PROCEDURE (CLIST) * * * * *
* $$ JOB  JNM=LISTLIBS,DISP=D,CLASS=A,NTFY=YES
* $$ LST  DISP=K,CLASS=Q,RBS=0
* $$ PUN  DISP=D,CLASS=A,RBS=0
// JOB     LISTLIBS
// LIBLIST PHASE,BG
// LIBLIST OBJ,BG
// LIBLIST SOURCE,BG
// LIBLIST PROC,BG
/&
* $$ EOJ
K889I  JOB LISTLIBS 06828 SUCCESSFULLY SUBMITTED ----- - STATEMENTS OUT=10
*PARTIAL END PRINT
```

Figure 9-3   Submitting a job to POWER using ICCF's submit-to-batch facility (part 3 of 3)

Depending on how your ICCF user profile is set up, the SUBMIT procedure may or may not alter the JECL statements you code in your job streams. So, if you submit a job with JECL and ICCF changes those statements when it transfers the job to POWER, consult your ICCF administrator.

At this point, the job has been submitted to POWER and is stored in the POWER reader queue. But when it's executed depends on how busy the system is. So don't assume that your job is executing because the SUBMIT procedure is finished—it probably isn't. To monitor the progress of your job and to control its output, you can use a set of special ICCF commands.

How to use ICCF system commands and procedures to monitor jobs and control output

Figure 9-4 illustrates the ICCF system commands and procedures you need to monitor the jobs you submit and to use their output. There are only two commands to monitor a job's progress: /DQ and /STATUSP (or /SP). The /DQ command displays all jobs, while the /STATUSP command lets you track a specific job. All of the other commands in figure 9-4 relate in one way or another to viewing or retrieving output. Since

Commands to monitor job status

Command	Function
/DQ	Display POWER queues; see figure 9-7 for details.
/STATUSP job-name [job-number] /SP job-name [job-number]	Display the current status of the specified job.

Commands to handle job output

Command	Function
/LISTP job-name [job-number] /LP job-name [job-number]	Display the list output for the specified job.
/SHIFT RIGHT n /SHIFT LEFT n	Move the display to the right n columns. Move the display to the left n columns.
/LOCP text	Locate the specified text in the list output being displayed (effective only within display from /LISTP).
/ERASEP queue job-name [job-number] /EP queue job-name [job-number]	Delete the output for the job from the specified queue (LST, PUN, or RDR).
/ROUTEP queue job-name [job-number] /RP queue job-name [job-number]	Route the output for the specified job in the specified queue (LST or PUN) to an appropriate output device at the central site.

Procedures to retrieve job output

Command	Function
GETL job-name [job-number]	Copy the list output of the specified job into the user's print area ($$PRINT).
GETL job-name [MEM = name] [job-number]	Copy the list output of the specified job into the named member in the user's primary library.
GETP job-name [job-number]	Copy the punch output of the specified job into the user's punch area ($$PUNCH).
GETP job-name [MEM = name] [job-number]	Copy the punch output of the specified job into the named member in the user's primary library.
GETR job-name [job-number]	Copy the specified job from the reader queue into a member named job-name in the user's primary library.
GETR job-name [MEM = name] [job-number]	Copy the specified job from the reader queue into the named member in the user's primary library.

Figure 9-4   Basic ICCF system commands and procedures for the submit-to-batch facility

you normally use the /STATUSP command before you use the output management commands for a particular job, I'll show you /STATUSP first.

How to monitor your job's progress   The LISTLIBS job submitted in figure 9-3 has been transferred to the POWER reader queue. To find out what POWER is doing with it, you use the /STATUSP system command. Just enter /STATUSP and follow it with the name of the member you submitted, like this:

```
/STATUSP LISTLIBS
```

Remember that the POWER job name is the same as the library member's name.

If you want to know the status of a particular job and there are multiple queue entries with the same job name, you also need to specify the job number on the command. For example,

```
/SP LISTLIBS 6828
```

would display the status of the job I submitted in figure 9-3, even if other queue entries named LISTLIBS were present on the system. If you don't specify the job number and there are multiple queue entries with the same job name, the first entry in the queue (the one with the lowest job number) is displayed. The same is true for the rest of the commands and procedures in this chapter.

The output you receive from a /STATUSP command is in the format

```
*STATUS = xy - job status
```

where x indicates the job's location and y indicates the job's disposition. To illustrate, I entered

```
/SP LISTLIBS
```

three times to display the status of the job. The result of my first inquiry was

```
*STATUS = RD - JOB AWAITING EXEC
```

RD means the job is in the POWER reader queue (R) and that its disposition is D. The job is awaiting execution because the background partition is currently executing another job.

The second /SP inquiry resulted in

```
*STATUS - R* - JOB EXECUTING
```

indicating that the job is running. Notice that the D for disposition has changed to an asterisk; this indicates that the job is executing.

```
/SHIFT RIGHT 20
...+....1....+....2....+....3....+....4....+....5....+....6. <==MORE==> .+..LS
// JOB     LISTLIBS                                              DATE 07/
// LIBLIST PHASE,BG

BG-TEMP ** NO LIBRARY INFORMATION AVAILABLE **

BG-PERM LIBNAME SUBLIB     STATUS   -PARTITIONS-
SEARCH  MMA     PROD                 012
 PRD1 BASE 012
        PRD1    CONFIG               012
        SOFTLIB SYSUTIL1             012

// LIBLIST OBJ,BG

BG-TEMP ** NO LIBRARY INFORMATION AVAILABLE **

BG-PERM LIBNAME SUBLIB     STATUS   -PARTITIONS-
SEARCH  MMA     PROD                 012
        PRD1    BASE                 012
        PRD1    CONFIG               012
        SOFTLIB SYSUTIL1             012
```

Figure 9-5   Using the /LISTP and /SHIFT commands to view job output (part 1 of 2)

After the job had been running for a moment, I entered the /STATUSP command again, and the result was

```
*STATUS = LK - JOB COMPLETED
```

The job has finished. The status entry indicates that the output is in the list queue (L) and that its disposition is K.

Now that the job has finished, I want to examine the output. Recall that because I didn't want the output printed at the central site, I entered RETURN on the SUBMIT procedure's command line. As a result, the output is held. (On this system, class Q isn't associated with any printer, so the output can't print automatically.) At this point, I have several options: I can (1) view the output, (2) delete the output, (3) route the output to the central site printer, or (4) retrieve the output and store it in my ICCF library.

How to view your job's print output   To view the output, enter /LISTP (or the abbreviation /LP) followed by the job name. Then, your terminal enters list mode and the output is displayed, as in part 1 of figure 9-5. Since this output was created for a printer, it's wider than your ICCF screen. As you can see, the date in the upper right hand corner is cut off. To move the display on the screen you enter the /SHIFT RIGHT or /SHIFT LEFT command followed by the number of columns

```
   ...+....3....+....4....+....5....+....6....+....7....+....8. <==MORE==> .+..LS
                                                DATE 07/05/88,CLOCK 14/05/42


   Y INFORMATION AVAILABLE **

   IB      STATUS  -PARTITIONS-
                   012
                   012
   IG              012
   TIL1            012




   IB      STATUS  -PARTITIONS-
                   012
                   012
   IG              012
   TIL1            012
```

Figure 9-5   Using the /LISTP and /SHIFT commands to view job output (part 2 of 2)

you want the display to move. So to see the rest of the output in part
1, I entered the command /SHIFT RIGHT 20. Part 2 of figure 9-5 shows
the resulting display. You can then enter the command /SHIFT LEFT
20 to return to the original display.

You can tap the enter key to page forward through the output or
you can use the /LOCP command to locate a particular text string within
it. Figure 9-6 shows the display that results after I entered /LOCP followed by PROC to locate the text string PROC in the output. The result
is that the output is positioned at the section for the procedure search
chain.

If you decide that you want a permanent copy of the job's output,
you can issue the /ROUTEP (or /RP) command to cause the listing to
be routed to the central site output device (printer for list output, card
punch for punch output). On the /RP command, you specify two operands: first the name of the POWER queue that contains the output
item (LST or PUN), then the queue entry name. So you enter

    /ROUTEP LST LISTLIBS

to cause the output of this job to print on the central site printer.

If you don't want to do anything with output in a POWER list,
punch, or reader queue, you should delete it with the /ERASEP (or

```
   ...+....1....+....2....+....3....+....4....+....5....+....6. <==MORE==> .+..LS
// LIBLIST PROC,BG

BG-TEMP ** NO LIBRARY INFORMATION AVAILABLE **

BG-PERM LIBNAME SUBLIB    STATUS  -PARTITIONS-
SEARCH  MMA     PROD              012
        PRD1    BASE              012
        PRD1    CONFIG            012
        SOFTLIB SYSUTIL1          012

EOJ LISTLIBS                                                    DATE 07/
*PARTIAL END PRINT
```

Figure 9-6   Using the /LOCP command to view job output

just /EP) command. Its format is just like /ROUTEP's. For example, you can enter

```
/ERASEP LST LISTLIBS
```

to delete the LISTLIBS output from the POWER list queue.

How to retrieve your job's output   In some cases, you may want to copy a queue item into a member in your ICCF library. To do that, you can use the ICCF procedure GETL and GETP to retrieve output from the list and punch queue, and GETR to retrieve a job stored in the reader queue. Figure 9-4 shows the formats of all three.

For GETL and GETP, the POWER queue entry you want to retrieve should have class Q; it will if you specified RETURN when you submitted the job. For GETR the job should have class A.

When you use these procedures, you can code several operands to control how they work. But figure 9-4 shows you only the simplest ones. For instance, to transfer the print output of LISTLIBS into a member named LLIBPRT, you enter

```
GETL LISTLIBS MEM=LLIBPRT
```

Then, to view the output, you enter

```
/LIST LLIBPRT
```

If you don't specify a member name when you use the GETL procedure, the output is stored in a temporary ICCF work area called the *print area*. Each user has a print area called $$PRINT. To retrieve the output from the job LISTLIBS and store it in your print area, you enter

```
GETL LISTLIBS
```

Then, to view the output, you enter

```
/LIST $$PRINT
```

The GETP procedure works similarly, only it stores output from the POWER punch queue in the *punch area* ($$PUNCH) if you don't specify a member name. The punch area is another ICCF temporary work area. Beware that both $$PUNCH and $$PRINT can be used for other functions, so output you store in them may be lost. If you want to store output permanently, you should use a library member.

Finally, with the GETR procedure, you can retrieve the contents of a POWER reader queue item. Unlike the GETL and GETP procedures, there is no temporary work area in which to store a job from the reader queue. So if you don't specify a member name on the GETR procedure, the output is stored in an ICCF file that has the same name as the job name you specify. Although you'll use GETR less often than GETL or GETP, it can be helpful in some situations.

How to use the /DQ command

Now, I'd like to show you one more system command you'll find useful as you work with the submit-to-batch facility: /DQ. This command lets you display the contents of POWER queues, much like a system operator can do with a POWER operator command.

Figure 9-7 illustrates the format of the /DQ command. As you can see, you can request information about the status of specific groups of queue entries with /DQ. Although the options for /DQ look imposing, they're easy to use. For example, to display all the jobs in the POWER reader queue that have class D or K, you enter

```
/DQ RDR FREE
```

To display all the jobs in the reader queue that begin with the letter C, you enter

```
/DQ RDR *C
```

If you experiment with the /DQ command, you'll soon find the combinations of operands that are most useful for you.

Command	Function
/DQ	Display all entries in all three POWER queues.
/DQ queue	Display all entries in the specified queue (RDR, LST, or PUN).
/DQ queue HOLD	Display all entries in the specified queue that are not available for processing.
/DQ queue FREE	Display all entries in the specified queue that are available for processing.
/DQ queue *abcedfgh	Display all entries in the specified queue whose names begin with the characters specified after the asterisk; you may specify from one to eight characters.
/DQ queue class	Display all jobs in the specified queue with the specified class.
/DQ queue name [job-number]	Display the entry in the specified queue with the specified name and number.

Figure 9-7   The format of the /DQ system command

Discussion
At this point, you should understand how POWER can operate on a cardless system. In effect, ICCF takes the place of a card reader as far as POWER is concerned. Although the submit-to-batch facility may seem like an obscure feature, it's one you are likely to use regularly.

Terminology
submit-to-batch facility
execution mode
print area
punch area

Objectives
1. Use the submit-to-batch facility of ICCF to submit a job to POWER.

2. Use the ICCF commands and procedures in figures 9-4 and 9-7 to monitor POWER job execution, control the output of POWER jobs, and view POWER queues.

Section 4

Advanced data management

The system considerations and job control statements you learned in chapter 4 for SAM DASD files were just enough to let you code basic job streams. But to work effectively in a production environment, you need to know more about data management. So in this section, you'll learn how to code job streams to process tape files and all types of DASD files.

This section contains four chapters. Since they're independent, you don't have to read one to use another. Chapter 10 describes VSE label processing and teaches you how to add label data to the label information area. Chapter 11 teaches you how to code jobs that use tape files with standard labels. (The tape processing examples in the previous chapters use unlabelled tapes.) Chapter 12 presents additional information on the DLBL and EXTENT statements for files that use native VSE access methods; it expands what you've already learned about SAM files and introduces ISAM and DAM files. Finally, chapter 13 presents VSAM. Specifically, it covers VSAM concepts, JCL, basic utility functions, and compatibility features.

Chapter 10

How to use standard labels

VSE uses the information you code on DLBL and EXTENT statements and TLBL statements to verify file processing operations. (The TLBL statement supplies label information for tape files; you'll learn how to code it in the next chapter.) This topic shows you how VSE uses that data, which it stores in its label information area. In addition, it teaches you how to make permanent entries in the label information area for frequently used files.

How VSE performs label creation and checking functions

When VSE performs label creation and checking functions, it uses data you supply in TLBL or DLBL and EXTENT statements. The job control program, using a VSE component called the *symbolic label access routine*, stores the data from the label statements in the label information area.

The label information area, you should recall, is part of the system residence file. It's a relatively small component of SYSRES. On an FBA device, its default size is 200 blocks; on a CKD device, it's from one to three cylinders, depending on the unit type.

When the job control program ends, the application program begins. Then, when the program opens a file, VSE performs its label processing functions. For instance, figure 10-1 shows what happens when an application program accesses an input DASD file. In this case, the symbolic label access routine transfers the label data from the label information area in SYSRES to an area in the partition's GETVIS area. Next, VSE's open routine retrieves the file's label from the VTOC of the volume that contains the file and stores that label data in another area in the partition's GETVIS area. Then, the label data from the label

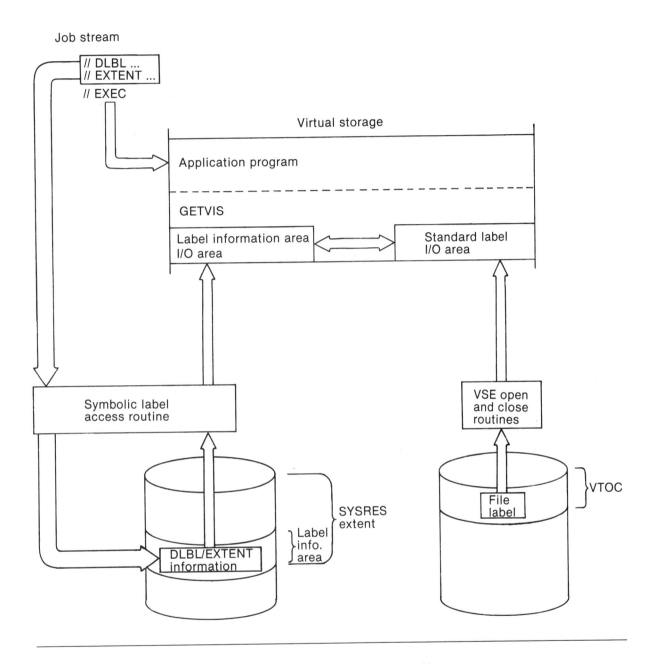

Figure 10-1   Label processing for an input DASD file

information area and the label data from the file itself are compared to insure that they're the same.

For an output file, the process is similar. Label data for the new file is transferred from the label information area through the two areas in the GETVIS area of the application program's partition. Then, VSE's open routines use that data to create labels for the new file. In addition, the open routines make sure that the area for the new file isn't already in use.

When you code label statements in routine job streams, they're in effect only for the duration of the job or, in some cases, only for a single job step. However, it's often more efficient to store label data for frequently used files permanently. To do this, though, you need to understand how the label information area is organized.

How the label information area is organized

The label information area is divided into three kinds of *subareas*. Each partition has one *partition temporary label subarea* and one *partition standard label subarea*. So on a system configured with 12 partitions, the label information area contains 12 partition temporary label subareas and 12 partition standard label subareas. In addition, the label information area contains one *system standard label subarea*.

Figure 10-2 shows these subareas within the label information area. Actually, though, the subareas aren't organized in sequence, as the figure shows, nor are fixed size sections of the label information allocated to them. Nevertheless, figure 10-2 should help you understand the concept of subareas. The shaded boxes in the figure represent the current label entries on a system configured with 12 partitions, but with only four in use.

Partition temporary label subareas   The temporary labels you create when you submit TLBL or DLBL and EXTENT statements are entries in your partition's temporary label subarea. They're called *user labels*, or *partition temporary labels*, and are in effect only for the duration of the job that contains them. In general, that's no problem because the label information you supply with an application job probably should be temporary.

Unfortunately, there is a problem if several steps within a single job each include label statements. Then, user labels submitted for one job step overlay those from a previous job step. So a sensible way to avoid this problem is to code all the label statements the job requires before the first EXEC statement in the job stream.

However, if the same names are used for different files in different steps, you may not be able to code all label statements at the beginning of the job. That was the case in the report-preparation job I showed you in topic 2 of chapter 4. As a result, I had to code duplicate label statements in that job.

In some shops, a partition may be used for the same sort of processing over and over, requiring the same files each time. In that case, if labels are stored temporarily, each similar job includes the same DLBL, EXTENT, and TLBL statements. Not only is that inefficient, it's also error prone because users have to code identical JCL statements repeatedly.

Label information area

Label subarea		Entries

Figure 10-2   Conceptual representation of the label information area in SYSRES

Partition standard label subareas   An effective alternative is to store information for frequently used files in a partition standard label subarea. *Partition standard labels* aren't cleared after each job step. Instead, they remain in effect until they're explicitly deleted. When label data for a file is stored in a partition standard label subarea, a job doesn't have to include label statements (TLBL or DLBL and EXTENT) for it. Since the data those statements would supply is already available, VSE can retrieve it for label creation and checking functions.

System standard label subarea   You can also store label information permanently for the entire system. These *system standard labels* are stored in the system standard label subarea of the label information area. Files that are used throughout the system, like libraries, should have system standard labels.

The LSERV program

If you want to list the contents of your system's label information area, you can execute an IBM utility program called LSERV. LSERV accesses the label information area and prints its entries. To invoke LSERV, you code a job like the one in figure 10-3.

Figure 10-4 illustrates part of the output from an LSERV job. Since the complete listing was 26 pages long, you can see I've omitted most of it. Even so, the entries in the figure should give you a good idea of what the listing can tell you. Although a complete listing contains a heading for each of a system's label information area subareas, figure 10-4 shows only three of them. One of the three is for system standard labels. The other two are for the background: one for user labels, the other for standard labels. (In a complete listing, there's a pair of headings like this for each partition.) If a subarea doesn't have any current entries, that's indicated by NONE, as under the heading BG USER LABELS.

Each label entry contains the data specified in its associated DLBL and EXTENT or TLBL statements. The three entries in figure 10-4 are for DASD files called IJSYSLN, IJSYSRS, and USRSLE. Although you haven't seen IJSYSLN before, you should recognize IJSYSRS as the system residence file and USRSLE as a private user library. It's possible to use just those names in application job streams (for instance, in LIB-DEF statements) because complete label data for the files is available in the label information area.

OPTION statement operands for label management

To make permanent entries in the label information area (either for a partition or for the entire system), you code a job with the appropriate label statements preceded by an OPTION statement that specifies a label management operand. That can be either PARSTD (for partition standard labels) or STDLABEL (for system standard labels). A third label management operand, USRLABEL, cancels the effect of both PARSTD

```
// JOB      LSERV
// EXEC     LSERV
/&
```

Figure 10-3   Job to print the contents of the label information area

and STDLABEL. If necessary, you can look back to topic 4 of chapter 5 to refresh your memory about how to code the OPTION statement.

Before I describe these operands, I want to warn you that you probably shouldn't use them in routine jobs. But I'm describing them anyway for two reasons. First, if you really do need to create standard labels, you'll know how. Second, if you know how to code these operands, you'll understand the effects of changing standard labels and you won't try it unless it's necessary.

Standard labels are typically created during system start-up. In other words, the DLBL and EXTENT statements (and, occasionally, TLBL statements) containing standard label data follow OPTION PARSTD or OPTION STDLABEL in the procedures that start the system. Then, when system initialization is complete, standard labels are already available in the label information area. As a result, you don't need to code them in application job streams.

If you do code OPTION PARSTD or OPTION STDLABEL in an application job and you aren't careful, you can destroy current standard label information. Because many jobs in your shop probably depend on those labels, this can cause serious operational problems. So if you think a standard label needs to be added, consult your systems programmer so she can add the appropriate label statements to the system start-up procedures. Now, with this warning out of the way, let me explain how to use the label management operands of OPTION.

The PARSTD operand   To store label information for a partition permanently, you code the OPTION statement with the PARSTD operand. If you need to use it in an application job, you should code it like this:

```
// OPTION    PARSTD=ADD
```

The ADD indicates that the DLBL and EXTENT statements that follow are to be added to existing partition standard labels. If you omit ADD and code simply

```
// OPTION    PARSTD
```

all of the partition standard labels already stored are deleted before the new labels from your job are stored.

```
BG USER LABELS (TEMPORARY PER PARTITION)

    NONE

BG PARTITION STANDARD LABELS (PERMANENT)

    IJSYSLN
        FILE IDENTIFIER                          BG.WORK.LINK
        FILE SERIAL NUMBER                       DOSRES
        VOLUME SEQUENCE NUMBER                   01
        CREATION DATE                            OMITTED
        RETENTION PERIOD (DAYS)                  0000
        FILE TYPE                                SEQUENTIAL

    EXTENT INFORMATION
        EXTENT SEQUENCE NUMBER                   000
        EXTENT TYPE                              1 (PRIME DATA)
        RELATIVE START ADDRESS IN TRACKS/BLOCKS  066676
        NUMBER OF TRACKS/BLOCKS                  003088
        SYMBOLIC UNIT                            SYSLNK
        VOLUME SERIAL NUMBER                     DOSRES
    . . .

STANDARD SYSTEM LABELS(COMMON TO ALL PARTITIONS)

    IJSYSRS
        FILE IDENTIFIER                          VSE.SYSRES.LIBRARY
        FILE SERIAL NUMBER                       DOSRES
        VOLUME SEQUENCE NUMBER                   01
        CREATION DATE                            OMITTED
        EXPIRATION DATE                          1999/365
        FILE TYPE                                SEQUENTIAL

    EXTENT INFORMATION
        EXTENT SEQUENCE NUMBER                   000
        EXTENT TYPE                              1 (PRIME DATA)
        RELATIVE START ADDRESS IN TRACKS/BLOCKS  002
        NUMBER OF TRACKS/BLOCKS                  055116
        SYMBOLIC UNIT                            SYSRES
        VOLUME SERIAL NUMBER                     DOSRES

                                    LOGICAL UNIT FORMAT: TYP=00,NUM=06
```

Figure 10-4   Output of the LSERV program on the sample system (part 1 of 2)

USRSLE

```
FILE IDENTIFIER                              USER.SLE.LIBRARY
FILE SERIAL NUMBER                           SYSWK1
VOLUME SEQUENCE NUMBER                       01
CREATION DATE                                OMITTED
RETENTION PERIOD (DAYS)                      1999/365
FILE TYPE                                    SEQUENTIAL

EXTENT INFORMATION
EXTENT SEQUENCE NUMBER                       000
EXTENT TYPE                                  1 (PRIME DATA)
RELATIVE START ADDRESS IN TRACKS/BLOCKS      115770
NUMBER OF TRACKS/BLOCKS                      005500
SYMBOLIC UNIT                                OMITTED
VOLUME SERIAL NUMBER                         SYSWK1

  . . .

END OF LABEL INFORMATION DISPLAY
```

Figure 10-4   Output of the LSERV program on the sample system (part 2 of 2)

All the DLBL and EXTENT statements that follow OPTION PARSTD (with or without ADD) are recorded permanently in the label information area and remain in effect after the job ends. However, since the effect of OPTION PARSTD lasts only until the end of the job, you don't need to worry that label statements in subsequent jobs will cause standard labels to be created. If you want to cancel the effect of OPTION PARSTD before the end of the job, you code another OPTION statement that specifies the USRLABEL operand.

The STDLABEL operand   To store system standard labels (that is, permanent labels for all partitions), you code the OPTION statement with the STDLABEL operand. It can only execute in the background partition, but, otherwise, it's just like OPTION with PARSTD.

If it's important not to delete partition standard labels by forgetting to code ADD with OPTION PARSTD, it's doubly important not to forget it with OPTION STDLABEL. You can cause serious systems problems if you accidentally delete system standard labels.

The USRLABEL operand   If you code the OPTION statement with USRLABEL, it cancels the effect of a preceding OPTION statement with either the PARSTD or STDLABEL operand. Then, it causes all subsequent labels created during the job to be user labels. However, in a production job that includes neither OPTION PARSTD nor OPTION STDLABEL, all labels are automatically created as user labels. As a result, you don't need to code OPTION USRLABEL unless you need to counter the effect of PARSTD or STDLABEL.

Discussion

As I stressed in this topic, you shouldn't use standard label options carelessly. Although you can correct damage to the label information area by rebuilding it, errors in many other jobs can happen in the mean time. And it might even be necessary to restart the system to restore the label information area if a job isn't readily available for this in the POWER reader queue. So be sure you have good reasons to code OPTION PARSTD and OPTION STDLABEL. And, if you use them, use them carefully.

Terminology

symbolic label access routine
subarea
partition temporary label subarea
partition standard label subarea
system standard label subarea
user label
partition temporary label
partition standard label
system standard label

Objectives   1. Explain how VSE uses the label information area to perform label creating and checking functions.

2. Given specifications for a job with several steps, describe the JCL alternatives for supplying the file label information each step requires.

3. Explain why it's sound practice not to code OPTION PARSTD or OPTION STDLABEL in routine application jobs.

4. Describe the JCL required to add and delete partition and system standard labels.

Chapter 11

How to process tape files

Mainframe systems have included tape units for decades. Although DASDs have become more and more important, many shops still use tape drives heavily because they can process sequential files efficiently and can store large files economically. And because most DASD units currently in use are fixed-media models, tapes provide the most convenient means to transport files from one system to another.

This chapter presents what you need to know to code job streams that do sophisticated tape processing, both with labelled and unlabelled tapes. First, it shows you how to manage processing of unlabelled tape files. Then, you'll learn how to initialize a labelled tape and how to use the TLBL statement to control the processing of labelled tapes. Finally, this chapter describes two operands of ASSGN that are specifically for tape processing: mode and ALT.

The MTC statement   If you want to control tape unit operations from a job stream, you can use the MTC statement. Figure 11-1 presents the format of the MTC statement. Its first two operands (operation and unit) are required; the third (count) is optional.

The operation operand   Figure 11-1 shows the values you can code for the operation operand of MTC. You're most likely to use BSF, FSF, REW, RUN, and DSE. REW, RUN, and DSE are useful for all tapes, regardless of whether they contain labelled or unlabelled files. BSF and FSF are most useful to position tapes that contain unlabelled files. Although you can use MTC with BSF or FSF to position labelled tapes, it's easier to use the TLBL statement, as you'll see later in this chapter.

The MTC statement

```
// MTC     operation,unit[,count]
```

Explanation

operation   One of the following three-character codes:

BSF	Backward space one tapemark
BSR	Backward space one record
FSF	Forward space one tapemark
FSR	Forward space one record
REW	Rewind but do not unload tape
RUN	Rewind and unload tape
WTM	Write a tapemark
DSE	Data security erase

unit   Address (cuu) or logical unit (SYSxxx) of the tape unit on which the operation is to be performed.

count   A two-digit value (01 to 99) that indicates how many times the operation should be performed.

Figure 11-1   The MTC statement

MTC also lets you perform other tape operations, but they aren't as useful as these five.

The unit operand   The other required MTC operand specifies the tape unit where the operation is to be performed. For this operand, you code either a physical address or a logical unit. For example, both

```
// MTC     REW,303
```

and

```
// ASSGN   SYS011,303
// MTC     REW,SYS011
```

cause the tape mounted on the unit at address 303 to rewind. If you code a symbolic unit, of course, you must already have assigned that unit to the correct tape device, as in the second of these examples.

| File 1 | TM | File 2 | TM | File 3 | TM | TM |

Figure 11-2   Tapemarks used to separate files on an unlabelled tape

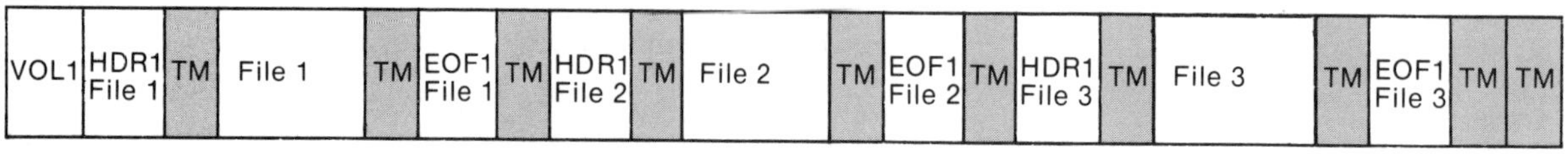

| VOL1 | HDR1 File 1 | TM | File 1 | TM | EOF1 File 1 | TM | HDR1 File 2 | TM | File 2 | TM | EOF1 File 2 | TM | HDR1 File 3 | TM | File 3 | TM | EOF1 File 3 | TM | TM |

Figure 11-3   Tapemarks used to separate labels and files on a labelled tape

The count operand   The count operand, MTC's only optional operand, lets you specify how many times the operation should be performed. If you omit the count operand, VSE defaults to 01. You can code values from 01 to 99.

You're most likely to use the MTC statement with the count operand to position a multi-file unlabelled tape volume at the proper file for processing. On an unlabelled tape, special characters called *tapemarks* separate files. To locate a file on a tape without internal labels, all you have to do is position the tape after a particular tape mark, and you're at the beginning of a file (or at the end of the data on the tape). Of course, you have to know how many tapemarks to skip to locate the file.

Depending on how the application programs that create the tape files are written, one or two tapemarks separate files on a tape. For instance, figure 11-2 shows one way files and tapemarks can be organized on a three-file tape. Here, one tapemark is use to separate files. In this case, to position the tape to read file 3, you code

```
// MTC      FSF,SYS016,02
```

assuming that the volume you want is mounted on a tape unit that's already assigned to SYS016. Because one tapemark separates each file, it takes two, not three, FSF operations for the tape to be positioned at the beginning of the third file.

Using MTC to position a tape with labelled files isn't as easy. That's because tapemarks separate not only files on a labelled tape, but also labels. For instance, figure 11-3 shows one way that three labelled files and tapemarks can be organized on a single tape. You can imagine,

```
//  JOB       INITTAPE
//  ASSGN     SYS000,300
//  EXEC      INTTP
//  INTT      SERIAL=(182006),CODE=(ECKOLS    )
/&
```

Figure 11-4   A sample job to initialize a tape with a standard VOL1 label

then, that using MTC with FSF to position a tape like this can be confusing. Fortunately, VSE lets you use an operand of the TLBL statement to position a tape that contains labelled files, as you'll see later in this chapter.

How to initialize
a tape

If you want to process labelled tapes, you need to make sure they have proper VOL1 labels. You do that by initializing them with the IBM utility program INTTP. With INTTP, you can perform special functions like initializing many tapes in one job and creating VOL2 through VOL8 labels. However, I'm only going to show you the simplest case: how to initialize one tape with a standard VOL1 label.

Figure 11-4 is a job stream you can use as a model for other jobs that initialize tapes. First, you assign SYS000 to the unit that contains the new tape; then, you code an EXEC statement to invoke INTTP. After the EXEC statement, you code an INTTP control statement.

Although the INTTP control statement looks like a job control statement because it begins with two slashes, it's not. On the SERIAL operand, you code the volser of the new tape; it's required. You must also include the CODE operand. The value you supply for it gets stored in a 10-character field in the tape's VOL1 label; it indicates who owns the tape. In figure 11-4, I just specified my last name. Notice that I padded it on the right with four blanks to make the value between the parentheses 10 characters long.

Shops that do a lot of tape processing usually have standards for what the code field of a VOL1 label should contain. As a result, if you need to initialize tapes for production files, be sure to find out what your shop's standards are.

The TLBL statement

To process a tape file with standard labels, you have to code the TLBL (tape label information) statement in your job stream. The job control program stores the data from a TLBL statement in the label information area just as it does for DLBL and EXTENT statements. And, as with DLBL and EXTENT, if a program processes a labelled tape file, the TLBL statement for it should precede the EXEC statement that invokes the program.

The TLBL statement

```
// TLBL     file-name,['file-id'],[date],[volser],[volseq],[fileseq],
          [generation],[version]
```

Explanation

file-name	A one- to seven-character name used by the application program to refer to the tape file.
file-id	A one- to 17-character name that's stored in the file-id field of the file's HDR1 label. The value you code must be bracketed by apostrophes. If you omit this operand for an output file, the file-name value is used.
date	For input files, specifies the creation date of the file in the format yy/ddd where yy is the year and ddd is the day of the year. For output files, specifies either the expiration date of the file or its retention period. To specify an expiration date, code the date in the format yy/ddd. To specify a retention period, code the date in the format dddd where dddd is a number of days from zero to 9999. If you omit date for an output file, VSE uses a zero-day retention period.
volser	A six-character value that specifies the volume serial number of the tape that contains the file.
volseq	A one- to four-digit value specifying the sequence number of a volume within a multi-volume file tape set. If you omit volseq, VSE assumes you coded 0001.
fileseq	A one- to four-digit value specifying the sequence number of the file on a multi-file volume. If you omit fileseq, VSE assumes you coded 0001.
generation	A one- to four-digit value specifying the generation number of the file. If you omit generation, VSE assumes you coded blanks.
version	A one- or two-digit value that qualifies the generation operand. If you omit version, VSE assumes you coded blanks.

Figure 11-5   The TLBL statement

It's possible to store tape label information from a TLBL statement permanently in the label information area as either a system or a partition standard label. When that's the case, job streams that execute programs that use the file don't have to include TLBL statements for it. However, permanent labels are more useful for DASD files; it's unusual to store tape labels permanently.

Figure 11-5 presents the format of the TLBL statement. The file-name operand is required; all the others are optional. Notice that the statement operands are positional. If you omit an operand but include a subsequent one, you must account for the position of the omitted operand with a comma.

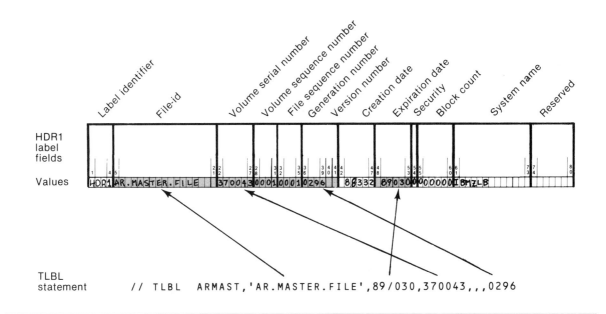

Figure 11-6   The relationships between HDR1 label fields and TLBL statement operands

All of the operands of TLBL except file-name have matching fields in the file's HDR1 label. Figure 11-6 will help you see the relationships between TLBL operands and HDR1 label fields. When an output tape file is created, the values for most of its HDR1 label fields come from the TLBL statement. When a job processes an input tape file, VSE compares the data you code for TLBL operands with the values in the corresponding HDR1 label fields. Now, let me describe the operands of TLBL.

The file-name operand   File-name, the only required TLBL operand, begins with a letter and is from one to seven alphameric characters long. It's the name the application program uses to identify the file. (In COBOL, it's the name you code in the ASSIGN clause of the SELECT statement; in assembler, it's the DTF name.)

The file-id operand   The file-id operand is the name that's stored in the second HDR1 label field. If you don't code the file-id operand of TLBL for a new tape file, VSE uses the value of the TLBL file-name operand. The value you code for file-id can be up to 17 alphanumeric characters long and must be enclosed between apostrophes.

If you code a value for file-id when you process an input file, VSE compares it with the value in the file-id field of the file's HDR1 label. If the values disagree, VSE issues a message for the system operator, who can let the job proceed or can cancel it. If you don't code file-id when you access an input tape file, VSE doesn't check the file-id field of the HDR1 label.

The date operand When VSE creates a tape file, it writes the current system date in the creation date field of the HDR1 label (positions 42 through 47 in figure 11-6). When you access a tape file for input, you can code a date value in its TLBL statement that VSE compares with the actual creation date recorded in the tape label. If they don't agree, the system operator must intervene to mount the correct tape or acknowledge the discrepancy and allow processing to continue.

The format of the creation date you code in the TLBL statement is yy/ddd, where yy is the year and ddd is the number of the day in the year. For instance, you'd code February 1, 1989 as 89/032. If you don't code a value for the date operand for an input file, date checking isn't done.

If you code the date operand when you create a file, the value is either the file's *expiration date* or its *retention period*. If you code a date in the format yy/ddd, VSE treats it as the file's expiration date. That means VSE won't let another file overwrite it until its expiration date has arrived. If you code the operand as a one- to four-digit decimal number with a value from 0 to 9999, VSE considers it to be a retention period. Then, the file is current for the number of days you specify. If you code a retention period, VSE converts it to an expiration date and stores it in the expiration date field of the new file's HDR1 label.

The volser operand For the volser operand, you code a value that VSE checks against the volume serial numbers stored in the file's HDR1 label and in the volume's VOL1 label. If you code the volser operand for an input file and VSE discovers a discrepancy, it issues a message to the system operator. For a single-volume file, the volsers stored in the file's HDR1 label and in the volume's VOL1 label are the same; VSE makes sure they agree when it creates the file. As a result, you can use the volser operand of TLBL to insure that the correct volume is mounted.

For a multi-volume file, the value in the HDR1 label's volume-serial-number field contains the volser of the *first* tape in the set for all segments of the file, regardless of the volser of the volume that contains the segment. To understand, consider figure 11-7. It illustrates a six-volume file with volume serial numbers from 182006 to 182011 (from the VOL1 labels of each reel). The volume-serial-number fields in the HDR1 labels for each segment of the file, however, all contain the same value: the volume serial number of the first tape in the set (182006). As a result, you don't use the volser operand to identify each segment of a multi-volume file. Instead, you refer to the volume-sequence-number field in the HDR1 label with the volseq operand of TLBL.

The volseq operand The volseq operand lets you specify that processing should begin with a tape in a multi-volume set other than the first. VSE compares the value you code for the volseq operand with

VOL1 label	HDR1 label		File segment
Volume serial number	Volume serial number	Volume sequence number	

First volume of set

| 182006 | 182006 | 0001 | File segment 1 |

Second volume of set

| 182007 | 182006 | 0002 | File segment 2 |

Third volume of set

| 182008 | 182006 | 0003 | File segment 3 |

Fourth volume of set

| 182009 | 182006 | 0004 | File segment 4 |

Fifth volume of set

| 182010 | 182006 | 0005 | File segment 5 |

Sixth volume of set

| 182011 | 182006 | 0006 | File segment 6 |

Figure 11-7   Volume-serial-number and volume-sequence-number fields in the HDR1 labels of the segments of a multi-volume file

the volume-sequence-number field in the file's HDR1 label. This field identifies the position of the segment in a multi-volume file. In figure 11-7, the values of the volume sequence number field range from 0001 to 0006.

If you want to start processing a multi-volume file with a segment other than the first, you code a four-digit value for the volseq operand of TLBL. For example, to use the tape set in figure 11-7 as input, but to begin processing with the third volume in the set, you code a TLBL statement like

```
// TLBL    INVMAST,,,,0003
```

When you use the volseq operand, though, you don't code volser. If you do, VSE may issue an operator message because the volser in a HDR1 label disagrees with the volser in the VOL1 label for all tapes in a multi-volume file except the first. If you omit the volseq operand when you code the TLBL statement, no checking is done. For most processing, you won't need to use the volseq operand.

The fileseq operand   The fileseq operand of TLBL lets you specify the position of an input file on a multi-file volume. The value you code is a four-digit number. If you omit the fileseq operand, VSE assumes you coded 0001. When you create output files on a tape, VSE automatically increments the values of the file-sequence-number fields in the HDR1 labels it writes.

You can use the fileseq operand of TLBL to position a tape at the proper location for processing when you're using a tape with standard labels. In this case, you don't have to worry about counting tapemarks, as you do with an unlabelled tape. For example, to access the fourth file on a tape, you code a statement like

```
// TLBL    ARMAST,,,,,0004
```

Of course, if you code other operands, they must agree with the values in the file's corresponding HDR1 label fields.

The generation and version operands   You can use the generation and version operands of TLBL to provide more detailed file identification data than the file-id field's 17 characters allow. Although generation-number and version-number are separate fields in the HDR1 label and generation and version are separate operands on the TLBL statement, they can work together.

The generation operand specifies a one- to four-digit number that identifies the generation number of the file to be processed. If you're familiar with IBM's MVS family of operating systems, you know that it provides sophisticated generation management facilities. But don't assume that MVS facilities are like those on VSE—they're not. If you want to use tape file generations on a VSE system, it's your responsibility to identify and manage each generation properly.

To illustrate the use of the generation operand of the TLBL statement, imagine that your shop performs special general ledger processing at the end of each month. Before the month-end processing, the general ledger master file is copied to a tape for permanent storage. In this case, you might code this TLBL statement for the file during February 1989's month-end processing:

```
// TLBL    GLARCH,'GEN.LEDGER.1989',,,,,2
```

Here, the file-id operand identifies the year the file was created, and the generation operand identifies the month (2).

If you omit a generation operand when you code the TLBL statement for an output tape file, VSE writes blanks in the generation number field of the HDR1 label. If you omit the generation operand when you code a TLBL statement for an input file, VSE doesn't check generation numbers.

Version number is a qualification of the generation number. For it, you can code one or two digits. As an example, suppose that the general-ledger file in the case I just described is archived daily instead of monthly. You could then use the version operand to specify the day of the month. For instance, you could code this TLBL statement for a job run on February 26:

```
// TLBL     GLARCH,'GEN.LEDGER.1989',,,,,2,26
```

As with the generation operand, version checking isn't done for an input file if you omit the version operand from the TLBL statement.

Keep in mind that generation tape processing is not automatic. As a result, the job that creates a file has to be changed to include new generation and version numbers each time it's run. That's why you probably won't use the generation and version operands of TLBL often.

ASSGN operands for tape processing

The ASSGN statement has two operands unique to tape units: mode and ALT. Mode lets you change a tape drive's processing mode and ALT lets you specify alternate units for overflow processing. If you code one of these operands, you can't code the other.

The mode operand When you execute a job that does tape processing, you may need to specify the tape drive's operating mode. You can do that with the mode operand of the ASSGN statement. For most tape units, the mode setting determines the drive's recording density. For the 8809 tape unit, mode specifies whether the drive should operate in start-stop mode or streaming mode and how large the gaps between the data blocks should be.

As a general rule, tape unit modes are set when the system is started and seldom need to be changed. If, for example, your installation has a tape drive that can process tapes with both 6250 and 1600 bpi densities, you're going to use 6250 almost all of the time. However, if your shop is upgrading to higher-density drives or you need to create tapes for other systems with tape drives that operate at a density other than your shop's standard, you have to be able to change modes.

The top section of figure 11-8 shows a subset of the mode values you can use to let your tape drives process different density tapes. Of course, not all units can process all tape densities. So you need to be sure that the unit you'll be using can process tapes at the density you request in the mode operand. If you need to specify a density other than those in figure 11-8, check the description of the ASSGN statement in *VSE/Advanced Functions System Control Statements*.

ASSGN statement mode operand values for non-8809 tape units

Recording density	Mode operand value
800 bpi	C8
1600 bpi	C0
6250 bpi	D0

ASSGN statement mode operand values for 8809 tape units

Operating mode	Mode operand value
Start-stop, short gap	60
Start-stop, long gap	50
Streaming, short gap	30
Streaming, long gap	90

Figure 11-8   ASSGN statement mode operand values

If your shop uses 8809 tape units, you can't change the recording density—it's fixed at 1600 bpi. However, you can use the mode operand to specify the operational mode of the unit: start-stop or streaming. The bottom section of figure 11-8 shows the four mode values you can code for an 8809 for all combinations of processing mode and gap size.

The ALT operand of ASSGN   If you're going to process a multi-volume file, it's efficient to use two tape drives. If you do, when one volume has been processed, processing can continue immediately on the second, called the *alternate tape unit*. Then, processing doesn't have to stop while the tape on the first drive rewinds and the operator mounts the next reel.

To specify an alternate tape unit, you code a pair of ASSGN statements for the same logical unit. The first assigns the primary tape drive, and the second assigns the alternate. For example, if a shop has two 3420 tape units at addresses 280 and 281, you could code these ASSGN statements:

```
// ASSGN    SYS010,280
// ASSGN    SYS010,281,ALT
```

Then, when a tape mounted on the unit at address 280 has been completely processed, processing can continue on the unit at address 281 without interruption.

Again, remember that you cannot code both the mode and ALT operands on a single ASSGN statement. If you need to use both for one drive, you have to code one ASSGN statement for that drive to set the mode. Then, you code another with ALT.

Discussion

Although the JCL to process tape files may seem complicated, it's straightforward in practice. If you work in a shop that does enough tape processing to warrant the use of the specialized features this chapter presented, you'll probably use them often. Then, as you gain experience with them, they'll become second nature to you.

On the other hand, you may work in a shop where tape processing is light. For example, you may use tape only to back up your system and to apply maintenance to your software products. If that's the case, you'll seldom need to use the specialized features this chapter presented.

Terminology

tapemark
expiration date
retention period
alternate tape unit

Objectives

1. Given specifications for a tape processing application that requires features described in this chapter, code an appropriate job stream.

2. Code a job to initialize a new tape.

Chapter 12

How to process DASD files with native VSE access methods

In chapter 4, you learned the basic JCL to define SAM files. However, you need to know some other operands of DLBL and EXTENT to process SAM files in a production environment. So that's what this chapter presents. In addition, it introduces you to ISAM and DAM files and shows you how to code label statements to identify them. Finally, it shows you how to code jobs to print DASD VTOC listings.

THE DLBL AND EXTENT STATEMENTS FOR SAM, ISAM, AND DAM FILES

The DLBL statement: Basic operands

Figure 12-1 gives the complete format of the DLBL statement for SAM, ISAM, and DAM files. (There are other operands you can code for VSAM files, but you'll learn them in the next chapter.) Since chapter 4 presented the first two operands of DLBL, I'm not going to cover them in this chapter. Instead, I'm going to show you how to use the DLBL operands that you haven't seen yet. Notice in figure 12-1 that the DLBL statement is a combination of positional and keyword operands. The first four operands are positional, and must be accounted for with commas if they're omitted and succeeding operands are coded. The rest of the operands are in keyword format. As indicated in the figure, you only need to code the commas for these operands if you code the operands themselves.

The date operand   Recall that one of the functions VSE performs when it creates a file is to check the DASD area the new file will use to insure that it's not already occupied. If it is, VSE checks the expiration date of the existing file (the expiration date is a field in the file's

The DLBL statement for SAM, ISAM, and DAM files

```
// DLBL    file-name,['file-id'],[date],[codes][,DSF][,BLKSIZE=n|,CISIZE=n]
```

Explanation

file-name
A one- to seven-character name used by the application program to refer to the DASD file.

file-id
A one- to 44-character alphameric name that identifies the DASD file in the VTOC. The value you code must be bracketed by apostrophes. If you omit this operand for an output file, the value you code for file-name will be used.

date
For output files, date specifies either the expiration date of the file or its retention period. To specify an expiration date, code the date in the format yy/ddd where yy is the year and ddd is the day of the year. To specify a retention period, code the date in the format dddd where dddd is a number of days from 0 to 9999. If you omit date for an output file, VSE uses a seven-day retention period for the file.

codes
A two-, three-, or four-character value that identifies the type of file. Possible values are:

SD	SAM file
DA	DAM file
ISC	ISAM file (creation only)
ISE	ISAM file (any other processing)

If you don't specify a value for the codes operand, VSE uses SD as the default.

DSF
Specifies that an output file is to be created as a data-secured file.

BLKSIZE = n
Specifies the number of bytes per block to be used for the file. Valid only for SAM files on CKD DASD.

CISIZE = n
Specifies the number of bytes per control interval to be used for the file. Valid only for SAM files on FBA DASD.

Figure 12-1   The DLBL statement for SAM, ISAM, and DAM files

label in the VTOC). If the expiration date has passed, the DASD space it occupies can be used for the new file. If the expiration date hasn't passed, VSE displays an error message that lets the operator decide whether to delete the existing file or cancel the job. If that happens, it's usually due to an error in the JCL, and the existing file probably shouldn't be deleted.

To access an existing file, don't bother to code the date operand; VSE ignores it. For new files, if you omit the date operand, VSE automatically assigns a seven-day retention period to the file. So you only need to code the date operand to create a file with a retention period that's other than seven days.

You can code the date operand in two ways: as a retention period or as an expiration date. For the retention period option, code the number of days the new file is to be retained (between 0 and 9999). Alternatively, you can code an expiration date in the format yy/ddd, where yy is the year and ddd is the day. For example, if a file created on February 5, 1989 is to be retained for 15 days, you could code either 15 as the retention period or 89/051 as the expiration date. Both would cause the file to expire on February 20, 1989.

The codes operand   The codes operand specifies the access method to be used for the file. If you omit this operand, VSE defaults to SD—the value for a SAM file. (None of the DLBL statements you've seen so far have used the codes operand because they've all been for SAM files.) Other values are DA (for DAM files) and ISC or ISE (both for ISAM files, but under different circumstances). You'll see examples of all of these values in this chapter.

Data-secured files and the DSF operand of DLBL

In the DLBL statement, you can code DSF if you want to create an output file as a *data-secured file*. When a program accesses a data-secured file, VSE issues a message for the system operator. At that point, the operator can let processing proceed or can cancel the job. Although the operator will probably let the job run, the messages VSE displays and the operator's replies are stored in the hard copy file. As a result, a complete record of access to the data-secured file is available.

You only need to code DSF when you create a file that you want to be data secured. To access an existing data-secured file for input processing, DSF isn't required. You can code DSF for files that will use any of the three native VSE access methods: SAM, ISAM, or DAM.

The BLKSIZE and CISIZE operands of DLBL

You can use DLBL's BLKSIZE and CISIZE operands only for SAM files. Both let you modify the default size of the physical block of data that's transferred to and from disk during I/O operations. BLKSIZE applies only to files on CKD units, and CISIZE applies only to files on FBA units. As a result, you can't code both on one DLBL statement.

The BLKSIZE operand for SAM files on CKD DASD   On CKD units, the unit of data transfer is a *physical block* that contains one or more *logical records*. (A logical record is an application program's view of the file.) For instance, the top section of figure 12-2 shows one way that logical records can be organized in physical blocks. Here, each physical block contains six logical records. Then, when an application program executes an I/O instruction for the file, the access method makes it look to the program like I/O operations are done on a record-by-record basis. Actually, though, I/O operations are done using the physical block rather than individual logical records.

Blocking on a CKD DASD

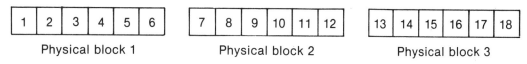

Blocking on an FBA DASD

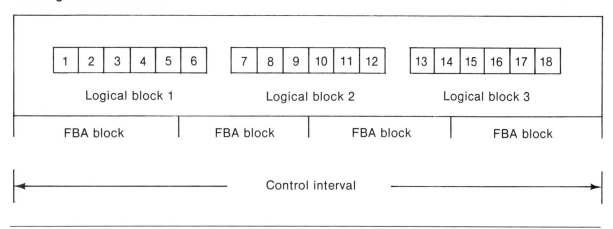

Figure 12-2   Blocking on CKD and FBA DASD

It's usually desirable to block records in a SAM file. If you do, fewer I/O operations are required to process the file and system performance is improved. The larger the block, the more records it contains and the fewer the I/O operations that are required to process the file. However, there is a trade-off between block size and program size: Larger block sizes mean that larger buffers are required in virtual storage to hold the block as records from it are processed by the program.

The application program usually specifies how many records are in a block. For example, in a COBOL program, you code the BLOCK CONTAINS clause in a file's FD entry. In some cases, though, you may want to override the value the application program specifies. When you create an output file, you can override the block size specified in the application program by coding the BLKSIZE operand on the file's DLBL statement. The value you code for BLKSIZE cannot be larger than 65536, and, for fixed-length records, it must be a multiple of the record length. Of course, once a file has been created, its block size is set, so you can't change it. As a result, you won't code the BLKSIZE operand on the DLBL statement of an input file.

You might want to use BLKSIZE to specify a more efficient blocking factor for a file if it's to be used on a DASD other than that for which its processing programs were designed. As a general rule, though, you should avoid the BLKSIZE operand. If you have a reason to change a blocking factor permanently, you should probably change the application program that creates the file.

The CISIZE operand for SAM files on FBA DASD   On an FBA DASD, data is not transferred in the same units as on a CKD device. Instead, it's transferred in units called *control intervals*. The bottom part of figure 12-2 shows how data might be organized on an FBA unit. Here, one control interval contains three *logical blocks* (the equivalent of the physical blocks in the top section of the figure), while the control interval consists of a string of 512-byte FBA blocks.

When you create a SAM file on an FBA DASD, the access method determines the proper control interval size. If you want to change it, you can code the CISIZE operand on the DLBL statement. The value you code must be a multiple of 512 bytes (the FBA block size) and cannot be greater than 32768. And if the value you code is greater than 8K, it must also be a multiple of 2K. As with the BLKSIZE operand for files on CKD units, you should have a good reason for using CISIZE.

The EXTENT statement: Basic operands

Figure 12-3 gives the complete format for the EXTENT statement. In chapter 4, you learned the logical unit, location, and size operands, so I'm not going to cover them again here. Instead, I'm going to focus on the other operands of EXTENT that you may need to use.

The volser operand   This operand specifies the six-character volume serial number of the volume that contains the extent. If you code it, VSE checks to make sure the correct pack is mounted on the unit you specify. If you don't code it, VSE doesn't check the volume label.

The type operand   You use the type operand when you process an ISAM file or a special kind of SAM file on a CKD device called a split-cylinder file. I'll show you how to code the type operand when I cover these two kinds of files.

Multi-extent files and the sequence-number operand of EXTENT

The label statements you've seen so far have all been for files that use only one extent—the simplest case. However, it's possible for a file to reside in more than one extent. This can happen if the file's too large to fit in the available space of one volume. Then, it's necessary to store it in two or more extents on two or more volumes if the entire file is to be available to the system at one time.

Files may also be stored in multiple extents on a single volume if the space allocations on the volume are so fragmented that no one extent is large enough to contain the entire file. Usually, this indicates that

The EXTENT statement

```
// EXTENT   [logical-unit],[volser],[type],[sequence-number],[location],
           [size],[split-cylinder-track]
```

Explanation

logical-unit	Specifies the logical unit assigned to the device that contains the extent. If omitted, the logical-unit operand from the preceding EXTENT statement is used; if no previous logical unit was specified, the logical unit the application program specified is used.
volser	The six-character volume serial number of the volume that contains the extent. If omitted, the volser value from the preceding EXTENT statement is used.
type	A one-digit value that identifies the type of extent. Possible values are:

	1	standard data area
	2	ISAM independent overflow area
	4	ISAM index area
	8	data area for a split-cylinder SAM file

The default is 1.

sequence-number	A one- to three-digit value from 0 to 255 that specifies the sequence number of the extent within a multi-extent file. The first extent of a file is considered to be extent 0; the default is 0.
location	For CKD devices, location is the relative track number where the extent begins. For FBA devices, it's the block number where the extent begins.
size	For CKD devices, size is the number of tracks the extent uses. For FBA devices, it's the number of blocks the extent uses.
split-cylinder-track	A one- to two-digit value from 0 to 29 that specifies the upper track number for a split-cylinder SAM file. This operand is valid only for SAM files and only on CKD DASDs.

Figure 12-3   The EXTENT statement

the files on the unit should be reorganized. However, if the DASD contains many files used by many jobs, it is time-consuming and error-prone to change all the affected job streams.

To use a multi-extent file, all you have to do is identify each extent with its own EXTENT statement. When you do this, you code the sequence-number operand of EXTENT to specify the position each extent occupies in the complete file. For example, figure 12-4 illustrates a job stream that invokes a program to process a three-extent SAM file stored on one FBA volume. Here, I've shaded the values I coded for sequence-number. As you can see, the first extent has sequence number 0, the second has 1, and the third has 2. Naturally, you can omit

```
// JOB      INV6220
// LIBDEF   PHASE,SEARCH=(USRSLE.INVNTORY)
// ASSGN    SYS005,SYSLST
// ASSGN    SYS014,251
// DLBL     INVMAST,'INVENTORY.MASTER,FILE',,SD
// EXTENT   SYS014,SYSWK4,,0,17864,240
// EXTENT   SYS014,SYSWK4,,1,54368,1660
// EXTENT   SYS014,SYSWK4,,2,124664,1000
// EXEC     INV6222
/&
```

Figure 12-4   Job that invokes a program to process a three-extent SAM file on one volume

the sequence-number operand when you process a single-extent file, because the operand's default value is 0. Notice in figure 12-4 that each EXTENT statement specifies different values for the location and size operands.

To process a file that's stored on more than one volume, all you need to do is specify the correct unit in its EXTENT statements. For example, figure 12-5 shows what the job in figure 12-4 might look like if the file used five extents instead of three. The first three extents are the same as in figure 12-4, but the fourth and fifth are on different volumes.

Don't let the JCL for multi-extent files scare you. As long as you include a correct EXTENT statement for each part of a multi-extent file, you won't have any problems. And don't think that you'll always have to code complete sets of label statements for complex multi-extent files. If your shop uses multi-extent files, label statements that identify them are probably stored as standard labels. Then, you don't have to include *any* label statements in your job streams to process those files.

Split-cylinder files on CKD DASD and the type and split-cylinder-track operands of EXTENT

Almost always, SAM files on CKD devices are allocated so they use complete cylinders. For some unusual applications, however, you might need to organize files so they share cylinders. Figure 12-6 illustrates this situation. It shows a section of an old 2311 DASD unit that contains three *split-cylinder files*, as well as the DLBL and EXTENT statements that define them. (Although 2311s are rarely used today, they make it easy to illustrate split-cylinder files because each cylinder contains only ten tracks.)

The beginning location of each split-cylinder file is computed using the relative track number technique. As you can see in the location operand of each EXTENT statement in figure 12-6, the three files begin at relative track numbers 700, 704, and 707. Then, the size operand in each statement specifies the number of tracks each file uses: 16, 12, and 12. In this example, though, the tracks the files use aren't con-

```
// JOB        INV6220
// LIBDEF     PHASE,SEARCH=(USRSLE.INVNTORY)
// ASSGN      SYS005,SYSLST
// ASSGN      SYS014,251
// ASSGN      SYS015,250
// ASSGN      SYS016,242
// DLBL       INVMAST,'INVENTORY.MASTER.FILE',,SD
// EXTENT     SYS014,SYSWK4,,0,17864,240
// EXTENT     SYS014,SYSWK4,,1,54368,1660
// EXTENT     SYS014,SYSWK4,,2,124664,1000
// EXTENT     SYS015,SYSWK3,,3,9288,2000
// EXTENT     SYS016,SYSWK2,,4,6524,2000
// EXEC       INV6222
/&
```

Figure 12-5 Job that invokes a program to process a five-extent SAM file on three volumes

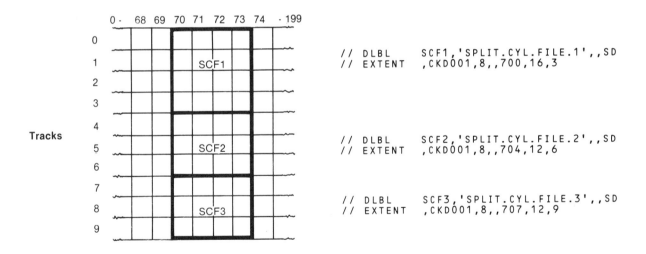

```
// DLBL    SCF1,'SPLIT.CYL.FILE.1',,SD
// EXTENT  ,CKD001,8,,700,16,3

// DLBL    SCF2,'SPLIT.CYL.FILE.2',,SD
// EXTENT  ,CKD001,8,,704,12,6

// DLBL    SCF3,'SPLIT.CYL.FILE.3',,SD
// EXTENT  ,CKD001,8,,707,12,9
```

Figure 12-6 Three split-cylinder SAM files on a section of a 2311 disk pack and the label statements that identify them

tinuous; they're split across four cylinders. To indicate that these are split-cylinder files, their EXTENT statements contain two new elements.

The first new element is the type operand, the third operand of EXTENT. (In the examples you've seen so far, it's been omitted.) The value 8 indicates that a file is a split-cylinder file.

The second new element is the last operand in each EXTENT statement: the split-cylinder-track operand. For this operand, you code the number of the last track in a cylinder that the file uses (*not* the relative track number). For the first file in the figure, that's track 3 (remember, track numbering on a cylinder begins with zero); for the second, it's 6; and for the third, it's 9.

It's unlikely that you'll use split-cylinder files. But if you do receive specifications for an application that requires them, there's nothing difficult about coding label statements for them. Remember that split-cylinder files can reside only on CKD DASDs, not on FBA units.

JCL FOR JOBS THAT PROCESS ISAM FILES

Sequential files, whether on tape or DASD, can be processed efficiently when most of their records are updated during a single run. However, sequential files just aren't well suited for applications in which current data from specific records must be readily available to users. One answer to this problem is to store an index to the data a file contains. Then, when a specific record needs to be accessed, it can be retrieved without having to process all the records that precede it in the file. In concept, that's how an ISAM file is organized.

For years, ISAM was heavily used on IBM mainframe systems, both DOS and OS, to implement files to be used in random processing. Today, however, VSAM is predominant because it's more efficient than ISAM. Even so, some shops still use ISAM files. So if you work in one of them, you need to understand the structure of ISAM files, and you must be able to code the JCL for jobs that process them.

Since ISAM is supported only on CKD devices, you shouldn't try to create an ISAM file on an FBA unit. An exception is if your shop uses the DASD compatibility feature to emulate CKD units on FBA DASDs. Then, you can use ISAM files on the emulated disks.

Components of an ISAM file

Compared to a SAM file, the structure of an ISAM file is complicated. It contains not only a sequential grouping of data records, but also index elements and, usually, overflow areas. To code JCL for jobs that process ISAM files, you have to understand these components.

The prime data area   The *prime data area* of an ISAM file is just what its name implies: It contains the bulk of the file's data records. Within the prime data area, records are ordered sequentially based on their key values.

Indexes   To retrieve records at random, ISAM requires an index structure. Every ISAM file uses two kinds of indexes to locate specific records: a *cylinder index* and *track indexes*. In addition, large ISAM files may use a third index type: a *master index*. After I describe cylinder and track indexes, I'll describe the master index.

The cylinder index contains one entry for each cylinder in the prime data area. Each entry contains two elements: (1) the highest key value

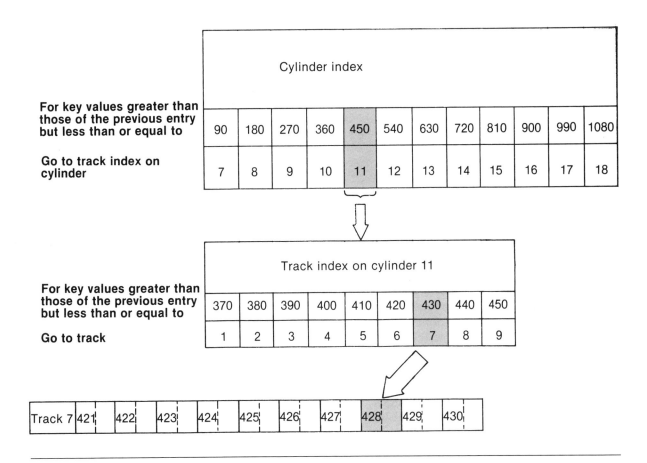

Figure 12-7   How ISAM searches cylinder and track indexes to locate a record

of the records stored in the cylinder and (2) the address of a lower level index for that cylinder, the track index. The track index, located at the beginning of each cylinder in the prime data area, contains one entry for each track within that cylinder. Like the entries in the cylinder index, each entry in the track index contains two elements: (1) the highest key value of the records stored on the track and (2) the track number itself.

Figure 12-7 illustrates how ISAM locates a record using the cylinder and track indexes. Here, the record with the key value 428 is to be retrieved. Searching the cylinder index, ISAM determines that the record is on cylinder 11. Then, searching the track index, ISAM determines that the record is on track 7 of that cylinder. Finally, by searching track 7, ISAM finds the record with key value 428. In contrast, if this were a sequential file, SAM would have had to read all the preceding records in the file to locate this record.

If an ISAM file is large, the cylinder index may require several tracks. When that's the case, the time required to locate an entry in it can be too time-consuming to be acceptable. If so, the file may be created with an optional master index. The master index points directly to each track of the cylinder index. As a result, the time required to search the cylinder index is reduced.

Overflow areas   ISAM files can include *overflow areas* that are used when records are added to the file. As a result, the entire file doesn't have to be rewritten to add new records in their proper positions within the key sequence, as is the case with a SAM file. When records are added to an overflow area, the index structure is updated so records can still be retrieved in key sequence. There are two kinds of overflow areas you should be familiar with: cylinder overflow areas and the independent overflow area.

One way to allow for file additions is to provide *cylinder overflow areas*. When you use this approach, part of each cylinder in the prime data area is reserved for inserted records. This is a function that you don't have to account for in your JCL. Instead, the application program that creates an ISAM file gives the specifications for cylinder overflow areas, and other application programs that process the file must agree with those specifications.

The other type of overflow area is a separate disk extent called the *independent overflow area*. You may use it instead of or in addition to cylinder overflow areas. However, because the independent overflow area is a separate disk extent, you have to include an EXTENT statement for it in the job streams that access the file.

When records are added to an overflow area, the index structure is adjusted to point to them. As more and more records are added to the file, it becomes necessary at some point to reorganize it. When a file is reorganized, the records in the independent overflow area are moved into the prime data area and the index structure is rebuilt. If ISAM files that have many insertions aren't periodically reorganized, serious performance degradation can result.

JCL elements for ISAM files

As you'd probably expect, the JCL to define an ISAM file is more complex than the JCL to define a SAM file. The formats of the DLBL and EXTENT statements for ISAM files are the same as for SAM files, except the split-cylinder-track operand of the EXTENT statement doesn't apply.

The codes operand of DLBL for ISAM files   On the DLBL statement for an ISAM file, you can code one of two values for the codes operand, depending on the operation you want to perform. If you're creating an ISAM file, code ISC (Indexed Sequential Create). If you're performing any other function, code ISE (Indexed Sequential Extend).

The type and sequence-number operands of EXTENT for ISAM files   An ISAM file always has at least two extents: the cylinder index and the prime data area. So when you code the label statements for

ISAM file area	Type operand value	Sequence-number operand value
Master index	4	0
Cylinder index	4	1
Prime data area(s)	1	$2,\dots,n$
Independent overflow area	2	$n+1$

Figure 12-8 Values for the type and sequence-number operands of the EXTENT statements for different areas of an ISAM file

an ISAM file, you'll have to code at least two EXTENT statements. And, if the file uses a master index, an independent overflow area, or additional prime data area extents, each of them also requires an EXTENT statement. As you can imagine, then, the complete set of label statements for a large ISAM file can be complicated.

On each EXTENT statement for an ISAM file, you code the type and sequence-number operands; they work together. Figure 12-8 illustrates the values you code for the different areas that can make up an ISAM file. As the sequence-number operand values indicate, you must code the EXTENT statements for an ISAM file's areas in the sequence in figure 12-8. As you can see, the first extent of an ISAM file isn't necessarily extent 0; if an ISAM file doesn't have a master index, the first extent is 1.

Figure 12-9 presents two sets of job control statements that identify the same ISAM file, along with a disk map to show where the file's areas are located. The first of the two sets of statements is for a job that creates the file; the second is for jobs that process the existing file. There's only one difference between the two sets: the codes operand of DLBL in the first set is ISC; in the second, it's ISE. (Here again, this illustration is for a 2311 disk drive because it only has 10 tracks per cylinder.)

The EXTENT statements in both sets of statements in figure 12-9 are identical. Since this ISAM file uses only a cylinder index and one prime data area, there's one EXTENT statement for each. The EXTENT statement for the cylinder index comes first. It begins at relative track number 300 and uses 10 tracks. (This is a large allocation for this file, but it's acceptable as an illustration.) The value of the type operand (4) and of the sequence-number operand (1) identify this extent as the cylinder index. Notice that the cylinder index extent isn't identified with sequence number 0, as the first extent of a SAM file would be. The prime data area is identified with type operand 1 and sequence-number operand 2.

Label statements to create a new ISAM file

```
// ASSGN    SYS015,290
// DLBL     ISAM1,'ISAM.TEST.FILE.1',0,ISC
// EXTENT   SYS015,CKD001,4,1,300,10
// EXTENT   SYS015,CKD001,1,2,310,90
```

Label statements to access an existing ISAM file

```
// ASSGN    SYS015,290
// DLBL     ISAM1,'ISAM.TEST.FILE.1',0,ISE
// EXTENT   SYS015,CKD001,4,1,300,10
// EXTENT   SYS015,CKD001,1,2,310,90
```

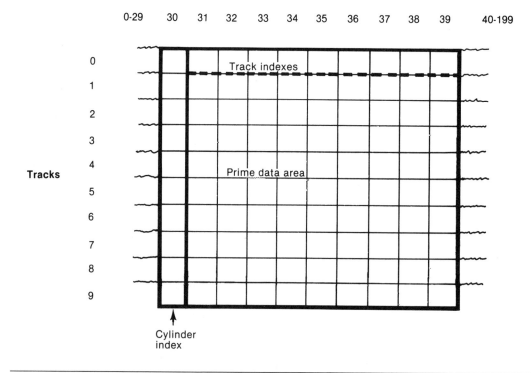

Cylinders available for user data

Figure 12-9   Label statements to identify a simple ISAM file for (1) creation and (2) later processing

Figure 12-10 illustrates similar sets of statements for a more complex file. This file uses a master index and an independent overflow area. The type and sequence number operands of the EXTENT statements identify each. For the master index, the type operand is 4 and

Label statements to create a new ISAM file

```
// ASSGN    SYS015,290
// DLBL     ISAM2,'ISAM.TEST.FILE.2',0,ISC
// EXTENT   SYS015,CKD001,4,0,1010,1
// EXTENT   SYS015,CKD001,4,1,1011,9
// EXTENT   SYS015,CKD001,1,2,1020,70
// EXTENT   SYS015,CKD001,2,3,1090,20
```

Label statements to access an existing ISAM file

```
// ASSGN    SYS015,290
// DLBL     ISAM2,'ISAM.TEST.FILE.2',0,ISE
// EXTENT   SYS015,CKD001,4,0,1010,1
// EXTENT   SYS015,CKD001,4,1,1011,9
// EXTENT   SYS015,CKD001,1,2,1020,70
// EXTENT   SYS015,CKD001,2,3,1090,20
```

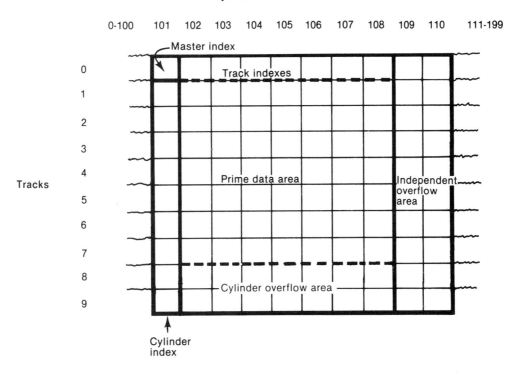

Figure 12-10   Label statements to identify a more complex ISAM file for (1) creation and (2) later processing

the sequence-number operand is 0. In the space allocations for the master index and the cylinder index, you can see that they occupy adjacent extents. (That's required if you use a master index.) The type operand of the independent overflow area is 2, and its sequence number is 3.

JCL FOR JOBS THAT PROCESS DAM FILES

DAM (Direct Access Method) files, unlike SAM files, allow direct access to specific records. And unlike ISAM files, records in a DAM file are created and retrieved based on actual disk addresses. Because direct file processing is complex from the viewpoints of programmers and system designers, DAM files are seldom used today. Even if you need to use direct processing, a VSAM relative-record data set is probably a more sensible choice than a DAM file. Nevertheless, because your shop may use some DAM files, I want to show you how to code the JCL for them. Fortunately, the JCL to define a DAM file is simple, even if the programming considerations to process it aren't.

The only difference between the JCL for a standard SAM file and a DAM file is the value you use for the codes operand. For a SAM file, it's SD; for a DAM file it's DA. So to access a DAM file, you use DLBL and EXTENT statements like those in figure 12-11.

HOW TO USE THE VTOC AS A VOLUME DIRECTORY

A DASD's VTOC contains entries that point to all the files on the volume. As a result, the VTOC is the place to look to find the location and size of an existing file or to determine what free space is available for a new file. To print the contents of a DASD's VTOC, VSE provides a utility program called LVTOC.

Figure 12-12 presents two job streams that run the LVTOC program. As you can see, they're simple. First, you code an ASSGN statement that relates SYS004 to the address of the the DASD for which you want the directory listing. Then, you code an EXEC statement to invoke LVTOC. Both jobs in figure 12-12 produce directory listings for the CKD DASD at address 290. This volume contains the files identified by the label statements in figure 12-6, 12-9, 12-10, and 12-11.

The first job in figure 12-12 is a model for one you would code to print a VTOC listing when you know the address of the unit. If you don't know the DASD's address, but you do know its volser, you can code a job like the second one in the figure. Notice on the ASSGN statement that I coded a generic device-class instead of a specific address; as a result, I included SHR.

The output from these jobs is in figure 12-13. Although I'm not going to explain all the information in the listing, I do want you to notice the shaded items. At the top of the first part of the listing, you can see that the report is for the volume CKD001. Next, there are entries for all of the files on the volume. The entries show, among other things, each file's id and extent usage. The last part of the report shows the free extents on the volume and their locations.

```
// ASSGN    SYS017,290
// DLBL     DAM1,'DAM.TEST.FILE',0,DA
// EXTENT   SYS017,CKD001,,,1200,50
```

Figure 12-11   Label statements to identify a DAM file

Option 1 (device address specified)

```
// JOB      LSTVTOC
// ASSGN    SYS004,290
// ASSGN    SYS005,SYSLST
// EXEC     LVTOC
/&
```

Option 2 (DASD volume serial number specified)

```
// JOB      LSTVTOC
// ASSGN    SYS004,DISK,VOL=CKD001,SHR
// ASSGN    SYS005,SYSLST
// EXEC     LVTOC
/&
```

Figure 12-12   Two job streams to produce a DASD VTOC listing

DISCUSSION   Although you need to be familiar with the material in this chapter, the chances are that much of the DASD file processing in your shop uses VSAM rather than the native VSE access methods. That's because VSAM offers significant advantages over ISAM and DAM processing. In the next chapter, then, I'll describe VSAM concepts and show you how to code job streams to create and process VSAM files.

Terminology

data-secured file
physical block
logical record
control interval
logical block
split-cylinder file
prime data area

cylinder index
track index
master index
overflow area
cylinder overflow area
independent overflow area

```
                        VTOC DISPLAY UTILITY  DATE - 11/28/88  TIME - 13:20

  LABEL IDENT - VOL1    VTOC LOCATION IS CYLINDER - 0    SERIAL NUMBER - CKD001    OWNER IDENT -

  T 1,R 1 FORMAT 4   LAST ACTIVE   UNUSED    ALTERNATE TRACK INFORMATION        EXTENT INFORMATION
                     FORMAT 1      LABELS    LOCATION     NO.OF TRACKS          SEQ TYPE   LOW    HIGH
                                   14        200  0       30                    0 PRIME    0  1   0  1

  T 1,R 2 FORMAT 5   USED ONLY BY OS, NOT SUPPORTED BY DOS/VS

  --------------------  FILE-IDENTIFIERS LISTED IN ALPHABETIC ORDER  --------------------

  T 1,R10 FORMAT 1   SER NUM-CKD001
  ------FILE IDENT------
  DAM.TEST.FILE
                     LENGTHS              DATES            SYSTEM       EXTENT INFORMATION
                     KEY BLOCK RCD    CREATE   EXPIRE      IDENT        SEQ TYPE   LOW     HIGH
                                      88 333   88 333      IBMDOSVS     0 PRIME    120  0  124  9

  T 1,R 4 FORMAT 1   SER NUM-CKD001
  ------FILE IDENT------
  ISAM.TEST.FILE.1
                     LENGTHS              DATES            SYSTEM       EXTENT INFORMATION
                     KEY BLOCK RCD    CREATE   EXPIRE      IDENT        SEQ TYPE   LOW     HIGH
                     6   94           88 333   88 333      IBMDOSVS     1 INDEX    30  0   30  9
                                                                        2 PRIME    31  0   39  9

  T 1,R 3 FORMAT 2
  INDEX   DATA IN CYL   CYL OFLOW   LENGTHS      HIGH'R'ON TRK      LAST RCD     LAST INDEX ENTRIES     TAG DEL   NON-FIRST   HIGH LEVEL
  LEVELS  FIRST LAST    TRACKS      KEY BLOCK RCD INDEX-PRIME-OFLOW SHARED TRK   TRACK CYLINDER MASTER  COUNT     OFLOW REFS  BYTE COUNT
  1       0  18  7      0           6   94        38   19   18      28           37 0 11  30 0 7        0         0           112

  PRIME   STATUS   INDEX ADDRESSES    LAST PRIME                        LAST OFLOW    OVERFLOW DATA
  RCDS    IND      CYLINDER LOW-MSTR  DATA RCD                          RCD ADDR      TRKS RCDS CYL
  968     '21'     30  0  0           37  5  17                         0  0  0       0    0    0

  T 1,R 9 FORMAT 1   SER NUM-CKD001
  ------FILE IDENT------
  ISAM.TEST.FILE.2
                     LENGTHS              DATES            SYSTEM       EXTENT INFORMATION
                     KEY BLOCK RCD    CREATE   EXPIRE      IDENT        SEQ TYPE   LOW     HIGH
                     6   94           88 333   88 333      IBMDOSVS     1 INDEX    30   0  30   9
                                                                        2 PRIME    102  0  108  9
                                                                        3 OFLOW    109  0  110  9

  T 1,R 3 FORMAT 2
  INDEX   DATA IN CYL   CYL OFLOW   LENGTHS      HIGH'R'ON TRK      LAST RCD     LAST INDEX ENTRIES     TAG DEL   NON-FIRST   HIGH LEVEL
  LEVELS  FIRST LAST    TRACKS      KEY BLOCK RCD INDEX-PRIME-OFLOW SHARED TRK   TRACK CYLINDER MASTER  COUNT     OFLOW REFS  BYTE COUNT
  2       0  18  7      0           6   94        38   19   18      28           105 0 7 101 1 4 101 0 1  0       0           16

  PRIME   STATUS   INDEX ADDRESSES    LAST PRIME                        LAST OFLOW    OVERFLOW DATA
  RCDS    IND      CYLINDER LOW-MSTR  DATA RCD                          RCD ADDR      TRKS RCDS CYL
  500     '23'     101  1  101  0     105  3  19                        109  0  0     20   0    0
```

Figure 12-13 LVTOC output (part 1 of 2)

```
                                     LENGTHS              DATES         SYSTEM      EXTENT INFORMATION
T 1,R 5 FORMAT 1   SER NUM-CKD001   KEY BLOCK RCD   CREATE EXPIRE       IDENT    SEQ TYPE  LOW   HIGH
---------------------FILE IDENT--------------------------------------------------------------------------
SPLIT.CYL.FILE.1                                    88 333  88 333   IBMDOSVS    0 SHARE   70 0  73 3

                                     LENGTHS              DATES         SYSTEM      EXTENT INFORMATION
T 1,R 6 FORMAT 1   SER NUM-CKD001   KEY BLOCK RCD   CREATE EXPIRE       IDENT    SEQ TYPE  LOW   HIGH
---------------------FILE IDENT--------------------------------------------------------------------------
SPLIT.CYL.FILE.2                                    88 333  88 333   IBMDOSVS    0 SHARE   70 4  73 6

                                     LENGTHS              DATES         SYSTEM      EXTENT INFORMATION
T 1,R 6 FORMAT 1   SER NUM-CKD001   KEY BLOCK RCD   CREATE EXPIRE       IDENT    SEQ TYPE  LOW   HIGH
---------------------FILE IDENT--------------------------------------------------------------------------
SPLIT.CYL.FILE.3                                    88 333  88 333   IBMDOSVS    0 SHARE   70 7  73 9

------------------------  LISTING OF FREE SPACE ON VOLUME  ------------------------

           RELATIVE TRACK                        EXTENT INFORMATION
           LOW    HIGH     FREE TRACKS          LOW         HIGH
            2      299         298              0   2       29  9
           400     699         300             40   0       69  9
           740    1009         270             74   0      100  9
          1110    1199          90            111   0      119  9
          1250    1999         750            125   0      199  9

                TOTAL FREE SPACE    1708

END OF VTOC DISPLAY
```

Figure 12-13   LVTOC output (part 2 of 2)

Objectives

1. Given specifications for a job that requires ISAM or DAM files, code appropriate job control statements to define those files.

2. Given specifications for a job that requires any of the following file-processing features, code appropriate job control statements to define the affected files:

   alternate block or control interval sizes (SAM files only)
   split-cylinder files (SAM files only)
   data-secured files (SAM, ISAM, or DAM files)
   multi-extent files (SAM, ISAM, or DAM files)

3. Given a DASD address or a volume serial number, code a job to print a listing of the unit's VTOC.

Chapter 13

How to process DASD files with VSAM

VSE/VSAM (Virtual Storage Access Method) is the predominant DASD access method on VSE systems. Because it's so widely used, you need to understand it to code production job streams for most VSE systems. VSAM does more than just replace SAM, ISAM, and DAM with its entry-sequenced data sets (ESDS), key-sequenced data sets (KSDS), and relative-record data sets (RRDS). It also provides efficiency improvements and better space management facilities than the native VSE access methods. In addition, it includes a multifunction utility program called Access Method Services (AMS) that lets you perform a variety of file-related functions. (AMS is also called IDCAMS; IDC is an IBM prefix associated with VSAM.)

Because VSAM is a comprehensive access method, this chapter presents a lot of information. Topic 1 introduces you to the VSAM concepts and terminology you need to know to use VSAM files. Topic 2 shows you how to code JCL for job streams that process VSAM files. Topic 3 shows you how to use basic AMS functions. Finally, topic 4 shows you how to use two VSE/VSAM features that are designed to make it easier for long-time DOS users to migrate to VSAM: the VSAM Space Management for SAM feature and the ISAM Interface Program (IIP).

TOPIC 1   VSAM concepts

This topic introduces you to the terms and concepts you need to under-stand to develop job streams that use VSAM files. First, it describes VSAM catalogs and areas; then, it shows you how the three kinds of VSAM files are organized. By the way, the facilities this topic describes are for VSE/VSAM release 3.0, so if you're using a different release, some details may differ. Nevertheless, the basic concepts are the same.

VSAM CATALOGS   DASD files that use VSE's native access methods are identified with labels stored in the VTOC of the volume where they reside. In con-trast, individual VSAM files don't have VTOC labels. They're identi-fied by information stored in VSAM *catalogs*.

VSAM uses two kinds of catalogs: a *master catalog* and *user cata-logs*. There's only one master catalog on a system. You might recall from earlier chapters the system logical unit SYSCAT; that's the VSAM master catalog. The master catalog stores label information for all user cata-logs and, in addition, may store information for some VSAM data files. More often, though, information for a VSAM file is stored in a user catalog. The file is then said to be "cataloged" in and "owned" by the user catalog.

Figure 13-1 shows the relationships among the master catalog, user catalogs, and files. The shaded areas in the figure represent areas under the control of VSAM. Notice that there's no more than one catalog on each volume; that's a VSAM rule.

A catalog can own items on more than just the volume where it resides. For instance, user catalog 3 owns VSAM files on volumes 3, 4, and 5. Notice also that a catalog can own VSAM files that are on volumes that have other catalogs. For instance, user catalog 3 owns VSAM files on volume 3, but volume 3 contains user catalog 2. It's even possible for non-VSAM files to be cataloged in a VSAM catalog.

VSAM AREAS   **Data spaces**   The sections of the volumes in figure 13-1 labelled "VSAM files" represent VSAM *data spaces*. As far as VSE is concerned, those extents are just that: VSAM space. The VSAM files that reside within a VSAM space—and there may be many—aren't recorded in the VTOC. What's in the VSAM spaces is transparent to standard VSE facilities.

In the simplest case, an entire DASD volume can be defined as one VSAM space. But it's also possible for only a part of a volume to be defined as a VSAM space. In figure 13-1, all of volume 4 is defined as VSAM space, but only part of volume 5 is. In addition, several VSAM data spaces can be defined on the same volume, as with volumes 1, 2, and 3 in the figure.

Clusters   In VSAM terms, a file, or data set, is a *cluster*. A cluster consists of a *data component* plus any indexes associated with it. Before any records can be written to a VSAM file, you have to use AMS to define the cluster. This is in contrast to files managed by the native VSE access methods. With them, all you have to do is open a file, and it's ready for use. However, once a cluster is defined, VSAM determines where the file is located. You don't have to worry about finding a free extent for it as you do with SAM, ISAM, and DAM files.

Control intervals and control areas   The unit of data VSAM transfers between DASD and virtual storage is the *control interval*. A control interval may contain one or more fixed- or variable-length records, but the control interval itself is always fixed-length. VSAM determines the optimum control interval size for a file based on the characteristics of the file and the DASDs that store it.

The VSAM control interval concept is much like blocking used with non-VSAM files. However, a control interval contains control information that isn't in a block. In addition, part of a control interval may be left empty so additions to the file can be made easily; that's not the case with blocks in files managed by the native VSE access methods.

A group of adjacent control intervals forms a *control area* within a data space. When you define a cluster, VSAM preformats control areas so they can be processed more efficiently. Just as sections within control intervals may be left empty to make additions easier, entire control intervals within control areas may be left empty.

Figure 13-2 illustrates the structure of a VSAM file's data component. Here, two control areas make up the data component of the cluster. Within each control area are two control intervals, each containing data records and control information. Of course, figure 13-2 is simplified. A VSAM file's data component can consist of many control areas, each with many control intervals.

VSAM FILE ORGANIZATIONS

The three VSAM file organizations parallel the native VSE access methods. An entry-sequenced data set is a VSAM file with sequential organization; a key-sequenced data set is a VSAM file with indexed sequential organization; and a relative-record data set is a VSAM file with direct organization. But don't confuse these VSAM organizations with the VSE native access methods. For example, even though a VSAM ESDS has sequential organization, SAM can't process it.

Key-sequenced data sets

Although key-sequenced data sets are the most complicated of the three file types, I want to describe them first for two reasons. First, most of the VSAM files you'll use will be key-sequenced. And second, once you're familiar with key-sequenced data sets, the other two VSAM file organizations will be easy to understand.

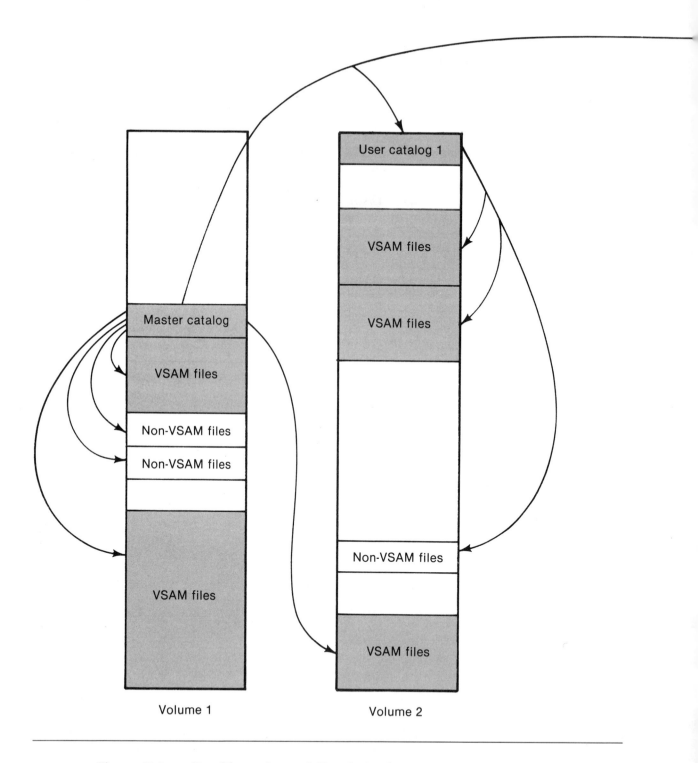

Volume 1   Volume 2

Figure 13-1   Possible catalog and file relationships

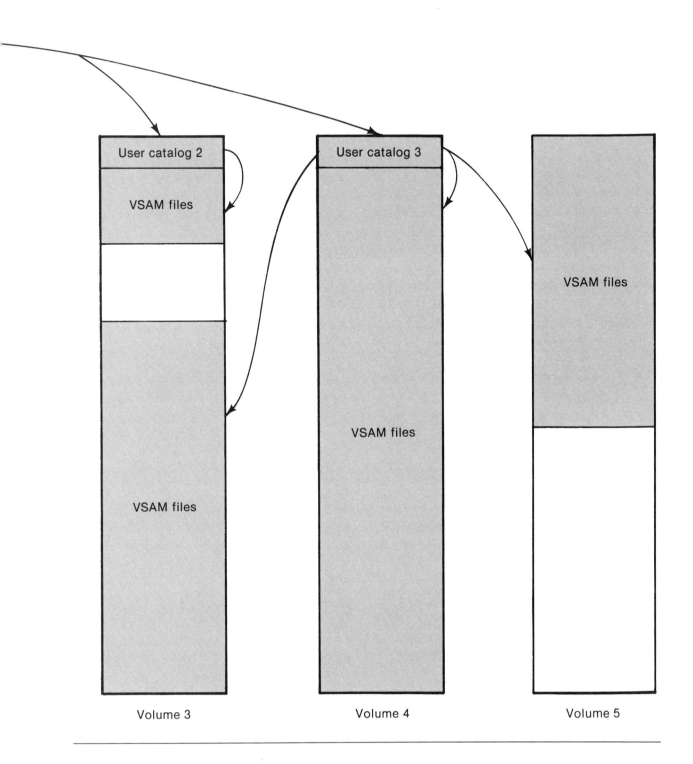

Volume 3   Volume 4   Volume 5

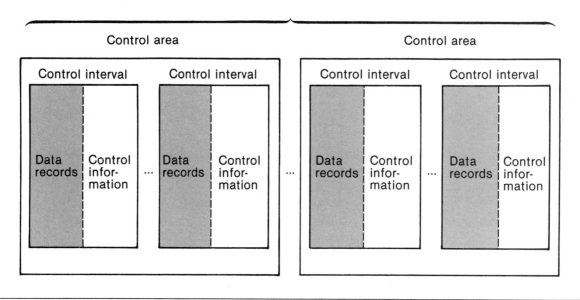

Figure 13-2   Structure of a VSAM file data component

A KSDS is similar in many ways to an ISAM file. In fact, one of the reasons IBM developed VSAM was to replace ISAM. However, VSAM uses an improved index structure and handles overflow processing more efficiently than ISAM.

Like an ISAM file, you can process a KSDS sequentially or randomly. When you use sequential processing, records are processed one at a time in the order of the key values stored in the file's index. When you use random processing, you supply the value of the key in the record you want to access.

A KSDS consists of two components: a data component and an *index component*. The data component contains the records, and the index component contains the indexes necessary to access them. Figure 13-3 illustrates these two elements of a KSDS.

The index component   As you can see in figure 13-3, the index component of a KSDS has two parts: a *sequence set* and an *index set*. The sequence set is the lowest level of the index. It's searched to determine the control interval in the data component that contains a particular record. The index set is a higher level index to the sequence set.

To understand how this works, consider the KSDS in figure 13-4. Here, the key value is a four-digit item number in a file of inventory records. The index set contains four entries, each with a pointer to a

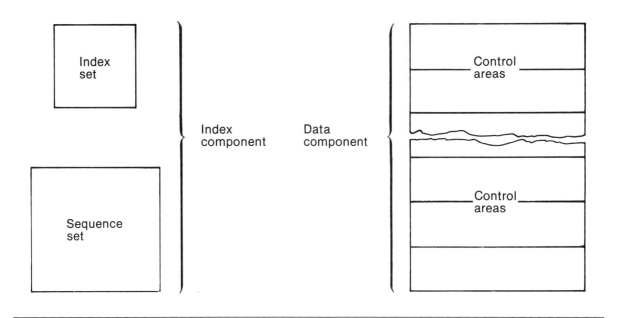

Figure 13-3   Elements of a KSDS

Index component					Data component						
Index set (level 1)		Sequence set									
Key	Pointer	Record	Key	Pointer	Control interval	Keys in control interval					
397	S1	1	187	C1	1	012	041	049	094	101	187
			284	C2	2	188	210	218	247	250	284
940	S2		322	C3	3	287	291	294	301	307	322
			397	C4	4	341	348	354	363	370	397
1391	S3	2	513	C5	5	410	415	420	434	470	513
			641	C6	6	585	592	601	615	621	641
1833	S4		787	C7	7	660	680	685	710	740	787
			940	C8	8	812	819	901	914	927	940
		3	991	C9	9	951	957	967	984	985	991
			1205	C10	10	1032	1105	1117	1121	1187	1205
			1297	C11	11	1207	1208	1231	1239	1250	1297
			1391	C12	12	1330	1337	1341	1355	1366	1391
		4	1522	C13	13	1410	1415	1423	1480	1481	1522
			1639	C14	14	1523	1530	1537	1539	1599	1639
			1740	C15	15	1641	1645	1691	1701	1703	1740
			1833	C16	16	1748	1780	1788	1790	1805	1833

Figure 13-4   Accessing a record in a KSDS

record in the sequence set as well as the highest key value referenced in that sequence set record. Each record in the sequence set in turn contains pointers to control intervals in the data component and the highest key value in each of them. In the data component, records are stored sequentially by key value.

To find a record, VSAM searches the index set sequentially for a key value greater than or equal to that of the desired record. When it's found, VSAM searches the indicated record in the sequence set sequentially to find the control interval that contains the record. Then, VSAM reads that control interval and searches it sequentially until it finds the data record.

For example, to retrieve the record with the key value 1239, VSAM first searches the index set in the index component to determine the record in the sequence set to access (record 3). Then, the entries in that sequence set record are searched to find the control interval in the data component that contains the record (control interval 11). Finally, VSAM reads control interval 11 and retrieves record 1239.

If you read in the last chapter how ISAM retrieves a record randomly, you can see that this is similar. However, from your point of view, a VSAM KSDS isn't tied as closely to the cylinder and track architecture of a particular DASD as an ISAM file is. As a result, the VSAM file is more flexible.

Free space in a KSDS   When a KSDS is defined, free space is reserved to accommodate new records. This space can be reserved in two ways: (1) space within each control interval may be left empty, and (2) entire control intervals may be left empty. When you define a KSDS with AMS, you can specify both types of free space, as you'll see in topic 3.

Figure 13-5 shows a control area that consists of four control intervals. Three of the four each contain three records and enough free space for two more, so 40 percent of the space is free in each of these control intervals. The numbers in each record area indicate key values; notice that they're in sequence. The fourth control interval contains no records. So 25 percent of the control intervals in the control area are free.

When a record is added to a KSDS, it's inserted in its correct sequential location in the data component and records that follow it in the control interval are moved down one position. That's what figure 13-6 shows. It indicates what the control area in figure 13-5 would look like after record 6494 is added to the file.

This is like what happens when a record is added to a track in an ISAM file that has free space in its cylinder overflow area. VSAM differs, however, because it moves records within the control interval in a virtual storage buffer. It doesn't actually rewrite the records on DASD until the space in the buffer is needed by another control interval. As a result, insertions in a KSDS can be processed more efficiently than insertions in an ISAM file.

Control area

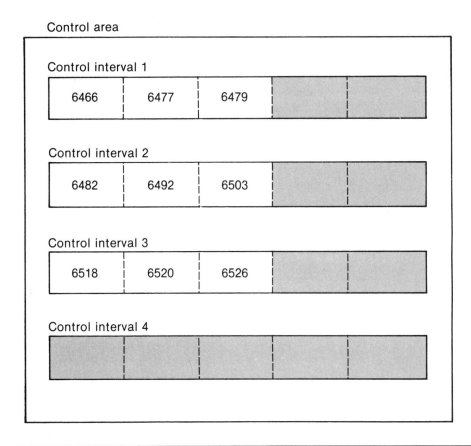

Control interval 1

| 6466 | 6477 | 6479 | | |

Control interval 2

| 6482 | 6492 | 6503 | | |

Control interval 3

| 6518 | 6520 | 6526 | | |

Control interval 4

| | | | | |

Figure 13-5   Free space distribution in the data component of a KSDS

If an insertion is to be made into a control interval that's already full, the records that would otherwise follow it are written to a free control interval (that would be the fourth control interval in figure 13-5 or 13-6). This is called a *control interval split*. Then, the free space in both the original control interval and the one used for overflow is available for insertions. Compare this to the relatively clumsy way ISAM handles insertions using its independent overflow area.

When a record is deleted from a VSAM KSDS, it's actually removed from its control interval and the space it occupied is available for a new record. Under ISAM, deletions are logical rather than physical; although they're no longer available to application programs, logically deleted records still remain in an ISAM file using valuable storage space. Because deletions don't waste space in the VSAM file and because insertions are handled more sensibly, a KSDS doesn't have to be reorganized as often as an equivalent ISAM file.

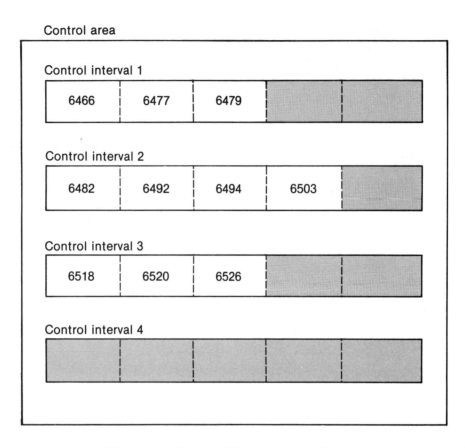

Figure 13-6   Free space distribution in the data component of a KSDS after adding a record

Entry-sequenced data sets

Compared to a KSDS, an ESDS is simple. It consists only of a data component, and all additions to it are made at the end of the file. Within an ESDS, records are identified by *relative byte addresses*, or *RBAs*. The RBA is an indication of how far, in bytes, each record is displaced from the beginning of the file. In an ESDS of 256-byte records, the first record has RBA 0, the second has RBA 256, the third has RBA 512, and so on.

Relative-record data sets

You can implement a VSAM file with direct organization as a relative-record data set (RRDS). Frankly, as with DAM files, there are few applications where an RRDS is a substantially better choice than a file with indexed sequential organization (a VSAM KSDS). Even so, I want to give you a brief description of an RRDS.

Control area

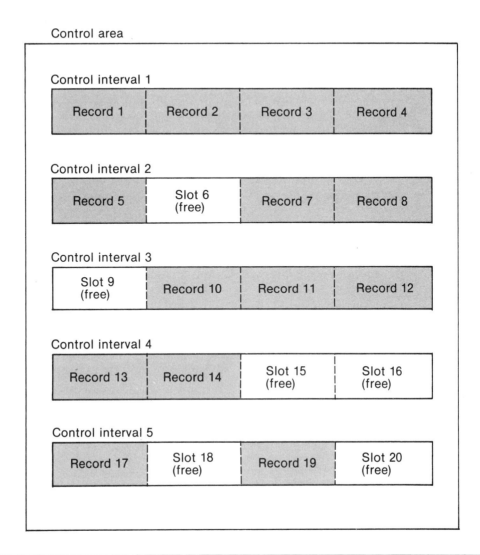

Figure 13-7   Record organization in an RRDS

Figure 13-7 shows a VSAM RRDS. The file consists of *record slots* that contain either data or free space. Each record slot is numbered, and it's those numbers, called *relative record numbers*, or *RRNs*, that identify records. When an RRDS is processed sequentially, the record slots are accessed in sequence. If a slot doesn't contain any data, it's skipped over. When a program processes an RRDS randomly, it accesses slots, not records, so it's possible for a program to access a slot that doesn't have a record in it. For example, in figure 13-7, that would happen if you accessed slot 6, 9, 15, 16, 18, or 20.

Additions to an RRDS can be handled in two ways. First, records can be added to the end of the file. Alternatively, records can be inserted in empty slots wherever they exist in the file. To do so, however, the application program has to be able to identify the slots that are empty.

Although records in an RRDS can be accessed randomly, that's done strictly based on the location of their record slots in the file. An RRDS doesn't have an index component; it consists solely of a data component. Because an RRDS doesn't have an index component, it can be processed more efficiently than a KSDS, so if an application lends itself to the RRN addressing scheme, an RRDS can be a practical alternative to a KSDS.

DISCUSSION   With all the new terminology you have to learn to use VSAM files, you might think that the access method is more complex than it has to be. Frankly, VSAM is complicated, but it's a significant improvement over the native VSE access methods. The efficiency improvements VSAM offers for indexed file handling and space allocation are reason enough to use it. However, another advantage of VSAM is that to define VSAM files in your job streams, you can code simpler JCL than you can for SAM, DAM, or ISAM files. That's what you'll learn in the next topic.

Terminology
catalog
master catalog
user catalog
data space
cluster
data component
control interval
control area
index component
sequence set
index set
control interval split
relative byte address
RBA
record slot
relative record number
RRN

Objectives
1. Describe the relationships among the VSAM master catalog, user catalogs, data spaces, and clusters.

2. Name and describe the three VSAM file organizations. Then, compare them to the VSE native access methods.

TOPIC 2   JCL to process VSAM files

In this topic, I want to show you how to code job streams to process VSAM files. You really only have to worry about coding DLBL statements, and they're the same for all three kinds of VSAM files. Because much of the data that identifies and locates VSAM files is stored in VSAM catalogs, you don't need to code EXTENT and ASSGN statements for them.

VSAM catalog considerations for coding job streams

Because the VSAM catalog structure is used to locate VSAM files, you have to include label statements for the catalogs that own the files your jobs use. That's why all jobs that access VSAM files require a DLBL statement for the VSAM master catalog. The name of the master catalog is *IJSYSCT*. As a result, its DLBL statement should look like this:

```
// DLBL     IJSYSCT,'VSAM.MASTER.CATALOG',,VSAM
```

No EXTENT statement is required.

Because it's a universal requirement for jobs that access VSAM files, this DLBL statement should be stored as a system standard label. If it isn't, have your systems programmer add the proper DLBL statement to the system start-up job stream that loads the label information area.

In addition to the master catalog, you also have to identify the user catalogs your job requires. I'll show you how to do that in a moment.

The DLBL statement for VSAM files

Figure 13-8 presents the format of the DLBL statement for a VSAM file. It includes five operands you haven't seen yet. I'll describe three of them (BUFSP, CAT, and DISP) in this topic. If you use the VSAM Space Management for SAM feature, you can code two other operands (RECORDS and RECSIZE). I'll describe them in topic 4.

The first four operands are the same as in the other DLBL statements you've seen. The file-name operand specifies the name the application program uses to refer to the VSAM file. The file-id operand (up to 44 characters long) is the name given to the cluster when it was defined. The third DLBL operand, date, doesn't have an effect for a VSAM file since the expiration date of a VSAM file is specified when the cluster is defined. As a result, I didn't include the date operand in figure 13-8, although I did account for its position with an additional comma. Finally, always code VSAM as the codes operand for a VSAM file, regardless of whether the file is a KSDS, an ESDS, or an RRDS.

The first four operands of the DLBL statement for a VSAM file are positional. The others you can code for a standard VSAM file are keyword operands: BUFSP, CAT, and DISP.

The DLBL statement for standard VSAM files

```
// DLBL     file-name,'file-id',,VSAM[,BUFSP=n][,CAT=catalog-name]
           [,DISP=disp][,RECORDS=records,RECSIZE=recsize]
```

Explanation

file-name	A one- to seven-character name used by the application program to refer to the file.
file-id	A one- to 44-character alphameric name that identifies the VSAM file in its catalog. The name you code must be the same as the one specified when the file was defined.
VSAM	For the codes operand, code VSAM for any VSAM file.
BUFSP = n	Specifies the size in bytes of the buffer VSAM uses for I/O operations for the file.
CAT = catalog-name	Specifies the file-name on the DLBL statement that identifies the catalog that owns the file.
DISP = disp	For reusable VSAM files, you can code one of these values on the DISP operand:

          NEW
          (NEW,KEEP)
          (NEW,DELETE)
          (NEW,DATE)
          OLD
          (OLD,KEEP)
          (OLD,DELETE)
          (OLD,DATE)
          (,KEEP)
          (,DELETE)
          (,DATE)

          See the text for details on their effects.

RECORDS = records	The primary space allocation for an implicitly defined SAM ESDS. If you specify records, you must also specify recsize.
RECSIZE = recsize	The average record size in an implicitly defined SAM ESDS. If you specify recsize, you must also specify records.

Figure 13-8   The DLBL statement for standard VSAM files

The BUFSP operand   VSAM uses buffers in virtual storage to transfer data to and from disk. It determines the default buffer size for a file based on control interval size and file type. If you have a good reason to alter a file's default buffer size, you can code the BUFSP operand on its DLBL statement. Code the number of bytes of storage, up to 999999, that should be allocated. If the value you code is less than the file's default buffer size, VSAM ignores your entry and uses the larger default size.

To decide on the proper amount of buffer space for a file, you need a detailed knowledge of VSAM functions and the structure of the file you're using. Usually, though, the standard buffer size VSAM calculates for a file is adequate. If you think you need to change it, you should read the chapter on optimizing VSAM performance in *VSE/VSAM Programmer's Reference*.

The CAT operand   You use the CAT operand of DLBL to specify what catalog owns the file you want to access. The value you code for CAT is the file-name of the catalog from a preceding DLBL statement. You don't always have to code the CAT operand, however, even though you almost always have to specify the user catalogs that own the files your job uses.

The usual way to specify a user catalog is to define a *job catalog* in your job stream. A job catalog is a VSAM user catalog that owns the files your job uses (or most of them). To specify a job catalog, you code a DLBL statement with the file-name *IJSYSUC*, like

```
// DLBL     IJSYSUC,'AR.USER.CATALOG',,VSAM,CAT=IJSYSCT
```

If you code a DLBL statement like this one, the system assumes that all VSAM files you want to access are owned by the user catalog you name as IJSYSUC rather than the master catalog. Since most applications are designed so related files are owned by the same catalog, this works well. Notice that I coded CAT=IJSYSCT to indicate the master catalog owns AR.USER.CATALOG.

To access a file that isn't owned by the job catalog, you can code the CAT operand on its DLBL statement. For that to work, you need to code a DLBL statement for the other user catalog with a name other than IJSYSUC. Then, the file name from the DLBL statement for the other catalog must agree with the name you code on the file's DLBL CAT operand.

For instance, suppose a program named AR9000 uses four VSAM files it calls CUSTMAS, OPNITEM, PDBILL, and BADDEBT. Their VSAM names are CUSTOMER.MASTER.FILE, AR.OPEN.ITEMS, AR.PAID.BILLS, and AR.BAD.DEBTS. All files are owned by AR.USER.CATALOG, except CUSTMAS; it's owned by MMA.USER.CATALOG. Figure 13-9 shows how you can identify these files. It includes DLBL statements for the two user catalogs the application requires. I used AR.USER.CATALOG as the job catalog because it owns three of the four files AR9000 uses. As a result, the CAT operand isn't required on the DLBL statements for those three files. However, the DLBL statement for the fourth file, CUSTMAS, does require CAT. The name I coded on the CAT operand is the same as the file-name on the DLBL statement for the catalog that owns it (MMACAT).

The DISP operand   You can code the DISP operand of DLBL to specify what's to be done with a *reusable file* when it's opened and closed.

```
// JOB      AR9000
// DLBL     IJSYSUC,'AR.USER.CATALOG',,VSAM,CAT=IJSYSCT
// DLBL     OPNITEM,'AR.OPEN.ITEMS',,VSAM
// DLBL     PDBILL,'AR.PAID.BILLS',,VSAM
// DLBL     BADDEBT,'AR.BAD.DEBTS',,VSAM
// DLBL     MMACAT,'MMA.USER.CATALOG',,VSAM,CAT=IJSYSCT
// DLBL     CUSTMAS,'CUSTOMER.MASTER.FILE',,VSAM,CAT=MMACAT
// EXEC     AR9000,SIZE=AUTO
/*
/&
```

Figure 13-9 Job stream to run a program that uses four VSAM files from two different catalogs

A reusable file is a VSAM file that can be used as a work file. Keep in mind that most VSAM files aren't reusable, and you don't code the DISP operand on DLBL statements for non-reusable files.

Figure 13-8 shows the values you can code for the DISP operand. The NEW and OLD options affect how the file is handled when it's opened for output. If you code DISP with NEW, the previous contents of the file are lost when it's opened and the effect is that you have a new, empty file. In contrast, if you code DISP with OLD, the contents of the file are retained when it's opened.

KEEP, DELETE, and DATE affect how the file is handled when it's closed. KEEP causes the contents of the file to be retained and DELETE causes them to be lost. (DELETE doesn't actually delete the file; it just causes it to be reset so it's empty.) DATE is conditional. If the file's expiration date hasn't been reached, DATE has the same effect as KEEP, but if it has, DATE has the same effect as DELETE. The default is (OLD,KEEP), so no data is lost when you don't code DISP.

The EXEC statement for programs that access VSAM files

As I pointed out in chapter 5, it is standard practice to code SIZE=AUTO on EXEC statements that invoke programs that use VSAM files. That's because VSAM requires a GETVIS area larger than the VSE default of 48K.

VSAM uses the GETVIS area to contain I/O buffers and control blocks. The exact size of the GETVIS area required varies from program to program. VSAM uses 40K for each open catalog, plus 12K for each KSDS, plus 10K for each RRDS and ESDS. In addition, if your program requires any VSAM modules that aren't resident in the SVA, the GETVIS area requirement is even larger. Fortunately, you don't have to calculate the exact size of the GETVIS area for an application. Just code SIZE=AUTO on the EXEC statement and, assuming the entire partition is large enough, you won't have any problems.

Discussion   At this point, I think you can appreciate how simple it is to code JCL for jobs that use VSAM files. You don't have to worry about coding the exact DASD addresses for the files a job uses. VSAM, through its catalog structure, keeps track of that information for you. As you code job streams that use VSAM files, you'll appreciate this more and more.

Terminology   IJSYSCT
job catalog
IJSYSUC
reusable file

Objective   Given specifications for a job that uses VSAM files, code appropriate DLBL statements for them.

TOPIC 3 How to use the Access Method Services program

This topic introduces you to AMS, the Access Method Services program. You can use AMS for practically any utility function involving VSAM files, including setting up the VSAM environment and managing it. In this topic, I'll show you how to code AMS job streams to define user catalogs, data spaces, and clusters.

HOW TO CODE AMS JOB STREAMS

JCL requirements

Whenever you run an AMS job, be sure a DLBL statement for the VSAM master catalog is available. It should be stored as a system standard label with the name IJSYSCT. On the EXEC statement, use the program name IDCAMS (not AMS) and code SIZE=AUTO.

Control statements

Immediately after the EXEC statement, you code control statements to tell AMS what you want it to do. Since most of the complexity in coding AMS job streams is in the control statements, I want to explain them now. An AMS control statement has two parts: the command and its operands.

AMS commands   Figure 13-10 illustrates the *functional commands* you can code in AMS control statements. With these commands, you can perform a variety of functions, such as creating and deleting catalogs, data spaces, and files; listing files and catalogs; and renaming, backing up, and restoring files. This topic shows you how to use the DEFINE command to define user catalogs, data spaces, and clusters for all three types of VSAM files. In chapter 18, I'll show you job streams to perform other AMS functions.

In addition to the functional commands, you can also code *modal commands* in an AMS job. Modal commands manage how IDCAMS executes based on conditions that arise during the job. Because modal commands are an advanced AMS feature, I'm not going to cover them in this book. If you're interested, refer to our book *VSAM Access Method Services and Application Programming* or to the IBM publication *Using Commands and Macros* for VSE/VSAM.

You can code the AMS command anywhere in columns 2 through 72, but I recommend you code it beginning in column 12 so it's aligned with your JCL. After the command, you code operands to provide more specific information about what you want AMS to do.

ALTER	EXPORT	LISTCRA
BLDINDEX	EXPORTRA	PRINT
CANCEL	IMPORT	REPRO
DEFINE	IMPORTRA	RESETCAT
DELETE	LISTCAT	VERIFY

Figure 13-10   Functional AMS commands

Control statement operands   When you code an AMS control statement, you often have to use several operands. As a result, most AMS control statements need to be continued. To continue a control statement, code one space followed by a hyphen immediately after the last element in the line.

To make your AMS control statements easier to read and change, I recommend you code one AMS operand per line on all control statements. Just as with the command component of a control statement, you can code operands between columns 2 and 72. If you align the operands, they're easier to read. For each operand, you code its name, then its value; the value is enclosed within parentheses.

BASIC AMS FUNCTIONS

This section shows you how to use AMS to define a user catalog, a data space, and clusters for all three kinds of VSAM files. All use the DEFINE command. I want you to realize, though, that my examples are simple. Since DEFINE has dozens of operands for a variety of specialized functions, you can also code commands of great complexity. If you need to use functions other than the ones I describe, you should refer to our book *VSAM Access Method Services and Application Programming* or VSE/VSAM's *Using Commands and Macros.*

How to define a VSAM catalog

To define a VSAM catalog, you invoke AMS and supply either a DEFINE MASTERCATALOG or DEFINE USERCATALOG control statement. However, you'll probably never use the DEFINE MASTERCATALOG control statement because each installation has only one master catalog that's created before any other VSAM work is done. So if VSAM is operational on your system, the master catalog is already defined.

In contrast, you may have occasion to define a user catalog. If you feel inclined to do so, be sure to clear it with your shop's management. To define a user catalog, you invoke AMS and supply a DEFINE USER-CATALOG control statement. A simplified format of this statement is presented in figure 13-11.

The NAME operand lets you supply a name for the catalog that can be up to 44 characters long. Figure 13-12 presents the rules for forming VSAM names that apply not only to catalogs, but also to clusters

The DEFINE USERCATALOG control statement

```
DEFINE USERCATALOG  ( NAME       (catalog-name)

                      VOLUME     (volser)

                      [ORIGIN    (location)]

                     ┌DEDICATE              ┐
                     │CYLINDERS  (cylinders)│
                     ┤TRACKS     (tracks)   ├        )
                     │BLOCKS     (blocks)   │
                     └RECORDS    (records)  ┘
```

Explanation

catalog-name	The one- to 44-character name of the new catalog. The name must follow VSAM naming rules. (See figure 13-12.)
volser	The volume serial number of the volume on which the catalog will reside.
location	Relative track number (for CKD units) or block number (for FBA units) of the starting location of the catalog.
DEDICATE	Specifies that all the available space on the volume is to be dedicated to the new catalog, and subsequent VSAM allocations will be made from that space.
cylinders tracks blocks records	The number of units of storage to be allocated to the catalog.

Figure 13-11   The DEFINE USERCATALOG control statement

and cluster components. And figure 13-13 shows you how to avoid some common errors when you form a VSAM name.

The VOLUME operand specifies the volume serial number of the DASD unit that will contain the user catalog. Remember that only one catalog may reside on a volume. Once you've identified the volume that will contain the user catalog, you have to indicate how large the catalog will be and where on the volume it will go. The other operands in figure 13-11 let you do that.

The simplest way to locate and allocate space to a user catalog is to code the DEDICATE operand. DEDICATE means that all of the space not in use on the volume will be owned by the catalog, even though the catalog requires only a small part of it. The space the catalog owns but doesn't use is then available for other VSAM files. In this case, VSAM determines the size of the catalog and locates it for you. If you code DEDICATE, you can't code the other space allocation operands

Length	1 to 44 characters
Characters	The 26 letters (A-Z) The 10 digits (0-9) The 3 national charcters (@, #, and $) The hyphen (-) The 12-0 overpunch
Segments	VSAM names with more than eight characters must be broken into segments that each contain from one to eight characters. Separate segments with periods.
First character	The first character of a VSAM name and of all segments within a name must be a letter or a national character.
Last character	The last character in a VSAM name may not be a period.

Figure 13-12   Rules for forming VSAM names

Invalid VSAM names

ACCOUNTS.RECEIVABLE.USER.CATALOG
  (Second segment too long.)

AR.TRANS.1984
  (Third segment starts with a digit.)

AR.TRANS.MAY + APR.YEAR1984
  (Third segment contains
  an invalid character.)

INVMAST.
  (Name ends with a period.)

ARCHIVE.GL.TRANS.FILE.7
  (Fourth segment starts
  with a digit.)

Valid VSAM names

ACCOUNTS.RECEIVBL.USER.CATALOG

AR.TRANS.YEAR1984
AR.TRANS84

AR.TRANS.APRIL.MAY.YEAR1984
AR.TRANS.APR-84.MAY-84

INVMAST

ARCHIVE.GL.TRANS.FILE.#7
ARCHIVE.GL.TRANS.FILE7
ARCHIVE.GL.TRANS.FILE.NO7

Figure 13-13   Invalid VSAM names with valid alternatives

(CYLINDERS, TRACKS, BLOCKS, or RECORDS), nor can you code the ORIGIN operand.

  To allocate an explicit amount of space to a user catalog, you code one of the other space operands. If the volume is an FBA device, you can specify the number of blocks the catalog will use with the BLOCKS operand. If the catalog will reside on a CKD volume, you can specify how large it should be with either the CYLINDERS or TRACKS operand. For either type of DASD, you can specify how many records the

```
// JOB      DEFUC
// EXEC     IDCAMS,SIZE=AUTO
           DEFINE USERCATALOG (NAME   (AR.USER.CATALOG) -
                               VOLUME (SYSWK3) -
                               ORIGIN (11616) -
                               BLOCKS (704))
/*
/&
```

Figure 13-14   AMS job to define a user catalog

catalog should contain with the RECORDS operand. Each catalog record requires 512 bytes.

Before you use any of these operands to specify the size of a new user catalog, you should determine how large that catalog should be. Usually, a systems designer decides on the proper size for the catalog. Then, it's no problem for you to code the AMS job to create it. However, if you have to decide for yourself how large the catalog should be, the situation is more complex since the amount of space a catalog requires varies depending on how many entries it will contain and what they are. Calculating catalog space requirements is a systems programming function that's beyond the scope of this topic. For more information, consult *Using Commands and Macros*.

If you code an AMS job with the DEFINE USERCATALOG control statement and you include NAME, VOLUME, and one of CYLINDERS, TRACKS, BLOCKS, or RECORDS, VSAM will decide where on the volume to create the catalog. VSAM searches for the first available extent on the volume that's large enough to contain the catalog. If you want to control where VSAM locates the catalog, you have to code the ORIGIN operand.

What you code for ORIGIN depends on the kind of DASD the catalog will reside on; it's the same as what you'd code for the location operand on an EXTENT statement. For a CKD device, you code the relative track number where the catalog will begin. For an FBA unit, you code the block number where the catalog will begin.

Frankly, coding an AMS job to create a user catalog isn't as hard as this description might make you think. The job in figure 13-14 is an example; its contents are straightforward. It creates a user catalog named AR.USER.CATALOG on SYSWK3, an FBA unit. The catalog begins at block 11616 and uses 704 blocks.

For VSAM performance reasons, the starting position of a catalog on an FBA device must be on a cylinder boundary. That means the origin value must be a multiple of 352 for a 3310 or a multiple of 744 for a 3370. Similarly, the size operand (BLOCKS) must be a multiple of one of those values. In the example in figure 13-14, the space occupied by the new user catalog begins at block 11616 (the 33rd cylinder on the pack) and uses 704 blocks (two 352-block cylinders). This is one

```
// JOB      DEFSPACE
// EXEC     IDCAMS,SIZE=AUTO
           DEFINE SPACE (ORIGIN  (12320) -
                         BLOCKS  (8800) -
                         VOLUMES (SYSWK3)) -
                  CATALOG         (AR.USER.CATALOG)
/*
/&
```

Figure 13-15   AMS job to define a VSAM space

of the rare cases in which you have to be concerned with the cylinder and track organization of an FBA DASD.

To define a catalog on a CKD volume, you code a relative track number for the ORIGIN operand, just as on an EXTENT statement for a file. For a catalog, the relative track number should be the first track on a cylinder. Again, that's for performance reasons.

After you've defined a user catalog with a job like the one in figure 13-14, you still can't put VSAM files on the volume. First, you have to define VSAM data space on it. To do so, you execute AMS and supply a DEFINE SPACE control statement. (If you define a catalog and specify DEDICATE in your AMS job, that causes space to be defined automatically.)

How to define a VSAM data space

Figure 13-15 is a simple job stream to define a VSAM data space owned by the catalog created by the job in figure 13-14. This job uses a DEFINE SPACE control statement, illustrated in figure 13-16.

The operands of DEFINE SPACE are much like those of DEFINE USERCATALOG. Both control statements specify a location and a volume. The difference is that while the job to define the user catalog specifies the new catalog's name, the job to define the data space names the catalog that will own the space (the CATALOG operand). The data space itself doesn't have a name you supply. Notice in figure 13-15 that there's no need for a DLBL or EXTENT statement for the master catalog, the user catalog, or the data space. VSAM manages that for you, as long as the label data for the master catalog is stored as a standard label.

Figure 13-17 shows a segment of a VTOC listing for the volume SYSWK3 produced after the user catalog and data space were defined by the jobs in figures 13-14 and 13-15. This only shows the two VTOC entries for those VSAM items. If you compare the extent information in the VTOC listing with the ORIGIN and BLOCKS operands in figures 13-14 and 13-15, you'll see they agree. So those areas of DASD storage are in use. And they're current too, as you can tell from the expiration dates of both: 99/366.

The DEFINE SPACE control statement

```
DEFINE SPACE        ( [ORIGIN        (location)]

                    ⎧DEDICATE                 ⎫
                    ⎪CYLINDERS     (cylinders)⎪
                    ⎨TRACKS        (tracks)   ⎬
                    ⎪BLOCKS        (blocks)   ⎪
                    ⎩RECORDS       (records)  ⎭

                    VOLUMES       (volser[ volser...]))

        [CATALOG                   (catalog-name)]
```

Explanation

location	Relative track number (for CKD units) or block number (for FBA units) of the starting location of the space.
DEDICATE	Specifies that all the available space on the volume is to be used for the new VSAM space.
cylinders tracks blocks records	The number of units of storage to be allocated to the space.
volser	The volume serial number(s) of the volume(s) to contain the VSAM space.
catalog-name	Name of the catalog that will own the space.

Figure 13-16   The DEFINE SPACE control statement

However, that's just about the limit of what VSE can tell you about these two data spaces. Notice the names; they don't make much sense. You can't tell from the VTOC listing that the extent beginning at block 11616 is AR.USER.CATALOG, nor can you tell what the other extent is for. Several VSAM files can reside within that one data space, but regardless of its contents, VSE looks at it simply as one extent.

How to define a
VSAM cluster

To create a VSAM file, you have to define its cluster with the AMS DEFINE CLUSTER control statement. Just what you need to code on the DEFINE CLUSTER control statement depends on the kind of VSAM data set the cluster is for (ESDS, KSDS, or RRDS) and on the characteristics of the file.

```
RRN- 15 FORMAT 1 DSF  SER NUM-SYSWK3                LENGTHS              DATES        SYSTEM      EXTENT INFORMATION
------------------------FILE IDENT-------------  KEY BLOCK   RCD     CREATE   EXPIRE    IDENT    SEQ TYPE    LOW   HIGH
                                                 ------------------  ------------------          --------------------
Z9999992.VSAMDSPC.T98528CF.T651F500                                 0  0   99 366  IBMDOSVS    0 PRIME  12320  21119


RRN-  5 FORMAT 1 DSF  SER NUM-SYSWK3                LENGTHS              DATES        SYSTEM      EXTENT INFORMATION
------------------------FILE IDENT-------------  KEY BLOCK   RCD     CREATE   EXPIRE    IDENT    SEQ TYPE    LOW   HIGH
                                                 ------------------  ------------------          --------------------
Z9999994.VSAMDSPC.T98528C3.T0C05F00                                 0  0   99 366  IBMDOSVS    0 PRIME  11616  12319
```

Figure 13-17 Partial VTOC listing showing entries for a VSAM catalog and a VSAM space

The DEFINE CLUSTER control statement

```
DEFINE CLUSTER      ( NAME                 (cluster-name)

                    [VOLUMES              (volser[volser...])]

                    {CYLINDERS            (primary[ secondary])}
                    {TRACKS               (primary[ secondary])}
                    {BLOCKS               (primary[ secondary])}
                    {RECORDS              (primary[ secondary])}

                    [RECORDSIZE           (averec maxrec)]

                    [{FOR                 (days)}]
                    [{TO                  (date)}]

                    [{REUSE   }]
                    [{NOREUSE }]

                    [{INDEXED    }]
                    [{NONINDEXED }]
                    [{NUMBERED   }]

                    [RECORDFORMAT         (format[(logical-rec-size)])]

                    [FREESPACE            (cipercent[ capercent])]

                    [KEYS                 (keylen offset)] )

        [DATA       ( [NAME               (data-comp-name)]
                      [VOLUMES            (volser[ volser...])] )]

        [INDEX      ( [NAME               (index-comp-name)]
                      [VOLUMES            (volser[ volser...])] )]

        [CATALOG                          (catalog-name)]
```

Figure 13-18   The DEFINE CLUSTER control statement (part 1 of 2)

A VSAM cluster is a logical structure that contains all the physical components of a VSAM file. For an ESDS and an RRDS, there's only the data component. Even so, two catalog entries are created for the file: one for the cluster itself and another for the data component. For a KSDS, there are three catalog entries: one each for the cluster, the data component, and the index component.

Figure 13-18 is a simplified version of the DEFINE CLUSTER control statement. As you can see, DEFINE CLUSTER is more complex than either DEFINE SPACE or DEFINE USERCATALOG. And the complete format, which you can see in VSE/VSAM's *Using Commands and Macros*, is even more complicated than the one in figure 13-18. The shaded operands are used only to define a KSDS cluster.

Explanation

cluster-name	The name of the cluster being defined. The name must follow VSAM naming rules.
volser	The volume serial number of the unit to contain the cluster, data component, or index component.
primary	The primary space allocation for the cluster, expressed in cylinders, tracks, blocks, or records.
secondary	The secondary space allocation for the cluster, expressed in cylinders, tracks, blocks, or records.
averec	The average length, in bytes, of the records in the file.
maxrec	The length, in bytes, of the longest record in the file.
days	The number of days (from 0 to 9999) the file is to be retained.
date	The date in the format yyddd (where yy is the year and ddd is the day) when the file is to expire.
REUSE	Specifies that the file is to be reusable.
NOREUSE	Specifies that the file is not to be reusable. This is the default.
INDEXED	Specifies that the file is a KSDS. This is the default.
NONINDEXED	Specifies that the file is an ESDS.
NUMBERED	Specifies that the file is an RRDS.
RECORDFORMAT	RECORDFORMAT is used only to define a cluster for a SAM ESDS. Refer to the next topic for details.
cipercent	The percentage of space to be reserved for added records in each control interval.
capercent	The percentage of space to be reserved for added records in each control area.
keylen	For a KSDS only, keylen specifies the length, in bytes, of the key field.
offset	For a KSDS only, offset specifies the displacement, in bytes, of the key field from the beginning of the record. (The offset is 0 if the key field is the first field in the record.)
data-comp-name	The name for the data component of the file.
index-comp-name	The name for the index component of the file.
catalog-name	The name of the catalog that will own the file.

Figure 13-18   The DEFINE CLUSTER control statement (part 2 of 2)

Notice that this control statement consists of sections called CLUS-TER, DATA, INDEX, and CATALOG. CLUSTER, DATA, and INDEX relate to the catalog entries that will be created for the cluster; CATALOG names the catalog that owns the cluster. By coding operands subordinate to CLUSTER, DATA, and INDEX, you can specify that values apply only to the data component (under DATA), only to the INDEX component of a KSDS (under INDEX), or to both (under CLUSTER). Although figure 13-18 doesn't indicate it, you can code most of the operands available at the CLUSTER level at the DATA or INDEX level as well. For instance, to fine-tune a running VSAM system, you might want to make different specifications for the data and index components of a cluster. At the level of this book, though, the only operands I want you to be aware of at the DATA and INDEX levels are NAME and VOLUMES.

The NAME operand   When you code a value for the NAME operand at the CLUSTER level, that name applies only to the cluster entry. Then, if you don't specify otherwise, VSAM creates a name for the data component (and, for a KSDS, for the index component) that will be long and cryptic. As a result, you'll be better able to manage your VSAM files if you assign meaningful names to them at the DATA and INDEX levels as well as at the CLUSTER level. You'll see examples of this later in this topic.

The VOLUMES operand   When you code the VOLUMES operand at the cluster level, you name the volume or volumes (up to 123) where the cluster will reside. If you don't code VOLUMES at the DATA and INDEX levels, VSAM decides where to locate the parts of the file. For performance reasons, though, you may want to locate the index and data components of a KSDS on different volumes. In this case, you specify the appropriate volume serial numbers on VOLUMES operands at the DATA and INDEX levels.

Space allocation and the RECORDSIZE operand   The size allocation operands (CYLINDERS, TRACKS, BLOCKS, and RECORDS) should be familiar to you from DEFINE SPACE and DEFINE USERCATALOG. For a cluster, you can specify both a primary and a secondary space allocation. The primary allocation is the space you expect the file to use. If the size of the file exceeds the primary allocation, VSAM allocates up to 15 additional extents per volume according to the secondary allocation you specify.

If you use the RECORDS operand in DEFINE CLUSTER, you also have to specify the size of the records that will make up the file by coding the RECORDSIZE operand. You code two values for RECORDSIZE: the size of the average record and the size of the largest record. So to specify that a file contains records with an average length of 80 characters, but with some that are as large as 160 characters, you code

```
RECORDSIZE (80 160)
```

Although it's an optional operand, you should always code RECORD-SIZE. And in an AMS job to define a cluster for an RRDS, the average and maximum record sizes must be equal.

The TO and FOR operands   You can code TO or FOR to specify how long the file you're defining should remain current. (You can't code both in the same DEFINE CLUSTER statement.) If you code neither, the cluster can be deleted at any time. If you code FOR, the value you include is the number of days (from 0 to 9999) that the file should be retained. If you code TO, the value you include is an expiration date in the format yyddd (with no slash). The yy is the year (from 00 to 99) and the ddd is the day (from 001 to 366).

The REUSE and NOREUSE operands   In the last topic, I described reusable VSAM files when I showed you how to code the DISP operand on the DLBL statement. To create a reusable file, you code REUSE in the job stream that defines the cluster. Omitting REUSE or explicitly coding NOREUSE makes the new file non-reusable.

The file-type operand   To indicate what type of cluster you're creating, you code INDEXED, NONINDEXED, or NUMBERED. Code INDEXED to define a KSDS, NONINDEXED to define an ESDS, or NUMBERED to define an RRDS. You may only code one of these operands in a DEFINE CLUSTER statement. The default is INDEXED.

The KSDS operands   When you define a cluster for a key-sequenced file, you should code two other operands: KEYS and FREESPACE. The KEYS operand specifies how long the key field is and where in the record it's located. The location is the key field's displacement in bytes from the beginning of the record. For example, if the key is four bytes long and occupies the first four bytes of the record, you would code this operand:

```
KEYS (4 0)
```

The FREESPACE operand lets you control the amount of free space within the data component of the KSDS. You can specify free space at one or two levels by coding one or two values on the operand. To specify the amount of space within each control interval that's to be reserved for insertions, you code a percentage as the first value for the operand. In addition, you can indicate that a certain percentage of the control intervals in each control area are to be left empty. For instance,

```
// JOB      DEFESDS
// EXEC     IDCAMS,SIZE=AUTO
           DEFINE CLUSTER (NAME        (AR.TRANS) -
                          VOLUMES      (SYSWK3) -
                          RECORDS      (500) -
                          RECORDSIZE   (256 384) -
                          NONINDEXED) -
                DATA    (NAME          (AR.TRANS.DATA)) -
                CATALOG               (AR.USER.CATALOG)
/*
/&
```

Figure 13-19   AMS job to define a cluster for an ESDS

you code

```
FREESPACE (30 20)
```

to specify that 30 percent of each control interval and 20 percent of each control area are to be left empty.

Since the system default is to allow no free space, you're wise to provide some additional space if additions to the file are likely. Also, you should be aware that the free space you request is not added to the space you allocate to the file; it's taken from it. So if you provide for free space, be sure to allocate enough space for the file to accommodate it and the initial number of records you expect. Otherwise, you defeat the purpose of providing free space.

The CATALOG operand   The last operand in figure 13-18, CATALOG, lets you specify the catalog that will own the cluster you're defining. If you omit it, the job catalog in effect when you execute AMS will own the file, and if no job catalog is in effect, the master catalog will own it.

How to define a cluster for an ESDS or an RRDS   Figure 13-19 shows a job to define a cluster for an ESDS. As you can see, it specifies NONINDEXED. The space allocation is in terms of records, since this is the most practical way to request space for a VSAM file. To specify space for a file in terms of cylinders, tracks, or blocks means you have to calculate what's adequate. When you use the RECORDS operand, VSAM does the calculation for you.

In this case, the file will have room for 500 records. The records average 256 characters, but may be as long as 384 characters. The file is to reside in VSAM space on SYSWK3, and it will be owned by AR.USER.CATALOG. The cluster as a whole is called AR.TRANS, and its data component is called AR.TRANS.DATA.

To name clusters and components, I recommend you adopt this standard: Add .DATA to the cluster name to form the name of the data

```
// JOB      DEFRRDS
// EXEC     IDCAMS,SIZE=AUTO
         DEFINE CLUSTER (NAME          (AR.TRANS) -
                        VOLUMES        (SYSWK3) -
                        RECORDS        (500) -
                        RECORDSIZE     (384 384) -
                        NUMBERED) -
              DATA      (NAME          (AR.TRANS.DATA)) -
              CATALOG                  (AR.USER.CATALOG)
/*
/&
```

Figure 13-20   AMS job to define a cluster for an RRDS

```
// JOB      DEFKSDS
// EXEC     IDCAMS,SIZE=AUTO
         DEFINE CLUSTER (NAME          (AR.TRANS) -
                        VOLUMES        (SYSWK3) -
                        RECORDS        (500) -
                        RECORDSIZE     (256 384) -
                        FREESPACE      (10 10) -
                        KEYS           (5 0)) -
              DATA      (NAME          (AR.TRANS.DATA)) -
              INDEX     (NAME          (AR.TRANS.INDEX)) -
              CATALOG                  (AR.USER.CATALOG)
/*
/&
```

Figure 13-21   AMS job to define a cluster for a KSDS

component. (Similarly, add .INDEX to the cluster name to form the name of the index component of a KSDS.)

To define a cluster for an RRDS, you code a job like the one in figure 13-20. In fact, to create AR.TRANS as an RRDS, only two changes to the job stream in figure 13-19 are required. In figure 13-20, I specified NUMBERED instead of NONINDEXED, and I changed the average record size from 256 to 384. That's because all the record slots in an RRDS must be the same size. In this case, some space will be wasted in record slots that contain records shorter than the full slot size.

How to define a cluster for a KSDS   It's only slightly more complicated to define a KSDS. As you can see in figure 13-21, I coded the KEYS operand and specified that the key is five characters long and begins at offset zero from the beginning of the record (the first byte).

I also specified that 10 percent of each control interval should be left empty for additions and that 10 percent of each control area should be left empty. Finally, I indicated that the data and index components of the file should be named AR.TRANS.DATA and AR.TRANS.INDEX.

DISCUSSION   With this background, you should be able to code jobs to define catalogs, spaces, and clusters. And if you have an application that requires advanced functions of DEFINE for these VSAM elements, you should be able to find what you need to know in our book *VSAM: Access Method Services and Application Programming* or in the IBM manuals. In chapter 18, I'll show you how to use other AMS utility functions to maintain catalog entries and to copy and print files.

Terminology   functional command
modal command

Objective   Given specifications for a VSAM user catalog, data space, or cluster, code an AMS job to define it.

TOPIC 4   VSAM compatibility features

This topic describes two VSAM features you might need to use in your shop. Both are designed to allow long-time DOS users with large investments in application programs that use native VSE access methods to continue to use those programs and at the same time take advantage of some of the facilities of VSAM. They're the *VSAM Space Management for SAM feature* and the *ISAM Interface Program (IIP)*. An additional use for the VSAM Space Management for SAM feature is to define and store VSE private libraries in VSAM space. You'll learn more about that process in chapter 15.

VSAM SPACE MANAGEMENT FOR SAM

The VSAM Space Management for SAM feature lets users define and process SAM files within VSAM data space. Such a SAM file is called a *SAM ESDS*. Although the file resides in VSAM space, programs that process it don't have to be modified to treat it like a VSAM file.

There are several advantages of storing a SAM file in VSAM space. First, you don't have to worry about finding free space on a DASD unit when you create a SAM ESDS. All you have to do is request a quantity of space and VSAM decides where to put the file. Second, the job control statements you code to process a SAM ESDS are simpler than the ones you would code to process the same SAM file. As with other VSAM files, you can omit ASSGN and EXTENT statements when you're processing a SAM ESDS. Third, when you use a SAM ESDS, you don't have to consider the organization of the DASD unit where the file will reside; VSAM manages that. As a result, a SAM ESDS has a device independence that a SAM file doesn't have. Finally, you can use AMS to perform utility functions on a SAM ESDS.

How to create a SAM ESDS

You can create a SAM ESDS in two ways. First, you can code an AMS job with DEFINE CLUSTER to define the new file explicitly. Second, you can create one implicitly by (1) providing enough information in a job stream to define the file and (2) invoking a program that opens it. When you create a SAM ESDS implicitly, however, it will be a reusable file. So if you want to create a non-reusable SAM ESDS, you have to define it explicitly.

Explicit definition   All you have to do to define a SAM ESDS explicitly is code a DEFINE CLUSTER job similar to the one to define a VSAM ESDS in figure 13-19. There are a couple of differences between the two types of jobs, as you can see in figure 13-22. This is a job to define a SAM ESDS cluster for a file with 256-byte records stored four per block.

```
// JOB     DEFSESDS
// EXEC    IDCAMS,SIZE=AUTO
         DEFINE CLUSTER (NAME          (AR.SAM.TRANS) -
                        VOLUMES        (SYSWK3) -
                        RECORDS        (500) -
                        RECORDSIZE     (1024 1024) -
                        RECORDFORMAT   (FIXBLK(256)) -
                        NONINDEXED) -
              DATA      (NAME          (AR.SAM.TRANS.DATA)) -
              CATALOG                  (AR.USER.CATALOG)
/*
/&
```

Figure 13-22   AMS job to define a cluster for a SAM ESDS explicitly

First, notice the RECORDSIZE operand. It specifies the physical size of the record. In figure 13-22, that's 1024 (four 256-byte records). This is different from the value you'd code for an equivalent standard ESDS, so don't let it confuse you.

Next, look at the RECORDFORMAT operand. On it, you code one of the values in figure 13-23. In the job in figure 13-22, the SAM ESDS I'm defining has fixed-length blocked records, so I had to code the logical record size (256 bytes). That's not required for an unblocked SAM ESDS or for one with variable-length records. (You'll code NOCIFORMAT on the RECORDFORMAT operand when you define libraries in VSAM space.)

Implicit definition   You can also define a SAM ESDS implicitly without coding an AMS DEFINE CLUSTER job, but it must be a reusable file. To define a SAM ESDS implicitly, you have to supply all the information required to define the file in its DLBL statement, as in figure 13-24. Here, I coded VSAM for the codes operand, and I used two new operands: RECORDS and RECSIZE.

For RECORDS, you code the number of logical records the file will contain. VSAM uses that value as the primary space allocation for the new SAM ESDS, and it uses 20 percent of it as the secondary allocation value. RECSIZE is the average logical record size. In figure 13-24, the primary space allocation for the SAM ESDS is 200 logical records, and the average size of a logical record is 256 bytes. The only time you use the RECORDS and RECSIZE operands of DLBL is when you're defining a SAM ESDS.

When you define a SAM ESDS implicitly, you have to code an EXTENT statement that specifies the volume that will contain the file. In figure 13-24, that's SYSWK3. The volume SYSWK3 must contain VSAM space owned by the file's catalog.

Record length	Blocked	RECORDFORMAT operand value
Fixed	No	(FIXUNB) or (F)
Fixed	Yes	(FIXBLK(logical-record-size)) or (FB(logical-record-size))
Variable	No	(VARUNB) or (V)
Variable	Yes	(VARBLK) or (VB)
Non-VSAM	No	(NOCIFORMAT)

Figure 13-23   Values for the RECORDFORMAT operand of the DEFINE CLUSTER control statement

```
// DLBL      IJSYSUC,'AR.USER.CATALOG',,VSAM
// DLBL      SAMWORK,'SAM.WORK.FILE',,VSAM,RECORDS=200,RECSIZE=256
// EXTENT    ,SYSWK3
```

Figure 13-24   JCL to define a SAM ESDS implicitly

How to process a
SAM ESDS

To process a SAM ESDS, the JCL you code is just what you use for any other VSAM file. The programs you run must be invoked with an EXEC statement that specifies SIZE=AUTO, even though they appear to use SAM rather than VSAM as their access method. (Remember, the application program is still written to process a SAM file.) If you're working with a reusable SAM ESDS, you can use the DISP operand of DLBL to control the file's disposition when it's opened and closed. If you need to, refer back to topic 2 to refresh your memory on DISP.

**THE ISAM
INTERFACE
PROGRAM**

If you work in a shop that hasn't completely converted from ISAM to VSAM, it's likely that many of your application programs still are written to process ISAM files. Since reprogramming is one of the greatest expenses in an ISAM to VSAM conversion, it may take years to complete. To make the transition from ISAM to VSAM easier, IBM includes, as part of VSAM, an interface program that lets application programs written to process ISAM files access and manipulate VSAM key-sequenced data sets instead. It's called the ISAM Interface Program, or IIP.

Although you don't have to change application programs that were written to use ISAM files when you use the IIP, you do have to change two other things. First, you have to convert your old ISAM files to VSAM key-sequenced data sets. And second, you have to change the JCL in jobs that process those files from ISAM to VSAM format.

How to convert an ISAM file to a VSAM KSDS

Converting an ISAM file to a VSAM KSDS is a two step process. First, you define the KSDS cluster with an AMS job like the one in figure 13-21. Then, you load data into the file. You can write an application program to convert an existing ISAM file to a KSDS, or you can use the REPRO function of AMS. Still another way is to use the utility program VSE/DITTO.

Regardless of the method you use to convert the file, if the original file contains logically deleted records, you don't want them copied into the KSDS. So if you have an existing program to reorganize the ISAM file, run it just before you convert the file.

How to code a job stream that uses the IIP

To process a VSAM KSDS with an application program that uses ISAM, all you have to do is code the JCL that defines the file in VSAM format. Figure 13-25 shows how two VSAM DLBL statements (one for the KSDS and the other for its catalog) can replace one DLBL, one ASSGN, and three EXTENT statements for an equivalent ISAM file. When you execute the application program, VSE opens the file expecting to find an ISAM file. When it finds a KSDS instead, it automatically starts the IIP. Notice in figure 13-25 that the EXEC statement in the job that processes the KSDS specifies SIZE=AUTO.

DISCUSSION

Both of the compatibility features in this topic serve as temporary substitutes as you convert your application programs to VSAM. However, VSAM Space Management for SAM can have some long-term applications. For example, some IBM program products (like the language translators) use SAM files, and you can't change them. However, you can define their work files as SAM ESDS's to take advantage of VSAM's space management services.

The IIP, on the other hand, should be used only for temporary compatibility since the IIP doesn't eliminate all of the inefficiencies of ISAM file processing. For example, deletions from a VSAM KSDS processed by the IIP work as they did under ISAM. In other words, records are deleted logically, not physically, so they continue to use file space after they're deleted. So if you're developing new applications, you shouldn't use the IIP.

A job to process an ISAM file

```
// JOB       AR8700
// LIBDEF    PHASE,SEARCH=(USRSLE.ACCTRCV)
// ASSGN     SYS006,SYSLST
// ASSGN     SYS020,291
// DLBL      OPNITEM,'OPEN.ITEM.FILE',0,ISE
// EXTENT    SYS020,CKD002,4,0,1410,1
// EXTENT    SYS020,CKD002,4,1,1411,9
// EXTENT    SYS020,CKD002,1,2,1420,70
// EXTENT    SYS020,CKD002,2,3,1490,20
// EXEC      AR8700
/&
```

A job executing the same program to process a VSAM KSDS

```
// JOB       AR8700
// LIBDEF    PHASE,SEARCH=(USRSLE.ACCTRCV)
// ASSGN     SYS006,SYSLST
// DLBL      IJSYSUC,'AR.USER.CATALOG',,VSAM
// DLBL      OPNITEM,'OPEN.ITEM.FILE',,VSAM
// EXEC      AR8700,SIZE=AUTO
/&
```

Figure 13-25   Jobs that execute the same program to process an ISAM file and a VSAM KSDS

Terminology   VSAM Space Management for SAM feature
ISAM Interface Program
IIP
SAM ESDS

Objectives   1. Code an AMS job to create a SAM ESDS explicitly.

2. Code a VSE job stream to create a SAM ESDS implicitly.

3. Code a VSE job stream that uses the DISP operand of the DLBL statement to process a reusable SAM ESDS.

4. Given a job stream that processes an ISAM file, change the job so it can process the same file converted to a VSAM KSDS using the ISAM Interface Program.

Section 5

Program development and library maintenance

In this section, I'll show you what you need to know about program development on VSE systems. The first chapter in this section, chapter 14, has two topics. The first shows you how to code job streams that use the VSE language translators and the linkage editor. The second shows you how to translate and test programs interactively using ICCF. Then, chapter 15 shows you how to use the VSE Librarian program. The first of its two topics introduces the Librarian program and its commands and teaches you how to print directory listings, how to print or punch individual members, and how to maintain VSE libraries. And the second topic presents some advanced Librarian commands.

Chapter 14

How to develop programs under VSE

In this chapter, you'll learn how to use VSE facilities as you do program development work. That doesn't mean this chapter teaches you how to code source language programs, but you will learn how to translate source programs into object modules and how to convert those object modules into phases you can execute. Topic 1 shows you how to create VSE job streams for program development. It covers the JCL and concepts you need to know to use the language translators and the linkage editor for most program development tasks. Topic 2 shows you how to develop programs interactively using ICCF. When you develop programs interactively, you don't have to code and submit jobs streams for execution. Instead, you issue commands at a terminal to perform program development tasks.

TOPIC 1   How to develop programs in batch

Figure 14-1 illustrates the sequence of steps in developing an application program on a VSE system. As you can see, the process has three steps: (1) language translation, (2) link editing, and (3) test execution of the application program. This topic shows you how to code job streams to perform the language translation and link editing steps. The JCL requirements for the test execution step depend on the program you're developing; you should be able to apply the JCL knowledge you've already picked up from this book to code this JCL.

Program-development job stream types

As you develop programs, you typically use a *translate, link, and go job*. This kind of job includes the statements necessary to run one of the language translators to convert your source program into an object module. In addition, it contains statements to invoke the linkage editor to convert the object module into an executable phase and statements to execute the phase. After you execute a translate, link, and go job, you evaluate the output of the test execution to determine if your program has logical errors. If it does, you correct them and run the job again. You'll see two ways to code a translate, link, and go job in this topic.

Because you may run the same translate, link, and go job several times before a program is error-free, you don't want to add the phase produced by each job to a sublibrary. As a result, the phase created in a translate, link, and go job is temporary; that is, it's only retained for the duration of the job.

After you're satisfied your program contains no logical errors, you store it permanently in a sublibrary. To do that, you execute a *translate and catalog job*. So I'll also show you an example of that kind of job in this topic.

Of course, depending on what you need to do, you may use other types of jobs as you develop programs. If you want to run the same version of a program repeatedly during testing, it's inefficient to use the translate, link, and go job for each run. Instead, you may want to run a translate and catalog job first to store the program in a sublibrary, then run an *execute-only job* to invoke the program as many times as necessary to test it thoroughly. Throughout this book, you've seen examples of execute-only jobs.

Don't think, though, that each time you want to run a different kind of program development job you'll have to code a new job stream from scratch. On the contrary, once you've coded one of each type, you'll only have to make minor modifications to them to use them for different programs. And the examples in this topic are models you can use for your first program development job streams. Before I present the model job streams, I want to describe in detail the two main steps in a program development job stream: the language translation step and the link edit step.

The language translation step

The name of the language translation step depends on the language translator you're using. If you use one of the high-level language translators (COBOL, PL/I, RPG II, or FORTRAN), this step is called the *compile step*, or a *compilation*. If you use the assembler, it's called an *assembly*.

As figure 14-1 shows, the primary input to a language translator is a source program, and its primary output is an object module. However, the language translation step can involve other elements. In addition to processing the source program as input, a language translator may also accept copy books stored in VSE sublibraries. And in addition to producing an object module as output, each language translator can produce a listing that contains many items of information about the source program.

Source program   The source program contains the instructions you want the program to execute, plus definitions of the data items the program processes. It's written using the conventions of one of the VSE-supported programming languages, and you use the translator for that language to convert the source program into an object module. For example, if you write a source program in PL/I, you use the PL/I compiler to convert it into an object module.

Source code is in card-image format. That means source programs consist of a series of 80-character records. The format of source program records varies depending on the programming language you use. As far as your JCL is concerned, the exact format of the source program records doesn't matter; you just need to know that they're in card format. Source program statements are in-line (SYSIPT) data in the job stream that invokes the language translator. Although the source program may be punched in cards, it's more likely that it will be stored on disk, probably in the ICCF library file.

Copy books   If the same segments of source code are used in several programs, it's efficient to store them in a sublibrary as a copy book. Then, your language translator can copy them into the source program at compile or assembly time. As you'll see in the next chapter, you use the VSE Librarian program to catalog copy books, and other source books, in sublibraries.

Record descriptions are among the most useful program elements to store in copy books because they're usually used without change in many programs. It would be a waste of time to have each programmer code the same description in his programs. In addition, each time a programmer codes a description, there's a chance for error. So copy books improve both programming efficiency and accuracy.

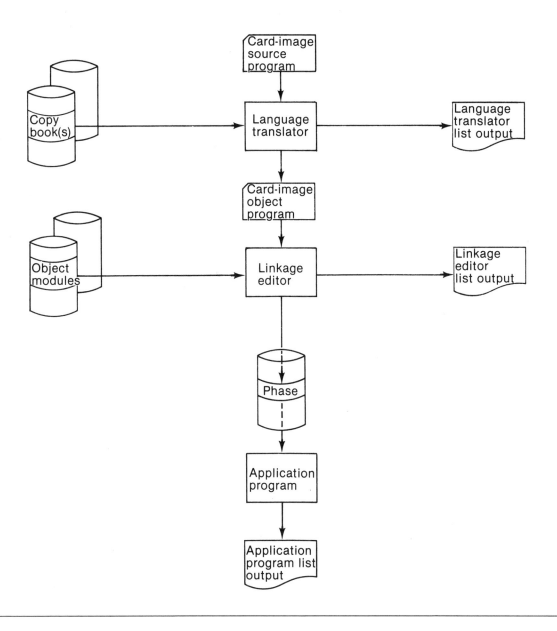

Figure 14-1   The program development process

Figure 14-2 shows how a copy book is used. The top part of the figure is a segment of a COBOL source program that includes a COPY statement for the member CUSTADR. The resulting source code is in the bottom of the figure. As you can see, it's as if the programmer had coded the record description directly in the source program. COPY is the statement you code in a COBOL, assembler, or RPG II program; %INCLUDE is the statement you code in PL/I.

Language translator listing Almost all the time, you'll want to produce a compiler (or assembler) listing when you translate a source program. The language translator listing can contain your source code, plus other information you will use as you test and debug your program. To get a language translator listing with a variety of components, you code appropriate values on the OPTION statement in your job stream. Chapter 5 introduced OPTION, and I'll give you more details about how to use it later in this topic.

Object module The primary output of a language translator is an object module. It's produced in card-image format, as figure 14-1 indicates. In some cases, you'll want the object module to be produced as actual punch output. For example, if you write a source program that's to be used as a subprogram by other application programs, you code a job that translates a source program and punches the object program. Then, you code a job that executes the VSE Librarian program to catalog the module into a sublibrary. (You'll learn how to do that in the next chapter.) It's also possible to include the object module for a subprogram directly in a job stream to be processed by the linkage editor, but you'll rarely need to do this.

In most cases, you'll simply want to execute the object module created by the translator so you can test it. You can't execute it directly, though, because it has to be converted into a phase first. To do that, you execute the linkage editor, which uses the object module in card-image format as input.

The link edit step

The linkage editor program (LNKEDT) converts an object module into a phase that can then be executed. The linkage editor can store the phase permanently or temporarily, depending on the options you code for the link edit step. I'll present those options in a moment.

The name of the linkage editor indicates two of its main functions. First, the linkage editor edits the object module so it's in an executable form. Second, if required, it can link separately compiled or assembled object modules together into a single phase. Usually, both steps are required when you develop a program in a high-level language. In addition, the linkage editor can catalog a phase into a sublibrary.

Editing relocatable object modules The instructions in an object module are in relocatable form. That means they reference storage addresses based on a starting address, or *load address*. However, in an object module, the load address isn't provided. The linkage editor provides the load address when it converts an object module into an executable phase. Usually, the load address is a *relative load address* that's set dynamically when the program is executed. Then, the program can run at any address rather than at a fixed address. The practical implication of this is that a phase created with a relative load address can run in any partition; it's not restricted to a particular partition because of addressing.

Source code

```
       .
       .
       .

    FD   CUSTADR
         LABEL RECORDS ARE STANDARD
         RECORD CONTAINS 90 CHARACTERS.
      ✷
      COPY CUSTADR.

       .
       .
       .
```

Source code after the compiler processes the COPY statement

```
       .
       .
       .

    FD   CUSTADR
         LABEL RECORDS ARE STANDARD
         RECORD CONTAINS 90 CHARACTERS.
      ✷
      COPY CUSTADR.
C     01   CUSTOMER-ADDRESS-RECORD.
C      ✷
C          05   CA-CUSTOMER-NUMBER          PIC X(5).
C          05   CA-CUSTOMER-NAME            PIC X(30).
C          05   CA-CUSTOMER-ADDRESS         PIC X(30).
C          05   CA-CUSTOMER-CITY            PIC X(18).
C          05   CA-CUSTOMER-STATE           PIC XX.
C          05   CA-CUSTOMER-ZIP-CODE        PIC X(5).

       .
       .
       .
```

Figure 14-2   Using a copy book in an application program

Linking object modules   The second function of the linkage editor is to combine two or more object modules into a single phase. If one object module contains references to others, they're treated as *unresolved references*. But the object module contains the information the linkage editor needs to resolve those references when it links it with other object modules.

When you develop a program in a high-level language, some functions are actually performed by *standard object modules* stored in a sublibrary. For example, a simple COBOL program can require several standard object modules in addition to the object module generated from your source program. When you link edit your program, its object module as well as required standard object modules are linked together. The standard object modules are supplied by IBM with the language translators.

It's also common to store user-written subroutines as object modules that the linkage editor can combine with calling programs. For example, common functions like editing a date or state code are often written as subprograms, converted by a language translator into object modules, and stored in a sublibrary. Then, many programmers can use those subroutines in the application programs they develop. All that's necessary is for the main program to contain the proper calling statements and for the linkage editor to link the modules together.

Cataloging program phases   After the linkage editor has processed one or more object modules to create a phase, that phase may be stored permanently in a sublibrary. So the third main function of the linkage editor is to catalog phases into sublibraries.

JCL to control the language translators

Now that you've learned a little about the input to and the output from the language translators and the linkage editor, I want to describe the JCL you need to know to control their operation. In this section, I'll describe the JCL considerations for the language translators. To run one of the language translators, all you have to do is code an EXEC statement that names the language translator program, then follow that EXEC with the source program statements.

Practically speaking, though, you need to do more than just invoke the language translator. For instance, you'll often want to exercise some degree of control over the output of the language translation process. And you'll want to specify that one or more sublibraries should supply copy books. To do that, you specify options for the language translation step.

Options and the language translators   What you have to do to get the language translator to work exactly as you want depends on the default values for the system standard options in effect on your system. To find out what they are, you can run a job like one of those in figure 14-3. Since both of these jobs invoke one of the language translators without specifying any overriding options, the result is that the language translator runs using the default options. Then, near the end of the job output is a list of the options in effect, as figure 14-3 shows.

Notice that more options are listed for the COBOL job than for the assembly job. That's because the COBOL compiler provides more options than the assembler. The assembler options are all set by the OPTION statement of VSE JCL, as are some of the COBOL options. The additional COBOL options are controlled by a special control statement processed by the COBOL compiler (the CBL statement). Although you'll see an example of the CBL statement later in this topic, I'm not

Job stream for assembler language

```
// JOB    LISTOPTS
// EXEC   ASSEMBLY
        .   ASSEMBLER LANGUAGE SOURCE PROGRAM
        .
/*
/&
```

Assembler output

. . .

OPTIONS FOR THIS ASSEMBLY - ALIGN, LIST, SXREF, NOLINK, RLD, NODECK, NOEDECK

. . .

Job stream for COBOL

```
// JOB    LISTOPTS
// EXEC   FCOBOL
        .   COBOL SOURCE PROGRAM
        .
/*
/&
```

COBOL compiler output

```
*OPTIONS IN EFFECT*  PMAP RELOC ADR = NONE   SPACING =     1    FLOW =      NONE
*OPTIONS IN EFFECT*  NOLISTX    QUOTE        SYM NOCATALR   LIST  NOLINK =   NOSTXIT    NOLIB
*OPTIONS IN EFFECT*  NOCLIST    FLAGW        ZWB NOSUPMAP   NOXREF ERRS      NOSXREF    NOOPT
*OPTIONS IN EFFECT*  NOSTATE    TRUNC        SEQ NOSYMDMP   NODECK NOVERB    NOSYNTAX   NOLVL
*OPTIONS IN EFFECT*  LANGLVL(2) NOCOUNT      ADV NOVERBSUM  NOVERBREF
*LISTER OPTIONS*     NONE
```

Figure 14-3 Sample jobs to determine current option defaults

going to describe the details of what you can use it for. Of course, if you develop programs in one of the languages that provides additional options, like COBOL or PL/I, you should know what those options are. To learn them, refer to the appropriate language reference manual.

Options that control listing output   LIST is the basic option you use to control the listing a language translator produces. If it's in effect, you get a source code listing, and if it's not, you don't. In addition to LIST, you can specify other options to control what the language translator listing contains. The top section of figure 14-4 presents the values you can code on the OPTION statement to do that.

The exact output each option causes to be produced varies depending on the language translator, but the figure indicates the content of each. Although your requirements may differ, the options you'll probably find most useful are LIST, ERRS, and XREF (or SXREF). LISTX and SYM can produce long listings that you may not use. However, if you find yourself with a debugging problem, they can be helpful.

Options that control object module output   The center section of figure 14-4 shows the values you can code on the OPTION statement to manage what the language translator does with the object module it produces. If the DECK option is in effect, the language translator produces the object module deck on SYSPCH. (This usually means that card output is routed into the POWER punch queue.) Although DECK is the standard default, it may have been overridden with STDOPT on your system. Unless you need an object module (most likely to catalog into a sublibrary), you should be sure NODECK is in effect before you execute one of the language translators. You're more likely to want to code one of the options that allow the object module to be link edited after the translation step: LINK or CATAL.

If you code either LINK or CATAL, the object module is written to SYSLNK, where the linkage editor can access it. (SYSLNK is a disk extent used as a work area by the linkage editor.) LINK implies that the phase the linkage editor produces from the object module should be stored only temporarily; CATAL implies that it should be cataloged permanently in a sublibrary. You usually use LINK when you're running translate, link, and go jobs to test a program; you use CATAL when testing is complete and you want to store the final phase.

Options that control copy books   To use copy books, you have to be sure that a sublibrary contains the books you want to use. As you learned in chapter 5, IBM system components use source books from specific sublibraries (C for COBOL, P for PL/I, or R for RPG II). The assembler, however, can use copy books from either sublibrary A or D. The last section in figure 14-4 shows the OPTION values that let you control the sublibraries that the assembler uses. (The E and F sublibraries are for edited macros.)

List output	LIST	(NOLIST)	Print a source code listing.
	ERRS	(NOERRS)	Print syntax errors detected in the source program.
	LISTX	(NOLISTX)	Print the object code (COBOL PMAP).
	SYM	(NOSYM)	Print the data definitions (COBOL DMAP).
	RLD	(NORLD)	Print the relocation dictionary (assembler only).
	{XREF SXREF}	(NOXREF)	Print a cross-reference listing of instructions and data names. (SXREF produces a sorted cross-reference listing.)
Object module output	DECK	(NODECK)	Write the object module on SYSPCH.
	LINK	(NOLINK)	Write the object module on SYSLNK and have the linkage editor convert it into a temporary phase.
	CATAL		Write the object module on SYSLNK and have the linkage editor convert it into a permanent (cataloged) phase.
Assembler copy book and edited macro input	{SUBLIB = AE		Use sublibraries A and E for copy books and edited macros.
	SUBLIB = DF}		Use sublibraries D and F for copy books and edited macros.

Figure 14-4   OPTION statement operands to control language translator and linkage editor functions

The sublibraries that contain the books you want to use must be specified in a sublibrary search chain. You should recall from chapter 5 that you set up a search chain for sublibraries with the LIBDEF statement. Just code either a single character library member type or SOURCE for the library type, SEARCH=, and from one to 15 sublibrary names inside parentheses. For instance

```
// LIBDEF  SOURCE,SEARCH=(USR1.AP2,USR3.AP3,USR2.AP4)
```

establishes a sublibrary search chain that consists of USR1.AP2, USR3.AP3, and USR2.AP4. The language translator searches those sublibraries in that order for members to be used in copy operations. As with LIBDEF in other situations, the library names you use must have already been defined with DLBL and EXTENT statements.

JCL to control the linkage editor

To invoke the linkage editor explicitly, you code an EXEC statement with the program name LNKEDT. Alternatively, you can code the GO operand on the EXEC statement that runs a language translator. In either case, you need to supply statements in your job stream to control the linkage editor. You need to be sure that the sublibraries the linkage editor will use are identified and that any required linkage editor control statements are included in the right positions.

JCL to control sublibrary usage by the linkage editor   When you run the linkage editor, you have to specify the sublibrary where the linkage editor will store the phase it produces. That's necessary only when the linkage editor is producing a permanent phase. To specify a sublibrary, code a LIBDEF statement with the CATALOG operand. For example,

```
// LIBDEF  PHASE,CATALOG=USR1.AP2
```

causes the linkage editor to store the phase it produces in USR1.AP2. When you code LIBDEF with CATALOG, you're not establishing a search chain; you're just naming the one sublibrary that will contain the new phase.

Additionally, if the linkage editor is to use any object modules stored in sublibraries, you must specify those sublibraries in a search chain. To establish this search chain for object modules, you code a statement like

```
// LIBDEF  OBJ,SEARCH=(USR1.AP2,USR3.AP3,USR2.AP4)
```

This causes the linkage editor to search USR1.AP2, USR3.AP3, and USR2.AP4 for the modules it requires.

The sublibraries that contain standard object modules will probably be identified in permanent search chains established during system start-up. In addition, the sublibraries that contain common user-written object modules should also be identified in permanent search chains. You'll only need to worry about setting up a search chain when the sublibraries that contain user-written object modules have not been previously identified.

Linkage editor control statements   In addition to specifying the sublibraries the linkage editor will use, you may need to code linkage editor control statements to specify the operations that the linkage editor will perform. There are only four: ACTION, ENTRY, PHASE, and INCLUDE. And the only one you have to know for typical program development jobs is PHASE.

If you're using the linkage editor to produce a phase that will be stored permanently in a sublibrary, you have to use the PHASE statement to name it. When you code it, it looks like this:

```
PHASE AR9000,*
```

Here, the phase will be named AR9000. If a phase with that name already exists in the CATALOG sublibrary, it will be replaced by the new phase. The asterisk indicates that the phase should be created with a relative load address. Because this lets the phase be executed in any

```
// JOB      TLG1
// OPTION   LIST,LINK,ERRS,NOSYM
// EXEC     FCOBOL,GO
         •
         •   COBOL SOURCE PROGRAM
         •
/*
/&
```

Figure 14-5   A translate, link, and go job that uses the GO operand of EXEC

partition, you'll code the asterisk almost all the time. When you code the PHASE statement, leave at least one blank at the beginning of the line.

The only confusing thing about this linkage editor control statement is that you code it before the EXEC statement that invokes the language translator. Although you would expect to code it after the EXEC, you don't because linkage editor control statements are stored on SYSLNK, and the PHASE statement must precede the object modules that will make up the new phase. As a result, you have to store the PHASE statement before you execute the language translator, which writes its object module on SYSLNK.

Model program development job streams

Two translate, link, and go job streams   Figures 14-5 and 14-6 present two translate, link, and go jobs. The first one uses the GO operand of EXEC to invoke the linkage editor and the newly linked program, following the execution of the language translator. To make this work, I added LINK to the OPTION statement. Recall that LINK specifies that the language translator should produce its object module on SYSLNK.

Because this type of translate, link, and go job consists of a single step, you need to supply all the job control statements required for the test step before the EXEC for the language translator. Also, if the application program requires any card input, you can include it in the job stream immediately after the source program deck. Just be sure to end both the source program statements and the input card data with end-of-data statements (/*).

In contrast to the job stream in figure 14-5, I prefer to code translate, link, and go as separate job steps, as in figure 14-6. In figure 14-6, I only added two statements to the job stream: EXEC LNKEDT and EXEC without a program name.

For the first step in the job, I once again coded LINK in the OPTION statement. After the end-of-data statement for the source program, I coded an EXEC statement that invokes the linkage editor.

After the link edit step, you code any additional JCL required to run the application program. If you need to assign devices or provide

```
// JOB       TLG2
// OPTION    LIST,LINK,ERRS,NOSYM
// EXEC      FCOBOL
     •
     •   COBOL SOURCE PROGRAM
     •
/*
// EXEC      LNKEDT
// EXEC
/&
```

Figure 14-6   A translate, link, and go job that uses three separate steps

label statements for the application program, this is the place to do it. Then, you code an EXEC statement without a program name to invoke the new phase. When you code EXEC without a program name, VSE uses the phase just processed by the linkage editor. So a translate, link, and go job stream is the only place you'll use EXEC without a program or procedure name. Finally, after the EXEC for the third job step, you can include any in-line card data the application program needs.

A translate and catalog job stream   Figure 14-7 is a translate and catalog job. To catalog the new phase into a sublibrary, I coded CATAL on the OPTION statement instead of LINK. CATAL indicates that the object module is not only to be linked, but also added permanently to the specified sublibrary. Then, I coded the linkage editor control statement PHASE. It specifies that the name of the phase to be stored in the sublibrary is PR4700. Remember that the PHASE statement must precede the object module on SYSLNK, so you code PHASE before the EXEC statement for the language translator. Finally, before I coded the EXEC statement for the linkage editor, I coded a LIBDEF statement that names the sublibrary the linkage editor will use to store the phase it creates. In this case, the phase will be stored in the sublibrary USRSLE.PAYROLL.

A more complex program development job stream   Part 1 of figure 14-8 illustrates a more complicated job that compiles a COBOL program that uses copy books, link edits the resulting phase with both COBOL standard object modules and user-written subprograms, and catalogs the phase into a sublibrary. The job stream that performs these functions is illustrated in part 2 of figure 14-8.

The OPTION statement in part 2 of figure 14-8 specifies that the COBOL compiler output should include a listing of the source program (LIST) and syntax errors detected by the compiler (ERRS). The

```
// JOB       TC1
// OPTION    LIST,CATAL,ERRS,NOSYM
   PHASE     CM4700,*
// EXEC      FCOBOL
     .
     .  COBOL SOURCE PROGRAM
     .
/*
// LIBDEF    PHASE,CATALOG=USRSLE.CUSTMAST
// EXEC      LNKEDT
/&
```

Figure 14-7   A simple translate and catalog job

output will not include a listing of the program's data definitions (NOSYM). In addition, it specifies that the object module should be link edited and cataloged into a sublibrary (CATAL).

The source program uses COPY statements that draw books from the sublibrary USRSLE.ACCTRCV, so the job includes a LIBDEF statement that sets up a sublibrary search chain for source books. That chain specifies just one sublibrary: USRSLE.ACCTRCV. If more than one sublibrary contained copy books used by this source program, I could have listed up to 14 more on that LIBDEF statement.

The PHASE linkage editor control statement supplies the name for the new phase (AR7740). Then, an EXEC statement invokes the COBOL compiler (FCOBOL). After that EXEC is a COBOL control statement (CBL) that specifies that copy books are to be used for the translation step (LIB). Next in the job stream is the COBOL source program itself.

Following the source program are two LIBDEF statements. One establishes a sublibrary search chain for user-written object modules. The link edit step for this program requires two sublibraries, as part 1 of figure 14-8 shows. USRSLE.USRUTIL1 contains user written subprograms and the other contains COBOL standard object modules. By coding USRSLE.USRUTIL1 in the LIBDEF statement, I established a temporary sublibrary search chain that the linkage editor uses to retrieve the user-written subprograms required to build the phase. I didn't need to specify the sublibrary for the standard object modules because it was already specified in the permanent sublibrary search chain set up during system initialization.

The next LIBDEF in the job in figure 14-8 specifies the CATALOG sublibrary where the linkage editor will store the new phase. Finally, an EXEC statement invokes the linkage editor (LNKEDT).

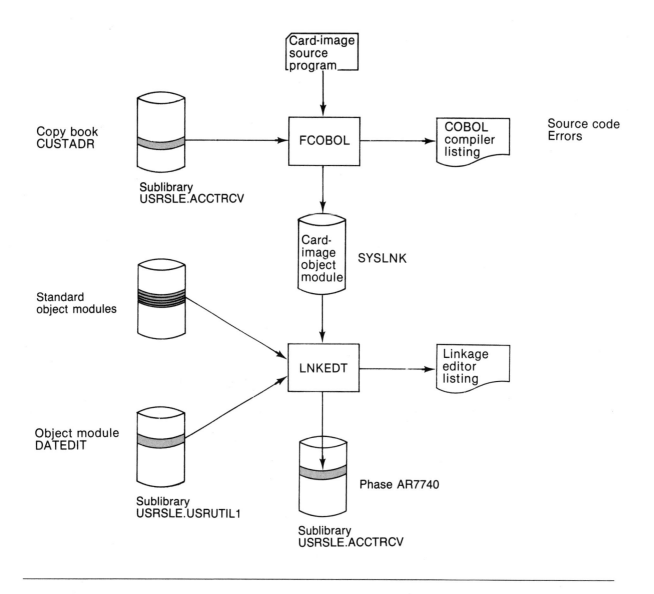

Figure 14-8   A more complex translate and catalog job (part 1 of 2)

Discussion   The program development job streams in this topic are models for the
types of jobs you'll use most often. Although you also need to have
a thorough understanding of the features of your language translator,
that's outside the scope of this book.

The linkage editor lets you perform functions other than those I've
described in this topic. For example, you can be specific about the modules you link together to form a phase and even include and exclude

```
// JOB     TC2
// OPTION  LIST,CATAL,ERRS,NOSYM
// LIBDEF  SOURCE,SEARCH=(USRSLE.ACCTRCV)
   PHASE   AR7740,*
// EXEC    FCOBOL
 CBL LIB
     .
     .   COBOL SOURCE PROGRAM
     .
/*
// LIBDEF  OBJ,SEARCH=(USRSLE.USRUTIL1)
// LIBDEF  PHASE,CATALOG=USRSLE.ACCTRCV
// EXEC    LNKEDT
/&
```

Figure 14-8   A more complex translate and catalog job (part 2 of 2)

parts of object modules. Nevertheless, the functions I described in this topic are the ones you'll use most of the time. For information on some of the more exotic uses of the linkage editor, refer to *VSE/Advanced Functions System Management Guide* and *VSE/Advanced Functions System Control Statements*.

Terminology

translate, link, and go job
translate and catalog job
execute-only job
compile step
compilation
assembly
load address
relative load address
unresolved reference
standard object module

Objectives

1. Describe the typical inputs to and outputs from one of the VSE-supported language translators.

2. Describe the three main functions of the linkage editor.

3. Code an OPTION statement to set language translator options to meet the requirements of a particular job.

4. Given application specifications, code a translate, link, and go job and a translate and catalog job to process a source program. The source program may use subprograms stored in one or more sublibraries.

TOPIC 2   How to develop programs interactively

Within ICCF, you can run programs in interactive partitions much as you can in VSE partitions. ICCF provides a set of job entry statements that control the execution of programs in interactive partitions just like VSE JCL statements control the execution of programs in VSE partitions. In this topic, I'm not going to show you how to write ICCF procedures of your own because it's a complex and detailed undertaking. Instead, I'm going to show you how to use IBM-supplied procedures to perform standard program development functions. Specifically, you'll learn how to use ICCF procedures to run the language translators, and you'll learn how to use a special ICCF program that provides linkage editor functions: *LINKNGO*.

ICCF also provides areas in its library file that simulate unit record devices. As a result, when you run a program in an interactive partition, you can work independently of VSE devices and VSE/POWER. So, in this topic, I'll show you how to use these areas too.

Temporary user areas

To understand the ICCF temporary user areas, consider figure 14-9. This figure compares the way unit-record devices supply input to and accept output from a VSE partition with the way temporary user areas of ICCF do the same for an interactive partition. As you can see, the input area is the logical equivalent of a card reader; the punch area is the logical equivalent of a card punch; and the print area is the logical equivalent of a printer. All of these areas, however, are within the ICCF library file, and you can access them through your terminal.

When a program executing in an interactive partition produces list output, it isn't routed to a printer, but rather to your print area. After list output is stored in the print area, you can view it by entering

```
/LIST $$PRINT
```

Because you can access the output at your terminal, much of the paper-shuffling of batch program development is eliminated.

If a program running in an interactive partition produces punch output, it's stored in your punch area, called $$PUNCH. You'll use the punch area to store the object module produced when you run a language translator in an interactive partition. If an application program running in an interactive partition produces punch output, it too is routed to your punch area. If you want to list the contents of the punch area, you can enter

```
/LIST $$PUNCH
```

Unit record I/O in a VSE partition

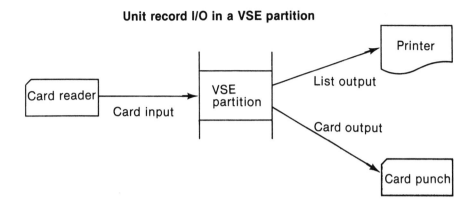

Unit record I/O in an ICCF interactive partition

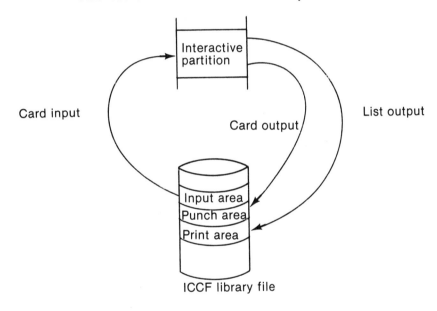

Figure 14-9   Unit record I/O in VSE partitions and ICCF interactive partitions

The input area serves the same function as a card reader for an interactive partition. So when you run a procedure in an interactive partition, its job entry statements are stored in the input area.

The language translator procedures

To execute a language translator in an interactive partition, you need to supply control statements to manage the translation, just as when you use a language translator in a VSE partition. However, those control statements are already coded and stored in standard procedures you use to invoke the language translators. Figure 14-10 presents the

```
ASSEMBLE source-member [OBJ object-member | OBJ *] [options]
COBOL source-member [OBJ object-member | OBJ *] [CBL] [options]
FORTRAN source-member [OBJ object-member | OBJ *] [PROCESS] [options]
PLI source-member [OBJ object-member | OBJ *] [PROcess] [options]
RPGII source-member [OBJ object-member | OBJ *] [options]
```

Figure 14-10   ICCF language translator procedure command lines

formats of the commands you enter to invoke the five ICCF language translator procedures.

For each procedure, you specify the name of the library member that contains the source program you want to translate. That's the first operand after the procedure name. That library member should contain only the source program; it should not contain test data, job entry statements, or job control statements.

The second operand, OBJ, lets you specify where the translator should store the object module it produces. You can direct the object module to a library member by specifying the member's name. The default, however, is for the object module to be stored in your punch area. That's what happens if you enter OBJ * or omit the OBJ operand altogether.

If you're using FORTRAN, COBOL, or PL/I, you can specify that ICCF should prompt you for additional language-specific operands. If you want to use language-specific operands, enter CBL, PROCESS, or PRO on the command line. If you don't want to use language-specific options, you can omit this operand.

For all of the language translator procedures, the last operand you enter consists of any options you want to be in effect for the translation. For this operand, you can code many of the values you can code on the OPTION statement in a batch job. Typically, you enter options that control list output.

Actually, the option values you code are used to generate ICCF /OPTION job entry statements. In addition to /OPTION values that have parallels on the VSE OPTION statement, there are several others that are unique to the ICCF environment. But, with one exception, you probably won't use them.

The exception is the GETVIS option. To insure that the proper amount of virtual storage is available in the interactive partition to execute the language translator, you can enter

```
GETVIS=0
```

or

```
GETVIS=48
```

Both cause the GETVIS area of the interactive partition to be set at its minimum size: 48K. If you don't code the GETVIS option, it's possible that the program area of your interactive partition won't be large enough to accommodate the language translator program.

Figure 14-11 illustrates a terminal session to compile and run a COBOL program. The source code is stored in a member called TRANLST. In part 1 of the figure, I specified that the object module should be stored in the punch area (OBJ *) and that the compiler should produce a listing. In addition, I entered GETVIS=48 to insure that enough storage is available for the compiler in the program area of the interactive partition.

When I tapped the enter key to start this procedure, the screen in part 2 of the figure was displayed. It indicates that my job will run in an interactive partition that was associated with class A when ICCF was started. The EX in the upper right corner of the screen shows that my terminal is in execution mode.

As long as the terminal is in execution mode, I have to wait for the job to complete before I can do other work. However, it is possible to continue with foreground work while you wait for a background job to finish. To do that, key in

```
/ASYNC
```

after your terminal enters execution mode. This command causes your terminal to enter *asynchronous execution mode*. This means the background execution you requested is no longer synchronized with what your terminal is doing. If you have to wait a long time for a background job, you should use /ASYNC so you can go on with foreground work. If you enter

```
/SYNC
```

your terminal is resynchronized with your background job.

When the job is complete, its list output is stored in your print area and displayed on your terminal screen, as illustrated in part 3 of the figure. The SP in the upper right corner of this screen indicates that the terminal is in *spool print mode*. In this figure, you can see that this is the output that would be routed to SYSLST if the compiler had executed in a VSE batch partition.

I can tap the enter key as many times as necessary to page through the output from the job. Part 4 of the figure shows the last screen of the list output. If I tap the enter key at this point, the terminal returns to command mode.

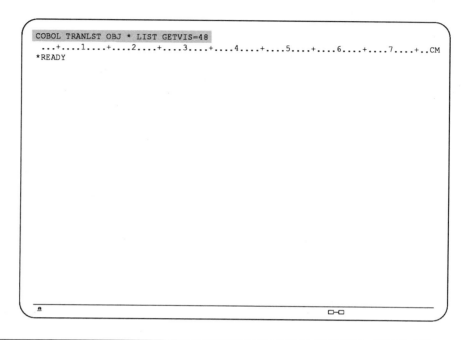

Figure 14-11   An interactive program development session (part 1 of 7)

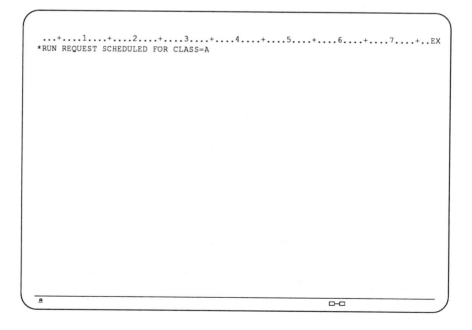

Figure 14-11   An interactive program development session (part 2 of 7)

```
   ...+....1....+....2....+....3....+....4....+....5....+....6....+....7....+..SP
   * * * * * START OF PROCEDURE (CLIST) * * * * *
   K867I  GETVIS SET TO 48K
   K859I  ALLOCATION FOR IKSYS11 - SERIAL=DOSRES UNIT=SYS013 LOC= 94780,640
   K859I  ALLOCATION FOR IKSYS12 - SERIAL=DOSRES UNIT=SYS013 LOC= 95420,640
   K859I  ALLOCATION FOR IKSYS13 - SERIAL=DOSRES UNIT=SYS013 LOC= 96060,640
   K859I  ALLOCATION FOR IKSYS14 - SERIAL=DOSRES UNIT=SYS013 LOC= 96700,640
       1  IBM DOS/VS COBOL                       REL 3.0            PP NO.
   00001        IDENTIFICATION DIVISION.
   00002        *
   00003        PROGRAM-ID.   TRANLST.
   00004        *
   00005        ENVIRONMENT DIVISION.
   00006        *
   00007        CONFIGURATION SECTION.
   00008        *
   00009        SOURCE-COMPUTER.   IBM-370.
   00010        OBJECT-COMPUTER.   IBM-370.
   00011        *
   00012        SPECIAL NAMES.
```

Figure 14-11   An interactive program development session (part 3 of 7)

```
   ...+....1....+....2....+....3....+....4....+....5....+....6....+....7....+..SP
   *OPTIONS IN EFFECT*    LANGLVL(2)  NOCOUNT      ADV          NOVERBSUM
   NOVERBREF
   *LISTER OPTIONS        NONE
       5        TRANLST       12.31.25      07/13/88
   CARD   ERROR MESSAGE

   00158  ILA4072I-W    EXIT FROM PERFORMED PROCEDURE ASSUMED BEFORE PROCEDURE-NA
   00166  ILA4072I-W    EXIT FROM PERFORMED PROCEDURE ASSUMED BEFORE PROCEDURE-NA
   00206  ILA5011I-W    HIGH ORDER TRUNCATION MIGHT OCCUR.

   END OF COMPILATION
   *PARTIAL END PRINT
```

Figure 14-11   An interactive program development session (part 4 of 7)

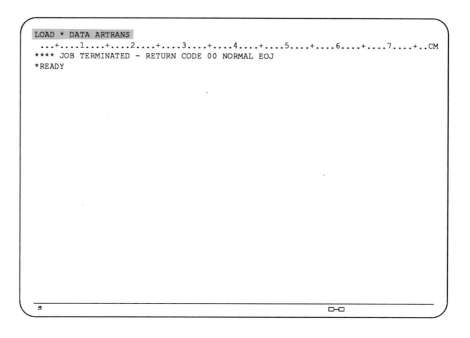

Figure 14-11 An interactive program development session (part 5 of 7)

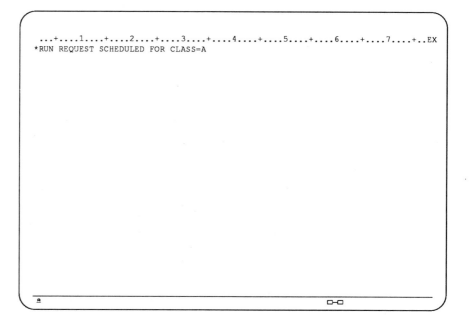

Figure 14-11 An interactive program development session (part 6 of 7)

```
...+....1....+....2....+....3....+....4....+....5....+....6....+....7....+..SP
* * * * * START OF PROCEDURE (CLIST) * * * * *
** ** ** BEGIN LINKNGO
     14,704 BYTES REQUIRED FOR PROGRAM STORAGE
PGM LOADED AT 8EDC00
XFER ADDRESS  8EDC00
** **
ACCOUNTS RECEIVABLE TRANSACTIONS
BRANCH  REP   CUST     TRAN    INVOICE TRANSACTION  PAY OR CR
  NO.   NO.   NO.      DATE      NO.      TYPE       AMOUNT
   1    19    01417  0A-20-88   23892   PAYMENT      0425600
   0    00    73280  07-2A-88   23921   PAYMENT      0000000
   4    41    52339  07-20-88   24830   NEW BILLING
   6    61    49872  07-20-88   24820   NEW BILLING
   8    86    32280  07-20-88   24812   NEW BILLING
   1    14    23052  07-20-88   24802   NEW BILLING
   2    21    16424  07-20-88   2904A   PAYMENT      0089000
   7    74    09822  07-20-88   24792   NEW BILLING
   6    51    02897  07-20-88   24203   CREDIT       0020000
   5    51    02897  07-20-88   23893   CREDIT       0040000
      10 TRANSACTIONS IN FILE
*PARTIAL END PRINT
```

Figure 14-11   An interactive program development session (part 7 of 7)

After this job has finished, the print area still contains the list output from the compilation, and I can review it by entering /LIST $$PRINT. The input area contains the job entry statements ICCF processed to perform the compilation, and the punch area contains the object module.

The LOAD procedure

To link, load, and execute the object module, I entered the command line in the top section of part 5 of figure 14-11. LOAD is the ICCF procedure that invokes the LINKNGO program. Recall that LINKNGO performs the functions of the linkage editor. Not only does it link an object module, but it also loads the resulting phase into an interactive partition and causes it to start executing.

In the command line in part 5, the asterisk indicates that the object module to be processed is in the punch area. If I had entered a member name instead of the asterisk, the LOAD procedure would have retrieved the object module from that member. In addition, the command line specifies that the program requires card data (DATA) and that the data is contained in a library member named ARTRANS.

When I tapped the enter key, the job was scheduled for execution, as part 6 of the figure indicates. As with the compile step, if the execution will take a long time, I can use the /ASYNC command to continue with foreground processing while waiting for the job to complete.

When the program execution has finished, its output is displayed on the terminal screen, just as in the compile job. Part 7 shows the output the program produced. It's stored in the print area, and I could retrieve it if I needed to. You should realize, though, that the output you see on your terminal screen doesn't reflect line spacing since blank lines are omitted from the display. As a result, you can't completely test report-preparation programs without printing the reports.

Discussion

This topic has presented just enough information about ICCF to let you translate and test simple card to printer programs in ICCF interactive partitions. However, most programs in a production environment are more complex than that. As a result, ICCF provides advanced features you can use to manage devices and files required by programs executing in interactive partitions. Unfortunately, they're outside the scope of this book. But if you want to learn how to use these features, I recommend my book *DOS/VSE ICCF*.

Although ICCF is a powerful program product, you should know that you can't always use it to develop a program in an interactive partition. For example, if you want to run the linkage editor, you can't do it in an interactive partition. And for system performance reasons, your shop may have a standard that requires some or all program development jobs to be executed in a VSE batch partition instead of in an ICCF interactive partition.

When that's the case, you still use ICCF to enter your source program and, possibly, to translate it to check for syntax errors. But to test the program, you code the proper JCL with the source program and submit the resulting job stream to POWER for execution in a batch partition. If you look back to chapter 9, you can refresh your memory about how to use the submit-to-batch facility to do that.

Terminology

LINKNGO
asynchronous execution mode
spool print mode

Objectives

1. Describe how ICCF uses temporary user areas to simulate unit-record devices for interactive partitions.

2. Use the appropriate ICCF language translator procedure to compile or assemble a source program in an interactive partition.

3. Use the ICCF LOAD procedure to link, load, and run an object module in an interactive partition.

Chapter 15

How to use the VSE Librarian

This chapter shows you how to use the VSE Librarian program. Topic 1 introduces you to the Librarian and shows you how to use the basic VSE Librarian commands to (1) print library directory listings, (2) retrieve data from VSE libraries (either in print or punch form), (3) add members, (4) rename members and sublibraries, (5) define new libraries and sublibraries, and (6) delete members, sublibraries, and libraries. Then, topic 2 shows you some advanced VSE Librarian commands you can use to copy and move libraries, sublibraries, and members, and to execute conditional Librarian commands.

You should realize, though, that you'll probably use the ICCF library file more than the VSE libraries. Today, source language programs that were once stored exclusively in VSE libraries are likely to be stored in the ICCF library file. And job streams stored in ICCF library members can be used instead of cataloged procedures. However, the size of the ICCF library file is limited, so not all source programs in a typical shop can be stored in it. Some are almost certain to be stored in private libraries. In addition, to take full advantage of the program development features you learned in topic 1 of the last chapter, you need to be able to use VSE libraries. So the emphasis in this chapter is on how to use the VSE Librarian for program development functions.

TOPIC 1   How to use basic VSE Librarian features

The VSE Librarian is a powerful program that lets you service and maintain system and user files. Prior to version 2.1 of VSE/AF, the Librarian consisted of different programs that were used to service and maintain each of the different types of libraries. Under VSE/AF version 2.1, however, a single program performs these functions, since libraries are no longer organized by the type of members they contain.

Another difference between the two versions of VSE is that with the older version, libraries could only reside in non-VSAM space. Under the current version, however, there is no restriction; libraries can reside in either VSAM or non-VSAM space. In either case, they're stored as SAM files.

As you learned in chapter 13, there are several advantages to storing SAM files in VSAM space. Because of those advantages, you should consider storing your files in libraries that reside in VSAM space. Throughout this chapter, I'll describe the coding required for maintaining files in both VSAM and non-VSAM space. But in most cases, the differences aren't significant.

To use the VSE Librarian, you need to know the JCL requirements and the rules for coding Librarian commands. That's what I'll present first in this topic. Then, I'll present the commands you'll use to perform typical Librarian functions.

HOW TO CODE VSE LIBRARIAN JOB STREAMS

When you code a Librarian job stream, you need to be sure that the libraries you'll be processing have been defined with DLBL and EXTENT statements. (Of course, if the libraries are defined in VSAM space, you don't need to code EXTENT statements.) If these statements aren't already available as system standard labels, you'll need to code them before invoking the Librarian. You code these statements the same way you'd code them for defining the libraries in a search chain, although search chains aren't required when you use the Librarian. Once you've defined the libraries to be processed, you're ready to invoke the Librarian.

How to invoke the VSE Librarian

To invoke the Librarian, you code an EXEC statement, just as you would for any other program; the name of the Librarian program is LIBR. If the library member you want to access is in VSAM space, you need to code the SIZE operand on the EXEC statement. Since the VSE Librarian requires a minimum of 256K of virtual storage, you'll probably code SIZE=256K most often. Note that SIZE=AUTO is *not* allowed when executing the VSE Librarian program. You follow the EXEC statement with a list of the library commands you want to execute. (I'll show you how to code them in a moment.) After the last command, you code an end-of-data statement (/*).

If you're only executing one library command, you can code it directly on the EXEC statement rather than coding a separate statement for it. To do that, you code the command on the PARM operand. For example, to print a library directory, you could code the following command:

```
// EXEC LIBR,PARM='LISTDIR LIB=USRSLE'
```

Note that you must enclose the library command with apostrophes when you code it on the PARM operand.

If you're using a later modification of VSE/AF 2.1, you can code more than one command on the PARM operand of EXEC. Just separate the commands with semicolons (;) and enclose the entire list with apostrophes. The only restriction is that the total number of characters can't exceed 100. (If you refer back to chapter 5, you'll see that this restriction applies to any data coded on the PARM operand.) Even though you can code commands on the PARM operand, I encourage you to code all Librarian commands as separate lines in your job streams. You'll have fewer restrictions, and your code will be more readable if you do.

How to code VSE Librarian commands

Figure 15-1 lists the VSE Librarian commands. As you can see, the Librarian lets you use abbreviations for these commands to make coding them easier. You can shorten commands by leaving off one or more letters from right to left. On the right side of figure 15-1, I've listed the shortest abbreviation of each command name. (By the way, just as commands can be abbreviated, so can their keyword operands; as I explain each command, I'll show you the shortest abbreviations for the keywords.)

I'll explain most of the commands in figure 15-1 in detail in this chapter. However, I've excluded some—BACKUP, COMPARE, INPUT, RELEASE, RESTORE, TEST, and UPDATE—because you won't use them very often. If you want more information on these commands, refer to the IBM publication *VSE/Advanced Functions System Control Statements*.

The basic format of the Librarian commands is similar to the format of JCL statements; you code the command name followed by at least one blank and the necessary operands. The only differences are that you don't begin the command with two slashes (//) and you can separate the operands with either commas or blanks. To make your job streams more readable, I recommend you code the command name beginning in column 4 and code the operands beginning in column 12. That way, your library commands will be aligned with your JCL statements.

Although the basic formats of library commands and JCL statements are similar, there are differences in the way you continue lines and code

COMMAND	SHORTEST ABBREVIATION
ACCESS	A
BACKUP	B
CATALOG	CA
CHANGE	CH
COMPARE	COM
CONNECT	CON
COPY	COP
DEFINE	DEF
DELETE	DEL
GOTO	GOTO
INPUT	I
LIST	L
LISTDIR	LISTD (or LD)
MOVE	M
ON	ON
PUNCH	PU
RELEASE	REL
RENAME	REN
RESTORE	RES
TEST	T
UPDATE	U
/.	/.

Figure 15-1 VSE Librarian commands and their shortest abbreviations

comments. In addition, you can use some advanced coding features with the library commands: generic references and multiple objects.

How to code continuation lines When you want to continue a Librarian command onto one or more lines, you code a continuation character in the continuation field (column 72), just like you do for JCL statements. For a Librarian command, however, the continuation character is a minus sign (-).

How to code comments Like JCL statements, you can code comments on library commands following any operands or on separate lines. However, unlike JCL statements, all comments must be preceded by /* and followed by */. Because the beginning of a comment looks like an end-of-data statement, be sure not to begin a comment in column one. As a general rule, I advise you to use comments sparingly, if you use them at all. They can make your coding difficult to read, and most Librarian commands are self-explanatory anyway.

How to code generic references In chapter 5, you learned that if you want to refer to all member types on a LIBDEF statement, you can code an asterisk (*) for the member-type operand. You can also use this type of specification, called a *generic reference,* on the Librarian commands for library member names and member types. For example, if you code XYZ.* on a library command, the Librarian will process all sublibrary member types with the name XYZ. Likewise, if you code *.PHASE, the Librarian will process all the phase members of the specified sublibrary. You can also use this type of reference to specify the last part of a member name. For example, INV*.OBJ refers to all object modules whose names begin with INV, such as INV100, INV2000, or INV4100A. Notice that it doesn't matter how many characters follow the INV. Finally if you code *.*, all the members of any type in the specified sublibrary will be processed by the command.

How to code multiple objects   Some Librarian commands let you specify multiple objects (libraries, sublibraries, or members) on which the function is to be performed. If this is allowed, you will see three dots (...) after the operand in the command's syntax. For example LIB=library... means you can specify more than one library.

You can specify multiple objects in several ways. For example, you can specify LIB1, LIB2, and LIB3 as multiple libraries as follows:

```
LIB=LIB1 LIB2 LIB3
LIB=LIB1, LIB2, LIB3
LIB=(LIB1 LIB2 LIB3)
LIB=(LIB1,LIB2,LIB3)
```

Although you can use any of these formats, I recommend you separate the objects by commas and enclose them in parentheses, as in the last example above. This is consistent with the way you code sublibrary lists in LIBDEF search chains.

BASIC VSE LIBRARIAN COMMANDS

Now that you know how to invoke the Librarian and how to code its commands, you're ready to learn the details of the basic VSE Librarian commands.

How to identify the sublibrary you want to access: The ACCESS command

Before you can perform any function on a library member, you need to specify the sublibrary in which it resides. To do that, you code an ACCESS command. Figure 15-2 shows its basic format.

For the SUBLIB operand, you code the name of the sublibrary you want to access, qualified by the name of the library in which it's located. The library and sublibrary you specify must already exist. Once you code an ACCESS command, it remains in effect until you code another ACCESS command, or the library or sublibrary being accessed is deleted or renamed.

You can also use the ACCESS command to find out what sublibrary is currently being accessed. You do this by coding a question mark (?) instead of the SUBLIB operand. This causes the name of the sublibrary to be displayed on either SYSLOG or SYSLST, depending on where you entered the command.

The ACCESS command

```
ACCESS  ({SUBLIB=library.sblibrary})
        {?                          }
```

Explanation

SUBLIB   Specifies the sublibrary to be accessed. This is the sublibrary the VSE Librarian will search when it encounters a command that has a member name and member type specification. SUBLIB may be abbreviated S.

?   Specifies that the name of the sublibrary currently accessed should be displayed.

Figure 15-2   The ACCESS command

How to retrieve data from libraries

One of the VSE Librarian functions you'll use often is printing directory listings. For example, if you try to execute a program from a VSE sublibrary and VSE doesn't find it, you'll want to know why. So you'll probably list the directory of the sublibrary to find out if you used the wrong program name or if a phase that should be in the sublibrary is missing. To do that, you use the LISTDIR command.

Sometimes, you may need to do more than just find out what members reside in a particular sublibrary; you may want to look at the contents of a particular member. To do that, you use the LIST or PUNCH command. I'll present all three of these commands—LISTDIR, LIST, and PUNCH—in this section.

How to print a directory listing for a library, sublibrary, or member: The LISTDIR command   The LISTDIR command lets you display the contents of a library or sublibrary directory or the directory information for a specific member. Figure 15-3 shows the format of the LISTDIR command.

The first operand specifies the kind of directory listing you want—library, sublibrary, member, or System Directory List—and its name. Notice that you can get multiple library or sublibrary directory listings or the directory information for more than one member with a single LISTDIR command. If you specify a library, the resulting listing includes the directories of all the sublibraries that library contains. If you want a member directory listing, remember that you first need to code an ACCESS command to specify the sublibrary in which the member is located.

The LISTDIR command

```
         (LIB=library...                )        (FULL  )
         {SUBLIB=library.sublibrary...  }         NORMAL
LISTDIR  {membername.membertype...      }  [OUTPUT={SHORT }]
         (SDL                           )        (STATUS)
```

Explanation

LIB
Specifies the libraries for which directory information is to be listed. The listing will include the directory contents of all the sublibraries in the specified libraries. LIB may be abbreviated L.

SUBLIB
Specifies the sublibraries for which directory information is to be listed. SUBLIB may be abbreviated S.

membername.membertype
Specifies the members for which directory information is to be listed.

SDL
Specifies that the System Directory List should be listed.

OUTPUT
Specifies the amount of information provided. FULL, NORMAL, and SHORT are applicable for libraries, sublibraries, and members. OUTPUT = NORMAL is the default. STATUS is applicable only for libraries and sublibraries. Do not specify the OUTPUT operand if you specify SDL. OUTPUT may be abbreviated O.

Figure 15-3   The LISTDIR command

You code the second operand (OUTPUT) to specify the amount of directory information you want. The four options—FULL, NORMAL, SHORT, and STATUS—differ primarily in the amount of member information they provide. As you might expect, FULL provides very detailed information about each member; NORMAL provides limited member information; SHORT provides only the member's name and type; and STATUS provides no member information at all. As a result, you can't code STATUS if you specify a member as the first operand. NORMAL is the default for this operand. If you want to display the System Directory List (SDL), you don't need to code the OUTPUT operand at all; the SDL is always displayed with the default value.

In figure 15-4, I've coded the JCL and Librarian commands needed to list a library directory, a sublibrary directory, the directory information for a member, and the System Directory List. Figures 15-5 through 15-8 show the output resulting from each LISTDIR command. Because I selected different OUTPUT options for each, you can see the different amounts of information available with this command.

```
// JOB      LISTDIR
// EXEC     LIBR
   LISTDIR LIB=USRSLE OUTPUT=SHORT
   LISTDIR SUBLIB=USRSLE.INVNTORY OUTPUT=STATUS
   ACCESS  SUBLIB=USRSLE.INVNTORY
   LISTDIR INV4800.PHASE OUTPUT=FULL
   LISTDIR SDL
/*
/&
```

Figure 15-4   Job to produce several directory listings

```
STATUS  DISPLAY         LIBRARY=USRSLE              DATE:88-06-23
                                                    TIME:12:04
---------------------------------------------------------------------

FILE-ID          : USER.SLE.LIBRARY

CREATION DATE    : 88-06-09    10:48

SUBLIBRARIES     :        7

LOCATION (BAM) : DEVICE=FBA      VOLID=DOSRES   BLK# = 389856 -   390255

LIBRARY BLOCK    : SIZE=  1024 BYTES    DATA SPACE=   988 BYTES

TOTAL    SPACE   :     200 LIBRARY BLOCKS    (100 %)
USED     SPACE   :     102 LIBRARY BLOCKS    ( 51 %)
DELAYED  SPACE   :      19 LIBRARY BLOCKS    ( 10 %)
FREE     SPACE   :      79 LIBRARY BLOCKS    ( 39 %)
```

SUBLIBRARY	CREATION DATE	SPACE REUSAGE	NO. OF MEMBERS	USED LB'S	DELAYED LB'S	% LIBR. SPACE
ACCTRCV	88-06-09	AUTO	0	1	0	1 %
COPYAR	88-06-22	AUTO	0	1	0	1 %
CUSTMAST	88-06-09	AUTO	4	17	0	9 %
INVAPPS	88-06-09	AUTO	0	1	0	1 %
INVNTORY	88-06-09	AUTO	4	49	0	25 %
PAYROLL	88-06-09	AUTO	0	1	0	1 %
USRUTIL1	88-06-09	AUTO	5	30	19	25 %

Figure 15-5   LISTDIR output for a library with OUTPUT=SHORT (part 1 of 2)

```
----------------------------------------------------------------
DIRECTORY DISPLAY        SUBLIBRARY=USRSLE.CUSTMAST    DATE: 88-06-23
                                                       TIME: 12:04
----------------------------------------------------------------

   M E M B E R              M E M B E R              M E M B E R
NAME      TYPE      .    NAME      TYPE           NAME      TYPE
----------------         ----------------         ----------------
CUSTADR   C              CM7740    PHASE          CUSTADR   S
CM4700    PHASE



DIRECTORY DISPLAY        SUBLIBRARY=USRSLE.INVNTORY   DATE: 88-06-23
                                                       TIME: 12:04
----------------------------------------------------------------

   M E M B E R              M E M B E R              M E M B E R
NAME      TYPE           NAME      TYPE           NAME      TYPE
----------------         ----------------         ----------------
INV4800   PHASE          INV5210   PHASE          INV5220   PHASE
INV4900   PHASE



----------------------------------------------------------------
DIRECTORY DISPLAY        SUBLIBRARY=USRSLE.USRUTIL1   DATE: 88-06-23
                                                       TIME: 12:04
----------------------------------------------------------------

   M E M B E R              M E M B E R              M E M B E R
NAME      TYPE           NAME      TYPE           NAME      TYPE
----------------         ----------------         ----------------
DATEDIT   OBJ            PRTDASD   PHASE          PRINTJOB  PROC
ABTERM    PHASE          ASSGN001  PROC
```

Figure 15-5   LISTDIR output for a library with OUTPUT=SHORT (part 2 of 2)

```
STATUS   DISPLAY            SUBLIBRARY=USRSLE.INVNTORY      DATE: 88-06-23
                                                           TIME: 12:05
-----------------------------------------------------------------------

CREATION DATE: 88-06-09    10:48

MEMBERS        :        4

SPACE REUSAGE: AUTOMATIC

USED     SPACE:        49 LIBRARY BLOCKS     ( 25% OF LIBRARY SPACE)
DELAYED  SPACE:         0 LIBRARY BLOCKS     (  0% OF LIBRARY SPACE)


-----------------------------------------------------------------------
```

Figure 15-6   LISTDIR output for a sublibrary with OUTPUT=STATUS

```
DIRECTORY DISPLAY           SUBLIBRARY=USRSLE.INVNTORY     DATE: 88-06-23
                                                          TIME 12:05
-----------------------------------------------------------------------
 M E M B E R
NAME     TYPE        M E M B E R    I N F O R M A T I O N
-----------------------------------------------------------------------
INV4800  PHASE       PUT INTO SUBLIB    : 88-06-17   16:01
                     LAST REPLACED      :   - -

                     NUMBER OF RECORDS  :          1
                     LOGICAL RECORD SIZE:       4928
                     LIBRARY BLOCKS USED:          5
                     FIRST LIBRARY BLOCK:     390170    (FBA BLOCK #)
                             ON VOLID: DOSRES
                     LAST LIBRARY BLOCK :     390178    (FBA BLOCK #)
                             ON VOLID: DOSRES

                     CONTIGUOUSLY STORED: YES
                     MSHP CONTROLLED    : NO
                     MSHP BYPASS USED   : NO
                     SYSIPT DATA        : NO

                     PHASE SIZE         :    4700     (HEX:   00125C)
                     LOAD   ADDRESS (HEX): 02D078
                     ENTRY ADDRESS (HEX): 02D078
                     SVA ELIGIBLE       : NO
                     RELOCATABLE        : YES
```

Figure 15-7   LISTDIR output for a member with OUTPUT=FULL

```
STATUS DISPLAY          SDL   AND   SVA              DATE: 88-06-23
                                                     TIME: 12:05
-----------------------------------------------------------------
SDL       TOTAL ENTRIES :     510   (100%)
          USED  ENTRIES :     333   ( 65%)
          FREE  ENTRIES :     177   ( 35%)


SVA       TOTAL SPACE   :   1636K   (100%)
          USED  SPACE   :   1579K   ( 97%)
          FREE  SPACE   :     57K   (  3%)


-----------------------------------------------------------------
DIRECTORY DISPLAY       SDL                          DATE: 88-06-23
                                                     TIME: 12:05

-----------------------------------------------------------------
M E M B E R    ORIGIN LOADABLE  LOADED   PHASE ADDRESS  ENTRY POINT
NAME     TYPE  SYSLIB INTO SVA INTO SVA  SIZE  IN SVA   IN SVA
-----------------------------------------------------------------
$$B$AU$$ PHASE   YES     YES      YES      792 E26B38    E26B38
$$BACLOS PHASE   YES     YES      YES      538 E14130    E14130
$$BATTF0 PHASE   YES     NO       NO       440   -         -
$$BATTNA PHASE   YES     YES      YES      971 E14350    E14350
$$BATTNB PHASE   YES     YES      YES      251 E14720    E14720
$$BATTNH PHASE   YES     YES      YES      844 E14820    E14820
$$BATTNK PHASE   YES     YES      YES      824 E14B70    E14B70
$$BATTNR PHASE   YES     YES      YES      389 E14EA8    E14EA8
$$BATTN2 PHASE   YES     NO       NO       944   -         -
$$BCEOV1 PHASE   YES     NO       NO        74   -         -
$$BCLOSE PHASE   NO      YES      YES     1105 E61A60    E61A60
$$BCLOS2 PHASE   YES     YES      YES      576 E154D8    E154D8
$$BCLOS5 PHASE   YES     YES      YES      272 E15718    E15718
$$BCLRPS PHASE   YES     YES      YES      608 E15828    E15828
$$BCVSAM PHASE   YES     YES      YES      528 E15A88    E15A88
$$BCVSO2 PHASE   YES     YES      YES      192 E15C98    E15C98
$$BFAQS  PHASE   NO      NO       NO        -     -         -
$$BFPSCL PHASE   NO      NO       NO        -     -         -
$$BFPSDI PHASE   NO      NO       NO        -     -         -
$$BFPSFO PHASE   NO      NO       NO        -     -         -
$$BFPSPR PHASE   NO      NO       NO        -     -         -
$$BFPSP3 PHASE   NO      NO       NO        -     -         -
$$BFPSSG PHASE   NO      NO       NO        -     -         -
$$BOCP01 PHASE   YES     YES      YES      972 E15D58    E15D58
$$BOCP03 PHASE   YES     YES      YES      864 E16128    E16128
$$BOCRTA PHASE   YES     YES      YES     1152 E16488    E16488
$$BOCRTC PHASE   YES     YES      YES     1200 E16908    E16908
$$BOCRTD PHASE   YES     YES      YES      810 E16DB8    E16DB8
$$BOCRTG PHASE   YES     YES      YES     1159 E170E8    E170E8
$$BOCRTH PHASE   YES     YES      YES      674 E17570    E17570
$$BOCRTI PHASE   YES     YES      YES      969 E17818    E17818
$$BOCRTJ PHASE   YES     YES      YES      884 E17BE8    E17BE8
$$BOCRTK PHASE   YES     YES      YES     1152 E17F60    E17F60
$$BOCRTQ PHASE   YES     YES      YES      723 E183E0    E183E0
$$BOCRTR PHASE   YES     NO       NO       631   -         -
$$BOCRTS PHASE   YES     NO       NO       691   -         -
$$BOCRTT PHASE   YES     NO       NO       609   -         -
$$BOCRTZ PHASE   YES     YES      YES     1152 E186B8    E186B8
   .
   .
   .
```

Figure 15-8   LISTDIR output for the System Directory List

The LIST command

```
LIST membername.membertype... [FORMAT=HEX]
```

Explanation

membername.membertype	Specifies the library members to be listed.
FORMAT = HEX	Specifies that the hexadecimal representation of each character string should be included in the ouput. This operand is not used with PHASE or DUMP member types. FORMAT may be abbreviated F.

Figure 15-9 The LIST command

How to print a library member: The LIST command The LIST command lets you print the contents of a library member. Its format is shown in figure 15-9. The first operand specifies the member name and member type of the library member you want to print. The second operand, FORMAT=HEX, is optional. If you code it, the character string representation of each record is followed by its hexadecimal representation. This option has no effect on PHASE or DUMP member types, since they're already represented by hexadecimal characters. Since you'll seldom want hexadecimal listings of other member types, you probably won't need to code this operand often.

Figure 15-10 shows a job that lists a procedure member in both character and hexadecimal format and shows its output. (Again, you'll probably never need a hexadecimal listing for a procedure; I'm using it here simply to illustrate the output format.) Notice that I had to code an ACCESS command (A) to define the sublibrary in which the member I want to list is located. Also notice the abbreviations I used for the LISTDIR command and the FORMAT operand.

How to punch a library member: The PUNCH command Occasionally, you may want to have the contents of a library member punched to the SYSPCH output device. For example, to make a change to a source or procedure library member, you can punch it, edit it, and then recatalog it. To punch a source book, object module, procedure, or phase, you use the PUNCH command. Its format is shown in figure 15-11. You can't use this command to punch dumps or user-defined member types.

The only required operand of the PUNCH command is membername.membertype. The two remaining operands are optional, and you probably won't use them often. You'll use the FORMAT=OLD operand only if you're transferring members from a current library to an old VSE library (VSE/AF version 1). Later modifications of VSE/AF 2.1

JCL for the job

```
// JOB      LISTMEM
// EXEC     LIBR
   A        S=USRSLE.USRUTIL1
   L        ASSGN001.PROC F=HEX
/*
/&
```

Output from the job

```
MEMBER=ASSGN001.PROC        SUBLIBRARY=USRSLE.USRUTIL1    DATE: 88-06-21
                                                          TIME: 15:37
```

```
// PROC     UNIT=250,VOLUME=,RCODE=0
664DDDC4444EDCE7FFF6EDDEDC76DCDCC7F44444444444444444444444444444444444444444444
110796300004593E250B563445EB93645E00000000000000000000000000000000000000000000

// IF       RCODE>6 THEN
664CC444444DCDCC6F 4ECCD444444444444444444444444444444444444444444444444444444
11096000000936 45E60385500000000000000000000000000000000000000000000000000000

// SETPARM UNIT=300,VOLUME=',VOL=007778'
664ECEDCDD4EDCE7FFF6EDDEDC776EDD7FFFFFF744444444444444444444444444444444444444
110253719404593E300B563445EDB563E0077780000000000000000000000000000000000000000

// ASSGN   SYS001,&UNIT&VOLUME
664CEECD444EEEFFF65EDCE5EDDEDC4444444444444444444444444444444444444444444444444
11012275000282001B045930563445000000000000000000000000000000000000000000000000
```

Figure 15-10   Job to list a member in both character and hex format and its output

also let you code FORMAT=NOHEADER. If you code FORMAT=NO-HEADER, only the contents of the member are punched. In contrast, if you don't code it, a CATALOG command with the appropriate operands and an end-of-data statement are included in the punched output so the member is prepared to be recataloged. (I'll present the CATA-LOG command later in this topic.) Since you'll usually punch a member so that you can change it and recatalog it, you'll seldom want to code FORMAT=NOHEADER.

The other operand, EOF, tells VSE whether or not it should add an end-of-file indicator (/*) to the end of your punch file. If you code EOF=YES or omit this operand, an end-of-file character is automatically added to the punch file when the command is completed. If you code EOF=NO, an end-of-file character is *not* added to the punch file. Then, you can collect multiple members in a single punch file. If you do that, be sure you specify EOF=YES for the last member added to the punch file.

The PUNCH command

```
PUNCH membername.membertype... [FORMAT={OLD      }] [EOF={YES}]
                                       {NOHEADER}         {NO }
```

Explanation

membername.membertype	Specifies the library members to be punched.
FORMAT	FORMAT = OLD allows members from a current library to be transferred to an old VSE library (VSE/AF version 1). FORMAT = NOHEADER specifies that the punch output should not include a surrounding CATALOG command and end-of-data indicator. This second option is only available with later modifications of VSE/AF version 2.1. FORMAT may be abbreviated F.
EOF	Indicates whether an end-of-file indicator (/*) should be added to the end of the punch file. EOF = YES is the default.

Figure 15-11   The PUNCH command

How to create a VSE library or sublibrary: The DEFINE command

Up to this point, the library commands I've presented operate on libraries and sublibraries that already exist. If you're working on a new application, however, you may want to create a new VSE library or sublibrary. To do that, you use the DEFINE command, shown in Figure 15-12.

The first operand of DEFINE specifies what you want to create, libraries or sublibraries. Although you use the DEFINE command to create both libraries and sublibraries, I'm going to present the procedures separately since the procedure for creating libraries is more complex.

How to create a VSE library   To create a library, you need to choose a library name and code JCL to define its location and size. A library name has one to seven alphameric characters, and begins with an alphabetic character. The only name you can't use is IJSYSRS, which is the name of the system library. Your shop probably has guidelines to help you select library names, so check with your supervisor.

As I mentioned at the beginning of this topic, libraries are SAM files that can reside in either VSAM or non-VSAM space. To define a library in non-VSAM space, you need to code DLBL and EXTENT statements before you invoke the Librarian. The most important thing to consider when coding the JCL to define a library is the size of the library.

To determine the size of your library, you first need to know the size of all the members you want to store in it. Then, you need to provide space for the library and sublibrary directories and for new members to be added in the future. The minimum library size is one track for a CKD device and ten blocks for an FBA device. Your library can

The DEFINE command

```
DEFINE  {LIB=library...                                    } [REPLACE={YES}]
        {SUBLIB=library.sublibrary... [REUSE=IMMEDIATE]}          {NO }
```

Explanation

LIB	Specifies the libraries to be created. Library names can have one to seven alphameric characters. The first character must be alphabetic. LIB may be abbreviated L.
SUBLIB	Specifies the sublibraries to be created. Sublibrary names can have one to eight alphameric characters. SUBLIB may be abbreviated S.
REUSE = IMMEDIATE	Indicates that library space is to be freed as soon as members of the library are deleted. This option only applies to sublibrary definitions. REUSE may be abbreviated REU.
REPLACE	Indicates whether or not the new libraries or sublibraries should be created if other libraries or sublibraries already exist with the same name. REPLACE = NO is the default. REPLACE may be abbreviated R.

Figure 15-12   The DEFINE command

have up to sixteen extents on different volumes, as long as the disk types are the same. For detailed information on estimating the disk space requirements of VSE libraries, refer to the IBM publication *VSE/Advanced Functions Planning and Installation*.

Figure 15-13 shows a job that creates a library in non-VSAM space. As you can see on the EXTENT statement, 1000 blocks will be allocated to the new library.

When you define a library in VSAM space, you have to go through two steps. First, you code an AMS DEFINE CLUSTER command (using the VSAM Space Management for SAM feature I described in chapter 13) to define the library to VSAM. When you code this command, be sure you specify NONINDEXED for the file-type operand. In addition, you must code NOCIFORMAT for the RECORDFORMAT operand. This specifies a special format used for files processed by certain programs, including the Librarian. You also need to code the operand SHAREOPTIONS(3) to allow unlimited access to the library. Of course, there is other information that has to be specified on the DEFINE CLUSTER command as well, including the name and size of the library. For more information on coding DEFINE CLUSTER for SAM ESDS files, refer to *VSE/Advanced Functions System Management Guide*.

After you define the SAM ESDS file, you use the Librarian's DEFINE command to create the library. Since you're using VSAM space, the coding is simpler than that in figure 15-13. You'll only need to code a DLBL statement and the Librarian commands.

```
//  JOB      DEFLIB
//  ASSGN    SYS014,251
//  DLBL     NEWLIB,'STEVE.NEW.LIB'
//  EXTENT   SYS014,,,,6524,1000
//  EXEC     LIBR
    DEFINE   LIB=NEWLIB
/*
/&
```

Figure 15-13   Job to define a library in non-VSAM space

On the DEFINE command for a library stored in either VSAM or non-VSAM space, you can code the REPLACE operand to tell the Librarian what to do if the library name you've chosen already exists. If you code REPLACE=NO or omit the operand as in figure 15-13, the new library won't be created. If you code REPLACE=YES, the new definition will replace the old one. Note, though, that even with REPLACE=YES, the Librarian will not replace a library if the old one is currently being used by another job.

How to define VSE sublibraries   Since most libraries are defined when a system is installed, you'll probably have more opportunities to create sublibraries than libraries. Fortunately, sublibraries are easier to define. For sublibrary definitions, you code the name of the sublibrary you want to create, qualified by the name of an existing library. A sublibrary name has one to eight alphameric characters. Again, you should check with your supervisor about your shop's naming guidelines.

You can also code the REUSE=IMMEDIATE operand when you define a sublibrary. It specifies that the space occupied by members will be freed immediately after the members are deleted. If you omit this operand, you may have to do some extra systems work to be able to use the space previously occupied by deleted members. So I recommend you code REUSE=IMMEDIATE whenever you define a sublibrary.

When you define a sublibrary, you don't need to code a DLBL or EXTENT statement for it like you do for a library. That's because the sublibrary space is suballocated from the space already allocated to its library. Actually, when a sublibrary is created, no space is allocated to it at all. Instead, the Librarian simply enters its name in the appropriate library directory. Then, when a member is added to the sublibrary, the required space is allocated for that member.

If the sublibrary you're defining already exists, you'll need to code the REPLACE=YES operand to replace it. If you don't want an existing sublibrary to be replaced, code REPLACE=NO or let it default.

```
// JOB      CRTSLIB
// EXEC     LIBR
   DEFINE SUBLIB=USRSLE.INVAPPS REUSE=IMMEDIATE REPLACE=YES
/*
/&
```

Figure 15-14   Job to define a sublibrary

Figure 15-14 shows a job that creates the sublibrary INVAPPS in the library USRSLE. Notice that I've coded the operand REPLACE=YES to specify that I want this new sublibrary to be created, whether or not another sublibrary with this name already exists.

How to maintain
VSE libraries

Now that you know how to create VSE libraries and sublibraries, you need to know how to maintain them. In this section, I'll present the commands that let you add and replace library members, delete libraries, sublibraries, and members, and rename sublibraries and members.

How to add members to a sublibrary: The CATALOG command
In chapter 5, I showed you how to catalog a dump by coding the SYS-DUMP system option. In chapter 14, I showed you how to catalog a phase when you link-edit a program. Now I want to show you how to catalog source books, object modules, procedures and user-defined library member types using the CATALOG command.

Figure 15-15 shows the format of the CATALOG command. As you can see, the only required operand is the member name and type. Notice that you can only specify one member on a CATALOG command. As you'll see in a moment, that's because the data to be cataloged must immediately follow the CATALOG command that names it.

The other operands of the CATALOG command are optional. The EOD operand defines the end-of-data indicator, which must be coded following the last line of data you want to catalog. It can be any two characters except the comma or blank. Usually, you'll use the default end-of-data indicator, /+. But if the characters /+ appear in the member that's being cataloged, you'll need to code an alternate end-of-data indicator using the EOD operand. There is one exception to this rule. If the characters /+ are used in a cataloged procedure as an end-of-procedure statement, the Librarian recognizes it as such and includes the statement at the end of the cataloged member. In addition, the Librarian assumes the end of the input data has been reached. Since there aren't many other cases in which you'll code /+, you probably won't need to change the end-of-data indicator often.

The DATA operand is used only with procedures. If the procedure contains any in-line data, you need to code DATA=YES. If it doesn't,

The CATALOG command

```
CATALOG membername.membertype [EOD=xx] [DATA={YES}] [REPLACE={YES}]
                                             {NO }            {NO }
```

Explanation

membername.membertype	Specifies the member name and member type of the data to be cataloged. The member type may not be PHASE or DUMP.
EOD	Specifies the two characters that will be used to indicate the end of the data being cataloged. EOD = / + is the default. EOD may be abbreviated E.
DATA	Applicable only with procedures. Indicates whether or not the procedure contains SYSIPT data. DATA = NO is the default. DATA may be abbreviated D.
REPLACE	Indicates whether or not the new member should be created if another member with the same member name already exists in the specified sublibrary. REPLACE = NO is the default. REPLACE may be abbreviated R.

Figure 15-15   The CATALOG command

you can either code DATA=NO or omit the operand. Note that if you're cataloging nested procedures, all the procedures in the nest must be cataloged with the same DATA option.

The REPLACE operand indicates whether or not a new member should be created if another member with the same name and type already exists in the specified sublibrary. If you code REPLACE=YES, the new member will be substituted for the old member. If you code REPLACE=NO or omit this operand, the new member will not be added.

To catalog source code into a sublibrary, you code a job like the one in figure 15-16. Here, the copy book CUSTADR with type S is cataloged into the sublibrary USRSLE.ACCTRCV. (You should recall from chapter 5 that the source book member type is a single character: A..Z, 0..9, #, $, or @. The member type SOURCE, used in the LIBDEF statement, is not used for cataloging source books.) I've also coded REPLACE=YES on the CATALOG command to indicate that the old version of the member should be replaced.

Following the CATALOG command are the source statements to be stored in the source book. As you can see, I've used the default end-of-data indicator, /+, to mark the end of the source data. Then, the /* statement signals the end of the Librarian command data, and the /& statement indicates the end of the job.

To add an object module to a sublibrary, you code a job similar to the one in figure 15-16. The only difference is that you code OBJ for the member type. To create the object module data that you would

```
// JOB       CATSRCE
// EXEC      LIBR
   ACCESS    SUBLIB=USRSLE.ACCTRCV
   CATALOG   CUSTADR.S REPLACE=YES
        01   CUSTOMER-ADDRESS-RECORD.
        ÷
             05   CA-CUSTOMER-NUMBER          PIC X(5).
             05   CA-CUSTOMER-NAME            PIC X(30).
             05   CA-CUSTOMER-ADDRESS         PIC X(30).
             05   CA-CUSTOMER-CITY            PIC X(15).
             05   CA-CUSTOMER-STATE           PIC XX.
             05   CA-CUSTOMER-ZIP-CODE        PIC X(5).
        ÷
/+
/÷
/&
```

Figure 15-16   Job to catalog a source book

include in the Librarian job stream, you have to execute one of the language translators with the DECK option.

By the way, it's possible to combine a language translation step and a CATALOG command step in one job. Although this job is more efficient than punching an object module and including it in another job to catalog it, it involves some complex device assignment considerations. If your shop uses subprograms extensively, though, you may want to try coding a model job to perform this function. On the other hand, if cataloging subprograms isn't a high-volume activity in your shop, you're probably better off punching and cataloging in separate jobs.

When you code a job to catalog a procedure, you need to be sure to code DATA=YES if the procedure contains in-line data. This is illustrated in the job in figure 15-17. You should recognize this job from chapter 6. Here, I coded DATA=YES on the CATALOG command because the procedure executes the SORT program, which requires control statements to be coded as input in the job stream. Notice that I did *not* code the EOD operand in this example, even though the procedure contains the characters /+. When this is the last statement in a procedure, a separate end-of-data statement for the Librarian isn't necessary.

In addition to cataloging source books, object modules, and procedures, you can also catalog members with user-defined member types. You do that using jobs similar to those I've already presented. In fact, you can use almost any of the Librarian commands on user-defined members that you can use on the pre-defined library members; you just can't process or execute the user-defined members using job control statements.

```
//  JOB      CATPROC
//  EXEC     LIBR
    ACCESS   SUBLIB=USRSLE.INVNTORY
    CATALOG  INV5200.PROC DATA=YES
//  LIBDEF   PHASE,SEARCH=(USRSLE.INVNTORY)
//  ASSGN    SYS006,SYSLST
//  ASSGN    SYS013,300
//  ASSGN    SYS015,250
//  DLBL     INVMAST,'INVENTORY.MASTER.FILE'
//  EXTENT   SYS015,,,,23120,3000
//  PAUSE    MOUNT TAPE FOR INVENTORY FILE ARCHIVE
//  EXEC     INV5210
//  DLBL     SORTIN1,'INVENTORY.MASTER.FILE'
//  EXTENT   SYS015,,,,23120,3000
//  DLBL     SORTWK1
//  EXTENT   SYS015,,,,26120,3000
//  DLBL     SORTOUT,'SORTED.INVENTORY.MASTER.FILE'
//  EXTENT   SYS015,,,,29120,3000
//  EXEC     SORT
    SORT     FIELDS=(21,8,CH,A),WORK=1
    RECORD   TYPE=F,LENGTH=256
/*
//  DLBL     INVMAST,'SORTED.INVENTORY.MASTER.FILE'
//  EXTENT   SYS015,,,,29120,3000
//  EXEC     INV5220
/+
/*
/&
```

Figure 15-17   Job to catalog a procedure member

How to delete libraries, sublibraries, or members: The DELETE command   When you want to delete libraries, sublibraries, or members, you use the DELETE command, shown in figure 15-18. As you can see, its format is simple. You only need to specify the libraries, sublibraries, or members you want to delete. For example, if you wanted to delete the procedure INV5200 that was cataloged in figure 15-17, you would code a job like the one in figure 15-19.

Although the DELETE command is simple, it's dangerous. When you use it, be sure you code the libraries, sublibraries, or member names carefully to avoid accidently deleting the wrong ones. To prevent you from deleting important parts of your library structure, the VSE Librarian imposes some restrictions. First, you can't delete a sublibrary if it's in use in another partition at the time the DELETE command is issued. Second, you can't delete the system library IJSYSRS or the system sublibrary IJSYSRS.SYSLIB. Finally, if the library or sublibrary you want to delete is specified in a current LIBDEF statement (either permanent or temporary), the LIBDEF statement must be dropped before you can issue the DELETE command. When a sublibrary is deleted, all ACCESS or CONNECT commands that are in effect for it are dropped.

The DELETE command

```
        (LIB=library...                 )
DELETE  {SUBLIB=library.sublibrary...   }
        (membername.membertype...       )
```

Explanation

LIB	Delete the specified libraries. The system library IJSYSRS cannot be deleted. LIB may be abbreviated L.
SUBLIB	Delete the specified sublibraries. The system sublibrary IJSYSRS.SYSLIB cannot be deleted. SUBLIB may be abbreviated S.
membername.membertype	Delete the specified members.

Figure 15-18   The DELETE command

```
// JOB      DELETE
// EXEC     LIBR
   ACCESS   SUBLIB=USRSLE.INVNTORY
   DELETE   INV5200.PROC
/*
/&
```

Figure 15-19   Job to delete a library member

How to rename sublibraries or members: The RENAME command   To change the name of a sublibrary or the name or type of a library member, you use the RENAME command. Its format is shown in figure 15-20. For each sublibrary or member to be renamed, you code the current name, a space or a colon, and the new name. For example,

```
RENAME SUBLIB=USRSLE.INVAPPS:USRSLE.INVBKUP
```

changes the name of the sublibrary INVAPPS located in USRSLE to INVBKUP. In addition, as you can see in figure 15-20, you can code more than one pair of names on the same command.

If an item with the new name you specify on the RENAME command already exists, the command is not executed. And, as with the DELETE command, you can't alter a sublibrary if it's currently being accessed by another VSE partition. Likewise, any LIBDEF search chains that specify the old sublibrary name must be dropped before the sublibrary can be renamed.

The RENAME command

```
RENAME {SUBLIB=library.oldsublibrary     [:]  library.newsublibrary...          }
       {oldmembername.oldmembertype       [:]  newmembername.newmembertype...    }
```

Explanation

SUBLIB	Specifies the old and new sublibrary names. The library name must be the same in both operands and can be specified in the second operand with an equal sign (=). SUBLIB may be abbreviated S.
membername.membertype	Specifies the old and new member names and types. The equal sign (=) can be used in the second operand if either the name or type is not changed.

Figure 15-20   The RENAME command

When renaming sublibraries, the library name must stay the same. Instead of coding the name twice, you can code an equal sign (=) for the second library specification. The equal sign signals the VSE Librarian that the name coded in the first operand is unchanged in the second operand. So in the above example, I could have coded

```
RENAME SUBLIB=USRSLE.INVAPPS:=.INVBKUP
```

The same shortcut can be used when renaming members if you want either the member name or type to stay the same.

When I introduced user-defined member types in chapter 2, I mentioned that you could use them to store several different versions of the same procedure in a sublibrary. A common use of the RENAME command, then, is to activate a procedure by giving it the PROC member type and by storing the other versions with alternate member types, like PROC1, PROC2, and PROC3. (Remember, you can't process a member with a user-defined type with JCL.)

Without user-defined member types, you'd have to give each version of the procedure a different member name. Then, when you wanted to switch to a different version of the procedure, you'd have to change the name in all the job streams that call it. If you store the different versions with the same name but alternate member types, however, you avoid having to do that.

DISCUSSION   Although VSE libraries and the programs that process them are important, program source code and copy books are commonly stored in the ICCF library so they're easily accessible to terminal users. However, you still need to be able to use VSE source statement libraries to store members for inclusion in jobs you assemble or compile in batch. And you still need to be able to use VSE relocatable libraries for the object code of the subprograms you use.

In many cases, source books and procedures are stored in both a VSE library and in the ICCF library file. Then, if you want to make a change to one of them, all you have to do is edit the ICCF version and replace the VSE version using the Librarian CATALOG command with the REPLACE=YES operand. In contrast, if the member isn't stored in an ICCF file, you have to punch it from the VSE library before you can edit it.

Objectives   Given appropriate specifications, code a job to:

1. Print a directory listing for a VSE library, sublibrary, member, or the System Directory List

2. Punch or print a member from a VSE library

3. Create a VSE library or sublibrary

4. Add a source book, object module, procedure, or user-defined member to a VSE sublibrary

5. Delete a VSE library, sublibrary, or member

6. Rename a sublibrary or member in a VSE library

TOPIC 2   How to use advanced VSE Librarian features

In topic 1 of this chapter, you learned the basic VSE Librarian commands that service and maintain libraries. In this topic, I'm going to discuss two more sets of commands you can use when working with the VSE Librarian.

The first set of commands provides additional maintenance functions. The CONNECT, COPY, and MOVE commands let you rearrange your library structure by copying and moving libraries, sublibraries and members. The second set of commands lets you establish conditions in your Librarian job streams, like the conditional JCL you learned in chapter 6.

How to copy and move libraries, sublibraries, or members

The COPY and MOVE commands both involve transferring data from one library or sublibrary to another. So, to make the following command definitions easier to follow, I'll refer to the data's original location as the from-library or from-sublibrary and the data's destination as the to-library or to-sublibrary. You code these specifications directly on a COPY or MOVE command when you want to transfer a library or sublibrary. But if you want to copy or move an individual member, you first have to code a CONNECT command to specify the member's from- and to-sublibrary.

The CONNECT command   In the first topic of this chapter, you learned that before you perform an operation on a library member, you need to specify the sublibrary in which it's located with an ACCESS command. But when you copy or move a library member, you need to access two sublibraries. To do that, you code a CONNECT command to "connect" the two sublibraries.

The format of the CONNECT command is shown in figure 15-21. For the SUBLIB operand, you code the name of the from-sublibrary, followed by a space or a colon, followed by the to-sublibrary. For example, if you code

```
CONNECT SUBLIB=USRSLE.INVTEST:USRSLE.INVAPPS
```

you can then copy or move the members in the sublibrary USRSLE.INVTEST to the sublibrary USRSLE.INVAPPS.

If the from-library is the same as the to-library, you can code an equal sign for it. So you could code the above example like this:

```
CONNECT SUBLIB=USRSLE.INVTEST:=.INVAPPS
```

You can also code an equal sign for the to-sublibrary if it's the same as the from-sublibrary.

The CONNECT command

```
CONNECT SUBLIB=from-library.from-sublibrary [:] to-library.to-sublibrary
```

Explanation

SUBLIB   Specifies the two sublibraries to be used in subsequent COPY or MOVE commands.
                          The from-sublibrary specifies the sublibrary where a member is presently located.
                          The to-sublibrary specifies the sublibrary to which you want a member transferred.
                          SUBLIB may be abbreviated S.

Figure 15-21   The CONNECT command

A CONNECT command remains valid until another CONNECT command is issued or until one of the sublibraries it specifies is deleted or renamed.

The COPY command   You can use the COPY command to copy libraries, sublibraries, or members. When you do, the data copied exists at both the old and new locations, even though it may be stored with different names.

The format of the COPY command is shown in figure 15-22. For its first operand, you specify the name of the library, sublibrary, or member you want to copy. Notice that you can copy multiple libraries, sublibraries, or members with a single COPY command.

When you copy libraries, you code the LIB operand with the name of the from-library, followed by a colon or a space, followed by the name of the to-library. For instance, if you code

```
COPY    LIB=USRSLE:SLEBKUP
```

all the sublibraries and members of the library USRSLE are copied to SLEBKUP. The to-library you specify, in this case SLEBKUP, must already be defined to the VSE Librarian with a DEFINE command. If it's not, the copy operation won't work.

In contrast, when you copy sublibraries, you can specify a to-sublibrary that hasn't yet been defined. When you do that, VSE creates that sublibrary in the specified to-library when it processes the COPY command. So you can code

```
COPY    SUBLIB=USRSLE.INVAPPS:SLEBKUP.=
```

even if the sublibrary SLEBKUP.INVAPPS doesn't exist. Note, however, that the to-library SLEBKUP must still already be defined to VSE. Notice also that you can code an = for the to-library or to-sublibrary when that name doesn't change.

The COPY command

```
      ⎧LIB=from-library [:] to-library...                                          ⎫
COPY  ⎨SUBLIB=from-library.from-sublibrary [:] to-library.to-sublibrary...⎬
      ⎩membername.membertype...                                                   ⎭

              [REPLACE=⎧YES⎫] [LIST=⎧YES⎫]
                      ⎩NO ⎭        ⎩NO ⎭
```

Explanation

LIB	Specifies the libraries to be used for the copy operation. All the sublibraries in the from-library are copied to the to-library. LIB may be abbreviated L.
SUBLIB	Specifies the sublibraries to be used for the copy operation. All the members in the from-sublibrary are copied to the to-sublibrary. If the to-sublibrary doesn't exist, it's created. SUBLIB may be abbreviated S.
membername.membertype	Specifies the members to be copied. The COPY command must be preceded by a CONNECT command that specifies the to- and from-sublibraries.
REPLACE	Indicates whether or not sublibraries or members that already exist in the to-library should be replaced. REPLACE may be abbreviated R.
LIST	Indicates whether or not the names and types of copied members, along with their corresponding to- and from-libraries and sublibraries, should be listed. LIST may be abbreviated LIS.

Figure 15-22   The COPY command

When you want to copy members, you must first code a CON-NECT command to specify the to- and from-sublibraries. Then, in the COPY command, you just code the names of the members you want to copy. In this case, it isn't possible to change the name of the member as you copy it from one location to another. To do that you need to use the RENAME command.

The COPY command also has two optional operands: REPLACE and LIST. The REPLACE operand indicates whether or not copied sublibraries or members should replace existing sublibraries or members with the same name. If you code REPLACE=NO or omit the operand, the existing sublibraries or members won't be replaced. In other words, the copy operation is not performed. If you code REPLACE=YES, the copied sublibraries or members will replace the existing ones.

The LIST operand indicates whether or not you want to list the members that are transferred during a copy operation. If you code LIST=YES, the copied members, along with their corresponding from- and to-sublibraries and libraries, are listed. This option is particularly useful if you code REPLACE=NO because, in that case, all of the members may not be copied. LIST=NO is the default.

```
// JOB      MERGE100
// EXEC     LIBR
   CONNECT  SUBLIB=USRSLE.INVTEST:=.INVAPPS
   COPY     *.* REPLACE=YES
/*
/&
```

Figure 15-23   Job that merges two sublibraries

With the new VSE Librarian program, there isn't a MERGE command that merges two sublibraries like there was with the old Librarian programs. But this function can be easily accomplished with the CONNECT and COPY commands. Figure 15-23 shows a job that does just that.

After the Librarian program is invoked, a CONNECT command specifies the two sublibraries that will be merged. In this case, the sublibraries are USRSLE.INVTEST and USRSLE.INVAPPS. Since USRSLE.INVAPPS is the to-sublibrary, it will be the location of the resulting merged sublibrary. Then, a COPY command coded with generic references specifies that all the members of all member types be copied. Since REPLACE=YES is coded on the COPY command, any member in USRSLE.INVAPPS that has the same name as a member in USRSLE.INVTEST will be replaced by that member.

As a result of this job, USRSLE.INVAPPS will contain all the members it previously contained (even though some of them may be different versions), plus all the members in USRSLE.INVTEST. And USRSLE.INVTEST will still contain all of its original members. If I hadn't coded the REPLACE=YES operand, members with duplicate names would *not* have been copied from USRSLE.INVTEST to USRSLE.INVAPPS.

The MOVE command   The MOVE command works just like the COPY command except that when an item is transferred to a new location, it's deleted from its previous location. The format of the MOVE command is presented in figure 15-24. As you can see, it's identical to the format of the COPY command. Since you should already understand how these operands are coded from my explanation of COPY, I'm not going to explain the MOVE command format in any more detail here.

You can use the MOVE command, just as you can the COPY command, to merge two sublibraries. The only difference is that, with MOVE, the from-sublibrary is emptied. (When you use a generic reference, you're only copying members, so the sublibrary itself isn't moved.) The only exception to this is if there are members with the same name in both sublibraries and the REPLACE operand is omitted or coded

The MOVE command

```
        (LIB=from-library [:] to-library...                                      )
MOVE    {SUBLIB=from-library.from-sublibrary [:] to-library.to-sublibrary...}
        (membername.membertype...                                               )
```

$$[REPLACE=\left\{{YES \atop \underline{NO}}\right\}]\ [LIST=\left\{{YES \atop \underline{NO}}\right\}]$$

Explanation

LIB	Specifies the libraries to be used for the move operation. All the sublibraries in the from-library are moved to the to-library. LIB may be abbreviated L.
SUBLIB	Specifies the sublibraries to be used for the move operation. All the members in the from-sublibrary are moved to the to-sublibrary. If the to-sublibrary doesn't exist, it's created. SUBLIB may be abbreviated S.
membername.membertype	Specifies the members to be moved. The MOVE command must be preceded by a CONNECT command that specifies the to- and from-sublibraries.
REPLACE	Indicates whether or not sublibraries or members that already exist in the to-library should be replaced. REPLACE may be abbreviated R.
LIST	Indicates whether or not the names and types of moved members, along with their corresponding to- and from-libraries and sublibraries, should be listed. LIST may be abbreviated LIS.

Figure 15-24   The MOVE command

REPLACE=NO. Then, members with duplicate names are not moved, and the from-sublibrary will still contain them.

How to use conditional Librarian commands

Just as you can control the sequence of execution of a job stream with conditional JCL, you can control the processing of a Librarian command stream with conditional Librarian commands. These commands—GOTO, label (/.), and ON—are equivalent to the JCL statements with the same names you learned in chapter 6. Notice, however, that the VSE Librarian doesn't provide an IF or SETPARM command.

The GOTO command   The format of the Librarian GOTO command is the same as the JCL GOTO statement, as you can see in figure 15-25. For its operand, you code the name of a label command that follows the GOTO command. Then, when the Librarian encounters the GOTO command, it branches to that label command and resumes processing. When you code a GOTO command, be careful that you code the name of a Librarian label command and not the name of a job control label statement.

The GOTO command

GOTO label

Explanation

label   Specifies the one- to eight-character operand of the label command (/.) where exe-
                         cution of the Librarian is to continue.

Figure 15-25   The GOTO command

The label command (/.)

/. label

Explanation

label   Specifies a one- to eight-character alphameric name.

Figure 15-26   The label command

The label command (/.)   Like the JCL label statement, the Librarian label command (/.) identifies a particular location in your Librarian
command stream. Its format is shown in figure 15-26. As you can see,
its only operand is a one- to eight-character alphameric name that can
be referenced by a GOTO command or the GOTO operand of an ON
command.

The ON command   The VSE Librarian issues a return code after
the execution of each command, just like the job control program issues
a return code after each step. Figure 15-27 shows the standard return
codes for Librarian commands. By testing these return codes with an
ON command, you can control the processing of your Librarian command stream. For example, before you try to move a sublibrary, you
can check whether the to-library is already defined. You do this by issuing a LISTDIR command for the to-library. If the return code is 4, the
library doesn't exist. Then, you can use an ON command to branch
past the MOVE command.

Like the ON statement you learned in chapter 6, the Librarian ON
command specifies a global condition. Then, a specified action is taken
if that condition is satisfied at any point during the Librarian command
stream.

RETURN CODE	MEANING
0	The command was completed successfully.
4	The command was completed, but an exceptional condition occurred, or the requested result already existed.
8	The command was only partly executed, but the Librarian program could continue processing.
16	A severe error occurred while processing the command. The Librarian program terminates.

Figure 15-27   Standard return codes for VSE Librarian commands

The ON command

```
ON $RC {>  n {GOTO label}
        {<    {CONTINUE }
        {=}
```

Explanation

$RC
Specifies the return code of the preceding Librarian command.

n
Specifies a decimal integer from 0 to 9999, which is to be used for comparison with the return code.

GOTO label
Specifies that processing should continue at the indicated label command if the indicated condition is true.

CONTINUE
Specifies that processing should continue if the indicated condition is true. CONTINUE may be abbreviated CONT.

Figure 15-28   The ON command

As you can see in figure 15-28, the ON command format differs from the JCL ON statement in the options available for specifying a condition. Here, you can only test return codes; there are no $ABEND or $CANCEL keywords. You're also limited in the types of comparisons you can make; the three choices are =, <, or >.

There are still two ways you can specify the action to be taken when the ON condition is satisfied. Using the GOTO command, you can specify that you want the Librarian to branch forward to a label command. Or, if you code CONTINUE, you can indicate that you want processing to continue with the next command.

```
//  JOB      MERGE200
//  EXEC     LIBR
    ON       $RC=8 GOTO LISTMEM
    CONNECT  SUBLIB=USRSLE.INVTEST:=.INVAPPS
    COPY     *.* REPLACE=YES
    GOTO     END
/. LISTMEM
    LISTDIR SUBLIB=(USRSLE.INVTEST,USRSLE.INVAPPS) OUTPUT=SHORT
/. END
/*
/&
```

Figure 15-29   Job that uses conditional Librarian commands

A sample job that uses conditional Librarian commands   Figure 15-29 presents a job that uses conditional Librarian commands. This job merges two sublibraries just like the job in figure 15-23. The added conditional commands provide an error checking routine.

After the Librarian program is invoked, an ON command specifies that if the return code from any command is equal to 8, processing should continue at the label command LISTMEM. Then, the two sublibraries USRSLE.TEST and USRSLE.INVAPPS are merged. If all the commands execute normally, the GOTO command directs the Librarian program to the END label command and the command stream is done.

However, if the COPY command issues a return code of 8, the ON condition is satisfied, and the job branches immediately to the LISTMEM label, skipping the GOTO command. Then, a LISTDIR command prints the directory of USRSLE.INVTEST and USRSLE.INVAPPS, so you can see what was and what wasn't copied. After that, the Librarian command stream ends.

Discussion   If you use the Librarian commands presented in this topic along with the commands presented in topic 1 of this chapter, you'll be able to code command streams for most of the functions you'll ever need. However, as I mentioned at the beginning of this chapter, there are some Librarian commands I haven't covered. Although you probably won't use these commands often, you might want to know what they are so you can use them if you ever need to. You can refer back to figure 15-1 to see what these commands are. If you want more information on them, refer to *VSE/Advanced Functions System Control Statements*.

Objectives   1. Code a job that copies or moves a VSE library, sublibrary, or member.

2. Code a job that uses conditional Librarian commands.

Section 6

Utility programs

All VSE shops have a set of IBM utility programs that are considered to be part of VSE itself. For example, the VSE Librarian program, LVTOC, INTTP, and the linkage editor can all be classified as utility programs. VSE also includes about a dozen others, most of them for systems programming functions I'm not going to describe in this book.

In addition to the utility programs VSE includes, most VSE shops use separately licensed utility programs. Two that are almost certainly available in your shop are DOS/VS Sort/Merge and VSE/DITTO. So chapter 16 shows you how to use Sort/Merge, and chapter 17 shows you how to use DITTO. Also, AMS, the VSAM Access Method Services program, provides a variety of utility functions you may need to use in addition to the DEFINE functions chapter 13 presented. So chapter 18 shows you how to use AMS to maintain VSAM catalogs and print and copy VSAM files.

Chapter 16

How to use DOS/VS Sort/Merge

Often, data stored in a file in one sequence needs to be reordered to produce a particular kind of output. For example, a sequential file of employee records stored in employee number sequence might have to be reordered so it's in sequence by employee name, social security number, department, job description, salary, hiring date, date of last promotion, or any other field its records contain. To resequence a file, you use the DOS/VS Sort/Merge program. The current Sort/Merge program available under VSE is DOS/VS Sort/Merge Version 2, or *SM2*.

As its name implies, Sort/Merge has two functions. The *sort* function assumes that all input records are out of sequence, and it puts them in the sequence you request. Resequencing a file is a sort application. The *merge* function assumes that records are in the right sequence, but are stored in separate files, so it combines them into one file, also in the right sequence. For example, suppose you have two files of general ledger transactions, both in account number sequence, but for different periods. If you want to combine them into a single file also in account number sequence, you use the merge function of SM2.

You can execute the Sort/Merge program in two ways. First, you can run it directly from a job stream, like any other application program. Alternatively, you can invoke it from a user-written application program. You'll learn the JCL considerations for both in this chapter.

HOW TO CODE JOB STREAMS TO INVOKE SORT/MERGE DIRECTLY

Already in this book, you've seen sample job streams that invoke Sort/Merge directly. In this section, you'll learn how to code the JCL to define the files SM2 uses, how to invoke SM2, and how to code the control statements that direct it.

Sort/Merge files

For the operations you're going to learn in this topic, Sort/Merge uses three kinds of files: output, input, and work files. Regardless of whether you want to perform a sort operation or a merge operation, SM2's output is always a single file. In typical operations, SM2 calls it SORTOUT and refers to it with logical unit SYS001.

Input, on the other hand, can come from up to nine files for either a sort or a merge operation. Sort/Merge refers to those files with the names SORTIN1 through SORTIN9 and the logical units SYS002 through SYS010. Although most sort operations use only one file (SORTIN1, SYS002), merge operations always use two or more files. For either operation, using the maximum number of input files Sort/Merge allows would be unusual.

Input and output files may be SAM or VSAM files. (Sort/Merge won't work with DAM or ISAM files.) The input and output files may be of different types. For example, the input file (or files) may be SAM files, while the output file is a VSAM file. However, all of the input files must be of the same type, although they may reside on different device types. For example, it's possible to combine and sort SAM files on tape, CKD DASD, and FBA DASD in one job step.

For a merge operation, all you need to worry about are the input and output files. However, for a sort operation, SM2 requires additional work space called *intermediate storage*. For very small sort jobs, that intermediate storage can be in virtual storage. But for most jobs, you need to provide intermediate storage on disk. (You may use either CKD or FBA DASDs, but not tape units, for work files.)

The exact amount of intermediate DASD storage SM2 requires depends on the files being processed and the SM2 functions you use. As a guideline, the amount of intermediate storage you need is about 125 percent of the total size of the input files. However, in some exceptional cases, the amount of required intermediate storage can be as much as the combined size of the input files plus 80 percent.

Rather than attempt to calculate the exact amount of intermediate storage required for an SM2 job, use 125 percent as a starting point. If the job will be used repeatedly and you expect the input files to grow, be sure to allow enough space in the work files for all the records the input files will eventually contain. I usually compute 125 percent of the total input file size, then increase that value to a round storage unit allocation. For instance, if I needed 770 FBA blocks for a work file, I'd probably allocate 1000. If you overallocate, be sure to specify a 0-day retention period for the work files so they won't unnecessarily use disk space.

You can allocate intermediate disk storage in one to nine work files, named SORTWK1 through SORTWK9. Their logical unit names begin with the next number after those used for the input files. So if a job uses three input files and three work files, their names and logical units are SORTIN1, SYS002; SORTIN2, SYS003; SORTIN3, SYS004; SORTWK1, SYS005; SORTWK2, SYS006; and SORTWK3, SYS007.

How many work files do you need for a particular job? It doesn't matter as long as the total intermediate DASD storage space available is sufficient for your job.

There are some peculiarities about SM2 work files you ought to know about. Specifically, SM2 lets you use a single DAM work file or multiple SAM work files. If you use a DAM file, you may have only one work file, but it may have multiple extents. If you use SAM work files, you can use from one to nine, but they may *not* have multiple extents. Because DAM files can't be used on FBA DASDs, I recommend you use SAM work files.

No matter what type of input, output, or work files you use, be sure you code the proper label and ASSGN statements to identify them. (If you're using VSAM files, you don't need ASSGN or EXTENT statements.) After you've identified the files, you can invoke the Sort/Merge program.

EXEC to invoke Sort/Merge

The phase name you use on the EXEC statement to invoke SM2 is SORT, regardless of whether you want to perform a sort or a merge operation. The Sort/Merge program requires a minimum of 32K of virtual storage in the program area of its partition. If no SM2 modules are stored in the SVA, the partition program area needs to be 12K larger. And the block sizes of the files you're processing must be included in the storage requirement. Even so, you'll seldom need to allow more than 64K for SM2. After the EXEC statement, you code the control statements necessary to specify the processing SM2 should do.

Sort/Merge control statements

You code Sort/Merge control statements like you code control statements for the linkage editor. Leave at least the first position of the statement blank. Then, separate the operation code from the operands by at least one blank. And if the statement requires more than one operand, separate them with commas.

There are more than a dozen SM2 control statements. In this topic, you'll learn the five you're most likely to use: SORT, MERGE, REC-

ORD, INPFIL, and OUTFIL. The others let you perform specialized functions like using alternate sorting sequences, omitting parts of records, and using exit routines. If you need any of these features, refer to *DOS/VS Sort/Merge Version 2 Programmer's Guide*.

For any execution of SM2, you must code the RECORD statement and either the SORT or the MERGE statement. The SORT and MERGE statements specify the operation the program should perform and supply additional control information. The RECORD statement specifies the format and size of the input records. The other control statements aren't required all the time, but may be necessary depending on your job. You can code SM2 control statements in any order.

The SORT and MERGE control statements   If you want SM2 to perform a sort operation, you code the SORT control statement. And if you want it to perform a merge operation, you code the MERGE control statement. Figure 16-1 illustrates both.

The purpose of the FIELDS operand in both statements is to tell SM2 the sequence in which you want the output to be. On this operand, you identify a field (or fields) in the input records that SM2 will evaluate to determine the positions the records will have in the output file. Each of these fields is a *control* (or *key*) *field*. You can specify from 1 to 12 control fields in the FIELDS operand of either the SORT or MERGE statement. For each control field, you supply four items: (1) position, (2) length, (3) format, and (4) sort sequence.

The position value you specify for a control field locates it in the record; it's the location of the first byte of the field. If a control field begins at the first byte in the input record, you code 1 for position. (Don't confuse this with offset, or displacement; that's zero for the first byte of a record.) Control fields must be located in the same positions in all the input records.

The second value you code is length. For it, supply the length of the control field in bytes. If a field contains signed data, the length should include the sign position (if there is one). The total length of all the control fields you specify cannot be greater than 256 bytes, and no control field may extend beyond byte 4092 in a record.

The third value you code specifies the format of the data stored in the control field. Figure 16-1 shows the most common data representations and the format codes you use for each. If all of the control fields you specify have the same format, you can omit the third value from the control field list and specify the format code with FORMAT= outside the list instead, as you can see in figure 16-1.

The last value you code for a control field specifies how SM2 should sequence the output. You may code either A for ascending sequence or D for descending sequence.

The sequence in which you code the control fields affects the output of SM2. The first control field you specify is the *major control field*; it determines the primary sequence of the output file. The other control fields are *minor control fields*. They also affect the sequence of the

The SORT and MERGE control statements of SM2

```
SORT  {FIELDS=(position,length,format,sequence...)          }
      {FIELDS=(position,length,sequence...),FORMAT=format}

      [,FILES=n]

     [{,EQUALS   }]
     [{,NOEQUALS}]

      [,WORK=n]


MERGE {FIELDS=(position,length,format,sequence...)          }
      {FIELDS=(position,length,sequence...),FORMAT=format}

      ,FILES=n
```

Figure 16-1   The SORT and MERGE control statements of SM2 (part 1 of 2)

output, but only within the sequence determined by the control fields specified to their left in the SORT or MERGE statement.

To understand how the control field values work, consider figure 16-2. It shows ten unsorted records, a SORT control statement that specifies how they should be ordered in the output, and the result of the operation: the sorted records.

In this example, the file is sorted based on three control fields. Since all of the fields contain character data, I omitted format values from the list of control fields and coded FORMAT=CH instead. According to the FIELDS operand of the SORT control statement, the program is directed to (1) sort the records in ascending sequence based on the six-byte field that begins in position 3 of each record; (2) within that sequence, sort the records in descending sequence based on the three-byte field that begins in position 11 of each record; and (3) within that sequence, sort the records in ascending sequence based on the three-byte field that begins in position 18 of each record.

In the bottom part of figure 16-2, the records are in ascending sequence according to the values in positions 3-8. For records that have the same data in that field (012345 and 019412), the records are in descending sequence according to the values in positions 11-13. For the records that still have the same control field values (019412 in the first field and 605 in the second field), the records are in ascending sequence according to the values in positions 18-20.

If all of the control fields in two or more records of a file being sorted are the same, the sequence of records in the output file depends on

Explanation

FIELDS   Specifies the control fields in the input records. You may code from one to 12 field specifications, each of which consists of four elements: position, length, format, and sequence. The elements are separated by commas.

    position   The location of the first byte of the control field in the input record.

    length   The length in bytes of the control field.

    format   One of the following two-character codes to identify the format of the data in the control field:

       CH   Character
       ZD   Signed zoned decimal
       PD   Signed packed decimal
       FI   Signed fixed-point binary
       BI   Unsigned binary
       FL   Signed normalized floating point

    If all control fields have the same format, you may omit this operand and instead code FORMAT = format to apply to all control fields.

    sequence   One of these one-character codes to identify the order in which the control field should be processed:

       A   Ascending sequence
       D   Descending sequence

FILES = n   Specifies the number of input files to be sorted or merged. You may omit this operand on the SORT statement. If you do, SM2 defaults to one input file. FILES = n is required on the MERGE statement.

EQUALS   Specifies that the order of the records in the input files should be preserved when all control fields are equal. Valid only on the SORT statement.

NOEQUALS   Specifies that the order of the records in the input files need not be preserved in the output file when all control fields are equal. Valid only on the SORT statement.

WORK = n   Specifies the number of work files to be used for a sort operation. Must be a numeric value from 0 to 9. If you code 0, SM2 attempts to use virtual storage for its work storage. If you omit this operand, SM2 defaults to 1.

Figure 16-1   The SORT and MERGE control statements of SM2 (part 2 of 2)

whether or not you code the EQUALS operand on the SORT statement. If you do, the order of the records from the input file is preserved. However, EQUALS makes SM2 execute less efficiently, so you should use it only when you need to. If you don't code EQUALS, or you code NOEQUALS, the order of the records from the input file may *not* be preserved. NOEQUALS is the default.

Unsorted records

Position	3-8	11-13	18-20
	012345	AAA	012
	012345	ABC	907
	011947	RB2	106
	047693	AAT	999
	142342	BBR	212
	002973	972	660
	112233	617	127
	019412	322	432
	019412	605	692
	019412	605	000

SORT statement

```
SORT FIELDS=(3,6,A,11,3,D,18,3,A),FORMAT=CH
```

Sorted records

	3-8	11-13	18-20
	002973	972	660
	011947	RB2	106
	012345	ABC	907
	012345	AAA	012
	019412	605	000
	019412	605	692
	019412	322	432
	047693	AAT	999
	112233	617	127
	142342	BBR	212

Figure 16-2   Example of the sort operation

If the three control fields I specified in figure 16-2 had different formats, I would have specified those formats in the FIELDS operand. For example,

```
SORT  FIELDS=(3,6,CH,A,11,3,PD,D,18,3,ZD,A)
```

specifies that the first field contains character data, the second contains packed decimal data, and the last contains zoned decimal data.

The MERGE statement works much like the SORT statement. To understand it, consider figure 16-3. It shows two files, already in the desired sequence, that I want to merge into a single sequential file. After SM2 has finished this merge operation, the output is in the same sequence as in the input, but the two files are combined into one sequential file. As you can see, the format of the FIELDS and FORMAT operands of MERGE are the same as for SORT.

	Input file 1		**Input file 2**	
Position	1-5	9	1-5	9
	01234	A	01234	B
	02694	A	01234	E
	02694	D	02988	A
	02988	R	06611	T
	05617	B	07122	R
	05617	C	88216	A
	98999	D	98999	A
	98999	E	98999	Z
	99667	X	99500	B
	99999	Z	99999	T

MERGE statement

```
MERGE   FIELDS=(1,5,A,9,1,A),FORMAT=CH,FILES=2
```

Merged file

01234	A
01234	B
01234	E
02694	A
02694	D
02988	A
02988	R
05617	B
05617	C
06611	T
07122	R
88216	A
98999	A
98999	D
98999	E
98999	Z
99500	B
99667	X
99999	T
99999	Z

Figure 16-3   Example of the merge operation

Notice in figure 16-3 that I coded the FILES operand on the MERGE statement. When you use MERGE, you must code FILES to specify how many input files SM2 should process. When you use SORT, you can omit FILES if only one input file is being processed, but it's required if you're processing two or more input files.

The RECORD control statement of SM2

For files with fixed-length records

```
RECORD TYPE=F,LENGTH=(record-length)
```

For files with variable-length records

```
RECORD TYPE=V,LENGTH=(max-length,,,min-length,modal-length)
```

Explanation

record-length	The length of the fixed-length records to be processed.
max-length	The length of the longest of the variable-length records to be processed.
min-length	The length of the shortest of the variable-length records to be processed.
modal-length	The length of the most frequently occurring record format.

Figure 16-4   The RECORD control statement of SM2

You might also need to code the WORK operand for a sort operation. It specifies how many work files SM2 will use; the default is 1. If you're sorting a small file and want to attempt a sort without a work file (in other words, if you want to use virtual storage for the intermediate storage SM2 requires), code WORK=0. And remember, you must supply a DLBL statement for each work file you indicate.

The RECORD control statement   In addition to coding either SORT or MERGE when you run SM2, you also must code the RECORD statement. RECORD, illustrated in figure 16-4, describes the records SM2 will process as input. If the file contains fixed-length records, you use the first format in the figure. Code F for TYPE (for fixed-length) and code the record length in bytes for LENGTH.

You use the second format in figure 16-4 for files with variable-length records. Code V for TYPE. Then, in the LENGTH operand, you code three record-length values: the maximum length, the minimum length, and the modal length. The modal length is the length of the most frequently occurring record format in the file. Although the values you code for these lengths are in bytes, they must be four bytes longer than the actual data record length when you use variable-length records.

Also, notice that two items on the LENGTH operand for variable-length files are omitted. Those items, which have parallels in the fixed-length format, are used when record lengths are changed by user exits. Since that's an unusual function, I'm not going to cover it.

The INPFIL control statement of SM2

```
INPFIL [BLKSIZE=n][,VSAM]
```

Explanation

BLKSIZE = n

Specifies, in bytes, the size of the largest input file block. You may omit this operand if the input files are VSAM, reside on FBA devices, or are unblocked. Otherwise, it's required.

VSAM

Required if the input files are VSAM. If you omit this operand, SM2 assumes the input files are SAM.

Figure 16-5   The INPFIL control statement of SM2

The INPFIL control statement   Unless you use an INPFIL control statement (illustrated in figure 16-5), SM2 expects to process SAM files with unblocked records as input. If you want to process VSAM files as input, you have to code the INPFIL statement with the VSAM operand. And if you want to process SAM files with blocked records on CKD DASDs or on tape devices, you have to code the BLKSIZE operand. For BLKSIZE, specify the maximum block size in bytes. If you want to use blocked SAM files that reside on FBA DASDs, BLKSIZE isn't required, nor is it required to process a VSAM file.

Recall that the input files Sort/Merge uses during one run must all be of the same type. So you can't mix SAM and VSAM files for input. That makes sense when you think about the INPFIL control statement. You code this statement only once for an SM2 run, and it specifies the input file type (VSAM explicitly or SAM by default).

The OUTFIL control statement   The OUTFIL control statement, illustrated in figure 16-6, is similar to INPFIL. If you want to create a blocked SAM file as output (on either CKD or FBA DASDs), you need to code the OUTFIL statement with the BLKSIZE operand to specify the largest block to be created. As with INPFIL, you don't code the BLKSIZE operand when the output is to be a VSAM file. But to specify that SM2 should create a VSAM file as output, you don't code VSAM, as you do with INPFIL. Instead, you specify the kind of VSAM file to be created: KSDS, ESDS, or RRDS.

Sample Sort/Merge jobs

Now, I want to show you three Sort/Merge jobs. All three use similar files, but present different Sort/Merge problems. The files these job use are sequential transaction files from a general ledger system. The control fields are transaction date and account number. The transaction

The OUTFIL control statement of SM2

```
OUTFIL [BLKSIZE=n][,VSAM-type]
```

Explanation

BLKSIZE = n

Specifies, in bytes, the size of the output file block. You may omit this operand if the output file is to be VSAM or is to be unblocked. Otherwise, it's required.

VSAM-type

If the output file is VSAM, you must specify one of these three values, depending on the type of VSAM file to be created:

KSDS
ESDS
RRDS

Figure 16-6   The OUTFIL control statement of SM2

date consists of three two-byte character fields: month beginning at position 27, day at position 29, and year at position 31. Account number is a six-byte character field beginning at position 41.

How to sort one file   The first example, illustrated in figure 16-7, is a sort that uses a single input file. The input file contains all the general ledger transaction records for one month (April, in this case). Within the input file, the records are in date sequence. However, the file needs to be reordered so it's in sequence by date within account number. That's so the output file can be used later in a job that runs a program to prepare a listing of transactions in date sequence, grouped by account number. In this sort, account number, not date, is the major control field.

The flowchart at the top of the figure gives the file names and logical units used in the job stream. If you study the JCL, you'll see that all three files used in this job reside on the DASD at address 242. Notice in the EXTENT statement for SORTWK1 that I allocated a work area that's 125 percent of the size of the input file (1250 FBA blocks compared to 1000). That should provide adequate work space for the sort.

On the EXEC statement that invokes the sort, I specified that the program area of the processing partition should be 32K. Then, the SORT control statement specifies the two control fields used for the sort: the major control field is account number and the minor control field is day. Since all of the records in the input file are from the same month, sorting by the day field results in the correct sequence. Alternatively, since the records in the input file are already in date sequence, I could have coded this SORT control statement

```
SORT FIELDS=(41,6,CH,A),EQUALS,WORK=1
```

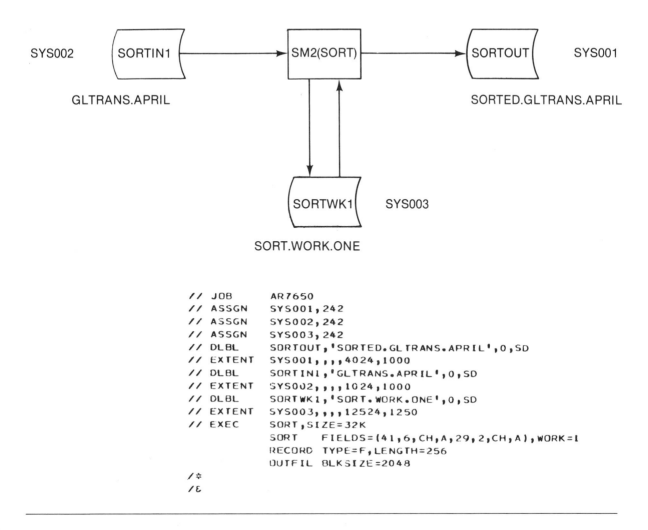

```
// JOB       AR7650
// ASSGN     SYS001,242
// ASSGN     SYS002,242
// ASSGN     SYS003,242
// DLBL      SORTOUT,'SORTED.GLTRANS.APRIL',0,SD
// EXTENT    SYS001,,,,4024,1000
// DLBL      SORTIN1,'GLTRANS.APRIL',0,SD
// EXTENT    SYS002,,,,1024,1000
// DLBL      SORTWK1,'SORT.WORK.ONE',0,SD
// EXTENT    SYS003,,,,12524,1250
// EXEC      SORT,SIZE=32K
            SORT    FIELDS=(41,6,CH,A,29,2,CH,A),WORK=1
            RECORD  TYPE=F,LENGTH=256
            OUTFIL  BLKSIZE=2048
/*
/&
```

Figure 16-7   Sorting one file

The EQUALS operand specifies that records with identical control fields should be retained in the same sequence as in the input file. But if you code EQUALS, SM2 has to do work it otherwise wouldn't do, so performance is reduced.

The input file contains fixed-length 256-byte records, as you can tell from the RECORD control statement. In this example, the input file is a blocked SAM file, but it resides on an FBA device. As a result, SM2 can process it without an INPFIL statement. However, if the blocked input file was on a CKD device, the INPFIL control statement with the BLKSIZE operand would be required. Because I wanted the output file to be created with the same blocking factor as the original file (8), I included the OUTFIL statement and coded BLKSIZE=2048 (8 X 256 = 2048) on it. Remember, OUTFIL is required if you want to create a blocked SAM file as output, regardless of the device type.

How to sort multiple files   The second example, illustrated in figure 16-8, shows you how to code a sort job that uses three input files. In this example, monthly transaction files from three months are to be combined and sorted to produce a transaction file for a quarterly period. The output file is again to be in date within account number sequence.

In this job, the three input files are SORTIN1, SORTIN2, and SORTIN3, associated with the logical units SYS002, SYS003, and SYS004. As a result, the sort work file, although named SORTWK1, is associated with logical unit SYS005. In this job stream, I specified that the work file should be allocated 3750 blocks.

Because I'm using three input files, I coded FILES=3 on the SORT control statement. Also notice on the SORT control statement that the second control field begins at position 27 and has length 4. As a result, it includes both the month and day fields within the date in the proper sequence for this sort application.

How to merge files   Figure 16-9 shows a job to merge the three monthly transaction files, assuming they're already in the correct sequence. The names and logical units in this example parallel those in figure 16-8, but the merge operation doesn't require a work file. On the EXEC statement, I coded SIZE=35K because a merge requires slightly more virtual storage than a sort. In the control statements in figure 16-9, I coded MERGE instead of SORT. Notice that I coded the FILES operand on the MERGE statement, which is required when you perform a merge operation. However, I didn't code the WORK operand because a merge doesn't use work files.

HOW TO CODE JOB STREAMS
TO INVOKE SORT/MERGE FROM AN APPLICATION PROGRAM

Sometimes it's better to code an application program that performs an *internal sort* than it is to use a *standalone sort* (one executed directly through JCL). When you use Sort/Merge through an application program, it's executed because of special statements you've coded in the program.

Figure 16-10 shows a job stream to execute a COBOL program that performs an internal sort. Here, GL6725, specified in the EXEC statement, is the application program. As a result, the job control statements you code to identify the files involved use the program names and logical units the application program specifies, not necessarily the SM2 default names. In this case, the COBOL application program uses GLTRANS.APRIL as input to the sort and processes the sorted records returned to it to produce a report. Although this program doesn't produce a permanent sorted output file, others might.

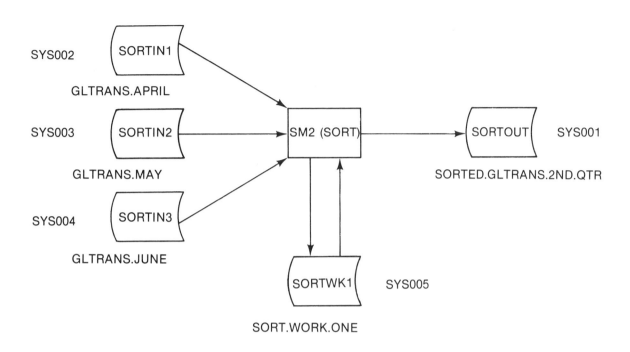

```
// JOB      AR7660
// ASSGN    SYS001,242
// ASSGN    SYS002,242
// ASSGN    SYS003,242
// ASSGN    SYS004,242
// ASSGN    SYS005,242
// DLBL     SORTOUT,'SORTED.GLTRANS.2ND.QTR',0,SD
// EXTENT   SYS001,,,,16274,3000
// DLBL     SORTIN1,'GLTRANS.APRIL',0,SD
// EXTENT   SYS002,,,,1024,1000
// DLBL     SORTIN2,'GLTRANS.MAY',0,SD
// EXTENT   SYS003,,,,2024,1000
// DLBL     SORTIN3,'GLTRANS.JUNE',0,SD
// EXTENT   SYS004,,,,3024,1000
// DLBL     SORTWK1,'SORT.WORK.ONE',0,SD
// EXTENT   SYS005,,,,12524,3750
// EXEC     SORT,SIZE=32K
          SORT    FIELDS=(41,6,CH,A,27,4,CH,A),FILES=3,WORK=1
          RECORD  TYPE=F,LENGTH=256
          OUTFIL  BLKSIZE=2048
/*
/&
```

Figure 16-8   Sorting three files

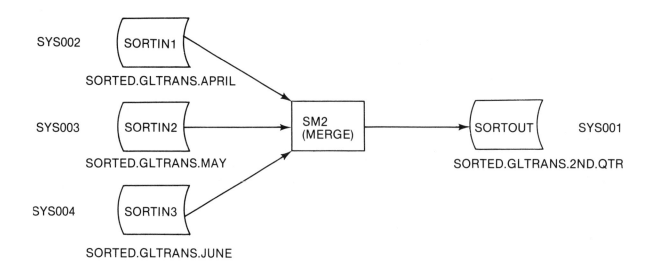

```
// JOB      AR7670
// ASSGN    SYS001,242
// ASSGN    SYS002,242
// ASSGN    SYS003,242
// ASSGN    SYS004,242
// DLBL     SORTOUT,'SORTED.GLTRANS.2ND.QTR',0,SD
// EXTENT   SYS001,,,,16274,3000
// DLBL     SORTIN1,'SORTED.GLTRANS.APRIL',0,SD
// EXTENT   SYS002,,,,12524,1000
// DLBL     SORTIN2,'SORTED.GLTRANS.MAY',0,SD
// EXTENT   SYS003,,,,13524,1000
// DLBL     SORTIN3,'SORTED.GLTRANS.JUNE',0,SD
// EXTENT   SYS004,,,,14524,1000
// EXEC     SORT,SIZE=35K
         MERGE   FIELDS=(41,6,CH,A,27,4,CH,A),FILES=3
         RECORD  TYPE=F,LENGTH=256
         OUTFIL  BLKSIZE=2048
/*
/&
```

Figure 16-9   Merging three files

The COBOL program specifies that the input file should be called SORTIN and that it should be associated with logical unit SYS008. It also specifies that the sort work file should be called SORTWK1 and should be associated with SYS001. You can see in the job stream in the figure that the DLBL and EXTENT statements I coded agree with this.

In the EXEC statement, I coded SIZE=(AUTO,32K) to insure that the program area will be large enough to accommodate the application program and SM2. As a result, VSE allows enough virtual storage for both programs.

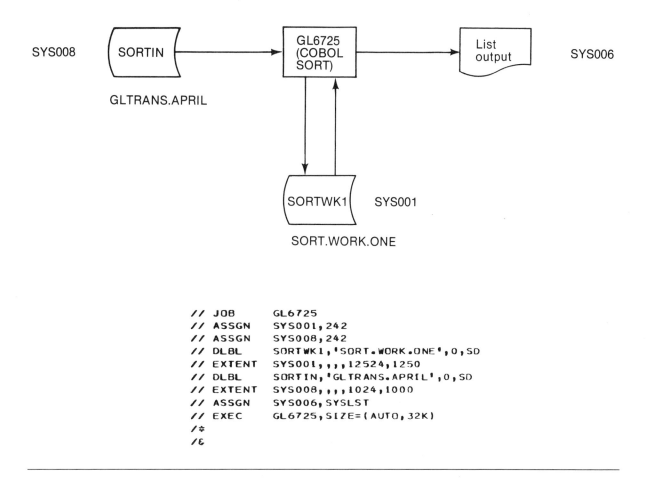

```
//  JOB      GL6725
//  ASSGN    SYS001,242
//  ASSGN    SYS008,242
//  DLBL     SORTWK1,'SORT.WORK.ONE',0,SD
//  EXTENT   SYS001,,,,12524,1250
//  DLBL     SORTIN,'GLTRANS.APRIL',0,SD
//  EXTENT   SYS008,,,,1024,1000
//  ASSGN    SYS006,SYSLST
//  EXEC     GL6725,SIZE=(AUTO,32K)
/*
/&
```

Figure 16-10   Invoking Sort/Merge from an application program

If an application program that does an internal sort requires other files or devices, you have to identify them in the JCL too. For example, in figure 16-10, the application program produces a report associated with SYS006 that should be printed on the central site printer. As a result, I coded an ASSGN statement to associate SYS006 with SYSLST.

DISCUSSION   When batch-sequential processing was the rule in data processing installations, Sort/Merge was used in many job streams. Although the continuing replacement of batch-sequential applications with interactive ones has reduced its use, sorting is still valuable in many circumstances. Remember, though, that Sort/Merge can process only SAM and VSAM files. You can't use it to process DAM or ISAM files.

Terminology   SM2
               sort
               merge
               intermediate storage
               control field
               key field
               major control field
               minor control field
               internal sort
               standalone sort

Objectives   1. Given specifications for an application that requires a standalone
                  sort or merge, code a job to execute the Sort/Merge program with
                  the appropriate file definitions and control statements.

               2. Given the requirements of an application program that performs
                  an internal sort, code the JCL to execute the program.

Chapter 17

How to use VSE/DITTO

VSE/DITTO, or just DITTO, is a multi-function program that lets you perform common data processing functions like printing, creating, and copying files. If you master the functions DITTO offers, you'll be able to perform a variety of program development and system management tasks easily and efficiently. In this chapter, I'll describe some of the functions you can perform with DITTO, show you how to code DITTO job streams, and give you examples of typical job streams.

DITTO has dozens of control statements that perform many functions. Some are more useful than others, but you may need to use a variety of them. Because there are so many, it's not practical for me to illustrate all of them. Instead, I'm going to show you how to use DITTO to produce a listing of its functions and the formats of its control statements. Then, I'll show you a few basic jobs that illustrate what you need to know to use DITTO for most applications. With that background, you should be able to use DITTO for the particular functions you need to perform.

DITTO can run in two ways: *console operation* and *batch operation*. Console operation lets the system operator run DITTO interactively. In this chapter, though, you'll only learn how to use DITTO in VSE jobs; that's batch operation.

DITTO functions   Essentially, what DITTO does is transfer data from one file to another, as its full name, Data Interfile Transfer, Testing, and Operations Utility, indicates. As a general rule, either the input or the output can be any kind of file. For instance, DITTO can copy a SAM input file to (1) cards, (2) tape, (3) another SAM file, (4) an ISAM file, (5) a VSAM file, or (6) a printer. As a result, you can use DITTO to print the contents of a SAM file or to convert a SAM file to almost any other kind of file. However, you can't create a DAM file, because DITTO doesn't support DAM for any operation. The input to DITTO isn't limited to SAM files; it can be cards, tape, or any disk file type except DAM.

In addition to providing a full set of file-processing functions, DITTO includes some special DASD and tape management functions. For disk, DITTO includes functions that let you display and alter the VTOC. For tape, DITTO includes functions that let you perform many of the operations of the MTC job control statement and the INTTP utility. Still other DITTO functions let you create files from data generated by DITTO itself; these functions are useful for building test files. You can imagine, then, how large the complete set of DITTO functions is. It's so large, in fact, that one of the functions of DITTO is to list its functions.

How to code a
DITTO job stream

Figure 17-1 is a DITTO job stream to produce a DITTO functions list. It also illustrates the basic JCL and control statement requirements for running DITTO.

JCL for a DITTO job   Notice after the JOB statement in figure 17-1 that I coded

```
// UPSI     1
```

DITTO uses the UPSI byte to determine whether it should operate in batch or console mode. If the first bit in the UPSI byte is on, DITTO operates in batch mode, so that's what you want when you execute DITTO from a job stream. If you don't include this UPSI statement, DITTO will begin to execute in console mode. Then, the system operator will receive a series of unexpected messages and prompts from DITTO. So be sure to code this UPSI statement.

To invoke DITTO, code

```
// EXEC     DITTO
```

If you need to use the SIZE operand of EXEC to process VSAM files, don't code SIZE=AUTO since it doesn't work as you'd expect with DITTO. Instead, code SIZE=128K. That should provide plenty of storage.

Although figure 17-1 doesn't illustrate it, if DITTO is going to do file-based operations, you have to code appropriate ASSGN, DLBL, and EXTENT statements, depending on the functions you request in DITTO control statements. DITTO control statements immediately follow the EXEC statement in the job stream.

DITTO control statements   To specify the function you want DITTO to perform and to supply additional control information for it, you use DITTO control statements; the job stream in figure 17-1 contains two.

```
// JOB      LISTFCTS
// UPSI     1
// EXEC     DITTO
$$DITTO XXX
$$DITTO EOJ
/&
```

Figure 17-1   Job to list VSE/DITTO functions

As you can see, they both begin with $$DITTO. You have to code $$DITTO in positions 1 through 7 of each DITTO control statement. After $$DITTO, you code the function code for the operation you want to perform. (XXX and EOJ are the function codes in the two control statements in figure 17-1.) You separate the function code from $$DITTO with one or more blanks. Figure 17-2, part of the output from the job in figure 17-1, illustrates all the DITTO function codes.

The XXX function is a simple one. For almost all others, you'll have to code one or more operands. You separate the operands from the function code with one or more spaces. Operands are separated from one another with commas, not spaces.

The specific operands you code vary depending on what you want DITTO to do. You can refer to another part of the function code listing to see the operands available with each statement. But I didn't include that section of the listing because it's long and you can easily get your own copy by running the job in figure 17-1.

You should know, however, that common operands for file-based functions are FILEIN and FILEOUT; they identify the DASD files to be used for the requested operation. On these operands, you code the file-name from the DLBL statement that identifies the related file. You'll see how this works in the sample job streams that follow.

Depending on the DITTO function you want to perform, a variety of other operands may be available. The examples in this chapter will help you understand how to use them. For the most part, they're self-explanatory.

In each DITTO job, the last control statement you code is

```
$$DITTO EOJ
```

This statement tells DITTO there are no more control statements in the job stream. So you don't have to code the end-of-data statement (/*) to mark the end of the DITTO control statements.

Sample DITTO jobs   In this section, I want to show you how to use DITTO to print, create, and copy files. In addition, the last example shows you how to use DITTO to list a DASD's VTOC. For each sample job stream, I've included the output from the job so you can better understand the DITTO function.

```
***********************************************************************
*   DATA INTERFILE TRANSFER, TESTING AND OPERATIONS UTILITY FOR VSE & VM   *
***********************************************************************
*                                                                     *
*                                                                     *
*   DITTO'S FUNCTIONS ARE GROUPED FOR CONVENIENCE AS FOLLOWS:         *
*                                                                     *
*          PROCESSING CONTROL FUNCTIONS                               *
*          CARD FUNCTIONS                                             *
*          TAPE CONTROL FUNCTIONS                                    *
*          BASIC TAPE FUNCTIONS                                      *
*          TAPE FILE FUNCTIONS                                       *
*          BASIC DISK FUNCTIONS                                      *
*          SAM FILE FUNCTIONS (VSE ONLY)                             *
*          ISAM FILE FUNCTIONS (VSE ONLY)                            *
*          VSAM FILE FUNCTIONS                                       *
*          DATA CREATE FUNCTIONS                                     *
*          BASIC DISKETTE FUNCTIONS                                  *
*          DISKETTE FILE FUNCTIONS                                   *
*          CMS FILE FUNCTIONS (CMS ONLY)                             *
*                                                                     *
*                                                                     *
*   THE INFORMATION BELOW PROVIDES SHORT DESCRIPTIONS OF EACH OF THE   *
*   FUNCTIONS, FOLLOWED BY DETAILED DESCRIPTIONS OF THE FUNCTIONS AND  *
*   THE PARAMETERS THEY USE IN BOTH BATCH AND CONSOLE MODE.            *
*                                                                     *
*                        •                                            *
*                                                                     *
*                   PROCESSING CONTROL FUNCTIONS                       *
*                                                                     *
*   XXX   LIST FUNCTIONS ON THE PRINTER                              *
*   SET   SET PROCESSING PARAMETERS                                  *
*   FMT   DESCRIBE DOUBLE BYTE CHARACTER SUPPORT (DBCS) FORMAT       *
*   CCL   CARD CLOSE - CANCEL CARD INPUT                             *
*   EOJ   END OF JOB                                                 *
*                                                                     *
*                        CARD FUNCTIONS                               *
*                                                                     *
*   CC    CARD TO CARD                                               *
*   CI    SAME AS CC WITH INTERPRETED CARDS                          *
*   II    INTERPRET PREPUNCHED CARDS                                 *
*   CP    CARD TO PRINTER IN CHARACTER FORMAT                        *
*   CD    CARD TO PRINTER IN CHARACTER AND HEXADECIMAL DUMP FORMAT    *
*   CT    CARD TO TAPE BLOCKED OR UNBLOCKED                          *
*   CSQ   CARD TO SAM FILE                                VSE ONLY   *
*   CVS   CARD TO VASM FILE                                          *
*                                                                     *
*                                                                     *
*                                                                     *
*                                                                     *
*                                                                     *
*                                                                     *
*                                                                     *
* * * * * * * * * * * * * * * * * * * * * * * * * * * * * * * * * * * *
```

Figure 17-2   VSE/DITTO functions (part 1 of 4)

```
✤ ✤ ✤ ✤ ✤ ✤ ✤ ✤ ✤ ✤ ✤ ✤ ✤ ✤ ✤ ✤ ✤ ✤ ✤ ✤ ✤ ✤ ✤ ✤ ✤ ✤ ✤ ✤ ✤ ✤ ✤ ✤ ✤ ✤ ✤ ✤ ✤
✤                                                                             ✤
✤                      TAPE CONTROL FUNCTIONS                                 ✤
✤                                                                             ✤
✤    BSF   BACKSPACE FILE                                                     ✤
✤    BSR   BACKSPACE RECORD                                                   ✤
✤    FSF   FORWARD SPACE FILE                                                 ✤
✤    FSR   FORWARD SPACE RECORD                                              ✤
✤    REW   REWIND TAPE                                                        ✤
✤    RUN   REWIND AND UNLOAD TAPE                                             ✤
✤    WTM   WRITE TAPE MARK(S)   (1 THROUGH 999)                              ✤
✤                                                                             ✤
✤                      BASIC TAPE FUNCTIONS                                   ✤
✤                                                                             ✤
✤    TB    TAPE BROWSE                                                        ✤
✤    TCN   TAPE TO CONSOLE                                                    ✤
✤                                                                             ✤
✤    TLB   TAPE LABEL DISPLAY                                                 ✤
✤    TMP   TAPEMAP (SHORT LIST OF A TAPE'S CONTENTS)                          ✤
✤                                                                             ✤
✤    TC    TAPE TO CARD BLOCKED OR UNBLOCKED                                  ✤
✤    TI    SAME AS TC WITH INTERPRETED CARDS                                  ✤
✤    TP    TAPE TO PRINTER UNBLOCKED IN CHARACTER FORMAT                      ✤
✤    TPD   TAPE TO PRINTER DEBLOCKED IN CHARACTER FORMAT                      ✤
✤    TD    TAPE TO PRINTER UNCLOBKED IN CHAR. AND HEX DUMP FORMAT             ✤
✤    TDD   TAPE TO PRINTER DEBLOCKED IN CHAR. AND HEX DUMP FORMAT             ✤
✤    TPV   TAPE TO PRINTER VARIABLE RECORDS CHARACTER FORMAT                  ✤
✤    TDV   TAPE TO PRINTER VARIABLE RECORDS CHAR. AND HEX DUMP FORMAT         ✤
✤    TFA   PRINT VSE SYSLST TAPES TYPE A FORMS CONTROL, CCW CODE    VSE ONLY  ✤
✤    TFD   PRINT VSE SYSLST TAPES TYPE D FORMS CONTROL              VSE ONLY  ✤
✤    TRS   TAPE RECORD SCAN                                                   ✤
✤    TRL   TAPE RECORD LOAD                                                   ✤
✤    TT    TAPE TO TAPE (01 THROUGH 999 FILES)                               ✤
✤    TTR   TAPE TO TAPE REBLOCKED                                             ✤
✤    TTC   TAPE TO TAPE COMPARE                                              ✤
✤                                                                             ✤
✤    ERT   ERASE TAPE (DATA SECURITY ERASE 3400/8809 ONLY)                   ✤
✤    INT   INITIALIZE TAPE                                                    ✤
✤                                                                             ✤
✤                      TAPE FILE FUNCTIONS                                    ✤
✤                                                                             ✤
✤    TFT   TAPE FILE TO TAPE FILE                                            ✤
✤    TSQ   TAPE (FILE) TO SAM FILE                                 VSE ONLY  ✤
✤    TIS   TAPE (FILE) TO ISAM FILE                                VSE ONLY  ✤
✤    TVS   TAPE (FILE) TO VSAM FILE                                          ✤
✤                                                                             ✤
✤                      BASIC DISK FUNCTIONS                                   ✤
✤                                                                             ✤
✤    DB    DISK BROWSE                                                        ✤
✤    DCN   DISK TO CONSOLE                                                    ✤
✤                                                                             ✤
✤    DVT   DISPLAY VTOC                                                       ✤
✤    PVT   PROCESS VTOC (RENAME/SCRATCH)                                      ✤
✤ ✤ ✤ ✤ ✤ ✤ ✤ ✤ ✤ ✤ ✤ ✤ ✤ ✤ ✤ ✤ ✤ ✤ ✤ ✤ ✤ ✤ ✤ ✤ ✤ ✤ ✤ ✤ ✤ ✤ ✤ ✤ ✤ ✤ ✤ ✤ ✤
```

Figure 17-2   VSE/DITTO functions (part 2 of 4)

```
* * * * * * * * * * * * * * * * * * * * * * * * * * * * * * * * * * * * * * *
*                                                                           *
*                    BASIC DISK FUNCTIONS (CONTINUED)                       *
*                                                                           *
*   DID   ALTER DISK VOLUME IDENTIFIER                                       *
*   DRL   DISK RECORD LOAD - KEY AND/OR DATA                                 *
*   EOF   WRITE DISK EOF RECORD                                              *
*                                                                           *
*     REPLACE FIRST D IN THE BASIC DISK FUNCTIONS BELOW WITH                 *
*     AN S (SPLIT CYLINDER) TO LIMIT PRINT OR SCAN TO SPECIFIC               *
*     TRACKS ON DESIRED CYLINDERS (CKD DEVICES ONLY).                        *
*                                                                           *
*   DP    DISK TO PRINTER UNBLOCKED IN CHARACTER FORMAT                      *
*   DD    DISK TO PRINTER UNBLOCKED IN CHAR. AND HEX DUMP FORMAT             *
*   DPD   DISK TO PRINTER DEBLOCKED IN CHARACTER FORMAT                      *
*   DDD   DISK TO PRINTER DEBLOCKED IN CHAR. AND HEX DUMP FORMAT             *
*   DRS   DISK RECORD SCAN - PARTIAL KEY OR DATA OR EOF                      *
*                                                                           *
*                    SAM FILE FUNCTIONS (VSE ONLY)                          *
*                                                                           *
*   SC    SAM FILE TO CARD                                       VSE ONLY   *
*   SI    SAME AS SC WITH INTERPRETED CARDS                      VSE ONLY   *
*   SPR   SAM FILE TO PRINT - CHARACTER FORMAT                   VSE ONLY   *
*   SDP   SAM FILE TO PRINT - HEX DUMP FORMAT                    VSE ONLY   *
*   SFA   PRINT SYSLST DISK FILE TYPE A FORMS CONTROL, CCW CODE  VSE ONLY   *
*   SFD   PRINT SYSLST DISK FILE TYPE D FORMS CONTROL            VSE ONLY   *
*   STP   SAM FILE TO TAPE (FILE)                                VSE ONLY   *
*   SSQ   SAM FILE TO SAM FILE                                   VSE ONLY   *
*   SIS   SAM FILE TO ISAM FILE                                  VSE ONLY   *
*   SVS   SAM DISK FILE TO VSAM DISK FILE                        VSE ONLY   *
*                                                                           *
*                    ISAM FILE FUNCTIONS (VSE ONLY)                         *
*                                                                           *
*   IPR   ISAM FILE TO PRINT - CHARACTER FORMAT                  VSE ONLY   *
*   IDP   ISAM FILE TO PRINT - HEX DUMP FORMAT                   VSE ONLY   *
*   ITP   ISAM FILE TO TAPE (FILE)                               VSE ONLY   *
*   ISQ   ISAM FILE TO SAM FILE                                  VSE ONLY   *
*   IIS   ISAM FILE TO ISAM FILE                                 VSE ONLY   *
*   IVS   ISAM FILE TO VSAM FILE                                 VSE ONLY   *
*                                                                           *
*                    VSAM FILE FUNCTIONS                                    *
*                                                                           *
*   VB    VSAM BROWSE                                                        *
*   VC    VSAM FILE TO CARD                                                  *
*   VI    SAME AS VC WITH INTERPRETED CARDS                                  *
*   VPR   VSAM FILE TO PRINT - CHARACTER FORMAT                              *
*   VDP   VSAM FILE TO PRINT - HEX DUMP FORMAT                               *
*   VTP   VSAM FILE TO TAPE (FILE)                                           *
*   VSQ   VSAM FILE TO SAM FILE                                  VSE ONLY   *
*   VIS   VSAM FILE TO ISAM FILE                                 VSE ONLY   *
*   VVS   VSAM FILE TO VSAM FILE                                             *
*   VRU   VSAM RECORD UPDATE (VRL)                                           *
*                                                                           *
* * * * * * * * * * * * * * * * * * * * * * * * * * * * * * * * * * * * * * *
```

Figure 17-2   VSE/DITTO functions (part 3 of 4)

```
* * * * * * * * * * * * * * * * * * * * * * * * * * * * * * * * * * * * * *
*                                                                         *
*                       DATA CREATE FUNCTIONS                             *
*                                                                         *
*    BDU  BUFFER TO DISKETTE FILE                                         *
*    BTP  BUFFER TO TAPE (FILE)                                           *
*    BSQ  BUFFER TO SAM FILE                                   VSE ONLY   *
*    BIS  BUFFER TO ISAM FILE                                  VSE ONLY   *
*    BVS  BUFFER TO VSAM FILE                                             *
*                                                                         *
*                       BASIC DISKETTE FUNCTIONS                          *
*                                                                         *
*    DKB  DISKETTE BROWSE UNBLOCKED IN CHARACTER FORMAT                   *
*    DKN  DISKETTE TO CONSOLE                                             *
*                                                                         *
*    DKI  PRINT DISKETTE INDEX TRACK (VTOC)                               *
*    DKP  DISKETTE TO PRINTER IN CHARACTER FORMAT                         *
*    DKH  DISKETTE TO PRINTER IN HEX CHARACTER FORMAT                     *
*    DKS  DISKETTE RECORD SCAN                                            *
*                                                                         *
*    DKL  DISKETTE RECORD LOAD (ALTER)                                    *
*    DKV  ALTER DISKETTE VOLID                                            *
*    IDK  INITIALIZE DISKETTE                                             *
*    DKE  EJECT AND FEED NEXT DISKETTE                                    *
*                                                                         *
*                       DISKETTE FILE FUNCTIONS                           *
*                                                                         *
*    DUC  DISKETTE FILE TO CARD                                           *
*    DUI  SAME AS DUC WITH INTERPRETED CARDS                              *
*    DUP  DISKETTE FILE TO PRINTER IN CHARACTER FORMAT                    *
*    DUH  DISKETTE FILE TO PRINTER IN HEX DUMP FORMAT                     *
*    DUD  DISKETTE FILE TO DISKETTE FILE                                  *
*    DUT  DISKETTE FILE TO TAPE                                           *
*    DUS  DISKETTE FILE TO SAM FILE                            VSE ONLY   *
*    DUV  DISKETTE FILE TO VSAM FILE                                      *
*                                                                         *
*    CDU  CARD TO DISKETTE FILE                                           *
*    TDU  TAPE (FILE) TO DISKETTE FILE                                    *
*    SDU  SAM DISK FILE TO DISKETTE FILE                       VSE ONLY   *
*    VDU  VSAM DISK FILE TO DISKETTE FILE                                 *
*                                                                         *
*                       CMS FILE FUNCTIONS (CMS ONLY)                     *
*                                                                         *
*    FPR  CMS FILE TO PRINT IN CHARACTER FORMAT                           *
*    FD   CMS FILE TO PRINT IN HEX DUMP FORMAT                            *
*    FDD  CMS FILE TO PRINT DEBLOCKED IN HEX DUMP FORMAT                  *
*    FTP  CMS FILE TO TAPE                                                *
*    TF   TAPE TO CMS FILE                                                *
*    FDU  CMS FILE TO DISKETTE FILE                                       *
*    DUF  DISKETTE FILE TO CMS FILE                                       *
*    FVS  CMS FILE TO VSAM FILE                                           *
*    VF   VSAM FILE TO CMS FILE                                           *
*                                                                         *
* * * * * * * * * * * * * * * * * * * * * * * * * * * * * * * * * * * * * *
```

Figure 17-2   VSE/DITTO functions (part 4 of 4)

How to print a file   Several of the DITTO functions let you copy different types of files to a printer. I'm going to show you how to use two (VPR and VDP) that let you print a VSAM file in character format or in character and hexadecimal dump format. The other print functions are similar, so after you've seen how to use VPR and VDP, they should be easy for you to understand and use.

When you use one of the print functions, you can specify where in the file you want to begin printing. You can supply either a record count or, for a VSAM KSDS or an ISAM file, a key value. In addition, you can specify that the listing should contain a certain number of records. So you don't have to print an entire file if you're interested only in a part of it.

Figure 17-3 presents two jobs to print a VSAM file. The two jobs are identical except for the DITTO control statement I coded. The first uses the VPR control statement to print the file in character format; the second uses the VDP statement to print it in both character and hexadecimal format.

For both control statements, I coded the same operands. Of the four, only FILEIN is required. It specifies the file-name operand on the DLBL statement that identifies the file to be printed (in this case, VSAM-IN). Notice that in both jobs, I coded a DLBL statement to specify a job catalog (IJSYSUC) for the VSAM input file.

If I hadn't coded any operands other than FILEIN, the entire file would be printed. However, by using the three optional operands, you can print just a segment of a file. If you code START and POSITION, you can begin printing at a position other than the beginning of the file. And if you code NLRECS, you can print a certain number of logical records rather than the entire file.

For START, you can code C or K. The value C causes DITTO to count forward, skipping the number of records you specify. If you code K, DITTO begins printing with the record that has the key value you specify. (K, of course, works with the VDP and VPR only for key-sequenced data sets and with the equivalent DITTO functions for ISAM files.)

To specify the number of records to skip (START=C) or the key value of the record where processing should start (START=K), code the POSITION operand. Because I coded 28 for this operand, DITTO will skip the first 28 records in the file and begin printing with the 29th.

When you code the POSITION operand to specify a key value, you need to code the key exactly as it appears in the record where you want to start. If you code a key value that's smaller than the key field in the file you want to print, DITTO pads the value on the right with binary zeros. So if you want to print a file beginning with key value 00123 and you code 123 for POSITION, printing starts at the record with key value 123LL, where the Ls are bytes of binary zeros. Then, if there is no record 123LL in the file, DITTO begins processing with the next record in the file whose key is greater than 123LL.

To print only a specified number of records, code the NLRECS operand. In the two jobs in figure 17-3, I wanted to print only three records.

Job to print the VSAM file in character format only

```
// JOB      PRTVSAM
// UPSI     1
// DLBL     IJSYSUC,'MMA.USER.CATALOG',,VSAM
// DLBL     VSAMIN,'CUSTMAST.MAILING.SEL',,VSAM
// EXEC     DITTO,SIZE=128K
$$DITTO VPR FILEIN=VSAMIN,START=C,POSITION=28,NLRECS=3
$$DITTO EOJ
/&
```

Job to print the VSAM file in character and hexadecimal formats

```
// JOB      DUMPVSAM
// UPSI     1
// DLBL     IJSYSUC,'MMA.USER.CATALOG',,VSAM
// DLBL     VSAMIN,'CUSTMAST.MAILING.SEL',,VSAM
// EXEC     DITTO,SIZE=128K
$$DITTO VDP FILEIN=VSAMIN,START=C,POSITION=28,NLRECS=3
$$DITTO EOJ
/&
```

Figure 17-3 VSE/DITTO jobs to list part of a VSAM file

If you examine the output of the two jobs, you'll see that's what I got in each case.

The output of the two jobs differ even though they printed the same data. In figure 17-4, the data records are printed in character format. That's fine for this file, because all the data in the records can be displayed in character format. However, if you want to print data that contains bytes that have values without character equivalents, like packed decimal fields, you'll probably want a listing that shows the data in both character and hex format. That's what figure 17-5 illustrates.

How to create a test file from card data   One of the most tedious parts of developing an application program is creating test data for it. But DITTO simplifies the task because it provides functions that let you create files from card-image data you key in at a terminal or from data generated by DITTO itself.

One of the easiest ways to create a small test file with content you control is simply to key in card images with the data you want. Then, you can use DITTO to convert those card images into a tape file or a SAM, ISAM, or VSAM file on DASD. Of course, if you're creating a SAM or ISAM file, you need to define it completely with DLBL and EXTENT statements. If you're creating a VSAM file, only a DLBL statement is necessary, but the file must be defined in a VSAM catalog. Figure 17-6 shows two job streams that create a SAM file from card input. One creates a file with one record per block, the other a file with two records per block.

Output from the PRTVSAM job

```
$$DITTO VPR FILEIN=VSAMIN,START=C,POSITION=28,NLRECS=3

* * * * DEVICE 242 SYS098,    FBA,  CUSTMAST.MAILING.SEL                    , VSAM              * * *

REC   29   DATA   256        28776JOHN WARDS AND ASSOC5600 N CLARK          CHICAGO     IL606030000557025000001230120606088002
                             5000002500000000000000000000000000000000000000000000000000000000000000000000000000000000000000000
                             000000000000

REC   30   DATA   256        29556NATIONAL INDUSTRIES 3879 NE FOOTE        WASHINGTON DC200190000774050000000080001230130606088000
                             0800000080000000000000000000000000000000000000000000000000000000000000000000000000000000000000000
                             000000000000

REC   31   DATA   256        29573UNIVERSAL SERVICES 2115 FULTON RD         POMONA      CA917680000119100000005000001230140606088005
                             0000050000000000000000000000000000000000000000000000000000000000000000000000000000000000000000000
                             000000000000

31 RCDS READ

$$DITTO EOJ
```

Figure 17-4   Output from a VSE/DITTO job that lists part of a VSAM file in character format

Output from the DUMPVSAM job

```
$$DITTO VDP FILEIN=VSAMIN,START=C,POSITION=28,NLRECS=3

** ** ** DEVICE 242 SYS098,    FBA,    CUSTMAST.MAILING.SEL            , VSAM                                                    ** ** **

REC  29  DATA  256   CHAR   28776JOHN WARDS AND ASSOC5600 N CLARK         CHICAGO          IL60603000557025000002500001230120608002
                     ZONE   4FFFFFDDCD4ECDCE4CDC4CEEDCFFFF4D4CDCDD4444444CCCCCCD4444CDFFFFFFFFFFFFFFFFFFFFFFFFFFFFFFFF
                     NUMR   0287761685061942015401226356000503319200000000038931760000936030005570250000025000012301206088002
                            01...5...10...15...20...25...30...35...40...45...50...55...60...65...70...75...80...85...90...95....

                     CHAR   500000250000000000000000000000000000000000000000000000000000000000000000000000000000000000000000
                     ZONE   FFFFFFFFFFFFFFFFFFFFFFFFFFFFFFFFFFFFFFFFFFFFFFFFFFFFFFFFFFFFFFFFFFFFFFFFFFFFFFFFFFFFFFFFFFFFFFFF
                     NUMR   500000250000000000000000000000000000000000000000000000000000000000000000000000000000000000000000
                            101...5...10...15...20...25...30...35...40...45...50...55...60...65...70...75...80...85...90...95....

                     CHAR   00000000000000
                     ZONE   FFFFFFFFFFFFFF44444444444444444444444444444444444444444444
                     NUMR   00000000000000000000000000000000000000000000000000000000000
                            201...5...10...15...20...25...30...35...40...45...50...55.

REC  30  DATA  256   CHAR   29556NATIONAL INDUSTRIES 3879 NE FOOTE        WASHINGTON       DC20019000774050000000800012301306088000
                     ZONE   4FFFFFDCECDDCD4CDCEEDCCE4FFFF4DC4CDDEC4444444CECCDCEDDA4444CCFFFFFFFFFFFFFFFFFFFFFFFFFFFFFFFFFFFFF
                     NUMR   0295565139651309544235993520387905506635000006123995736504320319000077405000000080001230130608088000
                            01...5...10...15...20...25...30...35...40...45...50...55...60...65...70...75...80...85...90...95....

                     CHAR   080000008000000000000000000000000000000000000000000000000000000000000000000000000000000000000000
                     ZONE   FFFFFFFFFFFFFFFFFFFFFFFFFFFFFFFFFFFFFFFFFFFFFFFFFFFFFFFFFFFFFFFFFFFFFFFFFFFFFFFFFFFFFFFFFFFFFFFF
                     NUMR   080000008000000000000000000000000000000000000000000000000000000000000000000000000000000000000000
                            101...5...10...15...20...25...30...35...40...45...50...55...60...65...70...75...80...85...90...95....

                     CHAR   00000000000000
                     ZONE   FFFFFFFFFFFFFF44444444444444444444444444444444444444444444
                     NUMR   00000000000000000000000000000000000000000000000000000000000
                            201...5...10...15...20...25...30...35...40...45...50...55.

REC  31  DATA  256   CHAR   29573UNIVERSAL SERVICES 2115 FULTON RD        POMONA           CA91768000119100000050000123014060880005
                     ZONE   4FFFFFEDCECDECD4ECDECCCE4FFFF4CEDED4DC4444444DDDDDC4444444CCFFFFFFFFFFFFFFFFFFFFFFFFFFFFFFFFFFFFF
                     NUMR   02957345955921302595935200211506433650940000764651000003191768000119100000050000123014060880005
                            01...5...10...15...20...25...30...35...40...45...50...55...60...65...70...75...80...85...90...95....

                     CHAR   000000050000000000000000000000000000000000000000000000000000000000000000000000000000000000000000
                     ZONE   FFFFFFFFFFFFFFFFFFFFFFFFFFFFFFFFFFFFFFFFFFFFFFFFFFFFFFFFFFFFFFFFFFFFFFFFFFFFFFFFFFFFFFFFFFFFFFFF
                     NUMR   000000050000000000000000000000000000000000000000000000000000000000000000000000000000000000000000
                            101...5...10...15...20...25...30...35...40...45...50...55...60...65...70...75...80...85...90...95....

                     CHAR   00000000000000
                     ZONE   FFFFFFFFFFFFFF44444444444444444444444444444444444444444444
                     NUMR   00000000000000000000000000000000000000000000000000000000000
                            201...5...10...15...20...25...30...35...40...45...50...55.

31 RCDS READ
$$DITTO EOJ
```

Figure 17-5 Output from a VSE/DITTO job that lists part of a VSAM file in character and hexadecimal format

Job to create an unblocked SAM file from card input, then list it

```
// JOB       FBASAMUB
// UPSI      1
// ASSGN     SYS001,241
// DLBL      NEWSAM,'SAM.TEST.FILE',0,SD
// EXTENT    SYS001,,,,10000,10
// EXEC      DITTO
$$DITTO CSQ FILEOUT=NEWSAM,CISIZE=512
00001  TEST RECORD 1
00002  TEST RECORD 2
00003  TEST RECORD 3
00004  TEST RECORD 4
00005  TEST RECORD 5
/*
$$DITTO SPR FILEIN=NEWSAM
$$DITTO EOJ
/&
```

Job to create a blocked SAM file from card input, then list it

```
// JOB       FBASAMBK
// UPSI      1
// ASSGN     SYS001,241
// DLBL      NEWSAM,'SAM.TEST.FILE',0,SD
// EXTENT    SYS001,,,,10000,10
// EXEC      DITTO
$$DITTO CSQ FILEOUT=NEWSAM,CISIZE=512,BLKFACTOR=2
00001  TEST RECORD 1
00002  TEST RECORD 2
00003  TEST RECORD 3
00004  TEST RECORD 4
00005  TEST RECORD 5
/*
$$DITTO SPR FILEIN=NEWSAM,RECSIZE=80
$$DITTO EOJ
/&
```

Figure 17-6   VSE/DITTO jobs to create a SAM file from card input, then list it

The DITTO function to create a SAM file from cards is CSQ. When you use the CSQ function, the output records are automatically 80 characters long. In these examples, I've chosen to use three operands: (1) FILEOUT, (2) CISIZE, and (3) BLKFACTOR.

The FILEOUT operand specifies the name from the DLBL statement that identifies the new SAM file. CISIZE, required only for files being created on FBA DASD, specifies the control interval size that's to be used. You follow the same rules for coding this operand that you do for coding the CISIZE operand on the DLBL statement. You can look back to chapter 12 to refresh your memory on how to do that.

Output from the FBASAMUB job

```
$$DITTO CSQ FILEOUT=NEWSAM,CISIZE=512

5 CARDS READ

5 BLOCKS WRITTEN

$$DITTO SPR FILEIN=NEWSAM


* * * * DEVICE  241  SYS001,    FBA,  SAM.TEST.FILE                              ,  SAM

BLOCK    1    DATA    80         00001    TEST RECORD 1
BLOCK    2    DATA    80         00002    TEST RECORD 2
BLOCK    3    DATA    80         00003    TEST RECORD 3
BLOCK    4    DATA    80         00004    TEST RECORD 4
BLOCK    5    DATA    80         00005    TEST RECORD 5

5 BLOCKS READ


$$DITTO EOJ
```

Figure 17-7 Output from a VSE/DITTO job that creates an unblocked SAM file from card input, then lists it

The BLKFACTOR operand specifies how many records should be stored per logical block in the new SAM file. You may code this operand for files on either type of DASD. If you omit it, each record will be stored in its own block.

After the CSQ control statement in the job stream, I included five data cards, and I indicated the end of the in-line data with an end-of-data statement (/*). After the input deck, I coded the SPR control statement to print the contents of the new file. The SPR function prints a sequential file in character format. Its FILEIN operand specifies that the file to be printed is the one with the DLBL name NEWSAM.

Figures 17-7 and 17-8 show the output from these jobs. For the CSQ function, DITTO printed the number of cards read and the number of output blocks written. Next in the output is the result of the SPR control statement I coded in both jobs. As you can see, each record in the new SAM file is printed. In addition, DITTO identifies the block numbers within the file and the number of bytes of data in each.

If you compare the output from the two jobs, you can see how blocking affects the output. Also, notice that on the SPR control statement in the second job I coded the RECSIZE operand to specify how large the logical records in the file are. If I had omitted this operand, DITTO wouldn't have deblocked the records when it printed them. In this case, the data would still have printed, but in a less readable form.

Output from the FBASAMBK job

```
$$DITTO CSQ FILEOUT=NEWSAM,CISIZE=512,BLKFACTOR=2

5 CARDS READ

3 BLOCKS WRITTEN

$$DITTO SPR FILEIN=NEWSAM,RECSIZE=80

* * * * DEVICE 241   SYS001,   FBA,   SAM.TEST.FILE      ,BLOCK   1   DATA   160

REC   1   DATA   80      00001   TEST RECORD 1
REC   2   DATA   80      00002   TEST RECORD 2

* * * * DEVICE 241   SYS001,   FBA,   SAM.TEST.FILE      ,BLOCK   2   DATA   160

REC   3   DATA   80      00003   TEST RECORD 3
REC   4   DATA   80      00004   TEST RECORD 4

* * * * DEVICE 241   SYS001,   FBA,   SAM.TEST.FILE      ,BLOCK   3   DATA   80

REC   5   DATA   80      00005   TEST RECORD 5

3 BLOCKS READ

$$DITTO EOJ
```

Figure 17-8   Output from a VSE/DITTO job that creates a blocked SAM file from card input, then lists it

Job stream

```
// JOB      BFRTOSAM
// UPSI     1
// ASSGN    SYS001,241
// DLBL     NEWSAM,'SAM.TEST.FILE',0,SD,CISIZE=512
// EXTENT   SYS001,,,,10000,10
// EXEC     DITTO
$$DITTO BSQ FILEOUT=NEWSAM,RECSIZE=48,BLKFACTOR=10,NLRECS=25,        X
$$DITTO     KEYLOC=1,KEYLEN=5,INCR=2,FILLCHAR=X
$$DITTO SPR FILEIN=NEWSAM,RECSIZE=48
$$DITTO EOJ
/&
```

Figure 17-9   VSE/DITTO job to create a SAM file from buffer input, then list it

How to create a test file from buffer data   If you need to create a test file and don't particularly care what the records in it contain, you can use one of the DITTO buffer functions. With them, DITTO stores data in a buffer, then transfers it to the file you specify. For example, figure 17-9 illustrates a job that creates a SAM file from buffer data.

The DLBL and EXTENT statements in this job are almost the same as in the ones in figure 17-6. In this example, I coded the CISIZE operand on the DLBL statement rather than on a DITTO control statement.

Notice the BSQ control statement. It specifies several operands. With them, I can control the format, size, and blocking of the new file. As in the jobs in figure 17-6, the FILEOUT operand names NEWSAM; that's the file-name I coded in the DLBL statement for the new file. The other seven operands on the BSQ statement are new to you.

Because this statement requires so many operands, I had to use a continuation line. To continue a DITTO control statement, code a comma after the last operand on the line; then, code a non-blank character in column 72. Begin the next line with $$DITTO; then, code the remaining operands, separating them from $$DITTO with at least one space.

In figure 17-9, I coded the operands of BSQ in two groups. Those in the first line specify the format of the new file, while those in the second provide information about what DITTO should write in each record. Although grouping the operands like this isn't required, it does make them easier to read.

After the FILEOUT operand in the first line of the statement, I coded the RECSIZE operand to define the record size for the new file (48 bytes). BLKFACTOR specifies how many records should be created per block (physical block for files on CKD DASDs, logical block for files on FBA DASDs); it's 10 in this example. Finally, NLRECS specifies how many logical records are to be created in the new file (25).

The operands on the second line of the statement specify what data should be written in each record. The first two operands, KEYLOC and KEYLEN, indicate that DITTO should create the file with a sequence field. In this case, the sequence field is at the beginning of each record (KEYLOC=1) and is five bytes long (KEYLEN=5).

If you request a key field by coding KEYLOC and KEYLEN and you don't specify otherwise, DITTO increments the key value by 10 for each record it writes. But you can specify otherwise by coding the INCR operand. INCR=2 in figure 17-9 tells DITTO to increment the field value by 2 instead of 10. Ditto also uses the increment value as the key for the first record.

Finally, the FILLCHAR operand specifies the value DITTO should write in the rest of the record. You can code only one character; in figure 17-9, it's the letter X. If you omit the FILLCHAR operand, DITTO fills in the records it creates with spaces.

The second control statement in figure 17-9 is again SPR, as in figure 17-6. Here, I coded the RECSIZE operand because the records in this output file will be blocked. If I had omitted RECSIZE, DITTO would not have deblocked the records when it printed them.

Figure 17-10 shows the job's output. You can see that DITTO separates each logical block in the file, identifies each record, and prints the contents of each. Notice that the first five characters in each record contain a sequence value that increases by 2 for each record. Also, notice that all the other positions in each record contain the letter X.

How to copy a file   Figure 17-11 illustrates a DITTO job to copy the SAM file created in figure 17-9 to a VSAM file. Before you can run a DITTO job to create a VSAM file, you have to define the VSAM cluster with AMS, as you learned in chapter 13. You specify the kind of VSAM file you're creating (ESDS, KSDS, or RRDS) when you define it, not in your DITTO job. If you're using DITTO to create a VSAM KSDS, it's your responsibility to avoid duplicate key values in the input data.

The control statement to copy a SAM file to a VSAM file is SVS. It requires both the FILEOUT and the FILEIN operands; they contain the file-name values I coded in the respective DLBL statements. Notice that I didn't have to code an EXTENT statement for the new VSAM file, although I did include a DLBL statement to define a job catalog (IJSYSUC).

The VPR control statement prints the contents of the new VSAM file, as you can see in figure 17-12. Notice here that the contents of the file are the same as in figure 17-10, but the records aren't blocked.

You can also use AMS, the VSAM Access Method Services program, to copy VSAM files and to convert SAM and ISAM files to VSAM files. However, the AMS control statements can be more complex than the DITTO control statements to perform the same functions. As a result, I encourage you to use DITTO to copy non-VSAM files to VSAM files.

Output from the BFRTOSAM job

```
$$DITTO BSQ FILEOUT=NEWSAM,RECSIZE=48,BLKFACTOR=10,NLRECS=25,        X
$$DITTO    KEYLOC=1,KEYLEN=5,INCR=2,FILLCHAR=X

3 BLOCKS WRITTEN

$$DITTO SPR FILEIN=NEWSAM,RECSIZE=48

* * * DEVICE 241 SYS001,  FBA,  SAM.TEST.FILE            ,BLOCK  1  DATA  480

REC   1   DATA   48   00002XXXXXXXXXXXXXXXXXXXXXXXXXXXXXXXXXXXXXXXXX
REC   2   DATA   48   00004XXXXXXXXXXXXXXXXXXXXXXXXXXXXXXXXXXXXXXXXX
REC   3   DATA   48   00006XXXXXXXXXXXXXXXXXXXXXXXXXXXXXXXXXXXXXXXXX
REC   4   DATA   48   00008XXXXXXXXXXXXXXXXXXXXXXXXXXXXXXXXXXXXXXXXX
REC   5   DATA   48   00010XXXXXXXXXXXXXXXXXXXXXXXXXXXXXXXXXXXXXXXXX
REC   6   DATA   48   00012XXXXXXXXXXXXXXXXXXXXXXXXXXXXXXXXXXXXXXXXX
REC   7   DATA   48   00014XXXXXXXXXXXXXXXXXXXXXXXXXXXXXXXXXXXXXXXXX
REC   8   DATA   48   00016XXXXXXXXXXXXXXXXXXXXXXXXXXXXXXXXXXXXXXXXX
REC   9   DATA   48   00018XXXXXXXXXXXXXXXXXXXXXXXXXXXXXXXXXXXXXXXXX
REC  10   DATA   48   00020XXXXXXXXXXXXXXXXXXXXXXXXXXXXXXXXXXXXXXXXX

* * * DEVICE 241 SYS001,  FBA,  SAM.TEST.FILE            ,BLOCK  2  DATA  480

REC  11   DATA   48   00022XXXXXXXXXXXXXXXXXXXXXXXXXXXXXXXXXXXXXXXXX
REC  12   DATA   48   00024XXXXXXXXXXXXXXXXXXXXXXXXXXXXXXXXXXXXXXXXX
REC  13   DATA   48   00026XXXXXXXXXXXXXXXXXXXXXXXXXXXXXXXXXXXXXXXXX
REC  14   DATA   48   00028XXXXXXXXXXXXXXXXXXXXXXXXXXXXXXXXXXXXXXXXX
REC  15   DATA   48   00030XXXXXXXXXXXXXXXXXXXXXXXXXXXXXXXXXXXXXXXXX
REC  16   DATA   48   00032XXXXXXXXXXXXXXXXXXXXXXXXXXXXXXXXXXXXXXXXX
REC  17   DATA   48   00034XXXXXXXXXXXXXXXXXXXXXXXXXXXXXXXXXXXXXXXXX
REC  18   DATA   48   00036XXXXXXXXXXXXXXXXXXXXXXXXXXXXXXXXXXXXXXXXX
REC  19   DATA   48   00038XXXXXXXXXXXXXXXXXXXXXXXXXXXXXXXXXXXXXXXXX
REC  20   DATA   48   00040XXXXXXXXXXXXXXXXXXXXXXXXXXXXXXXXXXXXXXXXX

* * * DEVICE 241 SYS001,  FBA,  SAM.TEST.FILE            ,BLOCK  3  DATA  240

REC  21   DATA   48   00042XXXXXXXXXXXXXXXXXXXXXXXXXXXXXXXXXXXXXXXXX
REC  22   DATA   48   00044XXXXXXXXXXXXXXXXXXXXXXXXXXXXXXXXXXXXXXXXX
REC  23   DATA   48   00046XXXXXXXXXXXXXXXXXXXXXXXXXXXXXXXXXXXXXXXXX
REC  24   DATA   48   00048XXXXXXXXXXXXXXXXXXXXXXXXXXXXXXXXXXXXXXXXX
REC  25   DATA   48   00050XXXXXXXXXXXXXXXXXXXXXXXXXXXXXXXXXXXXXXXXX

3 BLOCKS READ

$$DITTO EOJ
```

Figure 17-10 Output from a VSE/DITTO job that creates a SAM file from buffer input, then lists it

Job stream

```
// JOB       SAMTOVSM
// UPSI      1
// ASSGN     SYS001,241
// DLBL      IJSYSUC,'AR.USER.CATALOG',,VSAM
// DLBL      NEWVSAM,'VSAM.TEST.FILE',,VSAM
// DLBL      NEWSAM,'SAM.TEST.FILE',0,SD,CISIZE=512
// EXTENT    SYS001,,,,10000,10
// EXEC      DITTO,SIZE=128K
$$DITTO SVS FILEIN=NEWSAM,FILEOUT=NEWVSAM,RECSIZE=48,NLRECS=25,MODE=F
$$DITTO VPR FILEIN=NEWVSAM
$$DITTO EOJ
/&
```

Figure 17-11   VSE/DITTO job to copy a SAM file to a VSAM file, then list the VSAM file

Output from the SAMTOVSM job

```
$$DITTO SVS FILEIN=NEWSAM,FILEOUT=NEWVSAM,RECSIZE=48,NLRECS=25,MODE=F

3 BLOCKS READ

25 RCDS WRITTEN

$$DITTO VPR FILEIN=NEWVSAM


* * * * DEVICE   250   SYS098,    FBA,   VSAM.TEST.FILE                          VSAM


REC      1    DATA    48       00002XXXXXXXXXXXXXXXXXXXXXXXXXXXXXXXXXXXXXXXXXX
REC      2    DATA    48       00004XXXXXXXXXXXXXXXXXXXXXXXXXXXXXXXXXXXXXXXXXX
REC      3    DATA    48       00006XXXXXXXXXXXXXXXXXXXXXXXXXXXXXXXXXXXXXXXXXX
REC      4    DATA    48       00008XXXXXXXXXXXXXXXXXXXXXXXXXXXXXXXXXXXXXXXXXX
REC      5    DATA    48       00010XXXXXXXXXXXXXXXXXXXXXXXXXXXXXXXXXXXXXXXXXX
REC      6    DATA    48       00012XXXXXXXXXXXXXXXXXXXXXXXXXXXXXXXXXXXXXXXXXX
REC      7    DATA    48       00014XXXXXXXXXXXXXXXXXXXXXXXXXXXXXXXXXXXXXXXXXX
REC      8    DATA    48       00016XXXXXXXXXXXXXXXXXXXXXXXXXXXXXXXXXXXXXXXXXX
REC      9    DATA    48       00018XXXXXXXXXXXXXXXXXXXXXXXXXXXXXXXXXXXXXXXXXX
REC     10    DATA    48       00020XXXXXXXXXXXXXXXXXXXXXXXXXXXXXXXXXXXXXXXXXX
REC     11    DATA    48       00022XXXXXXXXXXXXXXXXXXXXXXXXXXXXXXXXXXXXXXXXXX
REC     12    DATA    48       00024XXXXXXXXXXXXXXXXXXXXXXXXXXXXXXXXXXXXXXXXXX
REC     13    DATA    48       00026XXXXXXXXXXXXXXXXXXXXXXXXXXXXXXXXXXXXXXXXXX
REC     14    DATA    48       00028XXXXXXXXXXXXXXXXXXXXXXXXXXXXXXXXXXXXXXXXXX
REC     15    DATA    48       00030XXXXXXXXXXXXXXXXXXXXXXXXXXXXXXXXXXXXXXXXXX
REC     16    DATA    48       00032XXXXXXXXXXXXXXXXXXXXXXXXXXXXXXXXXXXXXXXXXX
REC     17    DATA    48       00034XXXXXXXXXXXXXXXXXXXXXXXXXXXXXXXXXXXXXXXXXX
REC     18    DATA    48       00036XXXXXXXXXXXXXXXXXXXXXXXXXXXXXXXXXXXXXXXXXX
REC     19    DATA    48       00038XXXXXXXXXXXXXXXXXXXXXXXXXXXXXXXXXXXXXXXXXX
REC     20    DATA    48       00040XXXXXXXXXXXXXXXXXXXXXXXXXXXXXXXXXXXXXXXXXX
REC     21    DATA    48       00042XXXXXXXXXXXXXXXXXXXXXXXXXXXXXXXXXXXXXXXXXX
REC     22    DATA    48       00044XXXXXXXXXXXXXXXXXXXXXXXXXXXXXXXXXXXXXXXXXX
REC     23    DATA    48       00046XXXXXXXXXXXXXXXXXXXXXXXXXXXXXXXXXXXXXXXXXX
REC     24    DATA    48       00048XXXXXXXXXXXXXXXXXXXXXXXXXXXXXXXXXXXXXXXXXX
REC     25    DATA    48       00050XXXXXXXXXXXXXXXXXXXXXXXXXXXXXXXXXXXXXXXXXX

25 RCDS READ


$$DITTO EOJ
```

Figure 17-12   Output from a VSE/DITTO job that copies a SAM file to a VSAM file, then lists the VSAM file

Job stream

```
// JOB      LISTVTOC
// UPSI     1
// EXEC     DITTO
$$DITTO DVT INPUT=290,SORTBY=EXTENT
$$DITTO EOJ
/&
```

Figure 17-13   VSE/DITTO job to print a DASD's VTOC

How to print a DASD's VTOC   To print a listing of a VTOC, you use the DVT control statement. It has two operands: INPUT and SORTBY. For the INPUT operand, you code the address of the unit for which you want the listing. Figure 17-13 presents a job to print a VTOC listing for a DASD at address 290.

The SORTBY operand lets you specify the sequence of the listing. You can code NAME, EXTENT, or DATE as the value for the SORTBY operand. NAME causes DITTO to produce a listing in alphameric sequence by file name. DATE results in a listing in creation date sequence. And EXTENT, the value I coded in figure 17-7, causes a listing in disk address order to be prepared.

You can see what the output of the DVT function looks like in figure 17-14. The entries are in order by EXTENT location. Compare this listing with the one produced by LVTOC in chapter 12. Frankly, I think the options for sort order and the simpler format make a DITTO VTOC listing easier to use than an equivalent listing produced by LVTOC. In addition, when you use LVTOC to prepare a VTOC listing, the system operator may be prompted to authorize processing if the volume contains data-secured files. When you use DITTO, that doesn't happen.

Discussion   I think you'll agree that VSE/DITTO's functions can be useful in both program development and system management. Although the examples I've included give you the background you'll need to use all of the DITTO control statements, there are detailed differences from one statement to another. As a result, you may need more than the function list DITTO can produce for you. If you have difficulties when you try to use DITTO, refer to *VSE/Ditto Program Reference and Operations Manual*.

Terminology   console operation
batch operation

Objective   Given a program development or system management task that involves copying or printing files, use VSE/DITTO to do it.

Output from the LISTVTOC job

```
$$DITTO DVT INPUT=290,SORTBY=EXTENT

* * * * DEVICE   290  SYS098, VOLID=CKD001,  2311, WITH  200 CYLS, 10 TRKS/CYL, AND  3625 BYTES/TRK  --  SORTED BY EXTENT
```

---- FILE NAME ----	VOLSER	YY/DDD	EXT	TYPE	BEGIN-END				RELTRK/NUMTRKS
*** VTOC EXTENT ***			0	PRIME	0	1	0	1	1,1
*** FREE EXTENT ***			0	FREE	0	2	29	9	2,298
ISAM.TEST.FILE.1	CKD001	84/333	1	INDEX	30	0	30	9	300,10
ISAM.TEST.FILE.1	CKD001	84/333	2	PRIME	31	0	39	9	310,90
*** FREE EXTENT ***			0	FREE	40	0	69	9	400,300
SPLIT.CYL.FILE.1	CKD001	84/333	0	SHARE	70	0	73	3	700,34
SPLIT.CYL.FILE.2	CKD001	84/333	0	SHARE	70	4	73	6	704,33
SPLIT.CYL.FILE.3	CKD001	84/333	0	SHARE	70	7	73	9	707,33
*** FREE EXTENT ***			0	FREE	74	0	100	9	740,270
ISAM.TEST.FILE.2	CKD001	84/333	1	INDEX	101	0	101	9	1010,10
ISAM.TEST.FILE.2	CKD001	84/333	2	PRIME	102	0	108	9	1020,70
ISAM.TEST.FILE.2	CKD001	84/333	3	OFLOW	109	0	110	9	1090,20
*** FREE EXTENT ***			0	FREE	111	0	119	9	1110,90
DAM.TEST.FILE	CKD001	84/333	0	PRIME	120	0	124	9	1200,50
*** FREE EXTENT ***			0	FREE	125	0	199	9	1250,750

```
THIS VOLUME IS CURRENTLY  14 PER CENT FULL WITH  1708 TRACKS  AVAILABLE  (EXCLUDING FREE TRACKS IN SPLIT CYLINDERS, IF ANY)

$$DITTO EOJ
```

Figure 17-14   Output from a VSE/DITTO job that prints a DASD's VTOC

Chapter 18

How to use advanced AMS functions

In this chapter, you'll learn how to use some additional functions of AMS, the VSAM Access Method Services program. In chapter 13, you learned how to use AMS, or IDCAMS, to define VSAM catalogs, data spaces, and clusters. Now, you'll learn how to use AMS to list and maintain VSAM catalogs and to copy and print files.

How to use AMS to maintain VSAM catalogs

You should know how to use three statements for maintaining VSAM catalogs: LISTCAT, DELETE, and ALTER. LISTCAT lets you display the contents of a VSAM catalog. DELETE lets you purge a cluster from a catalog and, as a result, delete the associated VSAM file. And the ALTER statement lets you change a file's catalog entry; its most common use is to rename a file.

The LISTCAT control statement   Although you can use the LVTOC program or the DVT function of DITTO to display a volume table of contents, the files in VSAM space on that volume won't be on the listing. To find out what VSAM files are on your system, you run AMS and supply a LISTCAT control statement. When you use LISTCAT, the output is a listing of the contents of a catalog, not necessarily of a volume or of a single VSAM data space.

The LISTCAT control statement

```
LISTCAT [CATALOG (catalog-name)]
        [ENTRIES (entry-name...)]
        [entry-type]

        ⎡⎧NAME      ⎫⎤
        ⎢⎪VOLUME    ⎪⎥
        ⎢⎨ALLOCATION⎬⎥
        ⎣⎩ALL       ⎭⎦
```

Explanation

catalog-name	The catalog whose entries you want to list.
entry-name	The names of the entries you want to list. You may specify as many entry-name values as you wish. If you omit ENTRIES, all entries in the specified catalog are listed.
entry-type	Specifies the type of catalog entries you want printed (CLUSTER, DATA, INDEX, or SPACE). If both ENTRIES and entry-type are omitted, all entries of all types in the specified catalog are listed.
NAME	Specifies that only the names and types of the specified entries are to be listed. NAME is the default.
VOLUME	Specifies that the information listed by NAME, plus the history and volume locations of the specified entries, are to be listed.
ALLOCATION	Specifies that the information listed by VOLUME is to be printed, plus volume allocation data for data and index components.
ALL	Specifies that all catalog information for the specified entries is to be printed.

Figure 18-1   The LISTCAT control statement

Figure 18-1 shows the format of the LISTCAT control statement. The first operand, CATALOG, names the catalog whose contents you want to list. If you omit the CATALOG operand, the job catalog currently in effect (IJSYSUC) is used. If no job catalog is in effect, the master catalog is used.

The next two operands let you specify that AMS should list only particular entries in the catalog. With ENTRIES, you specify the names of the catalog entries you want to list. If you omit ENTRIES, all catalog entries of the type you specify will be listed. You can specify an entry type by coding one of four values: CLUSTER, DATA, INDEX, or SPACE. If you use one of these operands, only entries of that type will be listed. If you don't code a value for the ENTRIES operand or the entry-type operand, all entries of all types in the catalog will be listed.

Job stream

```
//  JOB      LISTCAT1
//  EXEC     IDCAMS,SIZE=AUTO
             LISTCAT CATALOG (AR.USER.CATALOG) -
                     NAME
/*
/&
```

Figure 18-2   AMS job to list a VSAM catalog

The last operand lets you indicate how detailed the information AMS will list should be. If you code NAME, only the name and entry type for each entry are printed. If you code VOLUME, AMS lists the name, entry type, owner-id, creation and expiration dates, and volume for each entry. If you code ALLOCATION, AMS prints all the information you get with VOLUME, plus data about DASD usage. And if you code ALL, all of the fields stored in a catalog entry are listed. This chapter includes examples of the output that results from all four of these values.

Figure 18-2 shows a job that prints the names of all the entries in a VSAM catalog. You might want to run a job like this to find out what names are in use in a catalog before you define a cluster. In this job, I coded NAME and omitted the ENTRIES and type operands. As a result, AMS printed the names of all of the entries in the catalog, as you can see in figure 18-3. The heading shows that the listing is for the catalog AR.USER.CATALOG.

If you specify VOLUME, ALLOCATION, or ALL instead of NAME, the listing you get contains progressively more information. As you get more information by coding these values, you need to be more selective about the entries you print.

For example, figure 18-4 shows an AMS LISTCAT job that prints the entries for the cluster AR.OPEN.ITEMS in the catalog AR.USER.CATALOG. In this job, I specified the VOLUME operand. You can see in figure 18-5 that its output includes not only the entry names, but also their history and the volume where they're stored.

Figure 18-6 shows the same job, but with the ALLOCATION operand instead of the VOLUME operand. Figure 18-7 shows this job's output. It includes the same data as in figure 18-5, as well as details about the file's DASD usage.

Output from the LISTCAT1 job

```
IDCAMS   SYSTEM SERVICES


                        LISTING FROM CATALOG -- AR.USER.CATALOG
CLUSTER ------- AR.BAD.DEBTS

    DATA ------- AR.BAD.DEBTS.DATA

    INDEX ------ AR.BAD.DEBTS.INDEX

CLUSTER ------- AR.OPEN.ITEMS

    DATA ------- AR.OPEN.ITEMS.DATA

    INDEX ------ AR.OPEN.ITEMS.INDEX

CLUSTER ------- AR.PAID.BILLS

    DATA ------- AR.PAID.BILLS.DATA

    INDEX ------ AR.PAID.BILLS.INDEX

CLUSTER ------- AR.USER.CATALOG

    DATA ------- VSAM.CATALOG.BASE.DATA.RECORD

    INDEX ------ VSAM.CATALOG.BASE.INDEX.RECORD

VOLUME --------- SYSWK3

CLUSTER ------- VSAM.TEST.FILE

    DATA ------- VSAM.TEST.FILE.DATA

    INDEX ------ VSAM.TEST.FILE.INDEX
```

Figure 18-3   Output from an AMS job that lists a VSAM catalog

Job stream

```
// JOB      LISTCAT2
// EXEC     IDCAMS,SIZE=AUTO
          LISTCAT CATALOG (AR.USER.CATALOG) -
                  ENTRIES (AR.OPEN.ITEMS) -
                  VOLUME
/*
/&
```

Figure 18-4   AMS job to list VSAM catalog entries (LISTCAT with VOLUME)

Output from the LISTCAT2 job

```
IDCAMS  SYSTEM SERVICES


                           LISTING FROM CATALOG -- AR.USER.CATALOG

CLUSTER ------- AR.OPEN.ITEMS
      HISTORY
           OWNER-IDENT-------(NULL)        CREATION---------84.346
           RELEASE----------------2        EXPIRATION-------00.000

  DATA ------- AR.OPEN.ITEMS.DATA
      HISTORY
           OWNER-IDENT-------(NULL)        CREATION---------84.346
           RELEASE----------------2        EXPIRATION-------00.000
      VOLUMES
           VOLSER-----------SYSWK3         DEVTYPE-------------FBA

  INDEX ------ AR.OPEN.ITEMS.INDEX
      HISTORY
           OWNER-IDENT-------(NULL)        CREATION---------84.346
           RELEASE----------------2        EXPIRATION-------00.000
      VOLUMES
           VOLSER-----------SYSWK3         DEVTYPE------------FBA
```

Figure 18-5   Output from an AMS job that lists VSAM catalog entries (LISTCAT with VOLUME)

Job stream

```
// JOB      LISTCAT3
// EXEC     IDCAMS,SIZE=AUTO
           LISTCAT CATALOG (AR.USER.CATALOG) -
                   ENTRIES (AR.OPEN.ITEMS) -
                   ALLOCATION
/*
/&
```

Figure 18-6   AMS job to list VSAM catalog entries (LISTCAT with ALLOCATION)

Finally, figure 18-8 shows the same job with the ALL operand. The output in figure 18-9 includes all the catalog information for the cluster AR.OPEN.ITEMS. As you can see, the output from this job shows useful information about the file: key position and length, record size, and number of records in the file. If you study the output from this job as well as from the preceding three, you should get an idea of which LISTCAT operands you should use to get the information you want.

Output from the LISTCAT3 job

```
IDCAMS  SYSTEM SERVICES

                LISTING FROM CATALOG -- AR.USER.CATALOG

CLUSTER ------ AR.OPEN.ITEMS
     HISTORY
        OWNER-IDENT------(NULL)      CREATION------84.346
        RELEASE----------2           EXPIRATION----00.000

DATA ------- AR.OPEN.ITEMS.DATA
     HISTORY
        OWNER-IDENT------(NULL)      CREATION------84.346
        RELEASE----------2           EXPIRATION----00.000
     ALLOCATION
        SPACE-TYPE-------BLOCK       USECLASS-PRI----------0     HI-ALLOC-RBA-------360448
        SPACE-PRI--------704         USECLASS-SEC----------0     HI-USED-RBA--------360448
        SPACE-SEC--------0
     VOLUME
        VOLSER-----------SYSWK3                                  HI-ALLOC-RBA-------360448
        DEVTYPE----------FBA         BLKS/MIN-CA----------32     HI-USED-RBA--------360448
        VOLFLAG----------PRIME       BLOCKS/CA-----------352
        EXTENTS:
        LOW-BLOCK--------13024       LOW-RBA---------------0     BLOCKS---------------704
        HIGH-BLOCK-------13727       HIGH-RBA--------360447

INDEX ------ AR.OPEN.ITEMS.INDEX
     HISTORY
        OWNER-IDENT------(NULL)      CREATION------84.346
        RELEASE----------2           EXPIRATION----00.000
     ALLOCATION
        SPACE-TYPE-------BLOCK       USECLASS-PRI----------0     HI-ALLOC-RBA--------16384
        SPACE-PRI--------32          USECLASS-SEC----------0     HI-USED-RBA---------3072
        SPACE-SEC--------0
     VOLUME
        VOLSER-----------SYSWK3                                  HI-ALLOC-RBA--------16384
        DEVTYPE----------FBA         BLKS/MIN-CA----------32     HI-USED-RBA---------3072
        VOLFLAG----------PRIME       BLOCKS/CA------------32
        EXTENTS:
        LOW-BLOCK--------13728       LOW-RBA---------------0     BLOCKS----------------32
        HIGH-BLOCK-------13759       HIGH-RBA---------16383
```

EXTENT-NUMBER------------1
EXTENT-TYPE--------X'00'

EXTENT-NUMBER------------1
EXTENT-TYPE--------X'00'

Figure 18-7   Output from an AMS job that lists VSAM catalog entries (LISTCAT with ALLOCATION)

Job stream

```
// JOB    LISTCAT4
// EXEC   IDCAMS,SIZE=AUTO
        LISTCAT CATALOG (AR.USER.CATALOG) -
                ENTRIES (AR.OPEN.ITEMS) -
                ALL
/*
/&
```

Figure 18-8 AMS job to list VSAM catalog entries (LISTCAT with ALL)

Output from the LISTCAT4 job

```
IDCAMS  SYSTEM  SERVICES

        LISTING FROM CATALOG -- AR.USER.CATALOG

REC-TOTAL---------3       SPLITS-CI-----------0    EXCPS-----------126     INDEX:
REC-DELETED-------0       SPLITS-CA-----------0    EXTENTS-----------1     LEVELS-------------2
REC-INSERTED------0       FREESPACE-%CI-------0    SYSTEM-TIMESTAMP:       ENTRIES/SECT-------9
REC-UPDATED-------0       FREESPACE-%CA-------0       X'9860 62C6483B0000'  SEQ-SET-RBA--------0
REC-RETRIEVED-----0       FREESPC-BYTES---13312                            HI-LEVEL-RBA----2048
ALLOCATION
SPACE-TYPE------BLOCK
SPACE-PRI--------32       USECLASS-PRI--------0    HI-ALLOC-RBA----16384
SPACE-SEC---------0       USECLASS-SEC--------0    HI-USED-RBA------3072
VOLUME
VOLSER------SYSWK3                                 HI-ALLOC-RBA----16384   EXTENT-NUMBER------1
DEVTYPE--------FBA        BLKS/MIN-CA--------32    HI-USED-RBA------3072   EXTENT-TYPE----X'00'
VOLFLAG------PRIME        BLOCKS/CA----------32
EXTENTS:
LOW-BLOCK-----13728       LOW-RBA-------------0    BLOCKS------------32
HIGH-BLOCK----13759       HIGH-RBA--------16383
```

Figure 18-9 Output from an AMS job that lists VSAM catalog entries (LISTCAT with ALL) (part 1 of 2)

Output from the LISTCAT4 job

```
IDCAMS  SYSTEM  SERVICES


                    LISTING FROM CATALOG -- AR.USER.CATALOG


CLUSTER ------ AR.OPEN.ITEMS
    HISTORY
        OWNER-IDENT------(NULL)        CREATION------84.346
        RELEASE----------2            EXPIRATION----00.000
        PROTECTION-------(NULL)
    ASSOCIATIONS
        DATA-----AR.OPEN.ITEMS.DATA
        INDEX----AR.OPEN.ITEMS.INDEX

DATA ------ AR.OPEN.ITEMS.DATA
    HISTORY
        OWNER-IDENT------(NULL)        CREATION------84.346
        RELEASE----------2            EXPIRATION----00.000
        PROTECTION-------(NULL)
    ASSOCIATIONS
        CLUSTER--AR.OPEN.ITEMS
    ATTRIBUTES
        KEYLEN--------8      AVGLRECL--------256      BUFSPACE-------5120      CISIZE---------2048
        RKP----------0       MAXLRECL--------256      EXCPEXIT------(NULL)     CI/CA-----------88
        SHROPTNS(1,3)  RECOVERY  SUBALLOC   NOERASE  INDEXED   NOWRITECHK   NOIMBED   NOREPLICAT
        UNORDERED   NOREUSE   NONSPANNED
    STATISTICS
        REC-TOTAL------800   SPLITS-CI--------0       EXCPS---------234
        REC-DELETED------0   SPLITS-CA--------0       EXTENTS---------1
        REC-INSERTED-----0   FREESPACE-%CI---10       SYSTEM-TIMESTAMP:
        REC-UPDATED------0   FREESPACE-%CA---10           X'986062C6278E0000'
        REC-RETRIEVED----0   FREESPC-BYTES----0
    ALLOCATION
        SPACE-TYPE-----BLOCK   USECLASS-PRI------0    HI-ALLOC-RBA-----360448
        SPACE-PRI------704     USECLASS-SEC------0    HI-USED-RBA------360448
        SPACE-SEC--------0
    VOLUME
        VOLSER--------SYSWK3   BLKS/MIN-CA-----32     HI-ALLOC-RBA-----360448   EXTENT-NUMBER-------1
        DEVTYPE----------FBA   BLOCKS/CA------352     HI-USED-RBA------360448   EXTENT-TYPE-----X'00'
        VOLFLAG--------PRIME
        EXTENTS:
        LOW-BLOCK-----13024    LOW-RBA----------0     BLOCKS-----------704
        HIGH-BLOCK----13727    HIGH-RBA----360447

INDEX ------ AR.OPEN.ITEMS.INDEX
    HISTORY
        OWNER-IDENT------(NULL)        CREATION------84.346
        RELEASE----------2            EXPIRATION----00.000
        PROTECTION-------(NULL)
    ASSOCIATIONS
        CLUSTER--AR.OPEN.ITEMS
    ATTRIBUTES
        KEYLEN--------8      AVGLRECL----------0      BUFSPACE----------0      CISIZE---------1024
        RKP----------0       MAXLRECL-------1017      EXCPEXIT------(NULL)     CI/CA-----------16
        SHROPTNS(1,3)  RECOVERY  SUBALLOC   NOERASE  NOWRITECHK   NOIMBED   NOREPLICAT   UNORDERED
        NOREUSE
    STATISTICS
```

Figure 18-9   Output from an AMS job that lists VSAM catalog entries (LISTCAT with ALL) (part 2 of 2)

As figure 18-9 illustrates, LISTCAT output can be lengthy. But frankly, most of it usually isn't relevant to you. And the more data AMS prints, the more difficult it is for you to use. If you run a job to print all the entries in a typical user catalog and you code ALL, the output can easily be hundreds of pages long. So you should be as specific as you can about the information you need when you run an AMS LISTCAT job. The less output you request, the simpler it will be for you to read and the less system time it will take to create and print it.

One of the main reasons you'll run an AMS LISTCAT job is to find out the names of the files currently defined in a catalog. Usually, you do that when you create a new file and you want the names to be consistent or you want to avoid using a name that's already in use. Other times, you'll need information about a specific file's characteristics and allocation. And in still other cases, you'll use LISTCAT output to make decisions about deleting or renaming a VSAM file. Now, I want to show you the AMS control statements you use to delete and rename files.

The DELETE control statement   You use the DELETE statement to remove entries from a VSAM catalog. Its formats, illustrated in figure 18-10, are simple. To delete a VSAM file, you use the first format in the figure. In it, you code the name of the cluster you want to delete and specify CLUSTER. If you want to delete the cluster regardless of whether its retention period has expired, code PURGE as well. The CATALOG operand lets you specify the catalog that owns the file to be deleted; it's optional. If you omit the CATALOG operand, you need to code a DLBL statement to specify a job catalog (IJSYSUC), unless the cluster is defined in the master catalog.

To delete a VSAM space, you first have to delete the VSAM files that reside within it. Then, you use the second format of the DELETE statement in figure 18-10. In it, you code the volume serial number of the volume that contains the space you want to delete and specify SPACE. Also, if you don't code a DLBL statement to specify a job catalog and the space isn't defined in the master catalog, you have to code the CATALOG operand to specify the catalog that owns the space you want to delete.

Figure 18-11 shows a job to delete the cluster VSAM.TEST.FILE from AR.USER.CATALOG. Because I coded the CATALOG operand, I didn't need to specify a job catalog with a DLBL statement. Since this file is a KSDS, this job causes three catalog entries to be deleted: the entry for the cluster itself as well as the entries for its data and index components.

The DELETE control statement

The DELETE command to delete a cluster

```
DELETE (entry-name...)
       CLUSTER
       [PURGE]
       [CATALOG (catalog-name)]
```

The DELETE command to delete a VSAM space

```
DELETE (volser)
       SPACE
       [CATALOG (catalog-name)]
```

Explanation

entry-name   The names of the entries you want to delete. You may specify as many entry-name values as you wish; separate individual entry-name values with spaces.

PURGE   Specifies that the cluster should be deleted whether or not its expiration date has arrived.

catalog-name   The catalog that contains the clusters or space you want to delete. If you omit the CATALOG operand, AMS uses the job catalog in effect or, if a job catalog isn't in effect, the master catalog.

volser   The volume serial number of the volume that contains the space to be deleted.

Figure 18-10   The DELETE control statement

```
// JOB      DELCLUST
// EXEC     IDCAMS,SIZE=AUTO
           DELETE  (VSAM.TEST.FILE) -
                   CLUSTER -
                   CATALOG (AR.USER.CATALOG)
/*
/&
```

Figure 18-11   AMS job to delete a file

The ALTER control statement to rename a VSAM file

```
ALTER   entry-name
        NEWNAME (new-entry-name)
        [CATALOG (catalog-name)]
```

Explanation

entry-name   The name of the entry you want to rename.

new-entry-name   The new name for the entry.

catalog-name   The catalog that contains the entry you want to rename. If you omit the CATALOG
                    operand, AMS uses the job catalog in effect or, if a job catalog isn't in effect, the
                    master catalog.

Figure 18-12   The ALTER control statement to rename a VSAM file

```
// JOB     RENAME
// EXEC    IDCAMS,SIZE=AUTO
        ALTER VSAM.TEST.FILE -
            NEWNAME (AR.WORK.FILE) -
            CATALOG (AR.USER.CATALOG)
/*
/&
```

Figure 18-13   AMS ALTER job to rename a file

The ALTER control statement   To rename a VSAM file, you use the AMS ALTER statement. ALTER has over 30 operands that let you change various characteristics of a VSAM catalog entry. Most are the same as the operands you can code when you define an entry: name, organization, allocation, protection, and so on. Although it's a versatile statement, the only operand I'm going to show you is NEWNAME, the operand you use to change the name of an entry.

Figure 18-12 shows the format of the ALTER statement to rename a catalog entry, and figure 18-13 shows a job stream that uses it. Notice that the original entry name follows ALTER and is *not* enclosed within parentheses. The new name for the entry, coded as part of the NEWNAME operand, is enclosed within parentheses. Again, since I coded the CATALOG operand, I didn't have to include a DLBL statement for a job catalog in this job stream.

How to use AMS to copy and print files

In addition to catalog maintenance, you can use AMS to copy and print files. For copy operations, you use the REPRO control statement; for print operations, you use PRINT. Although AMS can copy or print VSAM or non-VSAM files (SAM or ISAM only, not DAM), I'm only going to show you statement formats and job streams to process VSAM files.

Figures 18-14 and 18-15 present the formats of the REPRO and PRINT statements to process VSAM files. Since the statements are similar, I'm going to describe them together. REPRO requires two operands: INFILE and OUTFILE. PRINT requires only INFILE. For each of these operands, you code the file-name from the DLBL statement that identifies the file. (That's unlike the DELETE and ALTER statements in which you code the VSAM file-id directly.)

Figure 18-16 is an AMS REPRO job that copies a VSAM file to another VSAM file. Here, the input file is AR.OPEN.ITEMS and the output file is AR.OPEN.ITEMS.COPY. (Both are owned by AR.USER.CATALOG.) Notice in the REPRO control statement that I didn't use these names, but the names in the DLBL statements that identify the files. Don't forget that before you run a job that copies to a VSAM file, you must have already defined it.

PRINT is even easier to use. All you have to do is specify the file-name on the DLBL statement for the file you want to print on the INFILE operand, as the job in figure 18-17 shows. Notice in this job that I coded CHARACTER from the set of three optional operands CHARACTER, HEX, and DUMP. If you don't explicitly code one of these operands, AMS defaults to DUMP, and the result is a listing with both character and hexadecimal representations.

For both the REPRO and PRINT statements, you can code additional operands to control where the AMS operation begins in the input file and how many records it processes. The formats of these operands are the same for both statements, as figures 18-14 and 18-15 show.

To specify where processing begins in the input file, you can code SKIP, FROMKEY, or FROMNUMBER. To process a file beginning somewhere other than with its first record, code SKIP and specify how many records to bypass. You can use SKIP for any kind of VSAM file. For a KSDS, you can code FROMKEY with the key value of the first record you want to process. (If the key contains commas, semicolons, blanks, parentheses, or slashes, you must code the key between apostrophes.) For an RRDS, you can use FROMNUMBER with the relative-record number of the first record you want to process.

To specify where processing should end, you can code COUNT, TOKEY, or TONUMBER. COUNT indicates how many records should be processed; it's valid for any kind of VSAM file. For a KSDS or an RRDS, you can use TOKEY or TONUMBER to indicate where in the file to stop processing.

The REPRO control statement

```
REPRO   INFILE      (input-file-name)
        OUTFILE     (output-file-name)

       ⎡⎧SKIP        (count)  ⎫⎤
       ⎢⎨FROMKEY     (key)    ⎬⎥
       ⎣⎩FROMNUMBER  (number)⎭⎦

       ⎡⎧COUNT       (count)  ⎫⎤
       ⎢⎨TOKEY       (key)    ⎬⎥
       ⎣⎩TONUMBER    (number)⎭⎦
```

Explanation

input-file-name	The name of the file to be processed as input.
output-file-name	The name of the file to be created as output. The cluster must have already been defined with a DEFINE CLUSTER command.
SKIP (count)	For count, specify a numeric value to indicate the number of records to be skipped before the copy operation begins. Valid for all three types of VSAM files.
FROMKEY (key)	For key, specify the value of the key at which the copy operation should begin. Valid only when copying a KSDS.
FROMNUMBER (number)	For number, specify the relative record number at which the copy operation should begin. Valid only when copying an RRDS.
COUNT (count)	For count, specify a numeric value to indicate the number of records to copied. Valid for all three types of VSAM files.
TOKEY (key)	For key, specify the value of the key at which the copy operation should end. Valid only when copying a KSDS.
TONUMBER (number)	For number, specify the relative record number at which the copy operation should end. Valid only when copying an RRDS.

Figure 18-14   The REPRO control statement

To understand how to use these positioning operands and to see what character, hex, and dump output from PRINT look like, I've included three jobs to process the same input file in figures 18-18, 18-20, and 18-22. In each case, I coded SKIP(28) to bypass the first 28 records in the file and COUNT(3) to print only three records. As a result,

The PRINT control statement

```
PRINT   INFILE      (input-file-name)

        ⎡⎧CHARACTER⎫⎤
        ⎢⎨HEX      ⎬⎥
        ⎣⎩DUMP     ⎭⎦

        ⎡⎧SKIP       (count) ⎫⎤
        ⎢⎨FROMKEY    (key)   ⎬⎥
        ⎣⎩FROMNUMBER (number)⎭⎦

        ⎡⎧COUNT      (count) ⎫⎤
        ⎢⎨TOKEY      (key)   ⎬⎥
        ⎣⎩TONUMBER   (number)⎭⎦
```

Explanation

input-file-name	The name of the file to be printed.
CHARACTER	Specifies that the output of the print operation should be in character format.
HEX	Specifies that the output of the print operation should be in hex format.
DUMP	Specifies that the output of the print operation should be in both character and hex format. DUMP is the default.
SKIP (count)	For count, specify a numeric value to indicate the number of records to be skipped before the print operation begins. Valid for all three types of VSAM files.
FROMKEY (key)	For key, specify the value of the key at which the print operation should begin. Valid only when printing a KSDS.
FROMNUMBER (number)	For number, specify the relative record number at which the print operation should begin. Valid only when printing an RRDS.
COUNT (count)	For count, specify a numeric value to indicate the number of records to be printed. Valid for all three types of VSAM files.
TOKEY (key)	For key, specify the value of the key at which the print operation should end. Valid only when printing a KSDS.
TONUMBER (number)	For number, specify the relative record number at which the print operation should end. Valid only when printing an RRDS.

Figure 18-15   The PRINT control statement

```
// JOB      REPRO
// DLBL     IJSYSUC,'AR.USER.CATALOG',,VSAM
// DLBL     OLDVSAM,'AR.OPEN.ITEMS',,VSAM
// DLBL     NEWVSAM,'AR.OPEN.ITEMS.COPY',,VSAM
// EXEC     IDCAMS,SIZE=AUTO
          REPRO INFILE   (OLDVSAM) -
                OUTFILE (NEWVSAM)
/*
/&
```

Figure 18-16   AMS job to copy a VSAM file to a VSAM file

```
// JOB      PRINT1
// DLBL     IJSYSUC,'MMA.USER.CATALOG',,VSAM
// DLBL     ARMAST,'AR.CUSTOMER.MASTER.FILE',,VSAM
// EXEC     IDCAMS,SIZE=AUTO
          PRINT INFILE    (ARMAST) -
                CHARACTER
/*
/&
```

Figure 18-17   AMS job to print a VSAM file

these jobs print the 29th, 30th, and 31st records in the file. (Don't let the values in the first positions of the records in these figures confuse you; they're data, not record numbers.)

Figure 18-18 is an AMS PRINT job that uses the CHARACTER operand and figure 18-19 shows its output. Figures 18-20 and 18-22 illustrate the same job, only with the HEX and DUMP operands, and figures 18-21 and 18-23 show the jobs' output. I suspect that you'll use the CHARACTER operand most often. The DUMP operand produces output that's useful if you need to evaluate fields that contain data without character equivalents, like packed-decimal fields. The HEX operand, because it doesn't print character equivalents, isn't as useful as DUMP.

Job stream

```
// JOB      PRINT2
// DLBL     IJSYSUC,'MMA.USER.CATALOG',,VSAM
// DLBL     ARMAST,'AR.CUSTOMER.MASTER.FILE',,VSAM
// EXEC     IDCAMS,SIZE=AUTO
  PRINT INFILE (ARMAST) -
        CHARACTER -
        SKIP    (28) -
        COUNT   (3)
/*
/&
```

Figure 18-18   AMS job to print part of a VSAM file in character format

Output from the job PRINT2

```
IDCAMS  SYSTEM SERVICES

LISTING OF DATA SET -AR.CUSTOMER.MASTER.FILE

RBA OF RECORD - 8192
28776JOHN WARDS AND ASSOC5600 N CLARK          CHICAGO        IL60603000557025000002500001230120608002500000000000000
00000000000000000000000000000000000000000000000000000000000000000000000000000000000

RBA OF RECORD - 8448
29556NATIONAL INDUSTRIES 3879 NE FOOTE         WASHINGTON DC2001900007740500000000080001230130608800008000008000000000000000
0000000000000000000000000000000000000000000000000000000000000000000000000000000

RBA OF RECORD - 8704
29573UNIVERSAL SERVICES  2115 FULTON RD        POMONA         CA91768000011910000000500000123014060880050000005000000000000000
00000000000000000000000000000000000000000000000000000000000000000000000000000

IDC0005I NUMBER OF RECORDS PROCESSED WAS 3
```

Figure 18-19   Output from an AMS job that prints part of a VSAM file in character format

Job stream

```
// JOB      PRINT3
// DLBL     IJSYSUC,'MMA.USER.CATALOG',,VSAM
// DLBL     ARMAST,'AR.CUSTOMER.MASTER.FILE',,VSAM
// EXEC     IDCAMS,SIZE=AUTO
   PRINT INFILE (ARMAST) -
         HEX -
         SKIP    (28) -
         COUNT   (3)
/*
/&
```

Figure 18-20   AMS job to print part of a VSAM file in hex format

Output from the job PRINT3

```
IDCAMS  SYSTEM SERVICES

LISTING OF DATA SET -AR.CUSTOMER.MASTER.FILE

RBA OF RECORD - 8192
40F2F8F7F7F6D1D6C8D540E6C1D9C4E240C1D5C440C1E2E2D6C3F 5F6F040D540C3D3C1D9D24040404040404040C3C8C9C3C1C7D6404040 40C9D3F6
F0F6F03F0F0F5F5F7F0F2F5F0F0F0F1F2F3F0F1F2F0F0F0F0F0F040404040404040404040404040404040404040 40
F0F0F0F0F0F0F0F0F0F0F0F0F0F0F0F0F0F0F0F0F0F0404040404040404040404040404040 40
4040404040404040404040404040

RBA OF RECORD - 8448
40F2F9F5F5F605C1E3C9D6D5C1D34 0C9D5C4E4E2E3D9C9C5E240F3F8F7F940D5C540C6D6D6E3C54 0404040404040E6C1E2C8C9D5C7E3D6D540C4C3F2
F0F0F1F9F0F0F0F7F4F 0F5F0F0F0F0F0F0F0F0F0F0F0F0F0F0F1F2F3F0F1F2F3F0F0F0F0F0F040404040404040404040 40
F0F0F0F0F0F0F0F0F0F0F0F0F0F0F0F0F0F0F0F0F0404040404040404040404040404040 40
4040404040404040404040404040

RBA OF RECORD - 8704
40F2F9F5F7F3E4D5C9E5C5D9E2C1D34 0E2C5D9E5C9C3C5E24040 40F 2F1F1F54 0C6E4D3E3D6D54 0D9C44040404040404040D7D6D4D6D5C14040404040 40C3C1F9
F1F7F6F8F0F0F1F1F0F1F1F0F0F0F0F0F0F0F1F2F3F0F1F2F3F0F0F0F0F0F040404040404040404040 40
F0F0F0F0F0F0F0F0F0F0F0F0F0F0F0F0F0F0F0F0F0404040404040404040404040404040 40
4040404040404040404040404040

IDC0005I NUMBER OF RECORDS PROCESSED WAS 3
```

Figure 18-21   Output from an AMS job that prints part of a VSAM file in hex format

Job stream

```
// JOB        PRINT4
// DLBL       IJSYSUC,'MMA.USER.CATALOG',,VSAM
// DLBL       ARMAST,'AR.CUSTOMER.MASTER.FILE',,VSAM
// EXEC       IDCAMS,SIZE=AUTO
           PRINT INFILE (ARMAST) -
                 DUMP -
                 SKIP  (28) -
                 COUNT (3)
/*
/&
```

Figure 18-22   AMS job to print part of a VSAM file in dump format

Output from the job PRINT4

```
IDCAMS  SYSTEM  SERVICES

LISTING OF DATA SET -AR.CUSTOMER.MASTER.FILE

RBA OF RECORD - 8192
0000  40F2F8F7 F7F6D1D6 C8D540E6 C1D9C4E2   40C1D5C4 40C1E2E2 D6C3F5F6 F0F040D5   * 28776JOHN WARDS AND ASSOC5600 N*
0020  40C3D3C1 D9D24040 4040C3C8 F0F0F0F0   C9C3C1C7 D6404040 40C9D3F6 F0F6F0F3   * CLARK       CHICAGO      IL60603*
0040  F0F0F0F0 F5F5F7F0 F2F5F0F0 F0F0F0F0   F2F5F0F0 F0F0F1F2 F3F0F1F2 F0F6F0F8   *0000557025000002500000001230120608*
0060  F8F0F0F2 F5F0F0F0 F5F0F0F0 F0F0F0F0   F0F0F0F0 F0F0F0F0 F0F0F0F0 F0F0F0F0   *8002500000250000000000000000000*
0080  F0F0F0F0 F0F0F2F5 F0F0F0F0 F0F0F0F0   F0F0F0F0 F0F0F0F0 F0F0F0F0 F0F0F0F0   *0000000000000000000000000000000*
00A0  F0F0F0F0 F0F0F0F0 F0F0F0F0 F0F0F0F0   F0F0F0F0 F0F0F0F0 40404040 40404040   *0000000000000000000000*
00C0  F0F0F0F0 F0F0F0F0 F0F0F0F0 F0F0F0F0   F0F0F0F0 40404040 40404040 40404040   *0000000000000000*
00E0  40404040 40404040 40404040 40404040   40404040 40404040 40404040 40404040   *

RBA OF RECORD - 8448
0000  40F2F9F5 F5F6D5C1 E3C9D6D5 C1D34CC9   D5C4E4E2 E3D9C9C5 E240F3F8 F7F940D5   * 29556NATIONAL INDUSTRIES 3879 N*
0020  C540C6D6 D6E3C540 40404040 4040E6C1   E2C8C9D5 C7E3D6D5 40C4C3F2 F0F0F1F9   *E FOOTE         WASHINGTON DC20019*
0040  F0F0F0F0 F7F7F4F0 F5F0F0F0 F0F0F0F0   F0F0F0F0 F0F0F1F2 F3F0F1F3 F0F6F0F8   *000077405000000800001230130608*
0060  F8F0F0F0 F0F0F0F0 F0F0F0F0 F0F0F0F0   F0F0F0F0 F0F0F0F0 F0F0F0F0 F0F0F0F0   *8000080000000000000000000000000*
0080  F0F0F0F0 F0F0F0F0 F0F0F0F0 F0F0F0F0   F0F0F0F0 F0F0F0F0 F0F0F0F0 F0F0F0F0   *0000000000000000000000000000000*
00A0  F0F0F0F0 F0F0F0F0 F0F0F0F0 F0F0F0F0   F0F0F0F0 F0F0F0F0 40404040 40404040   *0000000000000000000000*
00C0  F0F0F0F0 F0F0F0F0 F0F0F0F0 F0F0F0F0   F0F0F0F0 40404040 40404040 40404040   *0000000000000000*
00E0  40404040 40404040 40404040 40404040   40404040 40404040 40404040 40404040   *

RBA OF RECORD - 8704
0000  40F2F9F5 F7F3E4D5 C9E5C5D9 E2C1D340   E2C5D9E5 C9C3C5E2 4040F2F1 F1F540C6   * 29573UNIVERSAL SERVICES 2115 F*
0020  E4D3E3D6 D540D9C4 40400F7D6   D4D6D5C1 40404040 40C3C1F9 F1F7F6F8   *ULTON RD        POMONA      CA91768*
0040  F5F0F0F0 F0F0F0F0 F1F1F9F1   F5F0F0F0 F0F0F1F2 F3F0F1F4 F0F6F0F8   *0000119100000050000001230140608*
0060  F8F0F0F0 F0F0F0F5 F0F0F0F0 F0F0F0F0   F0F0F0F0 F0F0F0F0 F0F0F0F0 F0F0F0F0   *8005000000500000000000000000000*
0080  F8F0F0F0 F5F0F0F0 F0F0F0F0 F0F0F0F0   F0F0F0F0 F0F0F0F0 F0F0F0F0 F0F0F0F0   *0000000000000000000000000000000*
00A0  F0F0F0F0 F0F0F0F0 F0F0F0F0 F0F0F0F0   F0F0F0F0 F0F0F0F0 40404040 40404040   *0000000000000000000000*
00C0  F0F0F0F0 F0F0F0F0 F0F0F0F0 F0F0F0F0   F0F0F0F0 40404040 40404040 40404040   *0000000000000000*
00E0  40404040 40404040 40404040 40404040   40404040 40404040 40404040 40404040   *

IDC0005I NUMBER OF RECORDS PROCESSED WAS 3
```

Figure 18-23   Output from an AMS job that prints part of a VSAM file in dump format

Discussion   As you work with VSAM files, you'll use the LISTCAT, DELETE, ALTER, REPRO, and PRINT control statements of AMS regularly. With REPRO and PRINT, you're not restricted to VSAM files; you can also use them to process SAM and ISAM files. (You can't process DAM files with AMS, however.) If you want to copy or print a SAM or an ISAM file, you have to supply additional identifying information in the control statements with the ENVIRONMENT operand. For example, you have to specify blocking and record format and, for ISAM files, device type. Frankly, though, you'll seldom need to use AMS to process a non-VSAM file, and the corresponding DITTO functions are easier to use. However, if you want to use REPRO or PRINT to process a non-VSAM file, you can refer to the description of the ENVIRONMENT operand in the appropriate sections of *Using VSE/VSAM Commands and Macros*.

Objectives   1. Code an AMS LISTCAT job to list VSAM catalog entries.

2. Code an AMS DELETE job to delete VSAM catalog entries.

3. Code an AMS ALTER job to rename VSAM catalog entries.

4. Code an AMS REPRO job to copy a VSAM file to another VSAM file. The copy operation may or may not involve all the records in the input file.

5. Code an AMS PRINT job to print a VSAM file. The print operation may or may not involve all the records in the input file.

Appendix A

VSE JCL reference summary

This appendix presents the formats of the VSE job control statements and the VSE/POWER job entry control statements that were presented in the figures in this book. Each statement includes a reference so you can look back to the complete figure to see what values you can code for the operands.

VSE JCL STATEMENTS

The ASSGN statement for any device

(Figure 5-11, part 1)

```
// ASSGN    SYSxxx,device[,TEMP|PERM]
```

The ASSGN statement for tape units

(Figure 5-11, part 2)

```
// ASSGN    SYSxxx,device[,mode|ALT][,TEMP|PERM]
         [,VOL=volser]
```

The ASSGN statement for DASDs

(Figure 5-11, part 3)

```
// ASSGN    SYSxxx,device[,TEMP|PERM][,VOL=volser][,SHR]
```

The DATE statement

(Figure 5-16)

```
// DATE    xx/xx/yy
```

The DLBL statement for VSAM files

(Figure 13-8)

```
// DLBL    file-name,'file-id',,VSAM[,BUFSP=n]
         [,CAT=catalog-name][,DISP=disp]
         [,RECORDS=records,RECSIZE=recsize]
```

The DLBL statement for SAM, ISAM, and DAM files

(Figure 12-1)

```
// DLBL    file-name,['file-id'],[date],[codes][,DSF]
         [,BLKSIZE=n|,CISIZE=n]
```

The EXEC statement to execute a procedure

(Figure 6-1)

```
// EXEC     PROC=procedure-name
```

The EXEC statement to execute a program

(Figure 5-1)

```
// EXEC     [[PGM=]program-name][,REAL][,SIZE=size]
          [,GO][,PARM='value']
```

The EXTENT statement

(Figure 12-3)

```
// EXTENT   [logical-unit,[volser],[type],
          [sequence-number],[location],
          [size],[split-cylinder-track]
```

The GOTO statement

(Figure 6-11)

```
// GOTO     {label}
          {$EOJ }
```

The ID statement

(Figure 4-8)

```
// ID       USER=user-id,PWD=password
```

The IF statement

(Figure 6-15)

```
// IF       ($RC                operator n    )
          {$MRC               operator n    }
          (parameter-name operator value)

[ ({OR }   {$RC                operator n    } ]
  {| }     {$MRC               operator n    }    THEN
  {AND}    (parameter-name operator value)
  {& }
```

The JOB statement

(Figure 4-3)

```
// JOB      job-name [accounting-information]
```

The LIBDEF statement

(Figure 5-3)

```
// LIBDEF  member-type
           [,SEARCH=(lib1.slib1,lib2.slib2,...lib15.slib15)]
           [,CATALOG=lib.slib]
           [,TEMP|PERM]
```

The LIBDROP statement

(Figure 5-9)

```
// LIBDROP member-type[,definition-type...][,TEMP|PERM]
```

The LIBLIST statement

(Figure 5-7)

```
// LIBLIST member-type[,partition]
```

The LISTIO statement

(Figure 5-12)

```
// LISTIO  type
```

The MTC statement

(Figure 11-1)

```
// MTC     operation,unit[,count]
```

The ON statement

(Figure 6-13)

```
// ON            {$RC operator n}
                 {$CANCEL        }
                 {$ABEND         }

   [{OR }  {$RC operator n}]  {GOTO {label}}
   [{ |  } {$CANCEL       }]  {     {$EOJ }}
   [{AND}  {$ABEND        }]  {CONTINUE     }
   [{ &  }                 ]
```

The OPTION statement

(Figure 5-22)

```
// OPTION   overriding-value[,overriding-value...]
```

The PROC statement

(Figure 6-17)

```
// PROC      [parameter-name=[value]]
             [,parameter-name=[value]...]
```

The RESET statement

(Figure 5-14)

```
// RESET    unit
```

The SETPARM statement

(Figure 6-18)

```
// SETPARM parameter-name= [{value}]
                           [{$RC  }]
                           [{$MRC }]

            [,parameter-name= [{value}]]...]
                              [{$RC  }]
                              [{$MRC }]
```

The STDOPT statement

(Figure 5-20)

```
// STDOPT   option-value[,option-value...]
```

The TLBL statement

(Figure 11-5)

```
// TLBL     file-name,['file-id'],[date],[volser],
           [volseq],[fileseq],[generation],[version]
```

The UPSI statement

(Figure 5-15)

```
// UPSI     nnnnnnnn
```

POWER JECL STATEMENTS

The JOB statement

(Figure 8-3)

```
* $$ JOB   [JNM=job-name]
           [,DISP=disposition]
           [,PRI=priority]
           [,CLASS=class]
           [,NTFY=YES]
           [,USER=user-information]
           [,PWD=password]
```

The LST statement

(Figure 8-4)

```
* $$ LST   [,DISP=disposition]
           [,PRI=priority]
           [,CLASS=class]
           [,FNO=form-number]
           [,JSEP=job-separators]
           [,COPY=copies]
           [,USER=user-information]
           [,PWD=password]
           [,TADDR=tape-unit]
           [,LST=list-unit]
           [,FCB=FCB-phase-name]
```

The PUN statement

(Figure 8-5)

```
* $$ PUN    [,DISP=disposition]
           [,PRI=priority]
           [,CLASS=class]
           [,FNO=form-number]
           [,JSEP=job-separators]
           [,COPY=copies]
           [,USER=user-information]
           [,PWD=password]
           [,TADDR=tape-unit]
           [,PUN=punch-unit]
```

Appendix B

Messages and codes

When VSE (or a VSE system component) encounters an unusual condition, it issues a message on the system console and writes it on the job's SYSLST output. To solve problems with job streams, you need to understand the format of these messages and you need to know how to find descriptions of them in the IBM manuals. Unfortunately, that's not always easy because VSE and its related components can generate hundreds of messages, and they're not all documented in the same place.

Although the format of a message varies depending on the system component that issues it, all system messages follow the basic format in figure B-1. As you can see, a message consists of five parts: (1) partition, (2) component-id, (3) message number, (4) action, and (5) text.

The partition component lets you know what partition caused the message to be generated. The partition identifier is more important for the system operator than for a programmer. If a job causes a message to be displayed, the operator needs to know where it's executing to correct the problem.

More important for you is the message identifier. It consists of the items labelled component-id, message number, and action in figure B-1. You use the message identifier to look up a detailed description of the message in a manual.

First, use component-id to decide what manual to consult. Figure B-2 lists the component-ids you're most likely to encounter and their related manuals. (The full titles of the manuals are at the bottom of the figure.) As you can see, if you know which manuals to go to, you can avoid a lot of unnecessary searching. (As a guideline, if you get a message code that doesn't begin with three letters, look in *VSE/Advanced Functions Messages*, unless the message begins with 42.

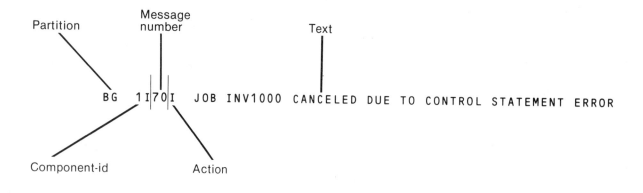

Figure B-1   The format of a VSE message

If it does begin with 42, look in *VSE/VSAM Messages and Codes*.) When you find the right component-id in the right manual, look sequentially through the entries for it until you find the entry with a matching number; that's the description of the message.

As you might expect, some messages occur infrequently, and others are common. The message in figure B-1 is one you're likely to see on your output as you test job streams. This is the message you get if you run a job that contains JCL with syntax errors. The first characters indicate that the message is from the background partition (BG). From the component-id (1I), you can tell the message is related to job control, and that you can find the message in *VSE/Advanced Functions Messages*. Since this message is obvious, you probably wouldn't need to look up it's meaning. But other messages can be brief and obscure, so you need to know how to find them in the messages manuals.

If you're using VSE as part of a system package, such as VSE/SP 3.1, you'll find that several manuals have been combined into the *VSE/SP Messages and Codes* manual. This two-volume manual includes information for VSE/AF, DITTO, POWER, and VSAM all in one reference. In most cases, that's the only manual you'll need.

Component-id	Related to	Manual
0C to OV	Supervisor, IPL, Console	VSE/AF
1A to 1P	Job control	VSE/AF
1Q	POWER	POWER
1R	POWER RJE BSC	POWER
1V	POWER RJE SNA	POWER
21	Linkage editor	VSE/AF
3M	Librarian	VSE/AF
40 to 41	I/O	VSE/AF
42	I/O and VSAM	VSE/AF and VSAM
43 to 49	I/O	VSE/AF
4A	VSAM	VSAM
7A to 7V	Sort/Merge	Sort/Merge
85 to 86	System utilities	VSE/AF
8C to 8X	System utilities	VSE/AF
A2	Assembler	VSE/AF
DFH	CICS	CICS
DLZ	DL/I	DL/I
DTO	DITTO	DITO
IDC	Access Method Services	VSAM
IKQ	Catalog Check Service Aid	VSAM
IPK	Assembler	VSE/AF
K0 to K9	ICCF	ICCF
L0 to L3	Librarian	VSE/AF
M0 to M5	Maintain System History Program	VSE/AF
P0 to P3	3800 Printing Subsystem	VSE/AF
S1 to S9	Standalone utilitites	VSE/AF
SE	Standalone utilitites	VSE/AF

Manuals

CICS	CICS/VS Messages and Codes
DITTO	VSE/DITTO Program Reference and Operations Manual
DL/I	DL/I DOS/VS Messages and Codes
POWER	VSE/POWER Messages
Sort/Merge	DOS/VS Sort/Merge Programmer's Guide
VSAM	VSE/VSAM Messages and Codes
VSE/AF	VSE/Advanced Functions Messages

Figure B-2 System message component-ids and related documentation

Index

Comment Form

Your opinions count

If you have comments, criticisms, or suggestions, I'm eager to get them. Your opinions today will affect our products of tomorrow. If you have questions, you can expect an answer within one week of the time we receive them. And if you discover any errors in this book, typographical or otherwise, please point them out so we can make corrections when the book is reprinted.

Thanks for your help.

Mike Murach
Fresno, California

Book title: DOS/VSE JCL, Second edition

Dear Mike: _____

_____

_____

_____

_____

_____

_____

_____

_____

_____

_____

_____

_____

_____

_____

_____

_____

_____

Name & Title _____
Company (if company address) _____
Address _____
City, State, Zip _____

Fold where indicated and tape closed.
No postage necessary if mailed in the U.S.

fold

fold

BUSINESS REPLY MAIL

FIRST-CLASS MAIL   PERMIT NO. 3063   FRESNO, CA

POSTAGE WILL BE PAID BY ADDRESSEE

Mike Murach & Associates, Inc.

4697 W JACQUELYN AVE
FRESNO CA 93722-9888

fold

fold

Order Form

Our Unlimited Guarantee

To our customers who order directly from us: You must be satisfied. Our books must work for you, or you can send them back for a full refund...no matter how many you buy, no matter how long you've had them.

Name & Title _____

Company (if company address) _____

Address _____

City, State, Zip _____

Phone number (including area code) _____

Qty	Product code and title	*Price
DOS/VSE Subjects		
___ VJLR	DOS/VSE JCL (Second Edition)	$34.50
___ ICCF	DOS/VSE ICCF	31.00
___ VBAL	DOS/VSE Assembler Language	36.50
Data Base Processing		
___ IMS1	IMS for the COBOL Programmer Part 1: DL/I Data Base Processing	$34.50
___ IMS2	IMS for the COBOL Programmer Part 2: Data Communications and MFS	36.50
___ DB21	DB2 for the COBOL Programmer Part 1: An Introductory Course	32.50
___ DB22	DB2 for the COBOL Programmer Part 2: An Advanced Course	32.50
OS/MVS Subjects		
___ TSO1	MVS TSO, Part 1: ISPF	$31.00
___ TSO2	MVS TSO, Part 2: Commands and Procedures	31.00
___ MJCL	MVS JCL	34.50
___ MBAL	MVS Assembler Language	36.50
___ OSUT	OS Utilities	17.50

Qty	Product code and title	*Price
CICS		
___ CC1R	CICS for the COBOL Programmer Part 1 (Second Edition)	$31.00
___ CC2R	CICS for the COBOL Programmer Part 2 (Second Edition)	Available October 1992
___ CREF	The CICS Programmer's Desk Reference	36.50
COBOL Language Elements		
___ SC1R	Structured ANS COBOL, Part 1	$31.00
___ SC2R	Structured ANS COBOL, Part 2	31.00
___ RW	Report Writer	17.50
___ VC2R	VS COBOL II (Second Edition)	27.50
VSAM		
___ VSMX	VSAM: Access Method Services and Application Programming	$27.50
___ VSMR	VSAM for the COBOL Programmer (Second Edition)	17.50

☐ Bill the appropriate book prices plus UPS shipping and handling (and sales tax in California) to my ___VISA ___MasterCard:

Card Number_____

Valid thru (month/year) _____

Cardowner's signature _____

☐ Bill me.

☐ Bill my company. P.O. #_____

☐ I want to **save** UPS shipping and handling charges. Here's my check or money order for $_____. California residents, please add sales tax to your total. (Offer valid in the U.S.)

* Prices are subject to change. **Please call for current prices.**

To order more quickly,

Call **toll-free** 1-800-221-5528

(Weekdays, 8:30 to 5 Pacific Standard Time)

Fax: 1-209-275-9035

Mike Murach & Associates, Inc.

4697 West Jacquelyn Avenue
Fresno, California 93722-6427
(209) 275-3335

fold

fold

BUSINESS REPLY MAIL

FIRST-CLASS MAIL   PERMIT NO. 3063   FRESNO, CA

POSTAGE WILL BE PAID BY ADDRESSEE

Mike Murach & Associates, Inc.

4697 W JACQUELYN AVE
FRESNO CA 93722-9888

I|.I....II.I...I..I.I..I.II.I..I..I.I..I.I...I..I..I.II

fold

fold

Order Form

Our Unlimited Guarantee

To our customers who order directly from us: You must be satisfied. Our books must work for you, or you can send them back for a full refund...no matter how many you buy, no matter how long you've had them.

Name & Title _____

Company (if company address) _____

Address _____

City, State, Zip _____

Phone number (including area code)_____

Qty	Product code and title	*Price
DOS/VSE Subjects		
____ VJLR	DOS/VSE JCL (Second Edition)	$34.50
____ ICCF	DOS/VSE ICCF	31.00
____ VBAL	DOS/VSE Assembler Language	36.50
Data Base Processing		
____ IMS1	IMS for the COBOL Programmer Part 1: DL/I Data Base Processing	$34.50
____ IMS2	IMS for the COBOL Programmer Part 2: Data Communications and MFS	36.50
____ DB21	DB2 for the COBOL Programmer Part 1: An Introductory Course	32.50
____ DB22	DB2 for the COBOL Programmer Part 2: An Advanced Course	32.50
OS/MVS Subjects		
____ TSO1	MVS TSO, Part 1: ISPF	$31.00
____ TSO2	MVS TSO, Part 2: Commands and Procedures	31.00
____ MJCL	MVS JCL	34.50
____ MBAL	MVS Assembler Language	36.50
____ OSUT	OS Utilities	17.50

Qty	Product code and title	*Price
CICS		
____ CC1R	CICS for the COBOL Programmer Part 1 (Second Edition)	$31.00
____ CC2R	CICS for the COBOL Programmer Part 2 (Second Edition)	Available October 1992
____ CREF	The CICS Programmer's Desk Reference	36.50
COBOL Language Elements		
____ SC1R	Structured ANS COBOL, Part 1	$31.00
____ SC2R	Structured ANS COBOL, Part 2	31.00
____ RW	Report Writer	17.50
____ VC2R	VS COBOL II (Second Edition)	27.50
VSAM		
____ VSMX	VSAM: Access Method Services and Application Programming	$27.50
____ VSMR	VSAM for the COBOL Programmer (Second Edition)	17.50

☐ Bill the appropriate book prices plus UPS shipping and handling (and sales tax in California) to my ____VISA ____MasterCard:

   Card Number_____

   Valid thru (month/year) _____

   Cardowner's signature _____

☐ Bill me.

☐ Bill my company. P.O. #_____

☐ I want to **save** UPS shipping and handling charges. Here's my check or money order for $_____. California residents, please add sales tax to your total. (Offer valid in the U.S.)

* Prices are subject to change. Please call for current prices.

To order more quickly,

Call **toll-free** 1-800-221-5528

(Weekdays, 8:30 to 5 Pacific Standard Time)

Fax: 1-209-275-9035

Mike Murach & Associates, Inc.

4697 West Jacquelyn Avenue
Fresno, California 93722-6427
(209) 275-3335

fold

fold

BUSINESS REPLY MAIL

FIRST-CLASS MAIL   PERMIT NO. 3063   FRESNO, CA

POSTAGE WILL BE PAID BY ADDRESSEE

Mike Murach & Associates, Inc.

4697 W JACQUELYN AVE
FRESNO CA 93722-9888

fold

fold